KEY CONCEPTS IN VICTORIAN LI

Palgrave Key Concepts

Palgrave Key Concepts provide an accessible and comprehensive range of subject glossaries at undergraduate level. They are the ideal companion to a standard textbook making them invaluable reading to students throughout their course of study and especially useful as a revision aid.

Key Concepts in Accounting and Finance
Key Concepts in Business Practice
Key Concepts in Drama and Performance
Key Concepts in Human Resource Management
Key Concepts in Information and Communication Technology
Key Concepts in International Business
Key Concepts in Language and Linguistics (second edition)
key Concepts in Management
Key Concepts in Marketing
Key Concepts in Operations Management
Key Concepts in Politics
Key Concepts in Psychology
Key Concepts in Strategic Management

Palgrave Key Concepts: Literature
General Editors: John Peck and Martin Coyle

Key Concepts in Contemporary Literature
Key Concepts in Postcolonial Literature
Key Concepts in Victorian Literature
Literary Terms and Criticism (third edition)

Further titles are in preparation

www.palgravekeyconcepts.com

Palgrave Key Concepts
Series Standing Order
ISBN 1–4039–3210–7
(outside North America only)

You can receive future titles in this series as they are published by placing a standing order. Please contact your bookseller or, in the case of difficulty, write to us at the address below with your name and address, the title of the series and the ISBN quoted above.

Customer Services Department, Macmillan Distribution Ltd
Houndmills, Basingstoke, Hampshire RG21 6XS, England

Key Concepts in Victorian Literature

Sean Purchase

palgrave
macmillan

First published 2006 by
PALGRAVE MACMILLAN
Houndmills, Basingstoke, Hampshire RG21 6XS and
175 Fifth Avenue, New York, N.Y. 10010
Companies and representatives throughout the world

PALGRAVE MACMILLAN is the global academic imprint of the Palgrave Macmillan division of St. Martin's Press, LLC and of Palgrave Macmillan Ltd. Macmillan® is a registered trademark in the United States, United Kingdom and other countries. Palgrave is a registered trademark in the European Union and other countries.

ISBN-13: 978 1–4039–4807–6
ISBN-10: 1–4039–4807–0

This book is printed on paper suitable for recycling and made from fully managed and sustained forest sources.

A catalogue record for this book is available from the British Library.

A catalog record for this book is available from the Library of Congress.

10 9 8 7 6 5 4 3 2 1
15 14 13 12 11 10 09 08 07 06

Printed and bound in Great Britain by
Creative Print & Design (Wales) Ebbw Vale

To Christelle, ma belle

Contents

Acknowledgements

A huge thank-you to John Peck, Martin Coyle, Carl Plasa, and to everyone who gave me friendship and encouragement during my time at Cardiff University. I am especially grateful to Irene Morra, for her immense knowledge of everything, her timely and spirited comments, and her remarkable supply of Jammie Dodgers (not always the cheap ones).

This book is also dedicated to my mother, Irene, and to the memory of my grandparents, Joyce Purchase, Albert Purchase, and Mabel Burdfield.

S.P.

General Editors' Preface

The purpose of Palgrave Key Concepts in Literature is to provide students with key critical and historical ideas about the texts they are studying as part of their literature courses. These ideas include information about the historical and cultural contexts of literature as well as the theoretical approaches current in the subject today. Behind the series lies a recognition of the need nowadays for students to be familiar with a range of concepts and contextual material to inform their reading and writing about literature.

This series is also based on a recognition of the changes that have transformed degree courses in Literature in recent years. Central to these changes has been the impact of critical theory together with a renewed interest in the way in which texts intersect with their immediate context and historical circumstances. The result has been an opening up of new ways of reading texts and a new understanding of what the study of literature involves together with the introduction of a wide set of new critical issues that demand our attention. An important aim of Palgrave Key Concepts in Literature is to provide brief, accessible introductions to these new ways of reading and new issues.

Each volume in Palgrave Key Concepts in Literature follows the same structure. An initial overview essay is followed by three sections – Contexts, Texts and Criticism – each containing a sequence of brief alphabetically arranged entries on a sequence of topics. 'Contexts' essays provide an impression of the historical, social and cultural environment in which literary texts were produced. 'Texts' essays, as might be expected, focus more directly on the works themselves. 'Criticism' essays then outline the manner in which changes and developments in criticism have affected the ways in which we discuss the texts featured in the volume. The informing intention throughout is to help the reader create something new in the process of combining context, text and criticism.

John Peck
Martin Coyle

Cardiff University

General Introduction

Queen Victoria reigned from 1837 to her death in 1901, and her name has become synonymous with the age. For students starting to study English literature, the term 'Victorian' suggests a quite specific historical juncture, tending to connote a peculiarly rigid set of ideas, circumstances, values and attitudes. These revolve around a number of concepts and themes, not to say clichés, which are frequently attributed to the Victorians, and they can be misleading. The Victorians are typically described as having lived rather drab lives that were little more than combinations of puritan ethics and repressions: severe moral probity, restraint, reserve, family values, a certain dourness or lack of humour, uncomfortable attitudes towards sex, stony faces in photographs, and black clothes. They are equally notorious for their intolerance towards social 'deviants' of all types. Criminals, lunatics, homosexuals and stray women were all treated severely or punished, and masturbation was discouraged by cold baths. In a society in which middle-class norms and attitudes rose to dominance, the working classes were also approached with caution and contempt, and foreignness in any shape or form was treated with suspicion and hostility.

As part of their complex middle-class ethos, the Victorians are just as famous for their liberalism and sense of industry. Concepts such as hard work, bustle, determination, energy, purpose and progress are all frequently attached to the Victorians, as are practical philosophies such as 'self-help' and 'philanthropy'. As these last two concepts suggest, however, the clichés surrounding the Victorian age, being clichés, turn out to be somewhat contradictory upon closer inspection: 'self-help' describes an ethos of self-sufficient individualism, while 'philanthropy' denotes an idea of charity or goodwill to others. As mutually defining oppositions, they are concepts which unsettle the clichés ascribed to the Victorians by operating as simultaneous attributes of the middle-class ethos. Similar contradictions appear when we consider the issue of sexual modesty. The general view is that the Victorians were prudish about the human body: everyone has an opinion, for example, about their reluctance to enjoy sex or reveal bits of their bodies. But this was an age when prostitution and pornography were rampant, homosexuals were jailed, transvestites roamed the nation's parks, population figures swelled, particularly in the crowded cities, and sex was discussed everywhere.

The contradictions and complexities of the Victorian period also have to be seen in the context of technological, and consequently social, change. In the aftermath of the Industrial Revolution, nineteenth-century Britain changed rapidly from a largely rural to a predominantly urban society, and the Victorians were unparalleled as innovators in the sciences and technology. Important engineering feats came to symbolize this change, especially the development of the railways from the 1830s onwards, one of the most singular and striking achievements being Isambard Kingdom Brunel's Great Western Railway linking London and Bristol, which was opened in 1835. A London to Birmingham railway was also in operation by 1838, and by the early 1840s the popular holiday destination of Brighton was served by a London to Brighton railway which cost around eight shillings (40p) for a cheap day return. By 1850, in fact, there were around six thousand miles of railway lines across Britain. For many Victorians, a better and faster railway system marked a better and faster Britain. The trains gave rise to greater efficiency in transport and communications, and enabled the swifter movement of vital resources and materials between the nation's core industrial centres.

Along with the railways came the new timetables drawn up to meet the increasing network of lines criss-crossing the country. British time was consequently forced to become synchronized and standardized, and this regulation determined a new sense of hourly structure and routine in daily life throughout the country. From that point onwards, Victorians would have to keep time with both the new trains themselves and the relentless chug of the modern world they inaugurated. Victorian engineers also undertook the construction of a series of massive bridge, tunnel and viaduct projects, primarily to facilitate better routes for the trains, and developments in communications technology enabled them to lay down longer and longer telegraph lines. After 1855, large-scale changes were also afoot in areas of health and sanitation. Engineers such as Joseph Bazalgette, for example, designed and constructed a sewerage system in London which eventually helped eradicate lethal diseases such as cholera. His project was encouraged by the outcry following the 'Great Stink' of 1858, which was caused by the pumping of raw sewage into the Thames.

Radical intellectual achievements were also beginning to shape and change the age. As with the railways, many Victorian theories and ideas would have an immeasurable impact on the way that people came to understand and live their lives. To draw upon only a few of the more obvious achievements, in chronological order, there was, for example, the publication of Karl Marx and Frederich Engels's work on the historical relationships between classes in *The Communist Manifesto*, which appeared in 1848 during a series of revolutionary upheavals throughout Europe. Eleven years later, in 1859, Charles Darwin published his theory of evolution in *The Origin of Species*. Although evolutionary ideas were not new to the Victorians (the work of Charles Lyell in 1830–3 and Robert Chambers in 1844 both held that organisms evolved from an original being created by God), Darwin's radical contribution was his theory of 'natural selection' and his stress upon the godless element of chance involved in evolutionary variation. His work posed the most lucid and persuasive challenge yet to religious orthodoxies, especially to the biblical idea of 'Creationism' and the notion of time, undermining centuries of Christian ideas about life on earth and the hierarchy of species. Towards the end of the century, Sigmund Freud's revolutionary ideas about psychosexual development, repression and the unconscious also began to receive recognition (and criticism). As with Marxism, psychoanalysis would have more impact in the twentieth and twenty-first centuries, and it originated in Continental Europe, not Britain. But, like Marxism, it is important to remember that it is a discourse rooted in nineteenth-century attitudes and anxieties, and that Freud's ideas germinated and came together in key publications such as *The Interpretation of Dreams* (1900), when Victoria was still alive.

To underline the influence of one of these intellectual achievements here, and its implications for modern literary criticism and theory, we can focus on Marxism. The construction of huge factories and mass industries throughout Britain in the Victorian period helped cultivate an increasingly class-conscious nation, and it is out of this context that Marx and Engels's ideas about the fundamentally exploitative nature of industrial capitalism became important for understanding the modern world. Their theories also, inevitably, informed the critical discussion of what is happening in, and how we interpret, Victorian literature although this has proved to be a far from simple story. It is, however, a far from simple story. In the early 'hungry forties', Engels witnessed at first hand what he described as the poverty and oppression endured by the British working classes in Manchester, then the centre of Britain's massive textile industry. He subsequently condemned the industrial-capitalist system in his polemical *Condition of the Working Classes in England* (1844). This text helped shape his collaboration with Marx, and the manner in which class relationships – which Marx and Engels saw as the driving force behind the history of the Western world – would be thought about and interpreted in the future. But Marx also developed theories about the way literature and culture participated in the spread and consolidation of 'ruling-class ideas'. One of the aims of this book, in this respect, is to demonstrate the various historical and theoretical ways in which Marx and modern Marxist literary critics have re-examined both 'ruling-class ideas' in Victorian literature and the tenets of basic Marxism.

The premise of basic or 'vulgar' Marxism is that the history of human relationships is governed entirely by the economic infrastructure of society. For some modern critics, especially postmodern critics, such an argument is reductive because it offers a far too sweeping 'grand narrative' of life and everything. Such reductionism, they maintain, fails to take account of the complex and ambiguous *other* movements of history, those which are made up, for example, of the numerous sexual, gender, or racial dimensions which cannot be simplified into a rigid, economic opposition between 'us' (the oppressed class) and 'them' (the dominating class). As with other critical and theoretical fields such as feminism, deconstruction, new historicism and psychoanalysis, and indeed the major Victorian ideas and attitudes themselves, *Key Concepts* provides crucial information on these complexities and some ideas about the various ways of approaching them. In doing so, the book demonstrates how and why a more complex approach to these ideas is important in any attempt to understand, and do justice to, the complexities of Victorian literature and culture.

II

Around the same time that Marx and Engels were establishing their social critique, Victorian writers also took up the cause of ordinary working people. In the 'Condition of England' or 'Social Problem' novels of the 1830s–50s, especially, the miseries and deprivations suffered by the British working classes came under increasingly heavy criticism. Two of the most famous and popular novels of this sub-genre were Elizabeth Gaskell's *Mary Barton* (1848) and Charles Dickens's *Hard Times* (1854). Gaskell's work is subtitled *A Tale of Manchester Life*, and Dickens's novel, although set in the fictional 'Coketown', is also a rendering of Manchester. Both novels deal with hardship, hunger, injustice and despair, and it is indicative of the changing role of fiction in the period, and the peculiarly Victorian confidence shared by Gaskell and Dickens, that they intended their works to be agents of social and economic reform.

In *Hard Times*, the weaver Stephen Blackpool is mistreated by the aptly named industrialist Josiah Bounderby, and just about everyone else in the novel (including his unpredictable wife). He is wrongly accused of theft, exiled by his union, made redundant, falls down an old mine shaft, and dies. And yet, as brutal and as unjust as conditions were, and however accurate Gaskell and Dickens were in reflecting these problems, in reality the new industrial systems proved to be hugely successful in terms of their overall contribution to the Victorian economy and the way that they sealed Britain's reputation around the world. Victoria's factories mass-produced a vast range of goods made from diverse natural and metallurgical resources – textiles (particularly clothes), steel, coal, hardware, household goods, pharmaceuticals, luxury goods – for a growing world market, and they ensured that the Queen would preside over the most powerful nation in history. With the Victorian industrialist and middle classes profiting from such growth, at the expense of workers such as Stephen Blackpool, Britain quickly became renowned as the 'workshop of the world'.

Given the importance of industry and trade, important shifts in the economic infrastructure of Victorian society are something that every student of the period needs to be aware of. In 1846, in the middle of the 'hungry forties', a new economic confidence slowly emerged in a climate of free trade heralded by the repeal of the Corn Laws (1846). Since 1815, the Corn Laws had imposed restrictive tariffs on imports of corn, and these led to inflated prices for domestic grain and home-baked bread. It was the Victorian poor who paid the price, in terms of deprivation, but also the poor who agitated against a law so weighted against their basic needs. The repeal of the Corn Laws signalled the slow retreat of some of the worst excesses and deprivations of the period, although not those associated with the concurrent Irish Famine (c.1845–52), which led to the starvation and emigration of millions from Ireland. However prematurely, a new decade, the 1850s, also indicated an era of prosperity after the 'hungry forties'. With a new spirit of confidence in place, in 1851 the Victorians undertook a grandiose project which seems largely to have been designed to show off their new-found prosperity to the world, and the 'workshop' of British superiority which made it possible.

The Great Exhibition (1851), heavily promoted by Prince Albert, took place fairly early on in Victoria's reign. It was a building which at once paraded Britain's economic success and imperial pre-eminence, and summed up the country's sense of a united purpose and identity. Housed in a Crystal Palace made almost exclusively of glass and iron, the exhibition dominated Hyde Park with all the robust British clarity, common sense and strength that the materials of its construction suggest. It was, to all intents and purposes, a kind of museum of modernity – British industrial-capitalist modernity – containing some 100,000 exhibits from around the world, and indeed it was British showpieces that dominated the floor space. On display were many of the instruments, apparatuses, designs, machines and tools (such as telegraphs and newfangled gadgets such as early cameras), which Victorians thought were making Britain 'great'. These included cotton-spinning and printing machines, industrial hammers, engines, locomotives, and the many other engineering and technological 'miracles' which were used in the nation's factories and mills. Records of the exhibition's floor plan indicate that although the nation's working classes were permitted entry, the exhibits were laid out in such a way that the role of the many Stephen Blackpools who operated them in reality was effectively downplayed. The Great Exhibition all but ignored, in other words, the human cost of Victorian industrialism.

Elsewhere in the exhibition, there were a range of international artefacts and curiosities on display, including the paraphernalia of empire such as Bengal ivories and stuffed elephants. All of the exhibits glamourized Britain's domestic and colonial achievements around the globe, and the stuffed elephants were, in this respect, more emblematic of British dominance in India than any celebration of Indian culture. Nonetheless, millions paid to come and see the exhibition over the six months it was open to the public. At the same time, the fact that Britain's economic gains and successes throughout the period, on the back of the Industrial Revolution, were also attributable to its prowess in world trade, is a significant factor in any understanding of the Victorians and their literature. The Great Exhibition celebrated an increasingly global market, but it also underlined the ambition, on the part of the Victorians, to establish the greatest empire the world had ever seen. By the time of Victoria's death in 1901, a full generation after she had been crowned Empress of India in 1876, the Victorians had succeeded in realizing this ambition. Following the last phase of the 'Scramble for Africa' campaigns, during which Britain carved out the lion's share of that continent, the British Empire had begun to govern around a quarter of the population of the globe. Back at home, meanwhile, as if pointing towards the hollowness of everything the Victorians achieved, both in Britain and abroad, the Crystal Palace was dismantled and relocated to South London. There it languished as a popular destination for day trips, before finally being destroyed by fire in 1936. After its months of glory in 1851, Joseph Paxton's tribute to Victorian might had become an empty and vulnerable shell.

If 1851 provides one key point of reference, we also need to be aware of the longer picture. Most commentators describe the Victorian era as part of a broader historical period known as the 'long nineteenth century'. This period, approximately 1815–1914, includes all of the events and affairs which distinguish British history throughout these years, from the end of one great European conflict, the Napoleonic Wars, to the outbreak of another, the First World War. In this respect, although this book deals specifically with key concepts in Victorian literature, the important point to make at this juncture is that this more extensive historical scope needs to be remembered when approaching the period. Quite obviously, many of the significant political and cultural events which shaped the age cannot easily be contained by the specific years defined by Victoria's reign. Neither did Victorian writers begin being 'Victorian' in 1837 and start being 'modernist' in 1901. Put another way, the Victorian age, its culture, ideas, problems and anxieties, the key concepts of its literature and their implications, are simply not as neat as the years 1837–1901 would suggest. When, otherwise, does the immediately preceding age of Romanticism (*c.*1789–1830) end, exactly, and to what extent do the ideas and concepts that characterize Romanticism still inform the Victorian age? Are there really discernible cut-off dates or points, and if there are, how do we account for the intervening years between 1830 and 1837, during William IV's short reign? For some critics, it is indeed the decline of the long 'Georgian' period (1714–1830), evidenced as early as the late eighteenth century in the so-called 'Romantic' decades, and not simply Victoria's accession to the throne, which marks the beginnings of 'Victorianism' as a definable concept. These were the tumultuous years of the French revolution (1789) and Britain's wars against Napoleonic France (1800–15). They were also the years leading up to the first great Reform Act (1832) and the New Poor Law (1834), when the notion of fundamental changes to the British constitution first seemed a real possibility and the nation's electorate was slightly expanded. At the other end of the nineteenth century, some commentators argue that the period considered by many to have succeeded Victorianism in literature and culture, modernism (*c.* 1890–1939), probably has origins as far back as the 1870s, more or less in the middle of Victoria's reign.

Evidently, the problems attendant on periodization underline why the many clichés and shibboleths ascribed to the Victorians need to be approached with caution. The entries in this book and the period covered by the chronology (1800–1914) have been selected with these problems specifically in mind. To that end, the book does not simply dispense with the clichés and the shibboleths. Rather, it re-examines them, in order to provide a more thorough research tool for twenty-first-century students of the period. Victorian Britain in the 1830s undoubtedly did undergo what Edward Bulwer Lytton, in *England and the English* (1833), described as an 'age of transition – an age of disquietude and doubt'. But this is not to suggest that other periods were not equally unsettled or transitory. More to the point, the reasons for these transitions and their implications are as many and complex as they are difficult to affix reliable dates to.

III

A few points about the structure and method of this volume are also required here. Over three sections, *Key Concepts* provides a series of small essays on a range of problems and issues associated with Victorian literature and its criticism. The first part, 'Contexts', deals with the numerous historical, political and cultural concepts which shaped the literature, and its scope is as broad as these categories suggest. Following the entry 'Age of Victoria', readers will find in the section alphabetical entries on a number of quite specific issues ranging from 'Architecture' to 'War'. Each of these will equip the reader with a three-step approach to the concept in question: the important historical and cultural facts required in order to contextualize a concept such as war in the nineteenth-century; the significant ideas surrounding the impact of war on Victorian consciousness; and lastly, by means of a series of close, theoretically informed readings, the ways with which to apply these facts and ideas to Victorian literature.

The same approach applies to the second and third parts of the book. Part 2, 'Texts', comprises discussions of the various literary genres and forms which make up Victorian texts. In this section, however, the emphasis is very much on genres, sub-genres and forms, rather than individual texts or authors. Hence there are a number of entries on subdivisions of the novel form but only one entry each on Poetry and Drama. The huge and diverse forms which make up Victorian poetry and drama cannot possibly be contained within a few paragraphs, and I have not tried to take on such a task in this section. It was, nonetheless, with some reluctance that due to restrictions on space and a need to prioritize what students are most likely to be interested in reading about, I allocated these concepts only two separate entries. Readers will, on the other hand, find discussions of Victorian poetry and drama integrated into various entries elsewhere in the book. The 'Contexts' section, for example, contains a separate entry on the poetry of the Pre-Raphaelite Brotherhood, one of the major poetic and artistic movements of the day, and the entry on 'Decadence and Aestheticism' incorporates a discussion of Oscar Wilde's dramatic works. Otherwise, as the entry on Poetry in 'Texts' attempts to show, many Victorian poets were great innovators in poetic form, and the 'dramatic monologues' form experimented with by major figures such as Alfred Lord Tennyson and Robert Browning were especially significant. Similarly, as I demonstrate in the entry on Drama, the theatre was immensely popular with the Victorian public. Although nineteenth-century plays were very much dominated by the genre of melodrama, social problem theatre also proved to be popular, and more controversial, towards the end of Victoria's reign.

Unavoidably, however, the preponderance of fiction in this section of the book also reflects the rise of the novel as the major form in Victorian literature. By mid-nineteenth century, after its emergence in the early eighteenth century, the novel had become truly pre-eminent, and for the first time its popularity eclipsed the previously dominant form in English literature, poetry. For the Victorians, fiction seems to have become the most suitable medium with which to reflect the 'age of transition' to the modern industrial world that they were building, and it is part of the task of Part 2 of this book to examine the historical and cultural reasons behind this development. The 'Victorian novel', at least as we have come to know it, has some of its roots in the early works of one of its great innovators, Charles Dickens. Intriguingly enough, *The Pickwick Papers* (1836–7) and *Oliver Twist* (1837) were even published during the first year of Victoria's reign. The novel's rise was then consolidated in what critics often describe as the peak years between 1847 and 1852, a period which the entry in this section on the Mid-Victorian Novel attempts to cover. At a glance, these years were certainly prolific for Victorian novelists. Publications included Charlotte Brontë's *Jane Eyre* (1847) and *Shirley* (1849), Emily Brontë's *Wuthering Heights* (1847), Elizabeth Gaskell's *Mary Barton* (1848) and William Thackeray's *Vanity Fair* (1847), as well as Dickens's *Dombey and Son* (1848) and *David Copperfield* (1850). *Key Concepts* sets out to explore the historical and cultural upheaval in which such a proliferation of novels were produced, and the many sociopolitical tensions and problems that resonate within them.

These days, Victorian studies are inseparable from modern developments in literary and critical theory, and this is why Part 3 of this book turns to 'Criticism'. Approaches to the period now come armed with an array of critical practices and 'isms', some of which can be bewildering for readers encountering them for the first time, and any list of them sounds exhausting: cultural materialism, new historicism, feminism, Marxism, postcolonialism, postmodernism, poststructuralism, structuralism, not to mention deconstruction, psychoanalysis, and queer theory. It is my intention in this section to clarify and explain these

approaches, but also to seek ways of applying them to Victorian literature. As with the preceding sections, each entry has a three-part structure. The concept of feminism, for example, is explained in terms of its
historical development (its rise in the 1970s, but also its origins in the
Victorian period); the major ideas underpinning feminism (its challenge
to patriarchal ideology); and some of the ways in which feminist critics
and theorists have approached Victorian literature (particularly the
portrayal of women by the literature of a male-dominated culture and
society). Each entry points out the distinguishing features of the separate
critical approaches and, where appropriate, their points of overlap. My
aim is to disentangle these approaches without reducing them, thereby
using them to read Victorian literature as closely, clearly – and politically
– as possible.

By way of example, let us say that the reader is researching the representation of 'food' in the mid-Victorian novel, and that he or she is also
interested in the broader historical problem of empire. The reader will,
to begin with, find an entry on Food and Famine in the 'Contexts' section
of this book. This situates the concept of food in Victorian literature
against its historical contexts, including the economic and industrial
crises of the 'hungry forties', the epoch-making potato famine in Ireland
(c.1845–51), and British colonialist ideas about the Irish that grew out
of centuries of tension between the two nations. With the aid of postcolonial theory, the entry then applies these ideas to a mid-Victorian
novel, Charlotte Brontë's *Shirley*, which refers, often obliquely, to all of
these problems and issues. As the structure of Food and Famine
suggests, *Key Concepts* is designed to work in a fairly specific kind of
way, and the entry can be read separately from other entries.
Alternatively, any reader wishing to expand his or her research on this
topic will also find entries from the other two parts of the book useful
and instructive. He or she can then, for example, cross-examine one
entry from 'Contexts' (Food and Famine), two related entries from
'Texts' (Mid-Victorian Novel and Social-problem Novel), and one entry
from 'Criticism' (Postcolonialism). The information contained at the foot
of each entry, under *See also*, is designed to indicate where the reader
might find an entry on another concept helpful. The section on Further
Reading should be self-explanatory.

A second example will clarify the way this book works. The entry on
Slavery, in the 'Contexts' section, begins with the significant dates and
events which defined British involvement in the Atlantic slave trade.
This information will furnish readers with the crucial facts about the
origins and abolition of the British trade (c.1562 to 1807), and the abolition of slavery as an institution throughout the British colonies (1833–4),

just a few years before Victoria's accession to the throne. As with the entry on Food and Famine, the important point to bear in mind here is that any representations of slavery in Victorian literature are better understood when the historical, conceptual and theoretical circum stances behind the topic are first clarified. Readers can then enrich their research by drawing on the information provided by related entries in 'Contexts', such as Empire, Nation, and Race, before turning to Postcolonialism or another such as Marxism, in the third section, on 'Criticism'.

The fact that Victorian literature is haunted by images of slavery has become increasingly important to modern critical approaches to the period. That such images appear so soon after the British government in 1833 dismantled the formal institutions that made slavery possible, begins to make more sense when Britain's status as one of the major slaving nations in modern history is explained. Postcolonial critics and theorists are then better-positioned to ask what this suggests about the Victorian imagination and its colonial consciousness, or about the peculiarly oppressive nature of the power struggles between men and women that form such a prominent feature of Victorian literature, and which some feminist and Marxist critics have suggested are akin to those relationships which underpin slavery. Researchers will also be in a better position to understand how Victorians understood and approached another important concept which finds an entry in 'Contexts', Race, a topic which is also, inevitably, touched on in entries on Slavery, Empire, Nation, Other, and so on.

In brief, postcolonial theory attempts to understand the ways in which Victorian literature can be read and interpreted in the light of nineteenth-century Britain's status as a colonial world power, of which slavery was pivotal. Postcolonial theorists and critics are also interested in the complex manner in which Victorian texts represent foreigners and foreign lands, especially, but not exclusively, those nations and territories colonized and enslaved by the British. The fact, at the same time, that the literature of the period is also bound up with what many critics describe as the Victorian 'invention' of British identity is also integral to the problem. Indeed, the chief aim of this book is to encourage the reader to read and think across a number of contextual, textual and critical categories. The researcher into a key concept such as slavery will then be poised to ask what the implications of all these problems are for the construction of British identity and the British Empire in Victorian literature, and how it might all be most intelligently and persuasively understood.

1 Contexts: History, Politics, Culture

Introduction

The logic of this section has to some extent been explained in the introductory essay to this volume. Here I want to clarify the scope – and the basis of selection – of the entries that appear in Contexts, and how they relate to what follows in the next two sections. In any historical period there are ideas, of a social, political, economic and ideological nature, that are central to people's thinking. In broad terms, we refer to the sum of these ideas as the cultural context in which people live. In the medieval period, for example, religion would have been a key factor in people's lives, and this continued to be the case in the Victorian period. But the Victorians experienced a different kind of religious faith, one which competed with a whole range of other key concepts: industrialism, capitalism, science, evolution, consumerism, the law, the nation, the ideology of family, to name only some of the most significant or obvious. All these concepts (and more) vied with religion for the hearts and minds of private individuals and public opinion alike, and it is these central aspects of Victorian life that are discussed in the essays in this section.

Contexts provides a starting point for a fairly specific kind of investigation. As comprehensively as possible, it covers the many ideas and concepts the Victorians clung to, or rather the complex array of issues and problems which underpinned their cultural framework and which both reassured them and caused them anxiety, often at the same time. The section ranges across obviously significant contexts, including Class, Religion, Science, Sex and War, to those less obvious, at least perhaps to literary critics, such as Architecture, Body, Clothing, Drugs, Madness and Music. Although it is, it need hardly be pointed out, within such contexts that literary texts are produced, literature is also our principal means of gaining access to the culture of attitudes and neuroses which have contributed to our understanding of the Victorians. At the same time, the section is designed to work in such a way as to encourage readers to think about the Victorians and their age from a combination of perspectives which should be construed as inseparable. The first is in terms of the broader historical picture of the nineteenth century provided by the section; the second is in terms of the endless churning of ideas, attitudes, contradictions, nuances and idiosyncrasies which made the Victorians tick and which are, crucially, such an integral and exciting feature of their literature. To that end, the entry on Childhood, for example, provides readers with vital information on the horrors facing Victorian children – especially poor Victorian children – such as infant mortality rates, child labour systems, prostitution, and the enduring miseries of nineteenth-century education systems. It proceeds from these facts to the highly sentimentalized and often paradoxical idea of childhood in Victorian consciousness, and from there to representations of childhood in Victorian literature. Each entry offers, along these lines, a detailed and thorough explanation of the key concept or context under discussion. Each, similarly, within the limited space provided, has the aim of arriving at as full a picture of the Victorians and their literature as possible.

'Contexts' is not, however, intended in any way to be encyclopaedic or comprehensive. On the contrary, it is intended to give readers a historical and contextual framework through which to approach Victorian literature, but with the added aim of encouraging readers to work out from each entry and pursue their research further. Readers of the section (as with the other two sections in the volume) can, with these objectives in mind, expect to find each entry supplemented by two sub-sections. The first is the 'See also' feature, which indicates where other entries elsewhere in the volume might be useful or helpful, either within the Contexts section itself or in the Texts and Criticism sections. The second, 'Further reading', provides suggestions for research outside of this volume. Both sub-sections can be found at the foot of each entry, and, as with the section as a whole, they have two major aims. One is to enrich the depth and scope of the reader's understanding of Victorian contexts, by encouraging a method of cross-examination, and the other is to urge readers to read Victorian literature critically and theoretically at all times. The suggestions for further reading, in particular, point readers towards the wide and ever-expanding world of modern literary studies and criticism. This is a world which, in its own richness and complexity, has contributed significantly to the rich and complex way in which the Victorians and their age must be understood.

Age of Victoria

Commentators tend to separate the Victorian age into early, mid and late periods. Victoria's reign (1837–1901) began shortly after the establishment in 1829 of Robert Peel's Metropolitan Police Force and the passage of the first great Reform Act of 1832. The police force heralded the new Victorian age of greater state discipline and a clampdown on crime, while the Reform Act, the first of three (one, it seems, for each of the early, mid and late Victorian periods) doubled a very small electorate. Although the proportion of Victorians eligible to vote rose again, following the subsequent great reform acts of 1867 and 1884–5, only around 12 per cent of the population were enfranchised in 1886, and women were all but excluded until 1918. Poor and destitute early Victorians also suffered under the Poor Law (Amendment) Act (1834), which forced more of them into the workhouse systems and orphanages famously condemned in Charles Dickens's *Oliver Twist* (1837). Meanwhile, early Victorians witnessed the dismantlement of slavery in the British colonies (1833–8), the age of working-class radicalism and the democratic reforms called for by the Chartist movement (*c*.1830s–40s), and momentous engineering and technological achievements such as the establishment of the railway system.

The economic depressions and the resultant socioindustrial crises of the 'hungry forties' and the Irish Famine (*c*.1845–1852), brought about other momentous events such as the repeal of the Corn Laws (1846). These laws, since 1815, had set British corn prices at an artificially (and unfeasibly) high rate, and they were blamed for causing much of the hunger and unrest in the period. Although Robert Peel's Corn Laws repeal legislation tends to sound somewhat insignificant in the more grandiose story of Victorian achievement and progress, it is important to stress that it did lead to two major developments, the impact and implications of which are obvious: cheaper bread (eventually) for starving Victorians, and the triumph of Britain's free-trade system. Indeed, the political and economic debates surrounding the repeal of the Corn Laws proved to be hugely influential. They had a direct bearing on the way the balance of power in nineteenth-century Britain was beginning to shift from the old landowner class to a burgeoning class of industrialists, manufacturers and tradesmen, who were spurred on by the new spirit of laissez-faire (non-state interference) economics heralded by repeal. Such a shift, albeit gradual, transformed Victorian Britain from a largely rural and agricultural society, based on a monopoly of landed and state-controlled interests, to an urban and industrial society, based on an increasing culture of individualism and capitalism. The change further ensured that Victoria reigned over a nation which, temporarily at least, had by the 1850s–60s begun to enjoy a period of relative prosperity and peace.

The new balance of power in society also intensified class tensions. Despite the creation of a disaffected but increasingly well-organized –

and in some quarters militant – working class, it was not, however, until 1871 that government legislation permitted the establishment of Trade Unions (the first Women's Trade Union League was formed in 1874). This legislation followed a history of complex 'Combination' laws typified by those promulgated before Victoria's reign. One, for example, in 1824, permitted the peaceful 'combinations' of some workers, while another, in 1825, swiftly prohibited them. A Factory Act of 1874 further recommended the relative leniency of a 56-hour week for the nation's workforce, although children under the age of 12 were still working in Britain's factories and industries as late as 1901 (the year of Victoria's death), when another Factory Act made this particular form of exploitation illegal. Although, then, the general story of the Victorian period is one of astonishing economic progress, the vast majority did not enjoy the benefits of prosperity. Indeed, by the last third of the century it begins to become clear that the Victorians lived under a capitalist system of free-trade economics which was at the increasing mercy of periodic booms and slumps. The most notable slump began in the early 1870s, when the 'great depression' set in, a downward trend which was to last well into the mid-1890s.

The economic changes of the Victorian period affected every aspect of life. Most obviously, Victoria presided over a population which after decades of industrialism and urbanization had swollen from around 9 million in 1801 to around 18 million in 1851. At her death in 1901, this figure had risen again to around 30 million. Intriguingly, though, the religious consensus of 1851 revealed that only a third of Britain's mid-century population attended church regularly. Although such figures do not necessarily mean that religion was less important to everyday British lives at a personal level, the faith of Victorians would nonetheless be increasingly shaken as the century wore on. It is illuminating, in this respect, to juxtapose these attendance figures with the fact that the 1851 census was carried out in the same year of the Great Exhibition in Hyde Park, that most visible monument to Victorian industrialism and capitalist might. That is to say, if Victorians were not worshipping at church, they were certainly worshipping their own less spiritual and more material achievements, and over 6 million paid to walk through the doors of the Crystal Palace in the half-year it was open to the public. Other Victorians adopted a more conservative religious stance in the period. The assertiveness of the Oxford Movement of Tractarians (c. 1830s–40s) for example – a complex but devout group that campaigned for greater spiritual observance in the face of industrial modernity, and which saw leading exponent John Newman's controversial conversion to Roman Catholicism in 1845 – reflected a grasping after traditional values. Such values were something perhaps particularly to be desired when the public and private consciousness of all Victorians, either consciously or otherwise, became subject to the increasing sway of more rationalist and scientific ideas and practices. Eventually, these influences led to the steady retreat or rather the displacement of faith, and the emergence of a more secular British society overall.

Underlying everything, however, was the economic strength of the nation. The early to mid-Victorian years, between roughly 1830 and 1875, were the triumphant years of British self-confidence, and in these decades the Victorians established a buoyant but increasingly productive economy, which ultimately created greater prosperity for a larger proportion of society. But they were also decades that witnessed a period of British isolationism from European affairs, a situation which, according to some commentators, only really came to an end after Victoria's death in 1901, with the *Entente Cordiale* (1904) between Britain and France. By that stage, in a context of increasing national hostilities and empire building, Britain had again started to cast about for European allies against the perceived new threat to national security posed by Germany. Although Victoria's 'dear soldiers', as she called them, fought in numerous imperial skirmishes and wars of conquest throughout the nineteenth century, in Europe they were involved in only one major conflict during her reign, the disastrously mismanaged Crimean War (1853–6). In this war, Britain allied itself with its historical enemy, France, against Russia, largely to prevent what the allies feared to be Russian expansionism south into Europe, Britain being largely concerned with protecting its maritime routes to its Eastern empire. In the British Empire itself, Victoria's armies became embroiled in other major incidents, especially, again, in the earlier period, and most notoriously during the Indian Mutiny (1857). But they were also involved in the later contexts of European nationalism and colonialism, in tumultuous events which were to reach their climax in the Boer Wars (1899–1902) in South Africa, between British forces and settlers of Dutch descent. At home, in the same period (c.1899), Victoria's shipyards and armaments factories had begun manufacturing again in earnest, primarily to keep up with Germany's increasingly dangerous-looking battleship programme. The subsequent naval race between Britain and Germany underlined the growing threat of national crises and conflict in nineteenth-century Europe, which would culminate in the First World War of 1914–18.

On the domestic stage, political affairs were dominated by tensions and rivalries which also climaxed in the late Victorian period. As if to underline the radical uncertainties and sociopolitical upheavals which would come to define the nineteenth century, in fact, between 1868 and

1892 virtually alternate governments were formed by the Liberal and Conservative parties, and by two of the most influential statesman and individuals of the age: the Liberal William Ewart Gladstone, and the Conservative Benjamin Disraeli. When, for example, Gladstone succeeded Disraeli as prime minister for the second time in 1880, he inherited, (along with a series of complex foreign affairs), one affair which was much closer to home, the implications of which would dominate British politics in the twentieth century and beyond. During the so-called 'Home Rule' crisis, late Victorians were repeatedly asked to reconsider Britain's long history of involvement and colonial settlement in Ireland. In the face of growing demands from Irish nationalists for Ireland's secession from Britain, Gladstone's mission was to disestablish the Irish church and 'pacify Ireland'. His 'Home Rule' bills were, however, successively defeated in parliament, first in 1886, and again in 1893, five years before his death in 1898.

Other important shifts in the sociopolitical and cultural contexts of the later Victorian period were signified by W. E. Forster's Education Act of 1870. This legislation eventually ensured that elementary education for all British children was compulsory, and it was instrumental in helping them out of the nation's industries and factories. In the same year, women gained better monetary rights (after marriage) over wages earned, and in 1878, after the passage of the Matrimonial Causes Act, they were permitted separation from their husbands on the grounds of assault or cruelty. Following the Married Women's Property Act (1882), women also gained full rights over their property. This act overturned a timeworn legal concept and custom known as 'coverture', which for centuries had effectively placed the woman – and everything she owned – under her husband's 'protection'. In 1886, women were also granted more equitable custody rights over their children, although only in the event of the father's death, and by the early 1870s–1880s, the so-called 'Woman Question' had increasingly come to the foreground in Victorian popular consciousness. Politically, the plight of women was made most visible (and audible) by the suffragette movement's calls for the women's vote, and culturally by the changing social roles and economic status of women dealt with in the controversial 'New Women' drama and literature of the day. Morever, the late Victorian period, even more so than earlier periods, was marked by growing anxieties about gender roles, promiscuity and sexuality in general. Such anxieties were signified, most obviously, by the raising of the age of consent to 16 in 1885, most violently, by the furore surrounding the 'Jack the Ripper' murders of prostitutes in Whitechapel in 1888, and, most controversially, by the Oscar Wilde trial for homosexuality in 1895.

In an age of conflicting ideas and changing attitudes, a range of celebrated social and political commentators emerged. The Victorians produced critics, essayists, historians, rhetoricians, polemicists, satirists, wits and moralists, most of whom seemed capable of holding forth on just about everyone and everything. Certain individuals did, more importantly, have a massive influence on the intellectual and cultural contexts of the age. Amongst the names which made such an essential contribution are: Thomas Carlyle, with his diatribes on everything from the so-called 'Condition of England Question', to the French Revolution, God, work, Chartism, the idea of the hero, the 'negro question', race and slavery; John Ruskin, with his influential criticisms of art, architecture and morality; the educationist and poet Matthew Arnold, with his speculative and satirical ideas about high and low culture; the utilitarian philosopher John Stuart Mill, with his writings on individual liberty and women's subjection; and Thomas Babington Macaulay, who was, amongst other things, a reactionary advocate of political 'evolution' or 'gradual' – and above all peaceful – progress. One must, inevitably, add to this list the ground-breaking scientific work of Charles Darwin, especially the publication of his *On the Origin of Species* (1859); the revolutionary writings of Karl Marx; and Sigmund Freud's controversial ideas about psychoanalysis towards the end of the century. All of these writers and thinkers (mainly, but not exclusively, men), form an integral feature of the intellectual, philosophical and ideological contexts of the Victorian period, and much of the social and political conflicts they gave rise to. It is, indeed, against the fervent and complex historical backdrop of such conflicts that we need to contextualize the broad changes and movements in Victorian literature.

See also General Introduction; *Contexts*: Economics; *Criticism*: Introduction.

Further Reading

Roberts, Adam C., *Victorian Culture and Society: The Essential Glossary* (London: Edward Arnold, 2003).
Wilson, A. N., *The Victorians* (London: Hutchinson, 2002).

Architecture

Architecture in nineteenth-century Britain is full of contradictions. On the one hand, the Victorians built largely to accommodate what was, by Queen Victoria's accession in 1837, the first and most heavily industrialized nation the world had ever seen. Their innovative designs for factories, railway stations, civic buildings and working-class terraced housing in industrial centres earned them their reputation for utility, purpose, common sense and functionalism. On the other hand, for all the British 'strength' and 'solidity' associated with Victorian building materials, such as red brick and ferroconcrete (concrete fortified with steel), and despite the fact that many Victorian architects removed stuccoed façades in order to expose the 'truth' or 'reality' of the rawer materials beneath, much of Victorian architecture remained elaborate, not to say fanciful. Many of the more functional designs were mixed with a rich sense of indulgence, flamboyance and some sentimentality. Richer Victorians, like their eighteenth- and seventeenth-century forebears, enjoyed splashing out on Tudor or Gothic manor-house retreats, and in major cities, such as London, an intricate array of fine Victorian public buildings and pleasure parks sprang up. At the same time, many British cities boasted a similarly eclectic mix of Georgian, Gothic-revivalist, Venetian and Dorian buildings, resplendent with their ornate facades, tall chimneys, formidable-looking gables, and porches.

There was conflict and considerable confusion in architectural debates surrounding public buildings of the period, with tensions between neo-classical and Gothic-revivalist ideas being particularly pointed. In short, some nineteenth-century architects, like their predecessors, tended to favour the rationalism of perpendicular angles and symmetrical lines over the often more asymmetrical designs associated with Gothic/mediaeval buildings, and there were instructive reasons behind their preferences. Greco-Roman façades, for instance, with their almighty pillars, dignified pediments and marble-white purity, lent buildings of the British Empire the lustre and splendour of classical empires, and this gave them an historical and forward-looking aspect. Alternatively, neo-Gothic architecture suggested a more romanticized and complex layering of the nation's relationship to its past. The 'Gothic revival' was part of the broader obsession with mediaevalism throughout Victorian culture and literature. Following the Church Building Act of 1818, the majority of British churches, including London's Church of All Saints (1859), were built or rebuilt in a Gothic or neo-Gothic style, only partly because this style was cheaper. The revival marked a return to those architectural designs which typify the Western Gothic tradition: pointed arches (rather than rounded), asymmetrical planning, mediaeval towers, long galleries, ornamental traceries, rose windows and gargoyles. Many Victorian houses also experienced a Gothic make-over throughout the century, as did numerous public buildings, and architects and builders of the mid-Victorian period, were particularly prolific. Although the fashion for neo-Gothic slowly declined towards the end of the century, it was this period which saw the erection of many of the

Gothic-inspired cathedrals and public buildings which dominate British townscapes to this day.

The Gothic revival was championed by the influential social commentator and art critic, John Ruskin. It was Ruskin who, in *The Stones of Venice* (1851–3), underlined the significance of the relationship between architecture and nationhood: 'All good architecture is the expression of national life and character.' The problem, however, lies in ascertaining what kind of nation, exactly, is 'expressed' by Victorian architecture, and what its implications are. To take just one famous example, one of the more famous and grandiose neo-Gothic projects undertaken by the Victorians was the Houses of Parliament, which after a fire in 1834 was redesigned and rebuilt by Charles Barry, with decorations and embellishments applied by the devout Augustus Pugin. Built during the early years of Victoria's reign (*c*.1837–60), this extravagant Gothic pile has dominated the London cityscape along the Thames embankment ever since. In many ways, Barry's architecture encapsulates the way in which the Victorians were masters at moving 'Britishness' forwards by constantly looking backwards (in Barry's case to mediaevalism). With all its robust stateliness and imploring spires and pinnacles, the building displays a conspicuously Victorian sense of ascendant world power and optimism. And because the building also resembles a church, Barry's monument to democracy has an air of religious grandeur which disguises its manifestly secular function. The Houses of Parliament consequently stand as a firmly modern achievement, but one which still seemed traditional for those Victorians who were determined to retain the nation's material connection with the past. Similarly, the Gothic revival and the testament, on the part of such buildings, to the power and might of Victorian Britain is characterized by the sheer size and presence of the other functional and secular projects the revival inspired, particularly London's daunting St Pancras Hotel (1868–74), and Alfred Waterhouse's colossal Manchester Town Hall (1868–77). All of these buildings reflect a nation that would, by the time of Victoria's death in 1901, form the hub of the most powerful empire in history. They are the bricks and mortar, in other words, of nineteenth-century capitalism and modernity.

The impact of architecture on Victorian consciousness is difficult to quantify. However, because its impact is invested with political dimensions, its implications for the literature of the day are far-reaching. Time and again, for example, a writer such as Charles Dickens places his individual heroes, such as Oliver Twist, Nicholas Nickleby or David Copperfield, in gloomy and oppressive buildings, in the architecture of Victorian discipline signified by the workhouse, the court, the prison, the ragged school and the factory. Oliver Twist is also led by the Artful

Dodger into the working-class disorder of labyrinthine streets and 'knots of houses', on the way to Fagin's den of pickpockets. He is then steered into the safe and more ordered interiors of the middle-class Brownlow and Maylie households, where he is eventually saved: 'a neat house, in a quiet shady street near Pentonville'. Buildings shaped the sense of space inhabited by individuals in Victorian literature. Their layout as *Oliver Twist* suggests, created and maintained the space between Victorian upper and working- or under-classes, just as it established a division between private and public space. As the century wore on, the space of work for most Victorians moved out of the home and increasingly became part of 'public' life, a separation marked by striking architectural differences between, for example, house and factory. It was a separation which was to have important implications for the domestic division of labour in Victorian society, particularly in terms of the role of women and the family.

One major effect of this division was that the integrity of 'home' as a space of privacy and intimacy became deeply enshrined in Victorian culture. Architects of the period ensured that middle- and upper-class households, at least, were divided into separate rooms to suit each function of the day: dining rooms, bathrooms, bedrooms, studies and so on, rooms that also acted as refuges for individuals. Yet whereas the popular novels of the day, like *Oliver Twist*, underline the Victorian ideals of domesticity, family and the sanctity of 'hearth and home', the idea of an individual space is taken to satirical extremes elsewhere in Dickens's work. In *Bleak House* (1853), for example, there is a 'Growlery', a room in which Mr Jarndyce goes, 'when I am out of humour', and in *Little Dorrit* (1857) there is a 'Snuggery', a Marshalsea prison 'tavern establishment'. Inmates would be snug, one presumes, in a Snuggery, away from the hurly-burly of Victorian prison life, and the room is described as 'convivial' in the novel. But the Snuggery is also, as Dickens puts it, as 'hot and strong' as 'grog for the ladies', and ironically, 'defective: being but a cooped-up apartment'.

The seclusion of space and the sanctuary held out by the reassuring idea of 'house and home' is rendered more complex by other works of Victorian literature. This is particularly the case with those novels written by women, whose role in the period was very much confined to the private and domestic sphere of 'house and home'. In Charlotte Brontë's *Jane Eyre* (1847), 'homes', and especially middle- and upper-class homes, often resemble prisons and asylums; they are, if anything, more like extensions of the architecture of discipline seen in Dickens's work than refuges for individuals. That the comfort and shelter provided by the house might also mean it is a place of restriction and correction is, for example, suggested by the novel's famous opening words: 'There was no possibility of taking a walk that day'. Indeed, as part of the overall theme of women's oppression in the novel, Brontë's novel is full of cell-like rooms. As a child, Jane Eyre is imprisoned in the 'red room' at Gateshead, and later in the novel it transpires that Bertha Mason, Rochester's first wife, is imprisoned as a 'madwoman' in the attic of Thornfield Hall.

In George Eliot's *Middlemarch* (1872), another best-selling novel written by a woman, the plucky heroine Dorothea Brooke finds, initially at least, a sense of liberation and delight in the interiors of her new marital home, Lowick House. This is despite the otherwise disconcerting mix of happiness and melancholy which seems mixed into the building's foundations:

> Dorothea, on the contrary, found the house and grounds all that she could wish: the dark book-shelves in the long library, the carpets and curtains subdued by time, the curious old maps and bird's-eye views on the walls of the corridor, with here and there an old vase below, had no oppression for her.

The sense of foreboding and disarray conveyed by the layout of Lowick House is, at this stage, more unsettling for the reader than for Dorothea. But amid its 'dark' book-shelves, 'subdued' soft-furnishings and dusty interiors, the building does suggest that something dismal is imminent. Moreover, it is instructive that Dorothea's positive first impressions of the building are described in terms of a quintessentially Victorian negative, 'had no oppression', rather than a positive, 'freedom', especially as her already unpromising marriage to the grimly academic Mr Casaubon is destined to dissolve into unhappiness, financial jeopardy and 'oppression' thereafter. As early as the next scene, in fact, when Dorothea is shown to her private chamber, the architecture of Lowick further betrays its brooding atmosphere of entrapment and decay. The room is, as in *Jane Eyre*, inhabited by the spectre of a repressed woman:

> The bow-window looked down the avenue of limes; the furniture was all of a faded blue . . . The chairs and tables were thin-legged and easy to upset. It was a room where one might fancy the ghost of a tight-laced lady revisiting the scene of her embroidery.

The narrative suggests that Dorothea's bedchamber is a room made suitable for prissy and angelic Victorian drudges, not for the spirited and beautiful likes of Eliot's heroine. The lovelessness and misery that over-shadows Dorothea's marriage is then described in the architectural terms of another mazy house-of-correction, in which, during the couple's honeymoon in the ruins of Ancient Rome, Eliot maps out the mind like plans for a building: 'How was it that in the weeks since her marriage, Dorothea had not distinctly observed but felt with a stifling depression, that the large vistas and wide fresh air which she had dreamed of finding in her husband's mind were replaced by ante-rooms and winding passages which seemed to lead nowhither?' That Dorothea gets 'lost' and confused between the metaphorical walls closing in on her, and that they signify the oppressions of her marriage to a cold and hardened older man, is an idea compounded when Eliot begins to mix her architectural metaphors with those of 'voyages' and 'seas'. There, when 'the door-sill of marriage' is 'crossed', as Eliot puts it, it is 'impos-sible not to be aware that . . . you are exploring an enclosed basin'. Her metaphors underline the point that, all too often in *Middlemarch*, as in many women's novels of the period, the Victorian family home is an emblem of the social and cultural architecture of patriarchal imprison-ment.

See also   *Contexts*: Cities and urbanization, Crime and punishment, Domesticity, Family; *Texts*: Sensation fiction; *Criticism*: Feminism.

Further Reading

Chase, Karen and Levenson, Michael, 'On the Parapets of Privacy', in *A Companion to Victorian Literature and Culture*, ed. Herbert F. Tucker (Oxford: Blackwell, 1999).

Body

The concept of the body was in crisis during the Victorian period. Indeed, the issues and questions which surrounded it intersected with a range of contemporary anxieties about sex and sexuality, gender, race and class, and these influenced concerns about hygiene, disease and medicine. Socially and politically, the Victorians took issue with the body on a number of levels, particularly the woman's body. The laws promulgated by the Contagious Diseases Acts of the 1860s, for example, which were only repealed in 1883, enabled the authorities to quarantine and inspect prostitutes suspected of carrying and transmitting venereal diseases. At the same time, as part of the Victorian mania for classifying everyone and everything, the bodies of criminals and lunatics also came under heavy scrutiny by dubious 'sciences'. The theories of an Italian criminal anthropologist, Cesare Lombroso, and a German physician-cum-journalist, Max Nordau, towards the end of the century, were particularly notorious. Lombroso 'discovered' that the bodies of criminals revealed all manner of deformities and sinister attributes which signified their degenerate state. He found, for example, that they possessed abnormal 'agility', misplaced 'depressions' on the skull, outsized 'jaws', morbid hairiness, and misshapen ears which pointed towards 'vampire' tendencies. For Nordau, social deviants were also marked by what he called bodily 'stigmata'. Their degeneracy, he argued, was betrayed by asymmetrical faces, more misshapen ears, snaggle teeth, webbed fingers and imbalanced craniums. As in Lombroso's work, such physical irregularities, for Nordau, matched the disorderly nature of the criminal mind. They made them 'impulsive', egotistical, and incapable of distinguishing 'right from wrong'.

The theories of Lombroso and Nordau have long since been discredited. However, in an age when other scientific ideas, such as those underpinning Darwin's theory of evolution, were still deeply unsettling, their points about the potential of the body to remain in – or regress to – a lower or more animal state were only extreme extensions of more general anxieties about the body in the period. Furthermore, by drawing on radical new ideas about the body, the Victorians projected the notion of an evolutionary scale onto their social hierarchy. In this respect, foreigners, particularly those the Victorians colonized or enslaved, such as Indians, Africans and the Irish, but also their own working classes and women, were placed somewhere at the bottom of the hierarchy, while the white, male middle classes positioned themselves at the top. Complementing this taxonomy, the typical, not to say clichéd notion of the ideal female body, and the one handed down to us in most literary, social and photographic portrayals from the period, was one that was asexual, passive and sedentary; it was a body which was carefully shrouded in voluminous clothes and confined to the domestic sphere of the home. The male ideal, on the other hand, was one of action, energy, vigour, strength and purpose, of power and prowess in all public spheres of Victorian life.

A fit and robust male body was widely considered to fortify the mind and purify the soul in the nineteenth century, and this partly explains the Victorians' preference for the athletic and hence productive physique. But it was also no coincidence that, as a result of this preference, such bodies, particularly working-class male bodies, would be better primed for working in the nation's heavy industries and fighting its many wars. As early as 1828, the public school reforms initiated by Thomas Arnold encouraged greater athleticism for men, and as the century wore on the establishment of team sports like football, cricket and rugby in public schools helped enforce the requisite physical discipline. Such sports also fostered notions of unity, nationhood and, in the cases of cricket and rugby, a certain masculine belligerence, which were exported into the empire. Around mid-century, Victorian obsessions with the body converged with a movement which promoted religious and missionary ideals about what constituted 'manliness' in the period: 'Muscular Christianity'. This movement, led by Charles Kingsley, writer of *The Water Babies* (1863) and an advocate of 'Christian Socialism', had the aim of purifying Victorians by redirecting their 'unwholesome' bodily and sexual impulses onto 'cleaner' habits such as outdoor pursuits, and especially regular exercise and sport. 'Muscular Christians' stressed action and vim. They placed emphasis on the hard, sinewy, vibrant and – however paradoxically for a religious movement – violent body of the ideal English man.

Recent commentators have argued that Victorian literature also configures an ideal English body. Such an ideal tends to be white, middle-class, male, asexual, handsome (but not pretty or effeminate), impermeable, classically proportioned and, better still, statuesque (Roman nose, 'stiff' upper lip), strong, and not given to 'wasting' its fluids as masturbators or homosexuals were perceived to do. Typically, however, all too often in Victorian fiction the body, ideal or otherwise, is read as an index of the mind, and it is in this respect that literary images of the body resemble those of the suspicious work of a Lombroso or a Nordau. Victorian texts linger on the surface attributes of the individuals they describe. They dwell on skin and flesh, and on the blood and bones encased within the body, only to establish, time and again, a picture of that individual's inner 'self' or identity. The following description of Tess Durbeyfield, from Thomas Hardy's *Tess of the D'Urbervilles* (1891), is a fairly typical example of this process: 'She was a fine and handsome girl . . . her mobile peony mouth and large innocent eyes added eloquence to colour and shape. She wore a red ribbon in her hair, and was the only one of the white company who could boast of such a pronounced adornment.' Tess is obviously very attractive, and she has alluringly red, flower-like lips, flowers having always been a conventional metaphor for vaginas in English literature. On the other hand, her eyes also contain an abstract, less physically 'present' quality – 'innocence' – the 'eloquence' of which 'speak' for her essentially guiltless nature throughout the novel (Hardy's novel is subtitled 'A Pure Woman'). Put another way, Tess's body is clearly an enticing prospect for the narrator, as it is for her two suitors in the text. But the ideal of her feminine purity is also inscribed on her flesh, as is her 'interior' life.

Hardy bases his descriptions on a simple literary dichotomy between 'white' and 'red', one which underlines Tess's simultaneously corporeal and ethereal presence in the novel. Whereas Tess's white skin, for example, connotes an angelic and maiden-like virginity – the 'absence' of bodily desire – her 'red' bits (lips, accessories such as ribbons) connote unease and physical 'presence' – the promise of sexual danger. From these puzzling and contradictory physical signifiers, readers receive the impression that a complex woman is being constructed, who, because of her 'natural' physical charms, is not sexually 'passive' but 'mobile', and potentially at odds with society. Her red bits act as warnings, in a sense, which signal her bloody fate in the novel, in which She is raped, loses a baby, murders, and is hanged. Similarly, Hardy fetishizes other bits of Tess's body throughout the novel: her breasts, her hair, her arms, and her sensuous but capable pink hands, especially, and most suggestively, when she is milking cows and churning butter.

Unsurprisingly, Hardy's work has been heavily criticized, most notably by feminist critics, for his desire to control and penetrate his women by way of such representations of the body, and particularly through the eroticized and vulnerable symbol of the mouth. Tess is, most notoriously, more or less force-fed strawberries by Alec D'Urberville early on in the novel – 'in a slight distress she parted her lips and took it in' – in an incident which acts as a prelude to her rape by the same man. But whether or not Hardy's sexual/textual politics also indicate a critique of Victorian ideas and attitudes about the body is difficult to ascertain. Either way, they point towards anxieties about the susceptible and permeable nature of body, the integrity of which always represents the integrity of the individual in Victorian literature.

See also *Contexts*: Clothing, Disease, Drugs, Food and famine, Other, Race, Sex and sexuality, Slavery, Violence; *Texts*: Crime fiction, Penny dreadfuls, Poetry, Sensation fiction; *Criticism*: Feminism, Queer theory, New historicism/Cultural materialism.

Further Reading

Poovey, Mary, *Making a Social Body: British Cultural Formation, 1830–1864* (Chicago, IL: Chicago University Press, 1995).

Childhood

Childhood in the Victorian period was frequently a cruel and brutal experience. Many of those children from impoverished and working-class backgrounds that escaped early deaths, either from hunger or disease, were forced into employment. From as young as four upwards, children worked in the nation's factories, mills and mines, in agriculture, as domestic servants, street vendors and chimney sweeps, generally in hazardous and unhygienic conditions. Other children drifted into vagrancy and crime. These, made notorious in the popular imagination by the orphans and ruffians of Dickens's novels, or by journalist and writer Henry Mayhew, were the 'street-children'. Typically, though, contemporary attitudes towards childhood were contradictory, not to say thoroughly hypocritical. On the one hand, there was much public hand-wringing about the plight of the working-class or destitute child throughout the period. On the other hand, it is easy to see why the exploitation of child labour was so profitable for Victorian industrialists, and why the system went on for as long as it did.

As the century wore on, government acts such as Lord Shaftesbury's Ten Hours Act (1847) did ease some of the most excessive hardships endured by children in the workplace, by limiting the hours worked by women and children to a moderately less harsh ten hours per day. It was only, however, after the passage of the Elementary Education Act in 1870 that children were eventually prised out of paid employment and placed into the embryonic forms of compulsory schooling. Otherwise, for most of the period schooling was at the mercy of church groups, philanthropists and social reformers such as Thomas Barnardo and Lord Shaftesbury. These figures enticed orphans and street children into an assortment of homes (the first Barnardo's home opened in London in 1870), religious schools, Sunday schools, voluntary schools, charity schools, and from 1846 the infamous 'ragged schools'. Some 'rescued' children, perhaps around 100,000 by the twentieth century, were even sent to the colonies, especially Canada, in order to work and 'better' themselves there. Statistically, in fact, a huge proportion of the Victorian population were children, and despite their high mortality rates their sheer numbers effectively gave them a more prominent place in Victorian consciousness. By 1884, the London Society for the Prevention of Cruelty to Children was established, even though the effects of this organization were limited early on. As late as 1875, for example, the age of consent was still 12, and for all the evangelistic and middle-class mixture of charity and pity which was publicly expressed in Victorian society, abuses such as child prostitution were rife.

The miseries associated with a poor Victorian childhood are well documented. Less well known is the intellectually appealing but slightly misguided idea that the Victorians all but invented the concept of 'childhood' itself, at least the idea of childhood as we understand it today. In many ways, rather, the Victorians mythologized, and to some extent sentimentalized, childhood. For some commentators, childhood represented humanity in its most natural and innocent, because non-sexual, state. Children were consequently perceived to be at the 'purest' stage of human development, and this marked them as a prelapsarian (unfallen) ideal, which in turn meant they signified a nostalgia for an equally 'natural' and 'purer' national past. The notion of childhood, in other words, helped Victorians envisage a more 'natu-ralistic' idea of Britain which was romantically associated with pastoral images of a preindustrial idyll. But such a notion was a legacy of eighteenth-century conceptions of childhood. More importantly perhaps, it had its roots in another concept, which links the idea of childhood to another form of wild or rather 'primitive' innocence in British consciousness: the 'noble savage'. The 'noble savage' was a term used by colonists and anthropologists to describe their encoun-ters with other races, and the contradictions inherent in the term resemble those which surround Victorian anxieties about childhood. The basic inference was that 'noble savages' were like children, funda-mentally because they were perceived to be uncivilized. In the context of imperial Britain, this process of making childlike, otherwise known as 'infantilization', proved to have complex and dangerous implica-tions for those nations subjected to British rule. It led to Indians, Africans and white colonial subjects such as the Irish, for example, being regarded as effectively the 'childhood' of humanity. This was an idea underpinned by contemporary representations of such people, most notably by Charles Kingsley, who in 1860 described the Irish people he saw in Sligo as 'white chimpanzees'. And, apes were, in Darwin's evolutionary scale of things at least, to all intents and purposes the 'childhood' of humanity. The infantilization of races colo-nized by the British was further underlined by an imperial discourse of family which had long since found its way into ostensibly 'innocent' terms such as 'mother country' and 'mother tongue', in which it was implied that the presence of the British Empire in other countries was justified because it was there to nurture, or rather civilize, the colo-nized 'children' in question. It was partly in this manner that Victorian conceptions of childhood, the 'noble savage', Britain and its empire, combined to use language in such a way as to lend what was actually a violent process of 'unnatural' relationships the 'naturalness' and 'inevitability' of that relationship between mother and child.

Victorian literature also played a decisive role in the sentimental construction of childhood. Even a cursory glance over Dickens's novels, for example, reveals that he was obsessed with children, although his work does contain a peculiar mix of grotesquely aged children and oddly childlike adults. There is, to draw on only the most extreme characters, the already aged Oliver in *Oliver Twist* (1837); the notoriously angelic and mumsy Little Nell in *The Old Curiosity Shop* (1841); the worn-looking Cratchit children in *A Christmas Carol* (1843); the unboyish title heroes of *David Copperfield* (1850) and *Nicholas Nickleby* (1838–9); the far too old-before-her-time Amy in *Little Dorrit* (1857); and Pip in *Great Expectations* (1861), whose destiny as a 'good' man seems to affect his curiously adult behaviour throughout. Many of these novels are *Bildungsromans*, 'education' novels which follow the lives of their heroes and heroines from childhood to maturity. Except in the case of Little Nell, who perishes in one of Dickens's more mawkish and drawn-out death scenes, most of Dickens's children begin in inauspicious circumstances and rise to happy endings. As suggested above, these children are all either innocent or corrupted by adults. Oliver Twist, famously, is innocent and pure at all times, but he effectively *does* nothing at all and has everything bad *done* to him. He endures the likes of Mr Bumble and the poor house, apprenticeships as an undertaker's 'mute' and chimney sweep; he then gets lured into the company of Fagin's dodgers, pickpockets and burglars, and he consorts with prostitutes. He remains, though, incorruptible throughout the novel, as if he is somehow innately good, and this is because, as suggested by his curiously inappropriate middle-class voice, he is destined for better things from the outset. Indeed, by the end of the novel, Oliver is saved both from a life of villainy and being working-class by the sanctuary provided by a well-to-do family, the Brownlows.

Dickens's nostalgia for the innocence of childhood, as the logic of his narrative implies, is ultimately a critique of the oppressions he associated with Victorian adulthood. Similarly, his queasy happy endings mark the straining point in which fiction resolves the contradictions in life created by the adult world. Any trace of romantic sentiment in his work is only, in this respect, as creaky and unpersuasive as the idea of childhood innocence itself in the period. It is also, however, what made his work so powerful in shaping the Victorian concept of childhood in the first place.

See also *Contexts*: Body, Death, Empire and imperialism; *Texts*: Children's literature; *Criticism*: Poststructuralism, Structuralism.

Further Reading

Kincaid, James, *Child-Loving: The Erotic Child and Victorian Culture* (New York: Routledge, 1992).

Cities and Urbanization

Following the Industrial Revolution, the nineteenth century saw a rapid growth in cities and urbanization. The population of Victorian cities swelled as more and more people moved out from rural or agricultural districts and gravitated towards the industrial centres looking for work in the nation's factories, mines and mills. The city of Bradford, for example, had around 8000 inhabitants in 1811. At Victoria's accession in 1837, this number had risen to around 25,000. In major inner cities such as London, this displacement caused massive problems in terms of housing, health and sanitation. For the poor, certainly the early system of shared housing and facilities occupied by separate families and neighbours, and typified by tenement living, only very gradually gave way to more separate homes with an emphasis on one family per dwelling.

For most of the century, housing for the majority of the poor in Victorian cities was notorious for its overcrowding and squalor, particularly in the slum districts, and the statistics are appalling. In an 1854 survey of tenement living in Newcastle it was found that there were approximately 9500 homes for over 20,000 families. By 1851, architects and city planners throughout the country were forced to face the fact that over half of the nation was now living in cities, and by 1871, only a quarter still lived in rural areas. The Lodging Houses Act and the Labouring Classes Lodging Houses Act (1851) were passed to prevent the worst squalors and 'indecencies' associated with overcrowded living and room-sharing, but any changes were slow in coming and gradual in effect. As a result, for every grand public building or elegant but useful railway station the Victorians constructed, such as London's neo-classical Euston station (1835–9) or the Gothic-inspired St Pancras (1868–74), for each library, leisure club, meeting house, hotel and bright new shopping arcade, and for every neat middle-class villa, just around the corner were crammed terrace houses and slum districts, urban hovels, and the decay of inner-city dwellings which were all but neglected for most of the period.

Worse still, working-class houses, where the majority of the British population lived, were badly built from poor materials, and initially they lacked water and sanitary facilities. Victorian planners built two major types of terraced house for the working classes: the more hygenic 'through terrace', with a small yard at the rear; and the notorious 'back-to-back', which came without a back yard and consequently without sufficient air or 'through' ventilation. Both houses were designed for one family, even though they often accommodated one family on each floor. The small but functional and endlessly cheap and reproducible Victorian streets of terraced housing still survive in former industrial centres, such as Manchester, Liverpool, Halifax, Birmingham, Cardiff and Newcastle.

Largely at the behest of middle-class planners, reforms in working-class housing gathered pace in the early 1840s, with the first slum-clearance projects in inner-city areas. Such moves were further prompted by anxieties about the cholera epidemic of 1853, which in city areas was linked to the general moral and physical degradation attributed to the working classes by those with the social and professional power to do so. Similarly, in the next decade, the working-class's back-to-back terraced housing was finally prohibited by law in 1864, as part of the Contagious Diseases Acts. These acts were largely aimed at prostitutes and sexually transmitted diseases, and their application to working-class housing only compounded the idea of a disease-ridden and 'contagious' lower order. The legislation, however, went unobserved for decades in many large towns such as Leeds, and in 1875 the Public Health Act issued another series of by-laws which enforced better sanitary conditions across the country. But local authorities were so remiss in redistributing the funds levied in rates back into working-class housing that many did not confront the problem until they were forced to do so by the Housing of the Working Classes Act in 1890, in the last full decade of Victoria's reign.

The demands on architects and urban planners to meet the changes of the nation's ever-expanding city populations further entrenched what was fast becoming a class-based society. With the rise and consolidation of Britain's industrialist, business and professional middle classes throughout the period, class and status increasingly began to be defined in terms of the material pleasures of bricks and mortar. That the Victorian middle classes aspired, it seems, to separate themselves from both the upper echelons of society, the old landed/aristocratic classes, and the growing working classes – as well as, needless to say, from each other – is an idea perfectly illustrated by their preference for detached and semi-detached housing in city and urban areas. These houses became the archetypal homes for a nation of 'self-helpers' and a symbol of Victorian individualism based on capitalist ethics.

Dickens was the great Victorian novelist of cities, especially London, and even early on in his career, London was the heaving centre of a growing British Empire. But just to say that Dickens's work is metrocentric or preoccupied with the city is to say nothing at all, especially because the concepts of cities and urbanization have a political dimension with profound implications for everything and everyone. Victorian cities and urban areas, as noted above, were designed with one eye on the separation of classes. However, the points at which the classes mingle or meet in the literature of the age are sources of considerable tension which signify in complex ways. The following, from *Sketches by Boz* (1836–7), is Dickens's description of 'Seven Dials', a notorious slum district in early Victorian London:

> From the irregular square into which he [the stranger stumbling across the 'Dials'] has plunged, the streets and courts dart in all directions, until they are lost in the unwholesome vapour which hangs over the house-tops, and renders the dirty perspective, uncertain and confined; and lounging at every corner, as if they came there to take a few gasps of fresh air as has found its way so far, . . . are groups of people, whose appearance and dwellings would fill any mind but a regular Londoner's with astonishment.

In Dickens's rendering, this part of London (near Oxford Street) is busy with class tensions. Note how 'irregular' the area is, and the way that Dickens's long and mazy sentence mimics the unplanned and haphazard nature of its streets and courts. The Dials, he suggests, is a degenerate area quarantined from the rest of London, one which is sequestered, the reader supposes, from other more 'regular' and ordered, better-off areas. But even amid Dickens's attention to the detail of 'dirt' – and the anxieties displayed by his sketch towards the fug of disease and the miasma of contagion it gives off, as an 'unwholesome vapour' – the general sense of disorientation and 'confinement' he found in the Dials says more about the observer than the observed. As Dickens's point about the 'astonishment' of those who are not 'regular' Londoners implies, the Dials is clearly an area that marks the proximity of respectable and ruffian zones in the inner-city area. Rather than any clearly demarcated separation between London's upper- and working-class areas, urban ramblers, such as Dickens himself, took a dim view of a city in which the borders of both seem dangerously permeable.

There is an important historical perspective behind such urban developments in Victorian London. In brief, during the course of the nineteenth century, architects and planners encouraged more 'open' layouts in inner-city areas. These had the aim of ensuring that the population was placed under greater surveillance and discipline by the newly established Metropolitan Police (1829), although they also enabled a street walker or flâneur, like Dickens, to stumble into areas like the Dials (even though Dickens was famous for actively going out and looking for them during his night walks). The question remains, however, why these undesirable areas were so endlessly attractive to Victorian writers. In the Dials, the streets clearly lack discipline. Moreover, the inhabitants of the area, like the streets, are portrayed as being of a distinctly lower and grubbier order than the refined narrator doing the walking and talking and writing. Yet the inhabitants of the Dials only feature as part of Dickens's tableau after he has set the scene; they seem to emerge, in other words, from the same walls and streets which dwarf and imprison them. In this respect, the Dials Londoners are part of the idle and 'loung-ing' classes that became such an affront to the purposeful and industri-ous Victorian middle classes who, steeped in their work ethic, were also popularized and satirized in best-selling literature such as Dickens's. Paradoxically, however, as his lingering in the Dials suggests, it was also Dickens – more than any other Victorian writer – who was most deeply attracted to, even while being repulsed by, the London labyrinth of narrow streets, walkways, tenements, alleys and wynds, and the homes they gave to the many burglars, prostitutes, orphans, pickpockets, eccentrics, pie-sellers and crossing-sweepers, that fired his imagination. At the same time, it is there, in the Dials, in this small, typically Dickensian London scene, that the reader becomes a voyeur, along with the narrator. Although the position Dickens offers is that of disgruntled but slightly amused middle-class observer, it is together that he and his readership witness the shaping of a specifically English identity, one which is divided along class lines in his work and writ small in the cultural politics of the Victorian city and its urban population.

See also   *Contexts*: Architecture, Class, Disease, Gaze; *Texts*: Crime fiction, Penny dread-fuls, Social-problem novel.

Further Reading

Briggs, Asa, *Victorian Cities* (Berkeley, CA: University of California Press, 1993).
Nord, Deborah Epstein, *Walking the Victorian Streets: Women, Representation, and the City* (New York: Cornell University Press, 1995).

Class

The term 'class' became general currency in the nineteenth century, when it replaced the old language of 'orders' and 'estates'. With industrializa-tion, a new Britain emerged, which divided Victorian society into roughly three sections which comprised an upper class (the old aristocracy and gentry), a middle class (industrialists, manufacturers, professionals such as lawyers, bankers and doctors), and a working class, which by the 1850s was so massive that it consisted of over half of Britain's adult population. There were also numerous sub-divisions of these classes: lower-upper, upper-middle, lower-middle, an upper or skilled working class, a lower or unskilled working class, and so on. The system was further supplemented by an underclass of criminals, vagrants, idlers, scroungers, ne'er-do-wells, street-children, and prostitutes, those not so easily assimilated into any economically definable group.

Victorian class distinctions were, however, often less rigid than is generally supposed, and there does seem to have been a limited degree of flexibility and class movement, upwards and downwards. Those Victorians that slid down the hierarchy gave rise to popular oxymorons such as 'shabby genteel'. Those on their way 'up', especially those lower-class individuals who rapidly attained wealth, the *nouveaux riches*, were frequently described as 'parvenus' or upstarts. On the other hand, marriage across class lines was still considered taboo, and any movement across classes seems to have unsettled Victorians greatly. Some aristocrats did, however, earn middle-class respect by becoming professional lawyers or businessmen, while middle-class bankers and professionals sought elevation by means of purchasing large estates and putting their children through public schools. The rise of public school-ing in later Victorian society was, in fact, one important factor in the unsettling of distinctions at the more well-heeled end of the Victorian class system. But generally speaking, this was still an era in which one eminent Victorian, Benjamin Disraeli, bemoaned the rise of the indus-trial middle class, while another, Matthew Arnold, heralded the decline of Britain's aristocracy, a class which dwindled, nominally at least, as the century progressed. Although the British aristocracy retained its social prestige, and still played a prominent role in political life, it was during the Victorian period that it eventually lost the real economic and political power it once had in society, largely because of the post-1875 agricultural depressions, the slow emergence of an unpropertied elec-torate, and the increasing prominence of the industrial middle classes in the House of Commons towards the end of the century. The story of the nineteenth-century class system is, in this respect, largely the story of the triumphant rise to power of the Victorian middle classes.

The concept of class in the period is intrinsically bound up with the nature of power. According to Karl Marx, the capitalist system consoli-dated by the Victorians fundamentally exploited the working classes, and time and again Victorian literature reflects this exploitation. Some of the literature also contains telling slippages between its terminology of class and that of nationalism and race. Benjamin Disraeli's 'Condition of England' novel *Sybil* (1845), for example, a tale of romance, strife, Chartism and murder by rioters, has an illuminating subtitle, 'Two Nations', which denotes the division between 'the rich and the poor' classes in Victorian Britain. However, Disraeli's use of the signifier 'nation' conjures up other images. It suggests, most obviously, that the concept of class is bound up with 'nationhood', with Englishness, and by extension that some classes in society are more English than others. Indeed, Victorian literature is full of references to the British working class as a sort of 'second' or foreign 'nation' within a nation, in a country increasingly dominated by middle-class conceptions of Englishness. In *Sybil*, this point is made explicit when Charles Egremont, the novel's hero, is taken to task by the radical journalist Stephen Morley, over Egremont's point that Victoria reigns over 'Two nations, between whom there is no intercourse and no sympathy . . . as if they were dwellers in different zones or inhabitants of different planets'. Disraeli's 'other' England also finds its way into some of his descriptions of the lower classes, such as Mr Diggs's son, Master Joseph: 'a short, ill-favoured cur, with a spirit of vulgar oppression and malicious mischief stamped on his visage. His black, greasy lank hair, his pug nose, his coarse red face and his projecting tusks . . .'. This description marks another conceptual slippage in Disraeli's work – that between the savage black other in Victorian consciousness and the British working classes – which is also present throughout Victorian literature. In *Sybil*, this slippage is signified by the 'blackness' of Master Joseph's hair and his generally dark and ferocious mien. It is underlined by his elephantine 'tusks' and flattened 'pug nose', the kind of snout which generally signifies 'primitive' working-classness in Victorian literature.

The Victorian novel, largely of middle-class orientation and authorship, was the perfect medium for disseminating middle-class ideologies and values. In an age of bourgeois 'free trade' individualism, the popular *Bildungsromans* (education novels), in particular, were preoccupied with charting the development of individuals towards their middle-class fate. Novels such as Dickens's *Oliver Twist* (1837) and *David Copperfield* (1850), and Charlotte Brontë's *Jane Eyre* (1847), all deal, in one way or another, with youthful hardships, coming of age, finding one's place in life through love and work, and the development of the self towards a resolution in better social and financial circumstances. But although Victorian literature is obsessed with class, often this is only to the extent that the hero or heroine's class status reflects on the status of the individual. The rise of Victorian men, for example, to the all-important status of 'gentleman', the social cachet of which exists somewhere at the intersection of middle-class respectability and aristocratic luxury and pleasure, is captured perfectly and most famously by Dickens's *Great Expectations* (1861). Intriguingly, Dickens's tale of Pip's rise to fortune from lowly beginnings, and his subsequent fall from fortune back to lowly beginnings, is underpinned by Dickens's insistence on the fundamental 'goodness' of his hero. Pip deserves his vaguely romantic fate with Estella, it seems, because he helped free a starving convict, Magwitch, on the marshes, and because his honest hard work at the Gargery forge – which would never alone make a gentleman (as Joe Gargery's fate testifies) – needed to be repaid somehow in the Victorian scheme of things. And yet, the fact that, as it turns out, Pip's sudden affluence and immediate snobbery is derived not from wholesome Victorian industry, but from Australian convict money, the filthy lucre of empire, seems to be what engineers his downfall back to the virtuous poor of the smithery.

Nonetheless, the idea of class consciousness in *Great Expectations* is ultimately founded on a notion of benign individualism which is unaffected by either rags or riches. The problem is, needless to say, that the category of benign individualism is itself a middle-class construction. This is why Dickens's novels tend to display affection and dismay, if not in equal measures, for the array of characters from across the Victorian class spectrum that his novels made famous. It is also why his world is full of eccentric 'individuals' who are all, in one way or another, at the mercy of the larger class system created by Victorian industrialism and capitalism.

See also *Contexts*: Body, Cities and urbanization, Clothing, Economics, Individualism, Industry, Reform, Slavery; *Texts*: Realist fiction, Social-problem novel; *Criticism*: Marxism.

Further Reading

Cannadine, David, *Lords and Landlords: The Aristocracy and the Towns, 1774–1967* (Leicester: Leicester University Press, 1980).
Davidoff, Lenore and Hall, Catherine, *Family Fortunes: Men and Women of the English Middle Class, 1780–1850* (Chicago, IL: Chicago University Press, 1987).

Clothing

After the French Revolution (1789), British men's clothing, hitherto often as fine and elaborate as women's, became more 'democratic' and less flamboyant. The reasons for this change are complex, but by the Victorian period, for the middle and upper classes at least, the change went hand-in-hand with the increasing divisions of labour in society. British men increasingly worked outside of the home in whatever public sphere they found themselves in, and women became more and more confined to the domestic or private sphere. Victorian clothes matched this division: dark, sober and functional for the men, leisurely and cumbersome, often extravagantly colourful, for the women. Clothing was an important signifier of one's position in life for the Victorians because it indicated status or class. It also had a part to play in distinguishing gender roles. In a society renowned, for example, for its problems with discussing sex and sexuality, clothes were supposed to shroud the body, and especially the bodies of women, in 'silent' modesty. This was, after all, a society in which even the humble trousers were often referred to as 'unmentionables' or 'unspeakables'.

The Victorian upper classes of both sexes did, nonetheless, continue to distinguish themselves from the lower orders with some fine and often intricate clothing. Although less elaborate overall than their extravagant eighteenth-century predecessors, richer Victorians maintained an attention to the details of their accoutrements and accessories: fancy cuffs, ties, collars, lapels. On the other hand, the cliché of middle-class male Victorian clothing in the latter half of the century, the one bequeathed by numerous portraits and photographs, does appear to have been fairly standard as well. Most ensembles comprised black, blue or grey frock coats, sober morning coats, top hats, combined with an array of tweedy attire for manly and more aristocratic pursuits in the country. Richer women, however, in spite of the clichés, were not forever wheeling about in crinoline or the dowdy black clothes associated with Victorian governesses and Queen Victoria herself, especially during her long mourning period after Prince Albert's death in 1861. The history of Victorian fashion finds women in a variety of tight skirts, corsage, ruffles, petticoats, bustles, bodices, boleros and boas. These garments were cut from a range of fabrics and materials from around the world, and in a range of styles which still looked to Paris as the fashionable centre of Europe. Stylish women in the 1830s, for instance, favoured the bell-shaped skirt, the result of multilayered petticoats. The fashion for wider and wider crinoline only really reached its height in the 1860s, after which tighter skirts became *de rigueur*.

Clothes also had a formal and ceremonial role to play for richer Victorians. Breakfast and dinner codes of dress needed to be observed, and there were rules for the theatre, clubs, town, trips to the country, and so on. For the majority of Victorians, the poor, spruced-up rags and second-hand clothing were all they could hope for. Indeed, although the Industrial Revolution put the British economy at the forefront of world trade, and despite the fact that the wealth created by the nation's textile industry in industrial powerhouses such as Manchester ensured that clothing eventually became cheaper and more available for everyone, the purchase of clothing was still, for many, a luxury. For the more affluent, on the other hand, the important technological developments of the period, such as the sewing machine in the 1850s and 1860s, only hastened the process of tailoring and adjustments in serving the cyclical demands of fashion.

Clothing provided an index for the Victorians in which the identity of the wearer could be read. The class, gender, sexuality, race and general disposition of an individual might all be known from the state of one's trousers, the cut of one's jacket, the length of one's lapels, or the shape of one's skirt; that is, by the outward and 'material' signifiers of one's position in life. The history of the crinoline, for example, contains an entire sexual politics all of its own. This wide bell of cloth and whalebone (or steel) seems to have been designed to prevent other bodies from coming too close, and while the 'cage' protected the woman's body, it also preserved the integrity of that most precious of Victorian categories, the individual. But the crinoline is also of interest because at the same time that it preserved the woman's modesty, its bottom-heavy shape inevitably drew the male gaze downwards, towards the woman's reproductive parts. In doing so, the bell effectively exaggerated the same hips and shapely promise of the body which it sought to conceal.

The crinoline also prevented the woman from doing any real physical labour. As with high heels, such clothing was not designed to help women move about and work as freely or in the same capacity as men, and the cage was more indicative of women's leisurely and sedentary confinement to the home. Frequently heavy and ungainly, albeit elegant, such items of clothing only inhibited women's bodies and rendered them less active. Similarly, after the mania for crinoline had declined somewhat in the 1870s, skirts then became so figure-hugging tight that some women could barely walk. This, needless to say, further restricted their ability to do anything useful and worthwhile outside of the home. The tighter skirts, however, along with further restrictions on the body made by garments such as corsets, were rejected by the 'new woman' movement at the end of the century, which promoted liberty for women in all walks of life. Symbolic of this movement was the founding, in 1881, of the Rational Dress Society, an organization which championed the cause of loose and free clothes.

There are many ways to read the politics of clothing in Victorian literature. In Charlotte Brontë's novels, women's clothing is associated with both sexual repression and the wider restrictions men placed on women throughout society. Governess Jane Eyre, for example, wears lots of mournful and shapeless black, and Brontë dwells on Lucy Snowe's frumpy 'grey' dresses throughout *Villette* (1853). In George Eliot's *Middlemarch* (1872), initially at least, Dorothea Brooke's beauty is curiously enhanced by the dignity of her 'poor dress' and 'plain garments', as they make her appear more classical and painterly, while the accessories of Thomas Hardy's Tess in *Tess of the D'Urbervilles* (1891), such as her 'red ribbon', symbolize both her nascent sexuality and the sexual violence and bloodshed to follow. In Dickens's *Great Expectations* (1861), Pip's fortune and immediate assumption of fine clothes is only one of the more famous examples of the 'worn' nature of class in Victorian litera-ture, as is the case in Dickens's sentimental attitude towards the black-smith Joe Gargery's buffed-up rags or 'shabby-genteel'. Other Dickens characters, and especially his ruffians and villains, often do with making the best of poor clothes, but this also enables them to transgress the hierarchy of class while doing so. One of the most entertaining purvey-ors of this transgression is the Artful Dodger in *Oliver Twist* (1837), who swaggers about London in his scruffy-aristocrat's garb of coat-tails and blucher boots, only to pick the pockets of the genuinely 'genteel'.

The significance of where some Victorian garments and materials originated should also not be underestimated. Victorian novels are full – consider, for example, the female characters in Thackeray's *Vanity Fair* (1847) – of women draped in Indian shawls, in the fabrics of empire such as cashmere (from Kashmir goats), and Victorians in general were fond of the colour and sensuousness associated with Oriental clothing and exotic dyes. Equally, the nineteenth century saw the triumph of cotton, and the fact that up until 1865, in America's deep South, much of this cotton was picked by slave hands before it was shipped to British working-class loomers and weavers, is all to easily forgotten. However, along with the class and sexual politics associated with clothing in the Victorian period, it underlies the way in which some fashionable mate-rials were steeped in the violence of British colonialism.

See also   *Contexts*: Body, Class; *Texts*: Mid-Victorian novel, Realist fiction, Social-problem novel; *Criticisms*: Marxism, Queer theory.

Further Reading

Harvey, John, *Men in Black* (Chicago, IL: University of Chicago Press, 1997).

Consumerism

Victorian Britain was at the centre of world capitalism and consumerism. Its dominance, however, was the result of a number of complex economic and political factors, which arose from Britain's status as the world's first and most successful industrialized nation. By the nineteenth century, after profits accrued from its superior balance of imports and exports, its reductions in trade tariffs, and especially the triumph of free trade after 1846 with the repeal of the Corn Laws, Britain became increasingly wealthy and prosperous. Much of this wealth was generated abroad and from the legacy of slavery (abolished in 1833–4), with around a quarter of British trade being transacted in its empire and colonies. At home, William Gladstone's 1850 and 1860 'free trade' bills put legal mechanisms in place which eventually facilitated a more effective economy for consumers on all levels of the capitalist system, from traders in world commerce to the humblest of shoppers. Other key developments included the growth of department stores, and in the 1840s a nationwide Co-operative Society. Initially a non-profit-making system, the 'co-ops' developed from trade unions. They worked along broadly socialist lines, in which working-class members invested a percentage of their earnings and then bought goods at lower or wholesale prices. In return, they received an annual dividend, depending on how much money they had invested.

Victorian capitalism established the idea of 'the consumer' as an endlessly desirous individual. In a period in which the need for immediate gratification became ever more apparent, capitalism, by selling 'things', sold a 'lifestyle', and with this came what Marxist critics call reification, or a rendering 'thing-like' of the individual. The idea of commodification is in fact central to Marx's ideas about the fetishism in western societies of the commodity, in which the actual relationships in history between people – for Marx, those classes that either control or are controlled by the material forces of production – are mistaken for relationships between 'things'. Commodification is also central to the intertwined histories of British capitalism and slavery, in which the slave was bought and sold in the same way as any other capitalist object, before frequently being worked to death and replaced with another. Marxist critics have argued that the working classes were condemned to a similar fate in Victorian consumerism, one which, by forcing them to sell their labour to the dominant owner classes, effectively made them 'wage slaves'.

The consumerism which underpinned Victorian culture and society also, then, 'consumed' individuals, and for some Marxist critics, Victorian literature became an integral part of this process. Many have argued, for example, that because the ideological destination of Victorian literature, directly or indirectly, is always the individual, just as it was in capitalist/consumerist ideology, the individual 'subject' also becomes an 'object' constructed in and by the language of the text. Indeed, consumerism is everywhere in Victorian fiction. It imbues everything that happens in the novels, and its ways and means both influence and connect up everyone. Thomas Hardy's *Tess of the D'Urbervilles* (1891), for example, is permeated by tensions between old and new consumerist systems. These become apparent in a scene at the market fair, where goods can still be exchanged for other goods, unlike the system of money and exchange which came to dominate the profit-driven economy of Victorian Britain. In a similar way, Dickens's novels are haunted by consumerism on both the largest and smallest scales of Victorian capitalism; they cover, in other words, both international trade and the transactions of pie shops. But Dickens's work is also crammed with the spoils of world consumerism, and his richer rooms and tables are resplendent with ornaments ('household gods'), elegant bits of furniture, 'Hindoo' chairs from India in *Bleak House* (1853), and a cornucopia of tea, sugar, coffee, tobacco, exotic fabrics and spices.

Of equal significance is the fact that the publication and circulation of Dickens's novels themselves, and their role in the development of English literature in the period, were not exempt from the Victorian consumerist enterprise. At the same time that English Literature rose as a scholarly discipline in the Victorian period, increasing rates of literacy stimulated the commodity status of books as consumer items, and books became cheaper and cheaper as the century wore on. But the distribution of novels was largely dominated, as it had been from the 1770s onwards, by commercial circulating libraries. In their Victorian heyday, the most powerful of these organizations was Charles Mudie's Select Library (founded in 1842), an organization that worked on a loan and subscription system, and which was not cheap, at least to begin with. Otherwise, novels were serialized in instalments through magazines and periodicals, a system which created the cliffhanger motif so beloved of consumers of fiction and popular culture in the nineteenth century. Books, with all the reassurance or escapism they offered, consequently became an increasingly successful commodity in their own right, and at any rate very desirable objects for consumers. Furthermore, preceding each instalment of, say, Dickens's novels, the most popular and commercially successful of Victorian writers, were advertisements for numerous other consumables, such as hair oil and soaps, cigars and clothing. It is in this respect that books were printed, promoted, circulated, sold and bought, as crudely and coldly as any other commodity, often as part of the same package.

It has also become a commonplace argument that realist Victorian fiction was initially written and 'consumed' by the capitalist bourgeoisie, whose largely patriarchal idea of the 'real' world was thereby at once reaffirmed or constructed by the same process. Yet in the period between *c*.1840 and 1890, in which British classic realism reached its apogee, Victorian novels were not only read by the middle classes – or by those with enough money and leisure time to buy and read them –

they were increasingly being purchased by an emergent and literate working class. As a result of such developments, the rise of the novel as commodity at once became more profitable for the publishing houses and more ideologically dominant throughout Victorian society. The idea, moreover, that the novel is somehow exempt from the grubby hands of capitalism is one of the greatest and most successful illusions created by the era of bourgeois economics and its reflection in Victorian literature, even when such novels appear to criticize the age of consumerism that produced them.

See also   *Contexts*: Class, Clothing, Economics, Food and famine, Industry, Travel; *Texts*: Penny dreadfuls, Realist fiction, Sensation fiction; *Criticism*: Marxism.

Further Reading

Lovell, Terry, *Consuming Fictions* (London: Verso, 1992).
Richards, Thomas, *Commodity Culture of Victorian Fiction: Advertising and Spectacle, 1851–1914* (London: Verso, 1991).

Crime and Punishment

The history of Victorian crime and punishment is complex. Statistically, for example, it may seem surprising that crime levels on the whole appear to have declined in the period, even though the figures depended on the way that the authorities defined criminal behaviour. Nonetheless, those whom Victorian society took to be criminals formed a rich and varied mix, and a list of those trhat made up the criminal underworld is inexhaustible: pickpockets, thieves, burglars, fences, murderers, rapists, rioters, Irish terrorists, religious dissenters, homosexuals, swindlers, fraudsters, embezzlers, forgers, card sharps, tricksters, vagrants, drunks, dodgers, 'toshers' (sewer-scavengers), mudlarks (riverside scavengers), river-dredgers, 'till-friskers', even 'cat and kitten hunters'. Given the fact that the Victorians are associated with taboos over sex and sexuality, it also often comes as a surprise to learn that crime figures for prostitution, especially child prostitution, reached unprecedented levels in the period. The Criminal Law Amendment Act (1885), for example, raised the age of consent from 13 to 16, in order to protect children from abuses, but this did not mean that such abuses did not continue. Even though prostitution has never technically been illegal in Britain – some Victorians, mostly men, even thought it was a 'necessary evil' – there were attempts at arresting 'streetwalking' prostitutes under vagrancy and soliciting laws. After the Contagious Diseases Acts of the 1860s, which were passed after scares that sexually transmitted diseases were rampant in the nation's armed services, prostitutes were also subject to police interrogation and physical examination for venereal disease. Their bodies were inspected by a surgical probing instrument called a speculum.

The Victorians also implemented laws which saw Britain gradually move away from the capital or corporal punishments for crimes against property associated with previous centuries. Between 1824 and 1829, home secretary Robert Peel's reform acts decreed that criminals should only suffer capital punishment for murder and treason, and those actually executed became fewer and fewer as Victoria's reign progressed. Records show that over 300 criminals were executed before 1820, for example, whereas only three died that way in 1871. By modern standards, though, Victorian forms of punishment remained severe. Corporal punishments, such as flogging, were used throughout the century, and until 1857 criminals were still being packed into the 'Hulks', which were decommissioned warships effectively acting as prisons. Worse, even if some Victorians considered it more 'humane' than confinement, around 160,000 criminals (25 per cent of whom were Irish) were transported to the Australian colonies between 1788 and 1868, the end of transportation coinciding with the year in which public executions such as hanging were outlawed. Britain's prisons also underwent reform in the period, particularly in the 1840s–50s, and Pentonville Prison (opened in 1842), with its revolutionary 'silent' and 'solitary' systems, boasted what became the most popular forms of confinement in the period. Other prisons used alternative forms of discipline. These included the repetitive and disciplinary tasks associated with the 'crank' and the treadmill, hard labour, and the so called 'wearying regime', in which criminals were weakened and rendered passive by meagre diets. Only the Prison Act of 1898 lessened some of the worst brutalities associated with Britain's disciplinary systems.

Broadly speaking, the institutional forces of discipline became an increasingly central feature of British society in the nineteenth century. They were typified by Robert Peel's Metropolitan Police Act (1829), which established London's first effective police force, and the foundation of a constabulary for each British county after further legislation made this possible in 1856. Gradually, as a result of these changes, crime, and the prevention of crime, increasingly became a matter of public, not private, responsibility in the period, although this distinction remained extremely ambiguous. The changes in policing were also connected with the growth in urbanization and a more regulated, time-structured society, yet whether or not this led to a more regulated and hence well-behaved citizenship which could be more easily policed is more difficult to assess. Indeed, with the rise of denser populations in more concentrated urban areas there arose, it seems, even greater chances for criminal activity. Some of these crimes, by being undetectable, remained invisible both to statistics and, consequently, contemporary moral opinion.

Not surprisingly, Victorian literature is full of references to crime and punishment, and the moral debates which surrounded them. The novels of Dickens, for example, the great social commentator of the age, are preoccupied with the criminal underworld. *Oliver Twist* (1837) alone contains pickpockets (Fagin's young rogues), a housebreaker (Bill Sikes), a fence for stolen goods (Fagin himself), a dodger (the Artful Dodger), a host of ruffians or shady characters up to no good like Monks, and even a sympathetic portrayal of a prostitute, Nancy. All of these characters are disciplined by the end of the novel, either by being transported, exiled, imprisoned, or in Nancy's case, murdered by her lover, Sikes. 'Twist', in fact, is a long-forgotten Victorian euphemism for the punishment of being 'hanged', and the hanging motif haunts the novel throughout. But Dickens's novel also satirizes the institutions of discipline and power which eventually brought these villains to justice. These institutions are the 'poor houses' and their representatives, the Bumbles (Parish Beadles), the courts, with their vampish magistrates such as Mr Fang, the prisons, and even two inexpert 'policemen', the unambiguously named Duff and Blathers.

Dickens's relationship to crime and punishment in *Oliver Twist* is, as these points suggest, more complex than might initially be the case. It begs the question as to why he lets Oliver fraternize with the criminal underclass in the first place, only to seek resolution in the happy ending of the Brownlows' rich and comfortable middle-class home. Another question readers might ask is to what extent the logic of Dickens's novel, at the same time that it 'disciplines' its criminals, 'disciplines' its readers to accept this logic and the inevitability of its happy ending. Oliver himself, in a cast of attractive villains, is a notoriously dull and colourless vehicle for this narrative process. On the other hand, his role in the novel is full of paradoxes. Although he does not say (or do) much, when he does talk he speaks fluent, untainted, middle-class English, and his guilded destiny, it seems, is inscribed in that voice. More importantly, the novel also contains a third-person narrative 'voice'. Ideologically speaking, third-person narratives act, as the literary theorist D. A Miller puts it in *The Novel and the Police* (1988), as anonymous forms of power and discipline; they perform, in other words, the same function in policing the individual reader as that performed by other invisible forces of authority in society. The act of reading third-person narratives and the false sense of reality they promote is, according to Miller, an act of discipline which effectively constructs the reader as an 'individual subject' who is 'subjected' to the image of the world established by the text. Indeed, the logic of Dickens's third-person narrative does appear to support Miller's arguments. Oliver is, as suggested above, somehow inherently good from the start, and Dickens's readers are, it seems, supposed to learn from his tale that the unimpeachably good will always triumph in the end. Yet, what is always implicit in this equation is the idea that 'goodness' equates with well-behaved middle-classness in the novel, as it so often does in Victorian literature.

Oliver Twist is often misread as a simplistic tale of one orphan's journey from rags to riches, one which roundly condemns the wretched state of Victorian Britain with its violent crimes and punishments. But there is, perhaps, as the work of Miller and others have demonstrated, another crime at work in the novel, one necessarily not recorded by Victorian crime statistics or by its literature. In the silent or invisible crime of ideology, in this respect, the unenlightened reader is quietly manoeuvred into the position of both bad detective and victim by the logic of Victorian narratives such as Dickens's. He or she is consequently disciplined and punished by the illusion of a bourgeois happy ending which pretends to resolve all of society's tensions and contradictions, and which holds out the idea that this illusion is the real and natural way of things in Victorian society.

See also *Contexts*: Cities and urbanization, Gaze, Gothic, Law, Madness, Reform, Violence; *Texts*: Crime fiction, Penny dreadfuls, Realist fiction, Sensation fiction; *Criticism*: Marxism.

Further Reading

Miller, D. A., *The Novel and the Police* (Berkeley, CA: The University of California Press, 1988).
Tambling, Jeremy, *Dickens, Violence and the Modern State: Dreams of the Scaffold* (Basingstoke: Macmillan Press, 1995).

Death

Mortality rates for the nineteenth century make shocking reading. The average life expectancy for most lower-class Victorians ranged from the mid to late 30s, early on in the period, to the late 40s, later on. It only reached the early 50s shortly before the First World War in 1914. Children suffered most. They accounted for around a quarter of all Victorian deaths, and infant mortality rates made up approximately one-fifth, with a disproportionately large number dying before the age of one. Premature deaths were due to a number of factors. They were mostly the result of wretched Victorian living conditions for the poor and working class in the cities, and especially lethal diseases such as typhoid and cholera, with outbreaks of the latter being particularly virulent in the 1840s and 1850s. As the century wore on, life expectancy gradually rose following the implementation of better sanitation and hygiene conditions, with Joseph Bazalgette's sewerage system in London in the 1850s and groundbreaking developments in medicine, particularly the invention of chloroform as an anaesthetic in 1847. Other developments had more grisly implications. The Anatomy Act of 1832, for instance, legalized the use of dead bodies from workhouses, hospitals and gallows, for use in medicinal science. Similarly, the sheer numbers and visibility of the dead throughout the country forced the authorities to construct more and more cemeteries, with eight new graveyards being built in London alone.

Unsurprisingly, then, the Victorians were obsessed with death, and above all with the ways and means of coping with it. But they are also often credited with the invention of British funeral rites, and especially the black pomp and splendour associated with the deaths of popular state figures and celebrities. When the Duke of Wellington died in 1852, for example, his hearse cost over £11,000, and over 1.5 million mourners lined the roads to watch his cortège. As the century progressed, the Victorians also ritualized the wearing of black clothes by mourners, in which changes in ensemble were supposed to correspond with the various stages of bereavement. This ritual became increasingly prominent after 1861, following Prince Albert's death from typhoid, when Queen Victoria in her sadness retreated from public engagements for decades. Some contemporary critics claimed that Victoria was ostentatious in her mourning, and outrageously sentimental even by Victorian standards; others said her grief was pathological. Either way, Victoria was rarely seen out of mourning black until her own death in 1901.

The ritualization of death and mourning, and the order and reassurance it provided, had important implications. It formed part of the regulation of conduct and the invention of British traditions and ethics so often ascribed to the Victorians. Funeral rites and the processes of mourning were a means of coping with the chaos and uncertainty of death. But they were also a means of coming to terms with the chaos and uncertainty of living. Moreover, the idea of death overshadows the Victorian age, and it is, perhaps, a sense of deathliness which gives the period its black, gloomy, oddly elegiac image. That is to say, the impression of Victorian society, at least the one handed down to posterity in countless unsmiling photographs, dark clothes, infant mortality statistics, stacked graves, and 'Books of the Dead', is one that is essentially moribund. Metaphorically speaking, the Victorian age also witnessed the slow 'death' of the religious certainties which helped Victorians cope with life and death. In 1859, Charles Darwin's theories on natural selection and evolution in *On the Origin of Species* helped inaugurate an increasingly secularized society, and with it the erosion of Christian faith. They underpinned one of the catalysts for change in society that German philosopher Frederick Nietzsche would later describe as the 'death' of 'God' in nineteenth-century consciousness.

Most Victorian novels feature at least one death. Many more provide a protracted and often extremely sentimental scene around a sickbed. So mawkish was one death, in fact, that a disgruntled Oscar Wilde was driven to write that one must have a 'heart of stone' not to 'laugh out loud' at the notoriously drawn-out and virtuous death of Little Nell in Charles Dickens's *The Old Curiosity Shop* (1841). But it would be a mistake to think that all Victorian literary deaths were as sentimental or manipulative as Little Nell's, or to suggest that they are entirely without moments of levity and downright strangeness. Even in Dickens's later novel, *Bleak House* (1853), for example, Krook's spontaneous combustion is treated with something approaching bemused indifference, although typically, as his name suggests, Krook is hardly one of Dickens's 'good' characters to begin with.

More intriguing, perhaps, is the concept of 'death in life', which is ubiquitous in Victorian fiction and poetry. Miss Havisham, for example, in Dickens's *Great Expectations* (1861), is famously jilted at the alter. Thereafter, she sits in Satis House in her bridal gowns, a vision of morbid whiteness, cobwebs and decay, enduring a 'living death' in which even the clocks have stopped. Indeed, in an interesting historical parallel with the publication of Dickens's novel, Queen Victoria became a lifelong 'widow' after Albert's death in 1861, and she confided in her letters that life without her husband was a 'death in life'. Furthermore, the idea that the lonely or bereft woman's life is a 'death in life' is a striking feature of the novels of Charlotte Brontë. Lucy Snowe in *Villette* (1853), for example, leads an ascetic and sexually repressed 'death in life', as does Jane Eyre, which makes her 'long to go' where there 'was *life* and movement'. For the latter, however, the idea of the woman's 'living death' is circumscribed by the image of 'sati', the Indian widow sacrifice, in which Hindu brides ritually immolated themselves (or were forced) on their husbands' funeral pyres. In *Jane Eyre* (1847), Brontë's heroine protests against the prospect of a 'deathly' marriage to Mr Rochester, because, as she puts it, 'I had as good a right to die when my time came . . . but I should bide that time, and not be hurried away in a suttee' ('suttee' being the Anglicized word for 'sati'). Jane Eyre's repressed 'living death' is haunted by images of the British Empire and colonialism. It links the woman's 'sacrifice' of her needs and desires to a patriarchal society with the colonial unconscious of Victorian literature.

Popular Victorian poetry was also preoccupied with the concept of 'living death'. Published in the same year as *Jane Eyre*, Alfred Lord Tennyson's elegiac lyric 'Tears, idle tears, I know not what they mean' (1847), sighs and fades away in iambic pentameters. But it closes, like death, after the last breath of a comma, on a more sombre and revealing note: 'O Death in Life, the days that are no more'. Bereaved at the loss of his close friend Arthur Hallam in 1833, the Victorian period's most celebrated poet also published a long collection of lyrical elegies, *In Memoriam A.H.H* (1850), and it is perhaps indicative of the age that it is this work, along with another that deals with the death of soldiers in the Crimean War (1854–6), *The Charge of the Light Brigade* (1854), which remain Tennyson's most famous and best remembered. Following the death of Prince Albert and the commencement of her own 'death in life', Victoria was, unsurprisingly perhaps, said to have found great comfort in Tennyson's work, and particularly in some of Tennyson's most famous lines from *In Memoriam*. These lines have long since passed into everyday usage, but they still seem marked by the essential deathliness of Victorian life: ''Tis better to have loved and lost / Than never to have loved at all'.

See also *Contexts*: Childhood, Disease, Gothic, Violence; *Texts*: Crime fiction, Penny dreadfuls, Social-problem novel; *Criticism*: Psychoanalysis

Further Reading

Bailin, Miriam, *The Sickroom in Victorian Fiction: The Art of Being Ill* (Cambridge: Cambridge University Press, 1994).

Decadence and Aestheticism

Decadence denotes moral, cultural or sexual degeneration. Aestheticism is defined as the perception or appreciation of beauty. In Victorian literature, these concepts are often best understood together, and certainly with the rise of the Oscar Wilde circle in the 1890s they became interchangeable. A quite specific 'aesthetic movement' is discernible in Victorian culture as early as the 1850s, one formed by a coterie of artists, writers, critics and designers, and their theories were often complex and contradictory. If we consider, for, example, the ideas of the influential art critic and social commentator John Ruskin in his monumental five-volume work *Modern Painters* (1843–60), aestheticism formed part of his broader argument that art had a role to play in being worthwhile, meaningful, and broadly 'realistic' in its depictions of nature. Ruskin, that is to say, advocated an art more faithful to reality than idealized. Although he would later contradict his own opinions, Ruskin's work came to typify mid-Victorian attitudes, in which he further argued that art should be didactic or morally instructive. The 'purpose' of art, according to Ruskin, was to reflect on society and to teach. Yet it should also be highly individualistic in its retreat from the decay of industrial modernity into the energy and 'beauty' of nature, largely because there was 'morality' in 'beauty'.

Aesthetes such as Walter Pater, on the other hand, argued that art and culture should be free from such Ruskinian burdens of social and political commitment, instructiveness, and above all 'usefulness'. Pater developed his theories in numerous works, but his *Studies in the History of the Renaissance* (1873) is where he revived an ancient formulation: '*l'art pour l'art*', or 'art for art's sake'. For Pater, art was aesthetically pleasing precisely because it was self-sufficient. His point was that art need not contain any ethical, meaningful or philosophical dimensions outside of its own artistry. The British decadent movement, as Pater's phrase '*l'art pour l'art*' suggests, was also largely inspired by the French nineteenth-century avant-garde, which was largely made up of writers and poets such as Baudelaire, Huysmans, Rimbaud and Verlaine. The problem with France, for many Victorians, was that it had long been Britain's historical enemy. To many conservative Victorians, Frenchness was decadent because it represented everything that was antithetical to Britishness. With their 'foreign' cultural and religious attitudes, and worse, their exotic language and stereotypically relaxed sexual attitudes, the French were what the British had defined themselves against for centuries. As a result, an idea such as '*l'art pour l'art*' was regarded with deep suspicion.

Decadent and aesthetic Victorian literature became inextricable from problems of sex and sexuality in the late Victorian period, especially when it contained a whiff of Frenchness. The cult of homosexuality and androgyny associated with Pater and the Wilde circle was deemed, in fact, to be particularly outrageous. Punished for being the most famous homosexual of his age, in an age when homosexuality and effeminacy were roundly condemned, Wilde underwent a trial for sodomy in 1895 and was imprisoned, at the same time that decadent literature, and particularly Wilde's, was celebrating its 'uselessness'. It did so, dangerously, in an age of utility, consumerism and productivity, in which the underlying idea of the 'uselessness' of homosexuals – in terms of the fact that they did not, most obviously, sexually 'reproduce' – was partly at least what made them appear so decadent to more conservative Victorians.

Wilde, a disciple of Pater, maintained the stress on individual self-expression central to Victorian aestheticism throughout his work. But he made his more provocative and decadent point about 'uselessness' in the preface to his only novel, *The Picture of Dorian Gray* (1891): 'All art is quite useless'. Wilde used, it seems, such comments to turn the great Ruskinian and Victorian social and cultural maxims on their heads. And yet, one of the paradoxes of decadent Victorian literature is that, despite its celebration of 'uselessness', it was 'useful' in terms of its revolt against Victorian morality and its middle-class ethos of purpose and productivity. In other words, Wilde 'used' his work to make a radically 'useful' political point about the 'useless' role of art in society, and by extension the 'uselessness' of Victorian ideas and attitudes. It is with this point in mind that the preface to *The Picture of Dorian Gray* (1891) begins to read like a decadent aesthete's manifesto, in which Wilde introduced his ideas in a series of famous aphorisms, perhaps the most notorious being the following: 'There is no such thing as a moral or immoral book. Books are well written or badly written. That is all.'

Aesthetic and decadent motifs resurface time and again in many of Wilde's legendary paradoxes and epigrams. In his plays, these had the effect of producing language which revolves back upon itself, as a series of 'plays' upon words within the ultimate medium of artifice and play, the theatre. Many aesthetes were dedicated to what they perceived to be the beautiful 'surface' of things, and Wilde's paradoxes appear decadent because they repeatedly toy with the 'surface' of language, with the signifier, with the slippery words which fail to 'produce' stable meanings and so lack any sense of logical or useful progression from sign to sense, or from word to reality. Algernon Moncrieff's comment in *The Importance of Being Earnest* (1895) is one example: 'The amount of women in London who flirt with their own husbands is perfectly scandalous. It looks so bad. It is simply washing one's clean linen in public.' And this is Cecily Cardew's point in the same play: 'Oh, yes. Dr Chasuble is a most learned man. He has never written a single book, so you can imagine how much he knows.' In these aphorisms and paradoxes, Wilde disputes a number of precious Victorian attitudes. As a result, faithful marriages, decency and cleanliness are all made to 'look bad', while the concept of 'knowledge', which underpinned the rationalist ideal of education and progress so vital to the modern world the Victorians built, is quietly inverted. Elsewhere, in *Lady Windermere's Fan* (1892), Lord Darlington expresses one of Wilde's most famous critiques of Victorian taboos on desire and sexuality: 'I couldn't help it. I can resist everything except temptation'. Similarly, in *A Woman of No Importance* (1893), Lord Illingworth informs Mrs Allonby that 'I adore simple pleasures. They are the last refuge of the complex', and later in Act Two, Lady Hunstanton, in typically aesthetic tones, praises Lady Stuttfield for the 'uselessness' of her language: 'How clever you are my dear! You never mean a single word you say'.

Wilde's writing demonstrates an overarching sense of fatigue in the face of a Victorian ethos which prided itself on concepts such as energy, productivity, truth, meaning, purpose and usefulness. Writing at the 'end of the century', or during the so-called *fin de siècle* period, his work signifies the decadent 'end' or rather the disintegration of Victorian Britain, just as we associate those years with the demise of the Victorian century itself and Victoria's death in 1901. The aristocratic milieu of *The Picture of Dorian Gray* takes this sense of weariness and decline further, and Wilde's main protagonists are decadent and aesthetic dandies. Dorian Gray, Basil Hallward and Lord Henry are effeminate men who recline on sofas all day looking bored, yawning, exchanging clever repartee, and generally doing nothing or being fed up, until they paint the all important picture of the gorgeous young Dorian. Their behaviour is profoundly anachronistic, in the sense of it being idle, non-productive, useless and therefore, most crucially perhaps, distinctly un-middle-class and hence un-'Victorian'. Aristocrats who uphold laziness and ennui as virtues are, needless to say, defying the Protestant work ethic so beloved of industrialist and bourgeois Victorians, and Wilde's fops smoke, drink and go to the theatre; as aesthetes, their only concern in life is with cultivating beauty and not being vulgar. They are dedicated to pleasure, leisure, the senses, to living life as art throughout the novel.

The Picture of Dorian Gray reads like a guide through aesthetic and decadent peccadilloes. Wilde explores the limits of indulgence in life's 'surfaces', in art, in the desire for ephemeral sensations; he lauds the ecstasy of intense moments, the orgasmic thrill of youth and, by placing Dorian in London's many houses of ill-repute, the darkness of its erotic undertones. Many, if not all of these peccadilloes come together through Lord Henry's eulogy on the bliss of cigarettes: 'Basil, I can't allow you to smoke cigars. You must have a cigarette. A cigarette is the perfect type of a perfect pleasure. It is exquisite, and it leaves one unsatisfied. What more can one want?' For a hardboiled aesthete and decadent such as Lord Henry, the beauty of the cigarette is that it provides 'exquisite', if only momentary, pleasures. But its ephemeral nature also, again, explains why it is so paradoxically 'useful' to aesthetes and decadents. Further, underneath this seemingly superficial discussion, lies Wilde's more telling critique, or perhaps his celebration, of the economic mechanism of desire which drove Victorian capitalism, and which, in the shape of 'perfect' commodities like cigarettes, created such pleasures by leaving one 'unsatisfied' in the first place. Cigarettes establish the desire to buy more cigarettes, and this is precisely the logic of capitalism. Likewise, Lord Henry's exhortation, as in much of Wilde's work, is suffused with a combination of sexual and economic longing with the language of desire, and one can surmise from his words that this is because the concepts of desire, the commodity, and the Victorian marketplace, are intimately connected. Lord Henry's praise of something as seemingly trivial and 'useless' as smoking is consequently as complex and ambiguous as it is portentous. It contains what is at once a hymn to the consummate capitalist product, the cigarette, one which is both aesthetically pleasing and decadent, and Wilde's critique of the modern Victorian world which made the cigarette available.

See also   *Contexts*: Pre-Raphaelitism; *Texts*: Drama, Poetry; *Criticism*: Marxism, Queer theory.

Further Reading

Sinfield, Alan, *The Wilde Century: Effeminacy, Oscar Wilde and the Queer Moment* (London: Cassell, 1994).

Disease

As a result of massive urbanization and swollen city populations, Victorian diseases were rampant. Of particular concern were the contagions and the ways and means of effective quarantine. The notorious Contagious Diseases Acts of 1864–9 (repealed in the 1880s), for example, put in place methods for the detainment and examination of Victorian Britain's many prostitutes and other 'fallen' women. Such methods were implemented because it was thought that the women were passing around venereal diseases such as gonorrhoea and syphilis, which were weakening the nation's soldiers and sailors. Another gruesome piece of legislation was the passage of the Anatomy Act in 1832. This law permitted the use of hanged criminals and the dead from workhouses and hospitals to be used in the interests of medicinal science, although it also heralded the decline of the age of the bodysnatchers. At the same time, although Victorian doctors and scientists were interested in 'alternative' or 'charlatan' therapies and remedies such as hypnotism, they did make major advancements in medicine and the eradication of disease. The groundbreaking work of Frenchman Louis Pasteur, for example, ensured that the science of bacteriology and macrobiology became better understood. Pasteur's germ theory eventually overtook miasma- or atmosphere-based theories about the origins of certain diseases. It was found that cholera, for example, of which there were massive epidemics in Britain from 1831 through to the 1840s and 1850s, was transmitted through bacteria in water and not, as was previously thought, through the air.

In 1847, the invention of chloroform as an anaesthetic helped Victorian surgeons combat numerous diseases and disorders. Doctors and scientists of the period, meanwhile, also developed more effective hypodermic needles, as well as the use of cocaine, opium and morphine as analgesics. Similarly, major developments in physics and chemistry improved medical biology, while ideas about cell theory, the cardiovascular system, digestion, endocrinology, pathology, vivisection and artificial insemination were all pioneered by Victorians. In 1882 and 1883 respectively, the German Robert Koch identified the bacilli for tuberculosis and then rabies, virulent diseases which for centuries had claimed thousands of lives. In 1885, Pasteur developed a successful vaccine for smallpox, which eventually became compulsory in Britain, and newly available medicines meant that incidents of sepsis and gangrene were also reduced. Alongside the steady professionalization of medicine in the Victorian period went the Victorian obsession with cleanliness and the repulsion of dirt. Following improvements in hygiene and sanitation conditions, as well as revolutionary designs for the nation's sewage systems, Victorians gradually began to live longer lives.

The contagiousness of various diseases spread alarm through all quarters of Victorian society. On a conceptual level, this took the form of anxieties about 'moral contagion', or rather a pathology of the social 'body'. In what became the dominant middle-class imagination of the period at least, anyone not white, male, middle class, English, and thus not 'healthy', 'sane' or 'rational', be they the French, Americans, the Irish, Africans, Indians, criminals, lunatics, homosexuals, masturbators, prostitutes, the British working classes, all seem to have been pathologized at some point. The differences between social classes, especially, were lent a distinctly pathological dimension. That the upper strata of society might be contaminated by the lower strata was a widespread anxiety, largely because it was thought that the 'disease-ridden' huddled masses in the cities led to the 'moral' contagions of rebellion, unrest and sexual vice. Indeed, the late-century 'science' of sexology pathologized as 'deviant' certain forms of sexuality, especially masturbation and homosexuality. These theories resulted in the identification of related but even more eccentric diagnoses in the period: monomania, spermatorrhea, the alleged 'lunacy' of the masturbator, and a raft of supposed 'cures' for these 'ailments', including mesmerism, clitoridectomies and cold baths. Furthermore, developments in the discourse of disease and medicine in the period are inextricable from the divisions in society wrought by the Victorian obsession with professionalization. The science of medicine saw the growth of specialisms such as paediatrics, anatomy, syphilology, gynaecology, as well as the idea of the general practitioner and the fully qualified nurse. These formed part of the Victorian desire to classify and categorize everything, and they reflect a peculiarly middle-class neurosis about order. As a discourse, in this respect, Victorian medicine was disciplinary in its aims and effects; it controlled the population by means of constant examination and segregation.

Most Victorian novels contain at least one incident of disease. Curiously, though, this is frequently mysterious, unspecified or undiagnosed, and it seems to transmit itself from an equally unknown or unacknowledged source. Protagonists will suddenly, for example, come over all faint and feverish in the afternoon. They will then lie down for a bit, become pale, before being condemned to their sickbeds for unreasonably long periods, until they slide into death or make complete (and often miraculous) recoveries. Middle-class female characters seem especially prone, and Shirley Keeldar and Caroline Helstone in Charlotte Brontë's *Shirley* (1849) both undergo nasty but vaguely defined disorders. Shirley's, the result of a dog-bite, at first seems to be a form of rabies. However, both women endure a similarly pernicious 'wasting' disease, during which they stop eating, that some recent commentators have argued shows symptoms of anorexia nervosa. Although an unclassified disorder at the time of Brontë's novel, for some critics the representation of a disease such as anorexia nervosa in literature written by women signifies a reflex to the patriarchal construction of female roles in the period. Shirley Keeldar and Caroline Helstone's 'refusal' to eat becomes a protest, in this respect, against the 'silence' of their oppressions under a male-dominated Victorian society, one projected onto their disease-wracked but 'eloquent' bodies. Other critics have argued that the sickroom scene is integral to Victorian fiction because it becomes, according to Miriam Bailin, a place of privacy and retreat from the chaos of Victorian public life, and the space in which all of life's terrors reach some form of resolution. The sickroom scene, based as it is so often at home, is in this sense 'therapeutic', and for critics such as Bailin it performs an ultimately reassuring 'social role' because of this location. Sickness, and the treatment of sickness in Victorian literature, consequently becomes about the integrity of community, and the social cohesiveness of those who gather about the sickbed to nurse and help.

The threat of women's contaminated bodies also, however, haunts the Victorian literary imagination in ways which are not so reassuring. In the 'Guinevere' section of Alfred Lord Tennyson's *Idylls of the King* (1856–74), a poem which deals with the legend of King Arthur, Arthur appears at a nunnery to reprove Guinevere for the 'shame' of her affair with Lancelot. Arthur can only, it seems, describe the now 'polluted', because eroticized, Guinevere, in distinctly pathological and contagious terms, in which the whole idea of the sexual woman becomes a simile of disease: 'She like a new disease, unknown to men / Creeps, no precaution used, among the crowd'. Like syphilis, it seems, Guinevere's desires are sickly because they elicit 'wicked lightnings of her eyes'. She also 'saps' / 'The fealty of our friends, and stirs the pulse / With devil's leaps, and poisons half the young'.

See also   *Contexts*: Body, Cities and urbanization, Death, Drugs, Madness, Science, Sex and sexuality; *Texts*: Sensation fiction; *Criticism*: Feminism, Psychoanalysis.

Further Reading

Bailin, Miriam, *The Sickroom in Victorian Fiction: The Art of Being Ill* (Cambridge: Cambridge University Press, 1994).

Domesticity

The Industrial Revolution and the rise of the middle class in the nineteenth century established the Victorian cult of domesticity. As Britain emerged as the world's richest and most successful nation, with a world-beating empire, this cult became increasingly entangled with notions of nationhood, although more insular Victorians continued to celebrate the idea of a supremacy built on Britain's geographically water-locked and isolated position. On the domestic front, the middle class and *nouveau riche* members of Victorian society, those largely responsible for the cult of domesticity, increasingly separated society along gender lines. The result of this division was a public sphere of work for men, and a private or domestic sphere for women. Based as it is largely around the figure of the woman, the emphasis on domesticity had the effect of at once performing and reinforcing patriarchal ideas about the role and status of women throughout society. It effectively restricted women's political, social and economic rights in the public sphere, restrictions which are still being dismantled in the twenty-first century.

As an important part of the cult of domesticity, there arose a series of didactic books aimed at the chaste and virtuous housewife, such as Isabella Beeton's *Book of Household Management* (1861) and Sophie Ellis's *The Women of England: Their Social Duties, and Domestic Habits* (c.1843). Ellis, for example, proclaimed that 'The sphere of woman's happiest and most beneficial influence is a domestic one.' Indeed, it is no accident, in this respect, that a verb related to the concept of domesticity, 'domesticate', means to 'train', 'breed' or 'tame', and that the 'domestic' domain – the integrity of the home in the Victorian imagination – became increasingly associated with the woman, and by implication her 'wild' propensities. But this is not to say that all Victorian women became domestic 'angels'. Although greater prosperity meant that many middle-class Victorian men could afford to leave their wives at home, many working-class women continued to work in the nation's factories and mills, alongside the men, throughout the century.

At the heart of Victorian ideas about domesticity, then, lies tension. That the the term 'domestic' can mean either 'of the family home', or something far broader in scope, as in 'home' nation or 'domestic affairs', increases the tension because it follows that everything which is not 'domestic' can mean 'unhomely' or 'foreign'. For the Victorians, the ideology of domesticity relates to something at once very private and extremely public, at once homely and alien. However, to situate this idea in the wider historical and political context of Victorian literature, one needs to dispense with what a recent commentator on this topic, Daniel Bivona, calls 'the unnecessary wall, at least in literary studies, between the "imperial novel" and its opposite number – the "domestic novel"'. This is because both 'genres' are inextricably linked to begin with; British 'imperialism' and British 'domesticity', in other words, haunt each other – they are 'of' each other in Victorian consciousness throughout the period.

There is a genre, or rather sub-genre, of Victorian writing known as 'domestic' fiction. This, as the name suggests, appears to have been focused solely on homely problems such as family, work, love, and the banality of everyday English life found in works as diverse as Anthony Trollope's *Barchester* series (1855–67) and George Eliot's *Middlemarch* (1872). On the other hand, there is the example of Charles Dickens, who was the most popular writer of 'domestic' fiction, and thus of Englishness and English ways, in his day. If, as suggested above, the cult of domesticity was integral to the Victorian construction of Englishness in the period, Dickens's role was pivotal. From his own inauspicious beginnings, he was widely praised as the champion and satirist of many causes and movements on the domestic front: reform, charity, the working classes, the underclasses, the dispossessed, the poor, as well as the mediocre, the kind, the criminals, the orphans, the prostitutes, the infirm, the sick, the mad, the silly and the strange. Of even greater significance, perhaps, is the idea that the invention of English domesticity, with its notions about the family, 'hearth and home', and especially the bonhomie associated with the English family Christmas promoted in works such as *A Christmas Carol* (1843), should also be attributed to Dickens's work. Intriguingly, Dickens's goodwill was notoriously partial, not to say extremely selective, and it did not often extend to those suffering in the margins of the British Empire, at least in his fiction. Nonetheless, his neglect of those problems which were not domestic, not directly affecting England, is precisely the point. Even if so-called 'domestic' Victorian literature is ostensibly not 'about' the world outside, then it remains, as suggested above, necessarily 'of' that wider context, or rather 'of' the British Empire. In other words, Dickens and the rest of Victorian literature was 'of' British power, 'of' its arrogance, of the liberty granted by its world dominance to do and say what it pleased. As a result of this, the cult of domesticity and the construction of Britishness created by Victorian literature is always, at the same time, a creation of the cult of otherness and the construction of what it means to be 'not British'.

Many of these ideas and problems impact upon the ideal of the 'domestic' woman in Victorian literature. 'The Angel in the House' (1854–63), for example, Coventry Patmore's self-righteously mawkish love poem, is only the most famous exploration of this ideal. Unavoidably, yet revealingly, Patmore's euphemistic description of the house-bound woman as 'angel' in this poem is full of the sexual politics of the day. 'Angels', being ethereal, are without 'material' bodies, and his suggestion, consequently, was that the domestic woman as 'angel' was above the sinful desires of the flesh. Ironically, of course, angels are generally depicted as either asexual or, in the case of Archangel Michael, more like men without genitals, if anything. But such ambiguities did not appear to have troubled Patmore and a few lines from the poem demonstrate his general ideas about the innocent angel's place in the Victorian ideal of domestic virtue: 'Marr'd less than man by mortal all / Her disposition is devout / Her countenance angelical'; 'Her modesty, her chiefest . . . ' ; 'She's not of the earth . . . '.

In the 'house' itself, with the marriage soon to come, Patmore clarifies the role of the domestic angel-wife as sacrificial slave to her husband: 'Her will's indomitably bent/On mere submissiveness to him / To him she'll cleave, for him forsake / Father's and mother's fond command! / He is her lord, for he can take / Hold of her faint heart with his hand.' Similarly, at the level of form, the poem's octosyllables are further instructive, as is the insistency of its rhyme schemes. This is because they seem to impose the structure and order of language on the 'angels' they describe, so that the form of his poem effectively becomes an integral part of the discourse of domesticity it promotes. At the same time, the inevitability of Patmore's metre, as light and insubstantial as angels, also implies the day-to-day rhythms of the ideal Victorian home, and with that the inevitable nature of the angel-woman's fate. The poem's formal constancy, it seems, enacts both the reassuring cosiness of the domestic ideal and the gloomy routine of being a Victorian woman.

Nonetheless, rather than just being an ethereal presence in the house, later in the poem Patmore compares his angel to a famous Indian diamond: 'A woman, like the Koh-i-noor / Mounts to the price that's put on her'. In brief, the Koh-i-noor diamond was stolen by the British Crown when the Punjab state was annexed in 1849, just five years before the poem began publication. And in Patmore's poem, the angel-woman becomes, albeit briefly, an exotic, sensuous object, like the diamond, with all of the Eastern promise that the image of India and its treasures gave to the British imagination; her body is eroticized, in this sense, but also objectified, commodified, 'priced', even 'stolen'. Moreover, just after the simile of the diamond, Patmore again describes the relationship between the conquest of the angel-woman's body and that of foreign territory as one and the same thing: 'A woman is a foreign land, / Of which, though there he settle young / A man will ne'er quite understand / The customs, politics, and tongue . . . '. This line is, in turn, quickly followed by an another unusual reference to the British Empire: 'For once, at Empire's seat, her heart / Then get what knowledge ear and eye'. It is in lines such as these that Patmore's ideology of the angel-women, who in the course of the poem becomes at once English and Indian, ethereal and physical, domestic and foreign, and the romantic conquest of her body thereof, intersects with that of the violent conquest of India made by the British Empire. The Victorian cult of domesticity fostered by the poem is, as these tensions suggest, haunted by the same 'foreign lands' which helped define and construct that cult, but also by the image of the eroticized woman made flesh.

See also *Contexts*: Body, Clothing, Family, Nation; *Texts*: Historical novel, Mid-Victorian novel, Realist fiction, Social-problem novel; *Criticism*: Feminism, New historicism/Cultural materialism, Postcolonialism, Structuralism.

Further Reading

Bivona, Daniel, *Desire and Contradiction: Imperial Visions and Domestic Debates in Victorian Literature* (Manchester: Manchester University Press, 1990).

Drugs

In the Victorian period, drugs such as cocaine, morphine and heroin were widely available and surprisingly accessible. Only the Pharmacy Act of 1868 prohibited the sale over the counter of the most widely used drug, opium, which for much of the period was easily bought in shops and chemists. Branwell Brontë, for example, the hapless brother of the famous literary sisters, took opium regularly, and the Haworth chemist he frequented in order to purchase the drug still stands. Although opium had been used medicinally in India and China for centuries, it was a relative newcomer to British medication. Victorian doctors prescribed it for the treatment of complaints such as diarrhoea and diseases such as tuberculosis, but it was also used purely for pleasure as a narcotic, or mixed with alcohol and drunk as laudanum. In its liquid form as laudanum, the drug was thought to be particularly effective in preventing fevers and gastrointestinal problems, and it was frequently used to temper the behaviour of unruly children.

The history of opium in Britain is also steeped in British imperial history. Although the majority of opium imports seem to have originated in Turkey, Britain became embroiled in what became known as the 'Opium Wars' with China in 1839–42 and in 1856–60. As far back as the eighteenth century, the British East India Company had been importing opium through Canton into China, in an attempt to open up the potentially massive and lucrative market in that country. At Victoria's accession in 1837, almost 4 million pounds of opium a year, in weight, were being trafficked in China. When the Chinese authorities attempted to block this traffic, the British foreign secretary at the time, Lord Palmerston, responded aggressively. His subsequent policy of 'gunboat diplomacy' led to the coast of China being heavily patrolled and bombed by British warships. The pressure of such brinkmanship eventually resulted in the Treaty of Nanking in 1842. It was this treaty that ceded Hong Kong to Britain, but it also sanctioned the British trade in opium and other goods through five different Chinese ports. The second outbreak of hostilities, in 1856, was due to British demands for further treaty ports. When these demands were also resisted by the Chinese, an Anglo-French force again bombed the Chinese coast into submission. The subsequent Treaty of Tientsin in 1860 gave Britain ten more trade ports and further legitimized its opium trade. Yet more Chinese resistance to these developments led to an Anglo-French invasion of Peking in 1860, after which another convention was set up that finally endorsed the Tientsin treaty and put an end to hostilities. The British import of Indian opium into China, however, continued apace throughout Victoria's reign, although by this stage the medicinal effects of the drug had became discredited, especially when its most potent alkaloid, morphine, was found to be highly addictive. This discovery partly explains why the drug had become, in conjunction with the political tensions with China, increasingly associated with the sinister opium dens inhabited by the East End of London's Chinese community.

The inscription of drugs, especially opium, in Victorian literature has profound cultural and political implications. It is everywhere bound up with anxieties about Orientalism, empire, nationhood and foreignness. The most famous account of opium-taking in the nineteenth century is that provided by Thomas De Quincey in *Confessions of an Opium-Eater* (1834). De Quincey describes opium as 'eloquent', because it appeared to 'speak' through him about the exotic worlds from which it was derived. In the passages of *Confessions* in which he describes his withdrawals from opium, for example, he feels tormented by 'crocodiles', by foreign and exoticized beasts. Much of his rhetoric also implies that he had been figuratively enslaved by opium, to the extent that the drug 'untwisted, almost to its final links, the accursed chain which fettered me'. He also refers to his 'fascinating enthralment' to the drug, recounting how opium forced him into a 'yoke of misery' and 'captivity so servile' which urged him 'knowingly to fetter himself with such a sevenfold chain'. The blissful fantasies De Quincey once enjoyed on opium – that is, the ability of opium to establish new territories in his mind – further led him to use an illuminating phrase to describe his withdrawals: 'opium had long ceased to found its empire on spells of pleasure'. In this case, De Quincey's reference to 'empire' implies that opium, and the otherworldliness it once created for the Englishman, acts to, as it were, counter-colonize his body. As with other drugs such as sugar and tobacco, which are steeped in British imperial history, the abuse of which also means their pleasures turn to pain, De Quincey's opium use appropriates his body, as if avenging the violence that was the drug's origin.

There are plenty of references to drugs and drug-taking in Victorian literature, some of which are more indicative of their historical contexts than others. In Charles Dickens's *Hard Times* (1854), for example, 'the whelp' Tom Gradgrind submerges himself in the 'complete oblivion' offered by opium, as if to escape from the daily 'grind' of his wretched English life, and it is opium which also results in the death of at least two of Dickens's characters. In *Bleak House* (1853), Captain Nemo's death chamber is acrid with both the 'odour of stale tobacco' and the 'vapid taste of opium'; with, that is, a lethal cocktail drawn from the eastward and westward reaches of empire. Similarly, in Dickens's later novel *Little Dorrit* (1857), opium destroys Mr Merdle, a man who commits suicide in successive draughts of liquid oblivion, after a life of mysterious colonial dealings abroad: 'on the ledge at the side were an empty laudanum bottle and a tortoise-shell handled penknife'.

Perhaps the most famous account of opium-taking in Victorian litera- ture is that provided by Dickens's last novel, *The Mystery of Edwin Drood* (1870). In this tantalizingly unfinished tale of disappearance, opium dens, snaggle-toothed drug-pushing crones, Lascars and Chinamen, the problems of counter-colonization and national identity indicated by De Quincey's addiction resurface. In this novel, however, opium creates androgynous English bodies; its altering properties seem to undo the gender categories so carefully constructed by the Victorians. Opium habituates John Jasper, for example, to an 'almost womanish' existence, and the opium crone, Princess Puffer, finds a brief moment of sanctuary from both womanliness and Englishness when she 'opium-smoked herself into a strange likeness of the Chinaman'. At the same time, Dickens's discussions of opium create confusing proper nouns, like 'Jack Chinaman', which suggests the inseparability of England and China after their opium wars. As in De Quincey's addiction, opium finds its 'empire on spells of pleasure' on Dickensian bodies, but in Dickens's work the Oriental origins of the drug also serve to, as it were, 'disorient' the English. Under the auspices of what Dickens calls an 'unclean spirit of imitation' throughout the novel, it is opium which unites his very English world with that of the Chinese other it fought and strived to subjugate.

See also   *Contexts*: Body, Death, Disease, Empire and imperialism, Madness, Orientalism; *Criticism*: Postcolonialism.

Further Reading

Barrell, John, *The Infection of Thomas De Quincey: A Psychopathology of Imperialism* (New Haven, CT, and London: Yale University Press, 1991).

De Quincey, Thomas, *Confessions of an English Opium-Eater Together with Selections from the Autobiography of Thomas De Quincey* (London: Cresset Press, 1950).

Economics

The Victorian economy was characterized by a periodic cycle of booms and depressions. Britain led world capitalism, but its familiar economic cycle of advance and retreat was determined by a number of factors: the annual success or failure rate of harvests; the overall influence of agri- culture; the success of British industries; conflicts such as the Crimean War (1854–6); and the triumph of free trade. The period saw the progres- sion from an economic system no longer based solely on the gold stan- dard (despite persistent cries of 'gold for ever!' and although the gold standard continued to be used until the twentieth century) to one based on bills of money, credit and debt. At the same time, frequent bad harvests had a knock-on effect throughout the Victorian economy. They increased the price of available food and further impoverished an already poor population. In turn, greater expenditure on food decreased the population's spending power for other goods, the result being problems of supply and demand for Britain's manufacturing industries. Despite a period of relative prosperity in Britain after the dip following the end of the Napoleonic Wars in 1815 – wars traditionally being good for the economy – the early years of Victoria's reign saw poor harvests in both 1838 and 1839. The decade which followed quickly become known as the 'hungry forties'. Widespread unemployment and starvation in these years led to working-class unrest, Chartist agitation over universal male suffrage, and increasingly vociferous calls for reform, while problems were compounded by the Irish Famine from c.1845 to 1852. This crisis, which was initially the result of a potato blight caused by the spread of a fungus, eventually led to the starvation and death of around one million Irish people, and the emigration of around a million more. Apart from the fungus itself, the socioeconomic and political problems caused by the famine were frequently attributed to the mismanagement and general indifference displayed by both the British government and the English landowner class in Ireland. Such an indifference was symptomatic, according to some commentators, of centuries of British colonialism in Ireland.

In the middle of these crises, another major economic and political event occurred. The repeal of the Corn Laws in 1846 is often taken as heralding the arrival of the era of free trade in Britain, and the beginnings of a new Victorian prosperity. Since the cessation of war with France in 1815, British government tariffs had imposed heavy duties on imported wheat, in order to protect the market for domestic producers. This meant that the distribution of foreign wheat in Britain was prohibited unless it sold at the fixed price of 80 shillings a bushel. Critics argued that this artificially high price restricted free trade and ultimately increased hunger and the spread of unrest throughout the country, which it did. More optimistic economists forecast that free trade, with its intrinsic competitiveness, would eventually force prices lower and keep them there. By the 1830s, the Corn Laws had become a byword for state interference in the economy, and in 1841 the Royal Commission on Import Duties concluded that free trade would reduce Britain's economic hardships, and that this was the way forward. After more and more calls for reform gave rise to the formation of the Anti-Corn Law League in 1838–9, in 1846 Robert Peel finally passed the crucial piece of legislation, the

Repeal of the Corn Laws Act. The effects of the act were to lessen duties on imported corn and stimulate growth in free trade, although ironically it did not immediately decrease the price of food. The first seven years of the decade after the act saw a boom in Britain's exports, particularly in the cotton trade. This led to a general upturn in the British economy during the 1850s, thanks largely to the fillip provided by both the new spirit of laissez-faire economics and the industrial demands of prosecuting the Crimean War (1854–6). Another depression began, however, in the 1860s–70s. One factor here was the outbreak of the American Civil War (1861–5), which led to restrictions on British imports of cotton – cotton having been the bedrock of the British economy for so long – and indeed the early 1860s became known as the years of the 'Cotton Famine'. This crisis was followed by more bad harvests in 1865 and 1866, and despite another boom towards the end of the decade, the bubble had burst again by the mid-1870s. The problems were such that commentators describe the period up to the 1890s and towards the end of Victoria's reign in 1901 as that of 'the Great Depression'.

The decades between the repeal of the Corn Laws in 1846 and the start of the depression around 1875 have been described by historian Eric Hobsbawm as the golden 'age of capital'. As Hobsbawm puts it, the mid-Victorian period was 'when the world became capitalist', the same period in which British and European history begins to become 'world history'. In short, this is the age in which Britain exported its capitalist ethos, its image of itself, into its empire. With its emphasis on 'individual' competition, the notion of 'free trade' underpinned the Victorian obsession with the idea of the 'individual', with 'self-help', with all the ideas of progress, industry, professionalism and purpose, associated with the Victorians. The doctrine of 'free trade' was discussed widely in the period, in particular by utilitarian thinkers such as John Stuart Mill in his influential *Principles of Political Economy* (1848). Mill's work, published in the same year as Karl Marx and Frederick Engels' *The Communist Manifesto*, with its emphasis on 'united' workers and 'collective' action, argued that 'free trade', albeit based on 'individual' competition, would eventually promote the happiness and economic well-being of everyone in society. For Mill, 'free trade' was part of the narrative of human perfectibility, progress and civilization which had gripped Western consciousness since the Enlightenment. But Mill was also heavily influenced by Malthusian economics. Thomas Malthus, a clergyman and political economist, had argued in his influential *Essay on the Principle of Population* (1798) that population growth tended to outstrip the amount of food available in society, and that this would eventually lead to starvation. His ideas are the point at which Victorian economic interests converge with political representations of class in the period. They took the form of anxieties about the masses crowded into Victorian cities and industrial areas, whose excessive reproduction and demands for food he thought would at once strain the economy and create social and industrial unrest.

In Victorian literature, many of the economic problems described above are prominent. They became collectively known in the 1840s as the 'Condition of England Question', a phrase which was first used by Thomas Carlyle in his essay, *Chartism* (1839). A series of novels, often called 'industrial' or 'social problem' novels, which grew up around this 'question', followed. These included works such as Charles Dickens's *Oliver Twist* (1837), Frances Trollope's *Michael Armstrong: the Factory Boy* (1839), the lesser-known Charlotte Tonna's *Helen Fleetwood* (1839), 1840s novels such as Benjamin Disraeli's *Sybil* (1845), Elizabeth Gaskell's *Mary Barton* (1848), Charlotte Brontë's *Shirley* (1849), Charles Kingsley's *Alton Locke* (1850) and Dickens's *Hard Times* (1854), the latter being largely a satire on political economy. Tensions between the economic and financial gain of individuals, and the social deprivation and absolute ruin of both the individual and the masses are central, however, to almost every published work of Victorian fiction.

See also *Contexts*: Cities and urbanization, Class, Consumerism, Individualism, Industry, Nation, Transport, War; *Texts*: Crime fiction, Penny dreadfuls, Realist fiction, Sensation fiction, Social-problem novel; *Criticism*: Marxism.

Further Reading

Guy, Josephine, *The Victorian Social-Problem Novel* (Basingstoke: Macmillan, 1996).
Shell, Marc, *The Economy of Literature* (Baltimore, MD: Johns Hopkins University Press, 1978).

Education

Free education for all was a late development in Victorian Britain. It was only with the Gladstone administration's Education Act of 1870 that state-funded primary education for all children was finally provided throughout England and Wales. In 1880, elementary education for everyone became compulsory until the age of ten. Secondary education only became more accessible with the passage of the Balfour Act in 1902, just after Victoria's death. Before these developments, the history of British education was one of poor planning, mismanagement, and squabbles between church and state. Although education became increasingly secularized as the nineteenth century wore on, the church continued to resist state interference. For most of the period, teachers occupied a relatively lowly status in society. Although the National Union of Teachers was founded in 1883, there had been a shortage of trained or qualified teachers since the early years of Victoria's reign, which led to the educationist James Kay Shuttleworth's introduction of the 'pupil-teacher' programme in 1846.

The raft of problems facing Victorian education ensured that adult literacy remained at persistently low levels. In the 1850s, for example, it is estimated that perhaps a half of women and a third of all men in England and Wales were illiterate. There were, however, boarding and public schools for the rich, such as St Paul's, Charterhouse, Winchester, Rugby, Eton and Harrow, and a series of expensive 'grammar schools' for the less affluent. There were also individuals, such as Thomas Arnold, educationist and headmaster of Rugby School from 1828, who developed an educational strategy which placed emphasis on rigour, discipline and intellectual endeavour. Arnold's public school model, in fact, became widely influential and much copied throughout the century. Unfortunately, most of these schools for the rich were solely for boys, and girls were all but excluded from the system. Poorer girls might, on the other hand, enrol at one of the many, penny-paying 'ragged schools', and richer girls might receive tuition from governesses. Later in the century, some middle-class girls were also able to attend the high schools provided after the passage by parliament of the Endowed Schools Act in 1869. At the boys' schools, the curricula were largely based on teaching classics such as Latin and Ancient Greek, and later, sport, particularly athletics. There the emphasis, and most conspicuously in the public schools, was on shaping young boys into fit, confident, well-mannered and, above all, patriotic 'gentlemen'.

In the latter half of the century, there were over five hundred private and public schools throughout Britain. Although intakes to these schools made up only a small percentage of the school population overall, their alumni generally went to Oxford and Cambridge, and students graduated from there to dominate positions in domestic and imperial politics, the Civil Services, the major professions, officer ranks in the army and positions in the church. Apart from Oxford and Cambridge (which only established women's colleges in the 1870s), other universities, some with small provisions for women, grew up and spread around British cities after the 1850s, the majority teaching new or 'modern' subjects such as English Literature. Prior to 1870, working-class children whose families could not afford the public or grammar school fees often went without education. Either that or they were already working in the nation's factories, industries and mills. Some attended the many parish-controlled 'voluntary' schools, Bible-based 'Sunday Schools' (dating from 1785), 'charity schools', rural 'dame schools' and 'ragged schools'. The latter were set up by philanthropists, leading to the formation of the Ragged School Union in 1844. Teaching in these schools was largely rudimentary, dealing with reading, writing and arithmetic, although some still taught basic handicrafts and domestic subjects. As the century developed, there was also a range of Bible study groups available to adults, as well as numerous academies, night schools (with fees at a penny a week), working-class colleges for artisans and labourers (The London Working Men's College was established in 1854), City and Guilds institutes, and various scientific or mechanical institutes.

It is no accident that the Education Act of 1870 and the Balfour Act of 1902 coincided with the rise to dominance of the British middle classes. By then, the emphasis in education was very much on foisting middle-class values and norms on what the system deemed to be an unruly working class. But the problems of Victorian education were more than just class-based. Most obviously, society only slowly conceded that the learning and intellectual capacities of women were equal to those of men. Until, that is, the middle classes decided that women needed to be better educated, women were only taught those domestic and oddly aristocratic subjects – sewing, music, conversation, etiquette – which would prepare them as 'better', albeit idle and mostly decorative, wives for their husbands. On this level, the history of Victorian education, like so much else, is predicated on a combination of tensions between class and gender difference. Indeed, if the exclusion of women and the working classes from education in the period is one thing, Victorian literature throws up even more complications around these issues. At first glance, for example, the unambiguously named Dotheboys Hall in Charles Dickens's *Nicholas Nickleby* (1839) is clearly an indictment of the misery and violence endured by boys at one of the period's many 'proprietary' schools, which were run entirely on a profit-making basis. The proprietor of this school is the equally well-named Wackford Squeers. Squeers repeatedly uses his cane, 'strong, supple, wax-ended, and new', to defile the flesh of his wretched and starving young charges, and one of his pupils, Smike, endures an almost ritual flagellation in the classroom. One of the more intriguing and illuminating aspects of Squeers's disciplinary methods, however, and the violence of bad 'education' it underlines, is that at one point he compares his lust for larruping small boys to 'A slave driver in the West Indies'. Squeers, Dickens writes, fantasizes that slave drivers, those notoriously brutal 'overseer' figures in the colonies, should crack the whip under him at Dotheboys Hall, in order, as he puts it, 'to do the same with *our* blacks'.

Nicholas Nickleby was published only six years after the laws which ended slavery throughout the British colonies (1833). Squeers's words are provocative, in this respect, because they turn the image of English boys into slaves, at the same time as they infantilize the real slaves hovering in the margins of Dickens's imagination. In doing so, the text reflects, inadvertently, one of the more violent myths established by the British Empire, which made a 'parent' of the aggressors ('Mother' England), 'children' of the dominated, and a naturalized 'family' of colonialism out of what was in reality a highly unnatural and often brutal relationship. Needless to say, the violence of whipping in the British colonies was aimed at 'educating' and disciplining the slave into complete submission, and this is precisely what Squeers, and his type of schooling, attempts to do with his 'blacks'. Famously, though, as part of Dickens's grim happy ending, Nicholas Nickleby gets revenge on the chief tormentor of his schooldays. By avenging the brutalities meted out against Smike, Nickleby thrashes Squeers until 'he roared for mercy', after which Squeers, as the symbol of bad education in Victorian society, is eventually transported for his crimes to the colonies himself, and the circle of Dickens's rhetoric is complete.

See also *Contexts*: Childhood; *Texts*: Children's literature.

Further Reading

Honey, J. R. de S., *Tom Brown's Universe: The Development of the Victorian Public School* (London: Millington, 1977).

Empire and Imperialism

Empire and imperialism are concepts described by Edward Said in *Culture and Imperialism* (1993) as the 'practice, theory, and attitudes of a dominating metropolitan centre ruling a distant territory'. They are terms which should be distinguished from *colony* and *colonialism*, even though they are often used interchangeably. Strictly speaking, colonialism refers to the development of actual settlements on the dominated territory in question, whereas imperialism, as Said suggests, has a less specific, but no less important, definition. The term 'British Empire' has, however, come to describe the history of British expansion in its entirety. It defines a long period of British supremacy and domination throughout much of the globe, the origins of which can be traced to the early British merchants who began trading in India in *c*.1608, or even further back to the beginnings of the Atlantic slave trade around 1562. By the end of the Victorian period, on the cusp of the twentieth century, the British Empire had grown to unprecedented proportions. It comprised Canada, parts of the West Indies and west Africa, and a line of countries which all but connected Egypt to South Africa. It also encompassed areas of the Middle East, including most of modern-day Iraq, India, Burma, areas of Malaysia and Borneo, New Guinea, Australia and New Zealand, a series of islands and smaller territories throughout the world, as well as territories closer to home, such as Ireland. The so-called 'long nineteenth century' following the Napoleonic wars and leading up to the Great War (1815–1914) was known as 'Pax Brittanica'. But it was hardly, as this suggests, a 'peaceful' period by any means. Throughout these years, the British found themselves fighting on a number of imperial and colonial fronts. Hostilities included the wars with Burma in 1824–6; the first 'buffer' wars with Afghanistan in 1838–42 to preserve the borders of India; the Opium Wars with China in 1839–42 and again in 1856–60; the Crimean War in 1854–6, in which Britain allied with France against Russia; the Zulu Wars of 1879 in South Africa; and numerous scrapes, slave insurrections and skirmishes, such as the infamous 'Morant Bay' Rebellion in Jamaica, of 1865.

One of the major conflicts was the Indian sepoy mutiny of 1857, the catalyst of which was the Indian soldiers' resentment at having to grease their rifles with cow and pig fat. British forces met the mutiny with brutal reprisals, and this resulted in the British government finally taking formal control of India from the British East India Company. In 1876, as if to make this transformation official, prime minister Benjamin Disraeli designated Victoria 'Empress of India'. When Victoria died in 1901, it was during the nation's involvement in one of its other more notorious wars of empire. This was the second Boer War (1899–1902) in South Africa between British forces and settlers of Dutch origin. The war, which eventually enabled Britain to tighten its grip on South Africa, represented the latest outbreak in what became known as the 'Scramble for Africa'. As the most recent phase of large-scale European expansion across that continent from the early 1880s onwards, the campaigns eventually saw the leading powers partition Africa between themselves at the Conference of Berlin in 1885, with the victorious British Empire gaining the lion's share.

The Victorian age of empire is also the age of capitalism. In this respect, left-leaning critics and commentators have long since identified a relationship between the aggressive forces of imperialism/colonialism and capitalism, especially when these forces combine, as they did in Victorian Britain, to extend one nation's export markets into another. In the mid-1840s, the first full decade of Victoria's reign and the years in which the English novel form rose to dominance, this relationship took the form of a conflict between 'old style mercantilism' and free trade. To summarize, in nineteenth-century Britain, mercantilism alluded to a system which prioritized exports over imports in the balance of trade. The rationale of old-style mercantilism, at least, was to place a greater and often more aggressive emphasis on international commerce. The obvious benefit of this system for early nineteenth-century Britain was that it was supposed to preserve the economic self-sufficiency of the nation-state, by selling 'out' rather than buying 'in', thereby creating more wealth. After the repeal of the Corn Laws in 1846, Britain became committed to the growth of laissez-faire economics, and this laid the basis for the triumph of British capitalism in its modern form and the expansions into empire it created. Laissez-faire, or 'free trade', as the latter term suggests, is defined by its 'freedom' from the trade restrictions and import tariffs associated with mercantilism. However, the philosophy and practice of free trade, linked as it became to contemporary Social Darwinian ideas about social competition, the survival of the fittest, and ultimately the encounters between 'superior' and 'inferior' people, had other implications. Free trade, and its underlying notion of the 'free individual' in British liberal society, became extended into the empire, as part of the British urge to replicate its image elsewhere. There, under the mask of civilization, capitalism was used to legitimate Britain's conquest of around one quarter of the world and its people.

The relationship between Victorian literature and imperialism is complicated. Some critics, such as Edward Said in *Culture and Imperialism* have discussed, for example, the way in which literature was central to the representation of the British Empire and the idea of Britishness both to Britain and around the world. But Said also conceded that in Victorian literature, images of empire and imperialism often amount to only a 'shadowy presence'. And, yet, this 'shadowiness' is precisely the point. Victorian fiction is typically uncomfortable with its images of the empire, and popular writers such as Dickens rarely, if at all, acknowledge it in their novels. When they do, on the other hand, it has profound implications. Dickens's *Dombey and Son* (1848), for example, follows the trials of a family-run business which has significant trade interests in the West Indies, an area which was once heavily involved in the British Atlantic slave trade. For recent postcolonial critics such as Suvendrini Perera in *Reaches of Empire* (1991), the Dombey family's involvement in these colonies is pivotal. Perera sees a complex interplay between empire and gender relationships throughout *Dombey and Son*. According to her interpretation of the novel, the emergence of free trade in the Victorian era, at the expense of the 'old style mercantilism' discussed above, contains a crucially gendered or sexual aspect.

Perera begins her thesis by drawing attention to the 'mid-Victorian debate over colonial policy'. At this stage in the debate, as she puts it, the 'ostensible pacifism of free trade, [was] often perceived as a softening or feminization of a more assertive expansionism'. In this way, as Perera puts it, the young Flo Dombey becomes the feminine symbol of passive 'free trade' in the novel, particularly after her brother Paul Dombey's death. At the same time, her estranged father, Mr Dombey, who is embittered by the loss of his son and heir, becomes the very pattern of patriarchy's cold and hardened colonial mercantilism, a man who for most of the novel refuses to countenance his daughter at all. According to Perera, the two are pitted against each other right from the beginning of the novel. Only when Dombey faces bankruptcy towards the close of the story does he eventually yield to both the love of his daughter and the effeminizing implications of laissez-faire economics she seems to bring with her. Perera thus reads the novel as an allegory of empire writ small in Victorian family strife. She describes a complex ideology of home and gender that is complicated by the family's involvement in the West Indies, but which Dickens resolves in a vaguely happy ending and a triumph for 'free trade'.

Towards the end of the century, as the British Empire expanded against an ever-darkening background of European nationalism and hostility, imperialism began to resonate more and more in Victorian society and literature. By the 1880s–90s, when it had reached the height of its popularity in Britain, places such as Africa and India found a series of complex representations in the popular novels and poetry of the day. These reaches of empire became especially prevalent in the work of writers who seemed to take the cultivation of imperial attitudes, Englishness and the idea of colonial adventure as their starting point, rather than their background, as in Dickens's work. The most popular of these works include Rudyard Kipling's *The Jungle Book* (1894), set in India; Rider H. Haggard's *King Solomon's Mines* (1886), set in Africa; and Joseph Conrad's brace of works, *The Nigger of the Narcissus* (1897) and *Heart of Darkness* (1902), which are set between Bombay and London, and Africa, respectively.

See also *Contexts*: Domesticity, Drugs, Economics, Evolution, Nation, Orientalism, Other, Race, Travel, War; *Criticism*: Postcolonialism.

Further Reading

Perera, Suvendrini, *Reaches of Empire: The English Novel from Edgeworth to Dickens* (New York: Columbia University Press, 1991).
Said, Edward W., *Culture and Imperialism* (London: Vintage, 1994).

Evolution

The publication of Charles Darwin's *On the Origin of Species* in 1859 proved to be momentous. Theories of evolution were not new to the Victorians, but Darwin's ideas were groundbreaking because, unlike his predecessors, Darwin had identified the actual biological mechanism for evolution, 'natural selection'. For Darwin, natural selection referred to a process by which species only survive if and when they adapt themselves to their environment, although crucially there is a random or chance element to this process of selection. Those species which vary successfully are henceforth in a better position to feed and reproduce themselves. The preservation and evolution of the species is consequently ensured via its inheritance of better and better genetic 'variations' by subsequent generations, and so on. According to Darwin, those species that do not adapt themselves to their available resources adequately, in what he called the 'struggle for existence', would either mutate into other species, or dwindle away towards extinction. Only in the *Descent of Man* (1871), however, did Darwin made the connection between natural selection and human beings more explicit. In this book, he outlined the connections between sexual reproduction and the evolution of the species, from one primordial organism through to apes and more primitive variations. But Darwin's theories and those of his contemporaries were not accepted uncritically at the time. This was largely because evolutionary theory and its implications went on to challenge just about every conceivable idea and attitude that the Victorians held dear.

Darwin's work on evolution crystallized centuries of suspicion towards the biblical idea of creation as expounded in Genesis. His theories heralded, more to the point, the next major victory for scientific rationalism over long-held ideas about God and 'Creationism'. Creationism refers to the idea that God created everything and everyone, and suggests that all organisms have more or less existed in their recognizable and immutable form since God created them. Evolutionary theory, in contrast, posited the idea that organisms are in a perpetual state of motion, variation and change. By the same token, in the biblical account of time, the world is also only a few thousand years old, and this is another idea which naturalists and scientists, particularly geologists, have contradicted, pointing, as they have done for centuries, to anomalies such as fossilization and dinosaurs.

To understand the underlying impact of evolution at the level of ideas for the Victorians presents something of a challenge. To begin with, it needs to be remembered that the widespread belief in God as the benign creator of everyone and everything had for centuries provided a sense of order, reassurance, truth; a rationale, in fact, for the very existence of the world and the role of 'mankind' in it. In what one critic, J. Hillis Miller, describes as the 'disappearance of God' in the Victorian age, evolutionary theory ushered in a more secular but also less certain view of the origins and destiny of life on earth. Consequently, Darwin's ideas about competition and survival eventually changed the way that the Victorians thought about their place in the world forever. His ideas helped consolidate a radical shift in consciousness which has frequently been compared to that of the Copernican revolution in physics. Following Copernicus's work in the early sixteenth century, the universe was no longer regarded as geocentric (Earth-centred), but heliocentric (sun-centred); his theories had effectively displaced planet earth from the centre of the universe, just as evolutionary theory removed both God and mankind from the centre of Victorian consciousness, replacing it with something infinitely more random and chaotic.

On a conceptual level, evolutionary ideas were taken up, extended and variously used and abused by numerous philosophers and social commentators throughout the Victorian period. The most important and influential of these was Herbert Spencer (1820–1903), whose work gave rise to a theory which became known as 'Social Darwinism'. It was Spencer, not Darwin, who discussed society as evolving like a biological 'organism', and it was Spencer who obsessed with issues about 'moral' fitness. Spencer also drew comparisons between the evolutionary ideas of 'natural selection' and the social, political and economic 'survival' of 'mankind' in general. By the Victorian period, especially from the late 1840s onwards, Britain was heavily involved in the 'competitive' arena of liberal free-trade economics, which would soon come to dominate the Western world. Spencerian ideas about the 'survival of the fittest' and the notion of superiority/inferiority they led to, were then used to legitimate the cycle of 'inevitable' and 'natural' inequalities established by British capitalism – as well its expansion throughout the world – as a means of legitimating colonial and imperial conquest. Evolution theory, with its emphasis on infinite motion and change through time (in the mid-Victorian period it was known as 'the Development Hypothesis'), was consequently used to consolidate a certain Victorian optimism about the 'growth' of 'mankind', itself the legacy of Enlightenment and rationalist ideals. It became associated, as this suggests, with Victorian ideas about betterment, transformation, the inexorable progress of humanity towards perfection. On the other hand, as is typical of the Victorians, some human beings were deemed to be more 'evolved' than others, whereas others still, particularly darker-skinned foreigners, the Irish, the British working class, even women, were thought to have either reached a point of stasis or to have regressed back along Darwin's evolutionary scale of things. It is at this point that evolutionary ideas intersect with the Victorian 'natural order' of society, with their mania for classification and hierarchy, and with their many anxieties about survival, extinction, dominance and power.

The concept of evolution influences just about every important theme and issue associated with the Victorians: class, race, gender, sexuality, the body, the nature of the individual in society. Major works such as George Eliot's *Middlemarch* (1872), for example, are full of references – some obvious, some oblique – to evolution theory and to Darwin in particular. The novel contains allusions to 'variation', 'natural selection', sexual rivalry, problems of origins, growth, and the interconnectedness of all people and things. Similarly, the level of structure and organization, on slightly more complex levels, in many Victorian novels, particularly classic realist novels, follow a pattern which enacts the logic of evolution itself. The protagonist of *Middlemarch*, for example, Dorothea Brooke, at first marries the 'wrong' man, before she marries the 'right' man. In other words, her story enacts a sense of development from one less suitable, or perhaps less well-'evolved', state of affairs, to one more suitable. In this way, Victorian novels generally take the form of exposition, complication and resolution; they move from disorder to order, or from imperfection to perfection. Although this process becomes more complicated, particularly towards the end of the century, early and mid-Victorian fiction – that typified, for example, by the works of Charlotte Brontë and Charles Dickens – frequently contrives a series of coincidences and mawkish happy endings, often extremely unlikely ones, in order to restore order. Problems arise because the typical resolutions found in Victorian novels are not just those discovered by those characters who appear most adaptable to their social environment. Indeed, those selected to attain wealth and marriage by the end of the novel as a testimony to their 'survival' as the 'fittest' of the species, often seem to have arrived there not so much by dint of their 'natural' place in society, as by moments of outrageous Darwinian 'chance'. This is certainly the case with Oliver Twist, whose fate pivots on a series of fluke encounters with those good and bad characters that would eventually shape his destiny.

In the far more gloomy Darwinian outlook of Thomas Hardy's novels, on the other hand, those protagonists less adaptable to society tend to fade and die by the end. The rakish Sergeant Troy in *Far from the Madding Crowd* (1874), for example, is shot; Jude in *Jude the Obscure* (1884) dies wretchedly, as does Michael Henchard in *The Mayor of Casterbridge* (1886); Giles Winterbourne in *The Woodlanders* (1887) becomes ill and dies in his cottage; and Tess Durbeyfield in *Tess of the D'Urbervilles* (1891) is raped and hanged. Similarly, in Alfred Lord

Tennyson's 'In Memoriam A. H. H.' (1850), a poem about mourning, the narrator grapples with a sense of loss which finds him pre-empting the struggle between Darwin's more malign or 'natural' order of things, and the benign order of God: 'Are God and Nature then at strife / That Nature lends such evil dreams?'; and 'I falter where I firmly trod . . . / I stretch lame hands of faith, and grope'.

Another way of approaching the concept of evolution in Victorian literature is to consider the manner in which Victorian novels so often draw evolutionary comparisons between class and race from the bodies of their characters. This is the point most obviously at which the 'scientific racism' that underpinned the period begins to impact on problems of nation and empire. In Dickens's novels, for example, there are references – some more subtle than others – to the similarity between the English working class and the various black foreigners that haunt his work. Both of these groups, it seems, are yet to have fully evolved in the Dickens world, and this is revealed, to explore just one instance in detail, through Dickens's representations of the nose. Dickens's noses tend to fall into two vastly opposing shapes, which at once signify the distinction between his working and upper classes, as well as that between his white and black characters. The first is the Greek, Roman or Coriolanian nose. This is a noticeably white, European, and imperial nose which is often referred to as 'aquiline'. Examples of these include 'Mr Wopsle, united to a Roman nose' in *Great Expectations* (1861), 'Mrs Sparsit's Coriolanean nose' in *Hard Times* (1854), and the Chuzzlewit line's 'chiselled noses' in *Martin Chuzzlewit* (1843). Their opposite is the less streamlined nose associated with Dickens's poor and servant classes. This nose tends to be broad, flat, pug, snub, snouty, or all at once; it is more erect than the 'Roman' and is indicative of a quietly simianized (made 'monkey'-like), less well-evolved and hence 'blacked' body throughout the novels. The Artful Dodger, for example, a member of one of Dickens's more infamous lower orders, pickpockets, 'is a snub-nosed, flat-browed' and dirty grown-up child . In *Dombey and Son* (1848) the 'mulatto' figure of Susan Nipper, although a good character, sports 'a little snub-nose and black eyes like jet beads' and in *The Old Curiosity Shop* (1841), Kit Nubbles, also a good character, has a 'turned up nose'. The evil rent-collector Daniel Quilp, on the other hand, is also stuck with a much-unloved retroussé nose in the same novel. At one point, when Mr Brass and Mrs Jiniwin stand about gossiping, hoping that Quilp is dead, the shape of Quilp's nose becomes the most imperative item for debate: '"Flat," said Mrs Jiniwin.' But this is the moment when Quilp himself springs into the room: '"Aquiline!", cried Quilp, . . . "Aquiline, you hag. Do you see it? Do you call this flat? Do you? Eh?"' Dickens's preoccupation with noses is part of the broader obsession in Victorian culture with outward and visible signs of social and racial status. It marks a fetishization of the body that, as part of the broader debate about evolution, became aligned with various, more disreputable nine-teenth-century 'sciences' such as craniology, phrenology and physiog-nomy. All of these sciences, and the 'social' debate about evolution in general, had a catastrophic impact on ideologies of class, sexuality and race throughout the Victorian period and beyond.

See also *Contexts*: Body, Class, Empire and imperialism, Gender, Individualism, Other, Race, Science; *Texts*: Mid-Victorian novel, Realist fiction; *Criticism*: Postcolonialism.

Further Reading

Beer, Gillian, *Darwin's Plots: Evolutionary Narrative in Darwin, George Eliot and Nineteenth-Century Fiction* (London: Routledge & Kegan Paul, 1983).
Oldroyd, David Roger, *Darwinian Impacts: An Introduction to the Darwinian Revolution* (Milton Keynes: Open University Press, 1980).

Family

The concept of 'family values' is frequently attributed to the Victorians, and at the public level the family ideal was promoted by the national figurehead herself, Queen Victoria. After her marriage to Albert in 1840, Victoria's life was held up as a paragon of wifely virtues, and her royal family, with its nine children, was portrayed as an English domestic idyll. When Albert died of typhoid in 1861, Victoria lost what she described in 1844 as 'our happy domestic home'. Thereafter, she became an increas-ingly home-bound and reclusive figure for the long 40 years of her remaining reign. Along with the royals, the wholesome or ideal Victorian 'family' was publicized by the increasingly efficient methods of communication available throughout the period. Newspapers, journals, pamphlets, reviews, images, cartoons, books on correct household management, and cooking manuals, all played their part in promoting the family idyll, as did other important cultural mediums such as novels and theatre. The census of 1851 reported that Victorian Britain had become a nation whose most popular and ideal family pattern was that of individual units living in separate homes. Yet even though well-to-do mid-Victorians do seem to have become extremely family-conscious and home-oriented – the ideal family unit becoming both a middle-class and working-class aspiration as the century wore on – many poor Victorian families were crowded together into dwelling houses or tene-ments in order to survive, particularly in inner-city and urban areas.

One major influence on these developments was the passage of important family-related legislation, especially in the early decades of Victoria's reign. The Infant Custody bill of 1839, for example, finally enabled divorced or estranged women to apply for access to their children, whereas under the aegis of previous legislation, custody went immediately to the father, regardless of how brutal, adulterous and generally unfit he was. Similarly, as with anxieties about extramarital desires and the spectre of prostitution, few things threatened the Victorians and their family ideals more than the prospect of divorce. In 1857, these threats were intensified by the Divorce and Matrimonial Causes Act. This piece of legislation enabled women to apply for divorce themselves for the first time in British history. Unfortunately, it also stipulated that for husbands, the wife's adultery alone was enough to warrant divorce. For wives, on the other hand, the husband's adultery was deemed to be insufficient grounds for divorce, and would have to be mitigated by other factors such as violence, desertion, bigamy, incest and bestiality. Furthermore, existing laws about women's unpropertied status in the Victorian family remained intact for decades. Only after the Married Woman's Property Acts in 1870 and 1882 were women able to retain their own property and money, which up until then were appropriated by their husbands under a system known as coverture.

The passage of the divorce act coincided with the Indian Mutiny of 1857. This imperial crisis, during which Indian sepoys revolted against British colonials, and in which the British alleged that British women were being raped by mutinous Indians, mirrored the crises of family and gender relationships on the domestic front. Victorian commentators began to draw various parallels between both crises. The British Empire, always paternalistic in its attitudes towards the colonies and their citizens, was construed as the dominant 'husband' in the imperial 'relationship'; India, in turn, was cast as the subservient but now rebellious 'wife' seeking 'divorce'. As it turned out, after British soldiers had brutally repressed the mutiny, the British government took control of Indian affairs from the East India Company (which had managed them since c.1607), in order to take an even more dominant and paternalistic role in matters of empire, and it is partly in this respect that the concept of family in Victorian culture becomes inseparable from constructions of Englishness and empire in the period. At the same time, as a microcosm of English society the family unit symbolized what was the most efficient unit of order and structure available to Victorians, one which underpinned the maintenance and reproduction of capitalism. The economically self-sufficient family functioned to define and preserve the well-being of the working patriarch, the role of women as 'angels in the house', and the successful nurture of obedient children who were born and bred to keep the whole process going.

The family ideal was further promoted by essentially didactic and corrective works such as *Beeton's Book of Household* Management (1861). In this popular text, Isabella Beeton reproves her readership – namely wives and mothers – with her claim in the Preface that 'there is no more fruitful source of family discontent than a housewife's badly-cooked dinners and untidy ways'. According to Mrs Beeton, in order to keep their 'men' interested in the family home, 'mistresses' must also become 'perfectly conversant with all the other arts of making and keeping a comfortable home', and her book contains plenty of tips on how to manage servants, children, clothing, money, gossips, 'light and cheerful subjects of conversation', and how not to be a 'sluggard'. For Beeton and other commentators, the Victorian family ensconced in their homes also acted as bastions of defence against the chaos of the outside world, against elements such as loners, criminals, gypsies, the mad, vagrant children, disreputable men, loose women and foreigners. Nonetheless, the two sets of categories – private (the family) and public (everything outside the family) – continually impinged on one another throughout Victorian society. This is why attempts were made to shore up family privacy within the architectural arrangements of the ideal Victorian house, which took the form of separate rooms for each member of the family. In richer homes, for example, segregated rooms divided the family from the servants, and family members from each other. Such arrangements also neccessitated the separation of sleeping chambers, as a means of prevention against sexual intercourse across classes and ultimate taboos such as incest. The Victorian family was, as Karen Chase and Michael Levenson put it, an at once 'spatial and social unit'. It had the very material design of 'hearth and home' built into the walls and foundations of its houses.

The private realm of the family was heavily discussed and publicized throughout Victorian literature. Indeed, by the time of Charles Dickens's success with *A Christmas Carol* in 1843, a story which pivots on the ideal, cosy Victorian family Christmas, the cult of the family presented by novels seemed to have been offering a literary refuge of sorts from the various economic and social problems wrought by the 'hungry forties'. The security and dignity of family and domestic life in Dickens is also, however, something of a fragile construction throughout his novels. For example, middle-class or affluent families, such as the Brownlows and the Maylies in *Oliver Twist* (1837), remain relatively intact. They signify the triumph of order, the resolution of complications, and a final haven for abject heroes like Oliver Twist. But for every respectable Dickens family, there are dozens of slightly less respectable or dysfunctional lower-class families, and an array of absent or bad mother and father figures. Such families include the fatherless Rudges in *Barnaby Rudge* (1841), the motherless Dombeys in *Dombey and Son* (1848), the imprisoned Dorrits in *Little Dorrit* (1857), the simultaneously humble, kindly and violent Gargerys in *Great Expectations* (1861), and the pillow-throwing Smallweeds in Bleak House (1853).

Another portrayal of a somewhat duff Dickens family is that found in the Jellyby household in *Bleak House*. The problem with Mrs Jellyby is not simply that she is a bad mother, and that her children tear about unkempt all day like 'red Indians' with 'tomahawks'. Mrs Jellyby neglects her children because she dabbles in a charitable concern in a corner of empire, Borrioboola-Gha in Africa. The implication is that Mrs Jellyby should be tending to 'family' matters, to matters of 'the home' rather than Africa. She forms an integral part of Dickens's satire – which he called 'telescopic philanthropy' in the novel – on the way that domestic problems and the 'condition' of England in general were being increasingly neglected because of Britain's growing world role. As the relationship between the 1857 divorce controversy and the Indian Mutiny, and Mrs Jellyby's own family of 'red Indians' suggest, the Victorian family ideal is, in fact, always bound up with both the integrity of Englishness and its role in empire.

See also *Contexts*: Domesticity, Gender, Nation; *Texts*: Children's literature; *Criticism*: Feminism, Psychoanalysis.

Further Reading

Chase, Karen and Levenson, Michael, *The Spectacle of Intimacy: A Public Life for the Victorian Family* (Princeton and Oxford: Princeton University Press, 2000).

Food and Famine

Industrialization and urbanization ensured that most Britons no longer produced their own food in the Victorian period. The population became increasingly dependent on a successful economy for sustenance, and by the first full decade of Victoria's reign Britain was undergoing a major depression. Since the passage of the Corn Laws in 1815, grain prices, and therefore a staple of the British diet, bread, were high, and this led to shortages of food and widespread hunger which earned the decade the name 'hungry forties'. The Corn Laws imposed heavy tariffs on imported and exported wheat. In a country already struggling to feed itself, they kept the price of bread at an artificially high price, and were only repealed in 1846 when, some commentators argue, the British government under Robert Peel felt compelled to respond to the Irish famine. Prior to 1850, in an age when any knowledge of vitamins and adequate nutrition was minimal, diets for the Victorian poor largely consisted of meagre, cereal-based meals. Generally, although by no means exclusively, more prosperous Victorians ate better, and those who could afford it treated themselves to the tropical delights of bananas and chocolate. Equally, the massive Victorian servant class, and especially those who lived and worked in more affluent homes, enjoyed better diets than others of a similar lower-class status.

Eating habits in the Victorian period depended on one's social standing and tended to revolve around work. Working-class Victorians, for instance, increasingly turned to a midday meal in order to sustain them for the long afternoon ahead. There were also important Victorian innovations in the preservation of foodstuffs, and early systems of mechanical refrigeration and canning were significant developments. Restaurants and grocery stores were also mid- to late-Victorian innovations, and fish and chip shops became popular in the late 1890s. There were, at the same time, numerous controversies over corrupt food producers in the period. Food swindlers adulterated their foodstuffs by adding, for example, chalk to bread, in order to create more 'bread' and increase profits, and such scandals went mostly unchecked until the passage of the Adulteration of Food, Drink and Drugs Act in 1872, when it was criminalized. By the end of the century, British agriculture and hence Britain's capacity to feed itself had shrunk considerably. It became so small that the nation's urban population had to be increasingly provided for by foreign imports of wheat, particularly imports from the colonies.

Hunger and desperation in the 1840s led to riotous and drunken lower-class Victorians. In an attempt to pacify these groups, philanthropical organizations such as the Temperance Movement rose up and attempted to encourage moderation. A welter of books aimed at both poorer and better-off Victorians also urged them to eat sparingly, with middle-class classics such as *Beeton's Book of Household Management* (1861) at the forefront. Isabella Beeton's exhortation to live and eat 'economically, tastefully and well', and the fact that she appended to each recipe 'a careful estimate of its *cost*, [and] the *number of people* for whom it is *sufficient*', became immensely popular in the period. Prior to this, however, as poorer Britons on the mainland starved throughout the 'hungry forties', 1845 also saw the outbreak of the Great Famine in Ireland (*c.*1845–52), the catalyst of which was a series of failures of the potato crop begun by a fungus called *Phytopthera infestans*. As this staple of the Irish diet vanished and people began to starve, successive British governments under Robert Peel and Lord John Russell were forced to act quickly. Although, however, these administrations provided public works, maize, and soup kitchens in Ireland, many commentators accused the British of indifference and procrastination. The authorities were blamed for putting limitations on money and vital resources after 1847, for not preventing the exportation of the 1846 grain harvest from Ireland, and for the ultimate failure to provide adequate relief for the worst excesses of the catastrophe. As a result of the famine, around one million died of starvation, and another million or so emigrated to mainland Britain or the colonies; in total, Ireland lost around 20 per cent of its population. Food and famine in Victorian literature and culture are closely linked to economic and class issues. But they are also, as the colonial relationship between Britain and Ireland suggests, linked to problems of nation and race.

The 'Condition of England' novels of the 1840s and 1850s reflect the wretched state of the nation in that period and, not surprisingly, they contain numerous images of starvation. Some of them also reflect massive upheavals such as the Irish famine. In Charlotte Brontë's *Shirley* (1849), Brontë's heroines, Shirley Keeldar and Caroline Helstone, are both middle-class English women who are sick with love for two brothers of Anglo-Belgian descent, Robert and Louis Moore. Intriguingly, though, both women also undergo problems with food, which is indicated by their refusal to eat and the appearance of an unnamed wasting illness. Prior to her illness, Shirley Keeldar is bitten by what seems to be a rabid dog, but some commentators interpret both her and Caroline Helstone's illness as showing symptoms of anorexia nervosa, although this disorder was not classified until much later in the century. For some critics, the important point about the inscription of food in Brontë's novel is the extent to which her 'anorexic' women use their bodies as sites of protests against Victorian patriarchy; anorexia and the refusal to eat becomes, in this respect, a physical reaction to the violence wrought on women's bodies throughout history.

In *Shirley* itself, these ideas are problematic. Although both of Brontë's heroines show symptoms of classic Victorian sexual repression, denial and the 'hunger' of desire, Shirley is also an independent heiress with 'manly' attributes. The novel, set in 1811–13, is also underpinned by the Luddite Riots. As the plot unfurls, Robert Moore introduces new machinery into his mill, but such machinery decreases the need for manpower. The result of such changes is unrest amongst his workers, who protest against the unemployment and hunger the new machines create. But although *Shirley* is set in to the latter years of the Napoleonic period, it can also be read as the projection of the historical concerns and anxieties which surrounded the novel's publication in 1849. With the spectre of working-class uprisings in the 1840s – those fomented by hunger and radical organizations calling for reform such as Chartism – not the least of these crises, it need hardly be said, was the Irish Famine. The novel's depictions of English working-class privation, patriarchal domination and a hungry, shillelagh-wielding Irishman called Malone, along with Shirley and Caroline's refusal to eat – not to mention the Brontë family's Irish heritage – can thus be interpreted as an unconscious reflex of all of these historical circumstances.

In the context of Ireland, the anorexic hunger of Brontë's women points towards a pathology of empire in the novel, where the unspeakable acts of British involvement in Ireland are projected onto the domestic context of 'English' problems. In other words, in what might be described as the colonial unconscious of Brontë's novel, which only ever permits Ireland and the Irish famine a marginal role, the violence of empire speaks out in the broader national crises of food and famine. However, in Brontë's novel, such crises appear on the sickly and famished bodies of middle-class Englishwomen, whose 'hunger', unlike the millions of dead and displaced Irish during the famine, is finally appeased by their inevitable marriages to Robert and Louis Moore, and by the nourishment and sustenance provided by the discourse of love.

See also   *Contexts*: Body, Consumerism, Domesticity, Family; *Criticism*: Postcolonialism.

Further Reading

Eagleton, Terry, *Heathcliff and the Great Hunger: Studies in Irish Culture* (London and New York: Verso, 1995).

Gaze

The nineteenth century saw the development of an increasingly well-policed and more rigorously disciplined society, which gave rise to an increasing culture of surveillance . Robert Peel's Metropolitan Police Act (1829) gave London its first effective police force, and a local constabulary for each British county was established from 1856 onwards. This development ensured that the question of obedience and punishment became a matter of public, as well as private, concern, and that all Victorians were encouraged to watch over and police everyone else. According to late twentieth-century theorists such as Michel Foucault, the result of these developments was that nineteenth-century society began to discipline itself automatically, by functioning along the lines laid down by the architectural design of prisons. One prison in particular, for Foucault, worked on the principle of visibility and the 'gaze'. Foucault based his concept of Panopticism, the 'all-seeing' society, from a diagram drawn up by the British utilitarian philosopher Jeremy Bentham in 1791. Bentham's Panopticon was a model prison in which supervisors could observe prisoners in their circle of individual cells without being seen themselves, and without seeing each other. This system was effective because prisoners, segregated from each other and subject to the constant gaze of the lone supervisor in a central watchtower, never knew whether or not they were being watched. Crucially, as Foucault describes it, the lone supervisor is 'invisible' to the prisoners, and in fact did not even need to be present in the watchtower in order for the discipline of his 'gaze' to become effective: 'he [the prisoner] is seen, but he does not see, . . . what matters is that he knows himself to be observed'. Foucault argued that this process of surveillance and visibility – this constant subjection to the gaze – was 'generalizable', that it was in fact central to the development of the disciplinary society throughout the Western world. In such a society, as Foucault concluded, 'the major effect of the Panopticon [is] to induce in the inmate a state of conscious and permanent visibility that assures the automatic functioning of power'. Put another way, that which exerts power and discipline in society effectively becomes 'invisible'; it is not, as Foucault goes on, reducible to one dominant or all-seeing 'individual'. But this very anonymity and invisibility ensures that individuals police themselves and each other, even if there is nobody actually in the vicinity to 'watch'. For Foucault, the notion of individualism in Western society is a direct effect of this culture of visibility, seclusion and the power of the gaze. The individual, having internalized the disciplinary power of penitentiary discourses, is partly a construct of such discourses, as with those proceeding from medicine, education and factory systems, with their numerous methods of segregation and social exclusion. These 'segregations' ultimately translate into the individualist ideals of privacy and sanctity, and the Western obsession with the freedom of the 'self'.

Foucault's ideas about the gaze have been applied to Victorian literature in numerous ways. One of the most illuminating to date is that made in D. A. Miller's work in *The Novel and the Police* (1988). One of Miller's central points is that the rise to dominance of the novel in the Victorian period coincides with the emergence of the police state and the culture of surveillance. Of particular significance is the omniscient narrator in the novel, which acts, according to Miller, like Foucault's lone supervisor in the Panopticon watchtower, as an anonymous form of power and discipline. The very anonymity and 'invisibility' of the omniscient narrator effectively operates like the 'invisible' powers of Foucault's Panopticon society; it 'sees' and 'watches' the reader without being seen or watched itself. Miller suggested that this process renders the 'individual' reader subject to the disciplining 'gaze' of the omniscient narrator. In other words, the narrator, whether representative of an essentially disciplinary and punitive society or not, effectively constructs the individual reader by policing him or her ideologically. Furthermore, in line with Foucault's ideas about the 'individual', Miller reminds us that the act of reading is itself solitary, private and individual act. In this respect, it is no coincidence that the rise of the Victorian novel is concomitant with the rise of bourgeois-capitalist and peculiarly Victorian notions of the 'free-thinking' individual. The act of reading subjects the reader to the gaze of invisible forces of discipline and power. These forces establish forms of consent and obedience in the reader which are everywhere disseminated in the pages of Victorian literature.

A society in which everyone appears to be watching and observing everyone else can be found in various nineteenth-century novels. The problem does, however, contain dimensions other than those described above. In Charlotte Brontë's *The Professor* (1857), for example, the reach of the gaze becomes extended into typically Victorian anxieties about gender, sexuality and desire. This novel is preoccupied with problems of visibility, and in particular the spectacle of womanhood, in which women seem subject to, and thus disciplined by, the male gaze throughout. Intriguingly, though, and uniquely for Brontë's novels, the protagonist and first-person narrator of this novel is a man. William Crimsworth is a miserable, sexually repressed and ascetic Englishman. Early on in the novel he is all but enslaved and heavily scrutinized by his overbearing, mill-owning brother, Edward: 'He [Crimsworth's brother] scanned me from head to foot.' Crimsworth eventually moves to Brussels to teach English in a girls' school and better himself. Once there he seems to do little but gaze at young women all day. He subjects his pupils to secretive observations from various vantage points, from which he is able to see, like Foucault's prison guard, without being seen himself: 'I thought it would have been so pleasant to have looked out upon a garden planted with flowers and trees, so amusing to have watched the demoiselles at their play; to have studied the female character in a variety of phases.' In the figure of Crimsworth, the idea of women as objects for study and 'knowledge' comes to the foreground in Brontë's novel, in a Victorian society obsessed with creating rational classifications and discourses about everyone and everything. It underlines Foucault's crucial point about the way in which the panopticon society empowers itself by gathering, via the gaze, a centralized and hence unified knowledge about the individuals under scrutiny.

Written after, but published before *The Professor*, Brontë returns to problems of the gaze in *Villette* (1853). In this novel, the Frenchman Monsieur Pelet assumes Crimsworth's role of patriarchal gazer upon women. He is particularly concerned with observing the novel's frumpy protagonist and narrator, Lucy Snowe: 'You [Lucy] need watching and watching over . . . I watch you and others pretty closely . . . '. But Lucy Snowe – as if in reaction to the male gaze – has also internalized the rules and methods about watching and learning in the Victorian panopticon, while remaining invisible herself: 'I had only meant to view him (Dr John(in the crowd, myself unseen'. Indeed, in this novel, in particular, but on various complex levels, Brontë's work operates like the panopticon society. It negotiates, in effect, a prison-house of individuals and individual readers, all of whom are made vulnerable – because visible and knowable – to the power and discipline of the Victorian patriarchal gaze.

See also *Contexts*: Architecture, Crime and punishment, Gender, Madness; *Texts*: Crime fiction; *Criticism*: Feminism, Poststructuralism.

Further Reading

Boone, Joseph A., 'Depolicing *Villette*: Surveillance, Invisibility, and the Female Erotics of "Heretic Narrative"', *Novel*, 25 (1992).
Miller, D. A., *The Novel and the Police* (Berkeley, CA: University of California Press, 1988).

Gender

The Victorians ordered their lives around a hierarchy of gender relationships which they constructed to suit themselves. With the obvious exception of Queen Victoria, men dominated every available public or social sphere. They were prominent in all areas associated with 'masculine' arenas of power and ambition: politics, government, the law, economics, industry, commerce, engineering, education, sport, the armed services, and the administration of Victoria's growing world empire. Women, at least in middle- and upper-class sections of society, were less active in the public sector. Men expected them to confine themselves to the private and 'passive' spheres of the home and the family, in domestic roles encapsulated by a comment in the influential *Edinburgh Review*: '[women] are the proper legislators for, as well as ministers of, the interior'. However, the Victorian patriarch was dominant in the 'interior' sphere as well. Due to the man's status as husband, father, breadwinner and owner of all family 'property', including his wife, he reigned supreme, to all intents and purposes, throughout Victorian society. In what was a century characterized by the emergence and consolidation of male-led, middle-class professions, male business-men and entrepreneurs, and the bourgeois cult of the gentleman, it therefore comes as no shock that a male, middle-class ideology of gender came to dominate Victorian society and culture.

Most Victorian men believed that women did not possess the intel-lectual capabilities which educated and industrious men were endowed with. Such an opinion served to distinguish women further from men, while preventing women from entering, earlier on in the century at least, the male-dominated fields of education, such as universities, scholar-ships and research. Regarded by men as not being 'of the mind' and so insufficiently 'cultured', women were treated as somewhat paradoxical figures 'of the body' and 'angels of the hearth', as at once physical and spiritual, as well as 'naturally' all heart, tenderness and submission, and so on. Men also thought that women and their 'natural' desires for reproduction were determined by their essential physicality, by what male-authored medical textbooks described as their 'uterine economy'. This biological determinism then became linked in Victorian conscious-ness with the motherly and wifely virtues of child-rearing and house-work that became associated with the role of women.

Such distinctions conveniently overlooked the very different plight of working-class women in the period. Far from being just biologically programmed for making babies and staying at home, working-class women were welcomed and very active in the public and 'male' spheres of the nation's factories and industries throughout the century. Indeed, as such contradictions suggest, the concept of gender was never really as secure in the Victorian period as history would have one believe. The very structure of gender roles and the apparently 'natural' differences and desires between men and women were everywhere undermined and contradicted by such discrepancies over class, but also by those which the Victorians classified as 'deviant' sexualities. For this was also an age of quietly insistent gender-bending, transvestism and homo-eroticism, all of which violated contemporary gender norms and sexual ideals. By the end of the century, the more flagrant antics of notorious decadents such as Oscar Wilde, who clearly upset the Victorian man–woman matrix with his effete ways, paradoxes, critiques of Victorian morality and preferences for men, had begun to besiege the Victorian order of things from all sides.

The literary and cultural spheres of Victorian society were also male-dominated, and this further enabled men to control and disseminate

what Karl Marx called 'ruling ideas'. In a context of increasing nationalism and imperialism, Victorian notions about the nature of writing and
literary form became increasingly gendered themselves. In one famous
incident, the much-ridiculed late-Victorian poet, Alfred Austin, took it
upon himself to defend the 'official' image of Britain as a nation of
macho and vigorous empire-builders, which he thought needed to be
reflected in the nation's poetry. Austin attacked his far more successful
predecessor as poet laureate, Alfred Lord Tennyson, for producing what
Austin called the 'feminine, narrow, domesticated, timorous Poetry of
the Period'. Another poet, Algernon Swinburne, also set about
Tennyson, in his claim that the latter's use of the 'idyl' form was unsuitable because unmanly. In comparison with the supposedly more
'masculine' forms of tragic or lyric poetry, Swinburne deemed the idyl
weak, womanly, and as 'the sole diet of girls'.

The great age of Victorian novel writing and its reception also created
problems that arose from anxieties about gender. It should not be
forgotten that, although the novel form was, for the most part, dominated by male writers, there were huge numbers of women novelists
writing for economic reasons (such as the prolific Margaret Oliphant, for
example), and the readership of novels was frequently considered to be
disproportionately made up of women. Unsurprisingly, this readership
was mostly comprised of middle- and upper-class women, those whom
men encouraged to lead more passive and sedentary lives; they were
women, that is to say, apparently with enough time to read novels and,
eventually, write them. Even though, as the *Quarterly Review* put it,
many novels were already seen as a corruptive force for the vulnerable
'fair one on the sofa', the writing of novels, in terms of Victorian gender
roles at least, was often considered a more 'active' and hence potentially
subversive task than reading. Women writers, in this respect, were
simultaneously perceived to be a threat to men, to other women, and to
themselves. Such anxieties partly explain why, generally speaking – and
with famous exceptions such as the Brontë sisters, George Eliot, and
poets such as Elizabeth Barrett Browning, Emily Dickinson and Christina
Rossetti, to name only the most obvious – women tended to be discouraged from entry into the writing profession.

In recent years, more and more Victorian women writers, published
and unpublished, have come to light, but it is estimated that only around
20 per cent of all published Victorian writers were female. The larger
proportion of these were novelists or writers of children's literature, and
the proportion of that group who ventured into literary criticism is even
smaller. As in all walks of private and public Victorian life (although
interestingly, writing and literature is where the private is *made* public),

the problems facing women writers seeking to get published in what was an extremely patriarchal society were many. The early writings of Charlotte Brontë, in particular, were subject to hostile comments from male reviewers. In 1837, Brontë sent some of her verse to the poet laureate and historian Robert Southey, whose response reveals many of the problems and struggles facing women writers in the period. Southey's letter begins with praise for Brontë's 'faculty of verse'. He then starts to accuse her of 'day dreams', before settling into an extraordinary discussion of why literature is unsuitable for women, whose 'proper duties', it seems, are elsewhere: 'Literature cannot be the business of a woman's life, and it ought not to be. The more she is engaged in her proper duties, the less leisure will she have for it, even as an accomplishment and a recreation.' In her riposte to these comments, Brontë's mood and tenor are quietly sarcastic: 'Sir, I cannot rest till I have answered your letter . . . In the evenings, I confess, I do think, but I never trouble any one else with my thoughts . . . I don't always succeed, for sometimes when I'm teaching or sewing I would rather be reading or writing but I try to deny myself.' Yet in spite of the eventual success of women such as the Brontë sisters, the problems that faced women writers in the period, especially lower-class women writers, remained formidable. This partly accounts for why, even towards the end of Victoria's reign, with the emergence of more vocal and better-organized women's groups, 1890s male writers such as Thomas Hardy and Joseph Conrad rose to prominence and popularity at the expense of a burgeoning school of contemporary 'new woman' writers, with their radical views on gender, sexuality, and the role of women both in and outside the home.

The discourse of Victorian gender is all about the nature of power. One popular contemporary poem, written by a woman, which reflects on this discourse – and the ideology of Victorian capitalism which underpins it – is Christina Rossetti's 'Goblin Market' (1862). The poem describes two young sisters, Laura and Lizzie, who leave the sanctuary of their home and linger in a glen by 'brookside rushes', where they are tempted by 'Goblin men'. Rossetti's goblins are actually indeterminate man/creatures, 'One like a wombat . . . / one like a ratel' , with cats' faces and swishing tails. They are alluring but ultimately sinister merchants who, with their relentless summons, 'Come buy, come buy', sell a cornucopia of English orchard and exotic fruits such as 'Lemons and oranges . . . / Figs to fill your mouth / Citrons from the South. Despite Laura's admonitions to Lizzie not to 'look at Goblin men' or 'buy their fruits', Laura is eventually tempted to 'buy' fruit with a 'golden lock' of her hair, after which she gorges herself. When the girls return home, Laura's indulgence appears to have turned her into an excessively desirous young woman, who longs for the pleasure of more indulgence. Her newfound needs for immediate gratification are 'baulked', however, and it turns out that she never hears or sees the 'goblin men' again, despite repeated returns to the glen. Unsatisfied, Laura begins to fade and sicken; she ages, withers, goes grey, and neglects her duties as a young Victorian woman: 'She no more swept the house / Tended the fowls or cows'. The frightened Lizzie, still able to hear the goblin's call, then decides to rescue her sister by buying 'fruit to comfort her'. But the goblin men do not accept Lizzie's offer of a 'silver penny' in exchange for the fruit. For reasons unspecified, they choose to bypass this simple capitalist transaction in order, it seems, to dine with Lizzie and to barter, if at all, on *their* terms. When Lizzie refuses, the goblin men become aggressive: ' [they] trod and hustled her / Elbowed and jostled her / Clawed with their nails . . . / Twitched her hair out by the roots . . . / Kicked and knocked her / Mauled and mocked her'. They also attempt to press fruit into Lizzie's body, as if to penetrate her physically on their own violent terms as well: '[they] Held her hands and squeezed their fruits / Against her mouth to make her eat'. Lizzie, however, who 'Would not open lip from lip', manages to resist the goblins, and eventually they slope off into the distance. Lizzie then runs home to Laura covered in fruit juice, where she exhorts her sister, in sensuous terms, to 'Hug me, kiss me, suck my juices' and to 'Eat me, drink me, love me'. When Laura dutifully performs these tasks, Lizzie is quickly restored to her old vitality.

The goblin fruit symbolizes both the poison and the cure in Rossetti's poem; it is at once the source of disease and the medicine. The poem, in this respect, works on numerous contradictory levels and sub-texts. Underpinned by gender conflicts, it is a violent drama about vicious men and vulnerable women, but it is also a hymn to pleasure, desire, temptation and sexuality. It is also, consequently, a biblical parable about the loss of innocence; an account of eroticism between women and sisters; and a pastoral fantasy about excess and death. Similarly, written in irregular, haphazard metres, the form of the poem enacts the gender, sexual and socioeconomic irregularities Rossetti discusses, and the general sense of danger and disorder central to its theme. At the same time, it is also cautionary and didactic in tone, a fairy tale with a syrupy happy ending. By the end of the poem, Rossetti's allegories of patriarchal oppression are contrasted sharply with Laura and Lizzie's older roles as virtuous and reflective 'wives' with children. Yet the sisters' newfound families remain curiously devoid of references to husbands, and the poem concludes in a celebration of 'sisterhood' which remains absorbed by its defiance of the powers of 'wicked' men: 'For there is no friend like a sister.'

See also *Contexts*: Body, Clothing, Family, Sex and sexuality, Violence; *Texts*: Drama, Historical novel, Poetry, Sensation Fiction; *Criticism*: Feminism.

Further Reading

Shires, Linda M. (ed.), *Rewriting the Victorians: Theory, History, and the Politics of Gender* (London and New York: Routledge, 1992).

Gothic

Gothic is a term derived from 'the Goths'. The Goths were Germanic tribes whose invasions in the third to fifth centuries were partly responsible for the decline of the Roman Empire and the onset of the 'dark ages'. Much later, Gothic came to be applied to a 'medieval' period in European architecture. It now has various definitions in numerous areas: history, architecture, art, literature, although it has retained its element of 'darkness'. By the time of the Victorians, the notion of Gothic 'darkness' had become mixed up with British anxieties about religious obscurantism, Catholicism and above all a sense of terror. The Victorians inherited an ethos of rationalism from the Enlightenment of the previous century. They lived in an age of science, industrialism, capitalism and imperialism, and they are renowned for their sense of progress, purpose, and their robust 'common sense'. But some Victorians also embarked on what became a massively popular 'Gothic Revival' in architecture. As part of their scholarly and artistic fascination with medievalism, this revival was characterized by the new design for the Houses of Parliament (1840–65). Augustus Pugin's and Charles Barry's grandiose neo-Gothic building is not, however, simply nostalgic: it is a monument to Victorian Britain's pre-eminence as a modern and increasingly secular (if outwardly pious) world power.

The Gothic renaissance in English architecture is also linked to the development of Gothic traditions in literature. As a genre, English Gothic fiction emerged during the Romantic period (*c*.1789–1830), and one of the first Gothic novels, Horace Walpole's *The Castle of Otranto: A Gothic Story* (1765), was written by a man who even turned his London home, Strawberry Hill, into a 'little Gothic castle'. Following Walpole's work, Gothic fiction achieved fame and notoriety by way of two 1790s novels in particular, Ann Radcliffe's *The Mysteries of Udolpho* (1794) and Matthew Lewis's *The Monk* (1796), and in the early nineteenth century with Mary Shelley's acclaimed *Frankenstein* (1818). In early Victorian literature, Gothic thrived in the popular 1830s and 1840s works of G. W. M. Reynolds, Edward Bulwer Lytton, G. P. R. James and William Harrison Ainsworth. Gothic themes and preoccupations also crept into a great deal of Victorian literature which is not deemed part of any recognizably Gothic genre as such, even that defined broadly as 'realism'. There are classic moments of Gothic suspense and melodrama, for example, in Charles Dickens's popular novels, which are a mishmash of harsh Victorian 'realities', the grotesque, the picaresque, Romanticism, and much more besides. Gothic chills and thrills are also integral to popular works such as Emily Brontë's ghostly masterpiece, *Wuthering Heights* (1847) and Charlotte Brontë's *Jane Eyre* (1847), and they underpin the so-called 'Sensation' fiction genre dominated by the novels of Wilkie Collins, especially *The Woman in White* (1860) and *The Moonstone* (1868). Gothic is, furthermore, a conspicuous feature of the decadent literature associated with the *fin de siècle* years, in particular Robert Louis Stevenson's *The Strange Case of Dr Jekyll and Mr Hyde* (1886), Oscar Wilde's *The Picture of Dorian Gray* (1891) and Bram Stoker's *Dracula* (1897).

That Gothic literature has its origins in the Romantic period is important to bear in mind because it helps to contextualize the problems and ideas that preoccupied the Victorians. In brief, late eighteenth-century Europe was overshadowed by two momentous events: the British Industrial Revolution and the French Revolution in 1789, and these upheavals produced, or rather reconfigured, two new spectres for Romantic and Victorian Britain. First, there was the creation of a potentially rebellious British working class; second, the resurgent image of the long-despised French. For centuries Britain's great Catholic enemy, after 1789 and with the rise of Napoleon the French haunted reactionary Britain with their radically republican and egalitarian ways. France, it seemed, epitomized all that was wild, irrational and terrible about foreignness. Unsurprisingly, in this respect, Gothic clichés in English literature such as the ruined abbey and furtive monk also point towards a residual Protestant and British anxiety relating to the 'foreignness' of the Catholic French. Moreover, the idea of the Gothic in Victorian literature is, both a reflection on, and a reaction to, all of these historical anxieties. It is, furthermore, characterized by the fear that that which is 'past', such as British Catholicism, that which should remain repressed or taboo, might return to haunt the present. Gothic signifies, for one recent commentator, Fred Botting, 'the writing of excess'; it is that which transgresses the 'bounds of reality and possibility'.

Gothic representations in texts are not necessarily subversive, however. Their disorders and transgressions also serve to underline the highly constructed order of rational 'reality' in the first place, itself a representation of the text. Gothic literature, as such, can only imply an 'unreal' dimension full of terror and macabre goings on, with well-known preoccupations including a certain taste for mystery, danger, dark secrets, suspense, melodrama, exaggeration, eeriness, ghosts, monsters, vampires, moving statues, blood, murder, rape, incest and vice. Vintage Gothic settings are equally well known. They include ruined abbeys, convents, graveyards, sinister castles, gloomy hallways and bedchambers, as well as lonely windswept landscapes with scudding clouds and moonlight. These settings, in turn, tend to be populated by a host of stereotypical, frequently somewhat wooden, characters. Gothic victims tend to be vulnerable and virginal women, whose bodies and minds are besieged by an evil villain in the dead of night. The villains, in turn, are frequently – but by no means exclusively – lusty and violent aristocratic men of mysterious origins. Although ghosts and vampires were not, even for Victorians, very realistic, their role in nineteenth-century culture in this respect betrayed fears and anxieties with very real implications for attitudes towards class, race and sexuality.

Many of the conventions that sustained Gothic fiction are still extant in late-Victorian literature. Although Bram Stoker's *Dracula* is an obvious example, the novel is revealing because it embodies almost every Gothic cliché imaginable, but it spices them up with specifically Victorian neuroses. Stoker's novel projects the full range of English, middle-class, male anxieties onto the threats embodied by one Gothic individual. Dracula, therefore, manages to be a vaguely 'aristocratic' monster, a decadent foreigner, a series of low animals and a lusty vampire cum vaporous 'devil' 'thing', all at once. Published in an 1890s Britain which had become increasingly anxious about class issues, nationalism, racial purity, empire, the evolutionary boundaries between humans and beasts, and, as ever, the role of its women, Stoker tells the story of how Dracula moves from Eastern Europe to the heart of the British Empire. Once there, in a series of increasingly unconvincing setpieces, the vampire sets about his desire for world domination by 'colonizing' the English. His aim, as Stoker suggests, is to 'contaminate' the English race by mixing it up with the vampire's alien blood and by sexually enlightening its chaste and virtuous women, who immediately become more sensuous and 'voluptuous' when bitten. In short, the novel articulates fears about the invasion and corruption of Englishness by irrational, 'un-English', Gothic forces. Its terror, where at all, lies in the fear that the rational and moderate English might be made 'foreign' to themselves by parasitic European nobles, and by un-Victorian sexual transgressions which are centred on men's struggles for women's bodies. But the bodies of Stoker's women also become, on a conceptual level, violent territories for the struggle for nationhood and 'empire' in the novel. In this interpretation, *Dracula* represents only one of the least ambiguous points in Victorian cultural history at which 'Gothic' signifies 'foreign'.

See also   *Contexts*: Architecture, Death, Madness, Other, Race; *Texts*; Crime fiction, Drama, Penny dreadfuls, Poetry, Sensation fiction; *Criticism*: Feminism, Psychoanalysis, Queer theory.

Further Reading

Botting, Fred, *Gothic* (London and New York: Routledge, 1996).
Punter, David, *The Literature of Terror: A History of Gothic Fictions from 1765 to the Present Day*, vol. 1 (London and New York: Longman, 1996).

Individualism

The concept of the individual is central to Victorian society and culture. Many contemporary books and public or legal documents testify to this fact, but three texts in particular, all published in the same year, proved to be especially influential. Charles Darwin's *The Origin of Species* (1859), John Stuart Mill's *On Liberty* (1859) and Samuel Smiles's *Self-Help* (1859) either deal explicitly with the individual, or were used to justify the ideology of the individual. Needless to say, Darwin's radical theories about evolution and 'natural selection' are not about the ethos of Victorian 'individualism' as such. They were, however, adapted to the political and socioeconomic spheres by the philosopher and sociologist Herbert Spencer (1820–1903). In what became known as 'Social Darwinism', it was Spencer, not Darwin, who applied the term 'the survival of the fittest' to society, and it was Spencer who drew parallels between the evolutionary ideas of 'natural selection' and the economic 'survival' of 'mankind'. Such ideas were then applied to the rise and consolidation of free trade in the period, which emphasized 'individual' enterprise and competitiveness; the development, that is, of a British economy unregulated by state intervention. At the same time, the integrity of the Victorian individual, especially the male individual, was enshrined in British law, particularly in terms of the preservation of individual property and liberty.

In the philosopher John Stuart Mill's *On Liberty* (1859), the emphasis is very much on the needs and desires of individuals. Mill argues in his essay for the individual's right to be 'heard' in society, and his famous introduction claims that the problem, broadly, is that of 'the nature and limits of the power which can be legitimately exercised by society over the individual'. For Mill, the individual was 'sovereign'. He or she should enjoy liberty of 'thought', 'feeling', 'expression', 'publication', and 'freedom of opinion on all subjects, practical or speculative, scientific, moral, or theological', as well as the freedom 'to unite' with other individuals. The only time, according to Mill, that society's 'power' should be exercised over the individual is in order to 'prevent harm to others'. And this stipulation only came about because the doctrine of utilitarianism advocated by Mill – the aim of which was to promote the greatest happiness of the greatest number – exposed the individual, as he put it, 'to external control, only in respect of those actions of each, which concern the interest of other people'.

As the most successful of many Victorian self-improvement books, Samuel Smiles's *Self-Help*, as its title suggests, is equally preoccupied with the individual. Smiles is unambiguous in his claim that it is the independent duty of the 'individual' to seek betterment, and that reliance on external help is 'enfeebling in its effects'. But although Smiles maintains, for example, that 'the spirit of self-help is the root of all genuine growth of the individual', his ideas are broadly similar to those contained in Mill's work, especially in terms of Smiles's claim that 'the duty of helping one's self in the highest sense involves the helping of one's neighbours'. On the other hand, Smiles's work, unlike that of Mills, reads more like a guidebook to Victorian virtues, particularly those of middle-class Victorians, and it emphasizes all of the following: 'self-reliance', 'self control', 'thrift', 'energy', 'industry', 'diligence', 'application', 'courage', 'perseverance'. Smiles's notion of self-help is, in fact, a national trait, and has always 'been a marked feature in the English character', despite his assumption that it marks an Englishness which remains, 'only an aggregate of individual conditions'. Smiles's book is important because it is a popular endorsement of the ascetic lifestyle and sense of industry which underpinned bourgeois capitalist individualism in the Victorian period. Equally, the ideas it contains are also, for Smiles, compatible with the Victorian sense of Christian duty and piety, a point evidenced by his opening dictum: 'Heaven helps those who help themselves'. The book goes on to recount a long list of successful 'individuals' who, by dint of their own application, eventually made good, often after humble or inauspicious beginnings. The list includes entrepreneurs, industrialists, inventors, producers, potters, scientists, artists and businessmen. One of the most famous success stories is that of Shakespeare, son of a 'butcher and grazier', whom, prior to his career as a writer, Smiles suspects of being a 'woolcomber'.

The work of Mill and Smiles points to a problem which preoccupied the Victorians. This was how to reconcile the ethos of individualism with the individual's requirement to participate in the construction of a better society for all. On the other hand, there was much opposition to the idea of individualism throughout the period. As early as the 1830s–40s, for example, Robert Owen fought for a society based on a 'social system'. The Owenites emphasized 'co-operation', 'community', and their movement was one of the earlier users of the term 'socialism'. There is also evidence of the development of a more 'unified' and non-individualistic working class in the period, which was exemplified by the growth of the many Methodist and Friendly Societies which preceded the trade union movements towards the end of the century. A more rigorously 'socialist' or Marxist critique of 'individualism' and the problems of free-trade economics in Britain did not, however, really take hold until the 1880s. Owenism, meanwhile – never really a mainstream idea – disintegrated by the mid-1840s. It broke up around the time of the successful passage of the Repeal of the Corn Laws Act (1846), an act which effectively heralded the triumphant era of free-trade economics and the ethos of 'individual' economic competition. Indeed, at the level of ideas, the important point about Victorian conceptions of the individual is that at root they were dominated by middle-class conceptions; they form part of an ideology which promoted and served the needs, desires, values and attitudes, of Britain's growing bourgeoisie. It is important to bear in mind that, for many Victorians, each individual was construed as no different from any other individual as such (as in the modern conception of individuality). The Victorian idea of individualism was based on more general assumptions about 'human nature', which was governed by intrinsic laws and remained fundamentally unchangeable. It was, nonetheless, as Marxist and left-wing orientated critics have consistently argued, the aim of bourgeois capitalist ideology to construct its subjects as free-thinking 'individuals', because then they chose their subjection 'freely'.

In terms of its dissemination in Victorian literature, the ideology of the individual is complex. Part of the problem to begin with is that Victorian novels, and certainly the classic realist novels which rose to prominence in the age of capitalism, are often preoccupied with individuals themselves. Even the briefest look at the titles of famous Victorian novels reveals that many have 'individual' names as titles, even when, as in the case of Benjamin Disraeli's *Sybil* (1845) or George Eliot's *Felix Holt* (1866), the works are also concerned with broader social problems: *Oliver Twist* (1837), *Sybil* (1845), David *Copperfield* (1850), *Jane Eyre* (1847), *Adam Bede* (1859), *Felix Holt* (1866), *Daniel Deronda* (1876),The *Picture of Dorian Gray* (1891), *Tess of the D'Urbervilles* (1891), *Jude the Obscure* (1894–5) *Dracula* (1897), and so on. In Victorian novels, as these titles suggest, the overarching spirit of individualism is everywhere. But even in the case of novels with more abstract titles, such as Anthony Trollope's *Can You Forgive Her?* (1864), the story contains representations of individualism which border on solipsism: 'Every man to himself is the centre of the whole world, – the axle on which it all turns. All knowledge is but his own perception of the things around him.' Time and again in Victorian literature, an individual is placed in conflict with his or her society. Their social environment is generally static, unchangeable, and it is against this environment that the individual protagonist struggles, and, by the end of the novel, generally changes for the 'better'. The individual 'becomes' individual, in other words, in the course of Victorian novels. He or she generally starts out poor, ill-educated or single. As the novel progresses, he or she becomes more self-aware or 'educated' about their status. Eventually, he or she is typically dealt a lucky or unlucky blow by fate, from which he or she becomes rich, married or dead. Classic realist Victorian fiction, in particular, deals with the psychological development of its individuals; it consistently provides the illusion that it can prise open the 'inner subjectivity' of its characters in order to describe their actions and motivations. To that end, individuals in these novels also tend to have a 'given' or 'essential' character which governs and limits their actions in society.

In George Eliot's *Middlemarch* (1871–2), for example, the social structure does not alter much by the end of the novel. However, Eliot's very individual heroine, Dorothea Brooke, has experienced a series of profound changes. The novel deals with many interlocking lives, and is crammed with self-absorbed and self-seeking individuals, such as Lydgate, Bulstrode, Rosamund, Casaubon and Fred Vincy, many of whom remain ignorant of each other's 'inward troubles'; Casaubon, for instance, as with the men in Trollope's novel, is described as 'the centre of his own world'. Nonetheless, the story still focuses on to one specific individual, Dorothea. Initially a flawed character herself, Dorothea changes – in the course of the novel – from the deluded pride and egoism of her early needs and desires, as both a 'blind' and 'wilful' individual, to accommodate a more objective vision of her status in life and a more sympathetic recognition of others, for whom she eventually provides 'beneficent activity'. It is in this respect that Dorothea 'becomes', as such, an individual in the novel. She is initially described as having less common sense than her sister, Celia, and her first marriage to Casaubon proves to be both ill-advised and unsuitable. As the marriage falls apart, Casaubon puts a codicil in his will which prevents Dorothea from marrying her next, more suitable suitor, Will Ladislaw, a move which would, as Casaubon has it, preclude Dorothea from gaining her inheritance. As the novel progresses, it becomes increasingly clear that Dorothea – very much an 'individual' woman by this stage – is up against the repressive forces of the patriarchal society represented by Casaubon. Fortunately, for Dorothea, she realizes that all the 'virtuous' and 'womanly' self-sacrifice and sense of duty she threw away on Casaubon is nothing to the romantic 'passion' she 'discovers' for Ladislaw. Indeed, the word 'discovers' is in fact, the key to understanding the situation in a novel very much of 'self-help' and 'self-discovery'. On the other hand, in the closing sentences of the novel, when Eliot briefly acknowledges the influence of society on Dorothea's plight – as well as the origins of her somehow 'natural' or 'intrinsic' 'noble impulse' – the inner subjectivity that bourgeois ideology claims that individuals are endowed with remains unexplained: 'Certainly the determining acts of her life were not ideally beautiful. They were the mixed result of young and noble impulse struggling against the conditions of an imperfect social state . . . For there is not creature whose inward being is so strong that it is not greatly determined by what lies outside it.' Dorothea's 'inward being' only gets to languish, it seems, as a significant, but rather vague, assumption of the individualist ethos in Eliot's novel.

For modern critics, novels such as *Middlemarch* also construct the 'individual' reader as subject. Novels 'subject' the reader, that is, to their ideological representations of bourgeois 'reality'. Emerging in the era of Victorian individualism, the effect of this dominant ideology is to 'police' the individual subject/reader by giving them the sense that they are free-thinking, autonomous individuals who know more (or at least as much as the narrator) about what is happening to the individuals in the text. Readers quickly acquire the sense in *Middlemarch*, for example, that one knows 'more' than Dorothea about her circumstances, and that her marriage to Casaubon is a bad idea, and it is in this respect that the 'individual' reader colludes with the 'individual' narrator. The act of reading itself is also essentially a private, solitary or rather 'individual' experience, and it is no coincidence that reading became an increasingly desirable pursuit in the Victorian age of capitalism, which is also the age of triumphant individualism.

See also *Contexts*: Class, Economics, Industry, Other; *Texts*: Mid-Victorian novel, Realist fiction; *Criticism*: Marxism, New historicism/Cultural materialism, Psychoanalysis.

Further Reading

Gagnier, Regenia, *Subjectivities: A History of Self-Representation in Britain, 1832–1920* (Oxford: Oxford University Press, 1991).

Industry

The Industrial Revolution (*c*.1780–1840) transformed Britain. During this period, Britain became the leading industrial nation, and up until around 1870 it was known as the 'workshop of the world'. From the 1820s to the 1850s, what are now some of Britain's major midland and northern cities such as Birmingham, Bradford, Leeds, Sheffield and Manchester, were transformed from small villages or towns to smoky and noisy but thriving centres of industrialization, which were crammed with factories and mills and linked by the emergent railway system. Manchester, for example, the city at the centre of Britain's huge cotton and textile industries, had by 1830 swelled to ten times the size it was around 1760. Significant developments such as the steam engine powered industrial Britain more quickly and efficiently. Steam, especially, boosted Britain's massive productivity in heavy industries such as coal, iron and, later in the century, steel, but it also underpinned the growth in Victorian transport and telegraphic communication systems, which in turn restructured Britain into modern 'industrial' time.

Life in industrial Victorian Britain was notoriously brutal and short for its growing working-class population, and it has been estimated that over half the workforce in Victorian mills, for example, were women. However, laws such as the Parliament Act of 1833, which excluded children under the age of 10 from working in factories, gradually removed some of the abuses. Similarly, by the 1860s, various industrial corporations had developed, which gave rise to the decline of the individual or independent capitalist, mill-owner or factory boss who typified the earlier industrial epoch. Trade Unions for the working classes, legalized in 1871, also became an increasing feature of industrial life from this period onwards, and the end of the century saw the formation of the Labour Party.

The concept of industry underpins all of those ideas frequently associated with the Victorians: energy, purpose, practicality, progress, creativity, inventiveness, application, professionalism. Crucially, the idea of Victorian industry is also closely bound up with the emergence of the bourgeois capitalist era – and is largely a projection of bourgeois values and attitudes – which partly explains why the more idle, criminal or aristocratic classes often appear to be suspicious, or subversive, in Victorian society and culture. In works of late-nineteenth-century literature, such as Oscar Wilde's *The Picture of Dorian Gray* (1891), there is, for example, the oddly anachronistic and aristocratic portrayal of Dorian Gray and his 'dubiously' homosexual friends. Gray lolls about all day yawning and being bored, in a distinctly non-industrious and purposeless manner, and his unmanly ways appear to serve as a critique of the

Victorian age of industry and application. Indeed, the age of industry brought with it a series of socioeconomic and cultural divisions which defined the Victorian century and beyond, those between work and leisure; the male sphere of work and the female sphere of the home (especially for middle-class families); city and country; and the 'industrial' north and the 'rural' south. Of particular concern, however, was the blurring of the division between the 'human' and the 'mechanical', which the Industrial Revolution also helped establish.

Victorian literature dealt with the industrial epoch in a range of 'industrial novels', which were often called 'social problem' or 'Condition of England' novels. As a sub-genre, the industrial novel peaks during the 1840s and 1850s, and then goes into decline after the 1860s. Titles include Frances Trollope's *The Life and Adventures of Michael Armstrong: the Factory Boy* (1839), Charles Kingsley's *Alton Locke* (1844), Benjamin Disraeli's *Coningsby* (1844) and *Sybil, or the Two Nations* (1846), Elizabeth Gaskell's *Mary Barton* (1848), Charlotte Brontë's *Shirley* (1849), Charles Dickens's *Hard Times* (1854) and George Eliot's *Felix Holt, the Radical* (1866), although industrial strife is also reflected in the work of Victorian woman poets such as Caroline Norton and Elizabeth Barrett Browning. Most of the novels contain set-piece industrial strikes, worker–industrialist tensions, problems of hunger or riots around mills. One of the major tensions in the texts is that of the transition from manual to machine-driven labour in the period. Stephen Blackpool in Dickens's *Hard Times*, for example, is one of many 'human' beings whose identity is both created by the age of industry, as a working-class man, and reduced in Dickens's language to a synecdoche, or 'hand'. He is deminished by the 'discourse' of Victorian industry, that is, to that most functional part of his body to which machines have also reduced him. Dickens's novel is set in the fictional industrial town of Coketown, in which industrial pistons nod like the heads of 'elephants'. Although Dickens protested that his story concerns 'working people all over England', it is more or less a fairly clear rendering of industrial Manchester. Although, in this respect, Stephen Blackpool's dialect is a mishmash of working-class Lancashire, his voice also marks him as distinctly 'other' in the text.

Hard Times is a complex industrial novel. On the one hand, it provides a sympathetic portrayal of Stephen Blackpool as a 'dignified' but lowly, and prematurely aged, power-loom weaver, who is very much the central working-class figure of the novel and who constantly describes his own plight in terms of confusion: 'awlus a muddle'. On the other hand, Dickens's sympathies towards the working-class miseries created by industry only extend so far. *Hard Times* provides a fairly unambiguous critique of early trades union movements, known then as Combinations. In the novel, these are represented by the uncompromising figure of Slackbridge the radical, and by the threat of working-class 'mob' violence that bedevilled the Victorians throughout the period. Oddly enough, however, Dickens's 'industrial' novel rarely ventures inside the industrial and factory spaces themselves, or rather into what Dickens calls Coketown's 'Fairy palaces'. Instead, it tends to focus on the numerous family and 'human' dramas that Dickens unfolds. Stephen Blackpool's story is, in fact, largely incidental to those of the Gradgrinds, Bounderbys and M'Choakumchilds which dominate the narrative, even though it is the industrialist Bounderby who 'owns' and controls Blackpool's life in the mill. Blackpool, as suggested above, is an unremarkable 'hand' in Dickens's novel, and this again is part of the point. He is a nonentity amongst thousands of industrial workers whom Dickens describes as 'people equally like one another'. Nonetheless, the weaver's succession of hard and harder times in the novel are at any rate quite remarkable in themselves: Blackpool loses his job after being wrongly accused of robbing a bank; he is besieged by his unlovely drunken wife; he fails to consummate his love affair with Rachael; he is accused by Slackbridge of being a union-breaking 'traitor' as bad as 'Judas Iscariot' or the hated 'Lord Castlereagh'; and he is 'sent to Coventry' by the Coketown community. Blackpool then disappears from town in disgrace, only to fall down a mine shaft into a 'black ragged chasm' which was left, symbolically, on the landscape by British industry, and is suitably known as the 'Old Hell Shaft'. There, eventually, he is found and rescued. However, despite having Blackpool's name cleared in Coketown, Dickens still contrives to kill him off at the end and ultimately, at the root of all of Blackpool's hard times, Dickens suggests, is the Victorian age of industry. The violence of this age, and all its implications, is unambiguously described by Dickens in one of the few mill scenes he does include, in which Blackpool works in a symbolically mixed metaphor of industry and ruralism – a 'forest of looms' – and on a 'crashing, smashing, tearing piece of mechanism'.

See also *Contexts*: Consumerism, Economics, Individualism, Science, Transport; *Texts*: Crime fiction, Historical novel, Mid-Victorian novel; *Criticism*: Marxism, Psychoanalysis.

Further Reading

Gallagher, Catherine, *The Industrial Reformation of English Fiction: Social Discourse and Narrative Form, 1832–67* (Chicago, IL: Chicago University Press, 1985)

Law

Victorian society inherited an array of common, civil and ecclesiastical courts of law, and the legal system was complex. Part of the complexity, and the confusion it gave rise to, lay in the fact that Britain had never had a written constitution on which to base its laws and judicial processes. Just before Victoria's accession, legal theorists, practitioners and intellectuals, such as Jeremy Bentham, attempted to establish a 'science' of British law, what Bentham called 'codification', along the lines of the French Napoleonic Code. The aim of codification was to simplify and rationalize the law, so it could be more easily read and understood by the public. Like-minded Victorians such as Thomas Babington Macaulay and the jurist James Fitzjames Stephen, against considerable resistance, took up Bentham's cause, and as a result Stephen published books with titles such as *A General View of the Criminal Law of* England (1863) and *Liberty, Equality, Fraternity* (1873). Although progress in the clarification of British law moved slowly in the period, the legal system itself managed to pass a number of significant laws which did instigate major changes to the lives of Victorians. The laws, for example, introduced after the passage of Robert Peel's Metropolitan Police Act of 1829 led to the successful growth of the nationwide police force. Less successful was the much maligned Poor Law (Amendment) Act of 1834, which was designed to provide relief for poverty, but which led to the squalid excesses of the parish 'workhouse' system famously criticized in Charles Dickens's *Oliver Twist* (1837).

Other important, if controversial, laws included the hated Contagious Diseases Acts of the 1860s, which focused on inspecting the bodies of prostitutes; laws which extended welfare and health provisions (1848, 1875); laws which increased the availability of education (1870, 1876); and laws which developed the powers of local government (1888, 1894). The three great Reform Acts of 1832, 1867 and 1884 eventually resulted in a more democratic and representative parliament, and the Repeal of the Corn Laws act in 1846 paved the way for the triumph of free trade. In 1861, capital punishment was finally limited to crimes of 'murder and treason', and in 1871 trade unions were legalized. At the level of the judicial system itself, the influential Judicature Acts of 1873–5 simplified the three major law courts of early Victorian Britain – the Queen's Bench, the Exchequer and the Common Pleas – into a unified High Court.

The Victorian legal profession itself remained rigidly divided for much of the period. Judges and barristers were at the top of the scale, often with public school and Oxford or Cambridge educations behind them, and they were widely regarded as respectable 'gentlemen'. Lower down were the solicitors, attorneys-at-law, and then the clerks, those who could not then plead in court, but whose careers, particularly those of the solicitors, rose in status as the century wore on. The stratified nature of the legal profession typifies Victorian obsessions with class and status, but the hierarchy it led to, significantly, all but excluded women. Consequently, as in other careers which middle-class men were to dominate, the Victorian legal system encoded its own system of patriarchal power, one which extended itself across all areas of society. By the same token, at its most fundamental level, Victorian law was concerned with the maintenance of discipline and order in society, and as the nineteenth-century legal and disciplinary system grew apace, it eventually encroached upon every aspect of British life. As a result, the law became the most conspicuous feature of the ever-growing culture of surveillance which was to spread itself throughout British society.

At the centre of Victorian law lay, however, a conflict of ideas. This took the form of a tension, throughout the period, between the authority of the law, on the one hand, and the ideology of individualism at the heart of Victorian culture, on the other, which the law both enshrined and sought to restrain. Unsurprisingly, for a nation at the forefront of world capitalism, the laws which governed the rights to an individual's 'property' were central to this ideology. And yet, ironically, it was also precisely the Victorian preoccupation with the individual's pursuit of 'property', and the entire commodification of British society that it led to, which created the pursuit of crimes against property in the first place. Such developments partly explain why punishments for theft such as hanging or transportation, up until 1861 at least, were so harsh. Moreover, the Victorians sought, often unavailingly, to reconcile the differences between individual rights and those of the wider society in general, and the tension can be witnessed at the level of the judicial process. What legal reformers and advocates of a more publicly owned 'codification' of the law tried to eliminate was what they saw as the far too 'individual' or 'discretionary' elements of Britain's judicial system, those enjoyed, for example, in the Court of Chancery. In Chancery, the judicial process was seen as far too subjective and it was, therefore, perceived as potentially unjust. As a sub-division of the earlier Victorian, three-part judicial system, Chancery was an 'equity' court which adjudicated over cases of trust funds and inheritance. Cases were sent to Chancery because decisions were supposed to be reached more quickly at the summary – and often seemingly arbitrary – 'discretion' of the Lord Chancellor. Such, however, were the arcane and labyrinthine processes of the British legal system under Chancery that some cases, prior to the Judicature Acts of the 1870s, went on for decades.

Much of Victorian literature looks quite favourably on British law and its institutions. The law in Mary Braddon's sensational murder novel, *Lady Audley's Secret* (1862), for example, or George Eliot's *Daniel Deronda* (1876), in which Rex Gascoigne describes his prospective career in 'law-rubbish' as no 'worse than any other sort', is seen often as an agent of stability and order in a far from stable world. Conversely, writers such as Charles Dickens did not appear to like lawyers or the legal process very much, even though he regarded policemen with bemused affection, and despite the fact that his stories are often celebrations of the restoration of legal order and justice by the end. Many of his novels contain satires on Victorian law, and his legal figures are frequently described as either incompetent, idle or slightly sinister. *Oliver Twist* (1837), for example, features a Gothic magistrate, Mr Fang, and a satire on the forerunners of the Metropolitan Police, the Bow Street Runners, in the shape of the loveable but largely ineffective 'Duff and Blathers'. In *Great Expectations* (1861), the mysterious role of solicitor/lawyer is played by the edgy-sounding Jaggers, and in *Bleak House* (1853) there are portrayals of the dark and vampish legal man, Mr Vholes, and the looming presence of the solicitor Mr Tulkinghorn. *Bleak House* also contains Dickens's most vigorous assault on Victorian law. This novel has become, in fact, the period's most famous critique of the endlessly complex rituals, protocols, procedures and bureaucracies which bedevilled the legal system and in which human beings, and by extension Victorian society in general, became entangled. Dickens reserves his particular spleen for Chancery law, which he describes as run by an incompetent 'wiglomeration'. His fictional case, 'Jarndyce and Jarndyce', is thought to have been based, in reality, on the notorious Jennings property case, which lasted for some 70 years in the nineteenth century. As 'Jarndyce and Jarndyce', as Dickens puts it, 'drones on' in Chancery, becoming a 'joke', even the members of the High Court of Chancery itself appear to have long since become trapped inside the 'walls of words' built up by the case. The chaos of language and paper left in the wake of 'Jarndyce and Jarndyce' then becomes indicative of the wider dilemma that *Bleak House* articulates. Like the system of law it savages, Dickens's novel is its own labyrinth of language, writing, ink and verbosity; it is, like the law, its 'own mountain of costly nonsense', full of delay, digression, obfuscation and, above all, words. The 'Jarndyce and Jarndyce' case is in fact so complex – 'no man alive knows what it means' – that any explanation here is pointless, except to say that this is precisely the problem, and the 'point' that Dickens's novel parodies.

Bleak House is, amongst other things, a legal mystery and a detective story. It is a novel full of secrets and passionate human conflict, which is simultaneously a satire on meaning, mystery, interpretation, fog and the threat of the unexplainable, with a case of 'spontaneous combustion' as one of its centrepieces. It is also a story of order and disorder, told through a series of confused and complex interlocked lives, which comprises one first-person narrative (Esther Summerson's) and a third-person narrative, which is anonymous. Stretching, as it does, to almost 1000 pages, the novel is as excessive in words as the language of law which it satirizes. Dickens's Britain, as he envisages it, and the laws upon which it is based, is a dirty, confused and hypocritical place, where in 'the midst of the mud and at the heart of the fog, sits the Lord High Chancellor in his High Court of Chancery'. There, as Dickens concludes, the Chancellor presides over a legal mess of 'trickery, evasion, procrastination, spoliation, botheration', that 'no man's nature has been made the better by'.

See also   *Contexts*: Crime and punishment; *Texts*: Crime fiction, Penny dreadfuls, Sensation fiction; *Criticism*: Deconstruction, Feminism, Poststructuralism.

Further Reading

Dolin, K., *Fiction and the Law: Legal Discourse in Victorian and Modernist Literature* (Cambridge: Cambridge University Press, 1998).

Madness

The Victorians were preoccupied with madness. As early as the years between 1829 and 1840, the Metropolitan Commission on Lunacy began to compile a series of medical reports and files on a range of cases. Doctors and physicians obsessed over causes and diagnoses, and successive governments produced a string of 'Lunacy Acts' in an attempt to deal with what was perceived to be a growing crisis. The years 1840, 1842, 1845, 1860, 1883, 1884 and 1890 all saw the passage of legislation which was aimed at everything from criminal lunacy to the better organization and monitoring of asylums. One particular case came to the attention of the Victorian public in 1843, when Daniel Macnaghten tried to assassinate Prime Minister Robert Peel, only to kill Peel's private secretary instead. The case set a precedent because Macnaghten was eventually acquitted for being insane, on the grounds of what physicians described as his 'persecution' complex. In his conclusions at the trial, Chief Justice Tindal summed up the new 'Macnaghten rules' as follows: 'he [Macnaghten] did not know he was doing what was wrong'.

In the 1850s, amid fears that Queen Victoria herself had lapsed into a hereditary mental condition known as 'porphyria', Britain underwent a 'lunacy panic'. Public anxieties and indignation became aroused when a number of individuals had been misdiagnosed as insane and wrongly committed to asylums. Although public pressure led to a committee of enquiry into these injustices, the problem for Victorians was always, in this respect, where and when to diagnose madness. Madness in the period was ascribed to anything from the inherited causes of bad blood or the wandering wombs of 'hysterical' women, to alcoholism, novel reading, excessive abstinence, sexual desire and masturbation. Treatments for such 'madnesses' included cold baths for self-abusers and genital ice treatments for overly sensuous women, while cliterodec-tomies were still seen as a suitable form of preventative for menstrual women and their 'psychoses' as late as 1880. As 'madhouses' were renamed 'asylums' and 'lunatics' became 'patients', however, the Victorians slowly turned to more didactic or restorative measures in the housing and 'nursing' of the mad. Such developments came about despite the fact that disciplinary methods such as strait-jacketing, opium sedatives, water therapies, restraint chairs and screw-locks were still in widespread use in asylums until at least mid-century. Later, indeed, with the new technology available, neurologists would administer to the mad an increasing amount of electric shocks as 'medicine'.

In his *Treatise on Insanity* (1835), and in distinctly Victorian tones, James Cowles Pritchard argued that madness represented a corrupt 'morality' rather than any damage to 'intellectual faculties'. Later in the century James Fitzjames Stephen, in *General View* (1863), took this idea even further, in his claim that British law should be based on the assessment of an individual's capacity for 'moral sanity' and 'moral distinctions'. Gradually, along these lines, Victorian doctors and physi-cians arrived at four basic categories of madness: 'moral insanity', 'melancholia', 'partial insanity' and 'mania'. As these classifications suggest, the concept of madness had became part of the Victorian discourse of medicine, a discourse which was itself a part, broadly speaking, of the West's enlightened 'knowledge' about the 'rational' and 'civilized world' it was making. By the 1890s, with the rise of psycho-analysis and Sigmund Freud's revolutionary ideas about the trauma and madness of repressed 'discontents' throughout Western 'civilization', the boundaries between madness and sanity, in every individual, became infinitely more uncertain.

Western civilization, of which Victorian Britain regarded itself at the forefront, predicates itself on the notion of rationalism – on, that is, the absence of madness. For influential writers and historians on this topic, such as Michel Foucault in *Madness and Civilization: A History of Insanity in the Age of Reason* (1967), however, the 'enlightened' West's construction of itself as a 'rational' and above all 'sane' civilization could only develop and sustain itself against that which it defines as madness in the first place. For Foucault, in other words, there is no rationality without irrationality, no sanity without madness, or vice versa, and the categories are mutually dependent in order to be in any way meaningful. The Western world developed, as Foucault puts it, only when its inhabitants became able to 'recognize each other through the merciless language of non-madness', and consequently the crucial moment in the history of madness is that break in knowledge which 'establishes the distance between reason and non-reason'. As with his ideas about criminals in prisons, Foucault also discussed the relationship in society that he saw between the solitary confinement of the mad in asylums and the idea of 'individuation' this confinement suggests. Such ideas led him to draw broader comparisons between the ideology of individualism established by Western capitalist societies, and that ideology which he saw as underpinned by a culture of surveillance in asylums, prisons, schools and factories, buildings which he thought all resembled each other. From these comparisons, he concluded that it is civilization itself that created an environment which is ultimately 'favourable to the development of madness'. In terms of the Victorians, the idea of madness also implied, to use Foucault's terms again, a form of 'non-being' for the individual in question. In the golden age of Victorian capitalism, madness came to represent a kind of death of the self in the midst of life.

There are many representations of madness in Victorian literature. From Alfred Lord Tennyson's account of love, loss and lunacy in *Maud: A Monodrama* (1855), where 'My life has crept so long on a broken wing / Thro' cells of madness, haunts of horror and fear', to the haunted questions of much of Emily Dickinson's verse, such as 'The first Day's Night had come'(1862), 'Could it be Madness-this?', madness is never far away from the ostensible order and rationalism of Victorian consciousness. In Robert Browning's 'Porphyria's Lover' (1835), in which insanity is feminized, Porphyria comes to the narrator like the madness of desire – 'she shut the cold out and the storm' – after which the narrator strangles her with her hair and kisses her corpse. Catherine Earnshaw's mental disintegration in Emily Brontë's *Wuthering Heights* (1847) has also been well documented – 'O let me not be mad' – as has Miss Havisham's maddened 'living death' in Charles Dickens's *Great Expectations* (1861), while in Wilkie Collins's 'sensation' novel *The Woman in White* (1860), Anne Catherick is wrongfully imprisoned in an asylum by Sir Percival Glide. Elsewhere, the very notions of Victorian propriety, common sense and sanity are consciously inverted in the topsy-turvy world of works such as Lewis Carroll's Alice tales (1865, 1871), where the pleasures of madness are usual, even 'sane', and where, as the March Hare/the Hatter puts it, 'we're all mad here'. Towards the end of the century, novels such as Robert Louis Stevenson's *The Strange Case of Dr Jekyll and Mr Hyde* (1886) also point towards the joy of madness. Dr Jekyll, like Alice, regularly escapes from Victorian taboos and repressions by taking 'the powders' and 'the blood-red liquor' in the phial. This is a tincture that, as Stevenson writes, 'shook the very fortress of identity', and from which the 'sane' Dr Jekyll is transformed into his unconscious other self – the 'mad' Mr Hyde – so that the man's desires, largely for drink, women and murder, are subsequently unleashed.

Time and again, however, it is women who are presented as more susceptible to madness in Victorian literature. The case of Bertha Mason in Charlotte Brontë's *Jane Eyre* (1847), although one of the more famous examples, is illuminating in this respect. Unbeknown to Jane Eyre, who becomes betrothed to Mr Rochester in the course of the novel, Mr Rochester is already married to Bertha Mason. Rochester brought Bertha back to England from his mysterious plantation in Spanish Town, Jamaica – in the novel's pre-narrative, as Brontë informs us – some 'fifteen years ago'. At Thornfield Hall, Bertha was then confined to the solitary space of the attic because, according to Rochester, 'she is mad; and she came of a mad family'. As the 'madwoman in the attic', Bertha is imprisoned in a space in which the Victorian 'home' is effectively transformed into an 'asylum' for women. There, watched over by Grace Poole, Bertha grovels about like some 'strange wild animal', and speaks only in mysterious grunts and gibbers.

Bertha Mason's madness in Brontë's novel has been interpreted as a sublimation of Jane Eyre's own repressed desires and sexuality, as her 'darkest double' or 'secret self' which rages against patriarchy. Before setting fire to Thornfield and eventually sacrificing herself, Bertha makes a foray down into Jane Eyre's bedchamber on the night before the wedding, whereupon she proceeds in an impassioned or rather 'maddened' manner to tear up the bridal veil. As a horrified Jane Eyre recounts to Mr Rochester the next day, Bertha appeared to her like the 'foul German spectre, the Vampyre' with a rolling 'savage' face and 'black' lineaments. Indeed, her depiction of Bertha in this scene demonstrates the invidious way in which race became Gothicized in the Victorian period, the way in which the 'irrational' colonial other – as represented by the 'Creole' Bertha – 'haunted' the British imagination. It draws a comparison, in this respect, between madness, the violation of black bodies, and the history of British involvement in Jamaican slavery that Rochester's relationship with Bertha suggests. As a result, in order for the story of the 'rational' Jane Eyre to complete itself, and so that her heroine can eventually marry Rochester after the revelation of Bertha's existence, Brontë must remove certain obstacles. Before order can be restored, and a suitably 'sane' conclusion reached, she must first kill off the threat posed by the other woman and the madness of foreign worlds she represents.

See also *Contexts*: Crime and punishment, Gaze; *Texts*; Poetry, Sensation fiction; *Criticism*: Postmodernism, Poststructuralism, Psychoanalysis.

Further Reading

Gilbert, Sandra M., and Gubar, Susan, *The Madwoman in the Attic: The Woman Writer and the Nineteenth-Century Literary Imagination* (New Haven, CT: Yale University Press, 1979).
Gilman, Sander L., *Difference and Pathology: Stereotypes of Sexuality, Race, and Madness* (Ithaca, NY: Cornell University Press, 1985).

Music

The Victorians are not renowned for their great composers or illustrious musical achievements. Ralph Waldo Emerson famously described nineteenth-century Britain as a land with 'no music'. Nonetheless, music did thrive throughout the period. A number of music colleges were established, including the Kensington Royal College of Organists (1864) and the Royal College of Music (1883). Similarly, Manchester's Hallé Orchestra was founded in 1858; Alfred Novello first published *The Musical Times* in 1844, and the *Gramophone Company* (HMV) for recorded music was created in 1898. Performances and concerts frequently attracted huge and appreciative crowds, and the Promenade Concerts given by Henry Wood, who had a mandate to promote Englishness in music, were especially popular in the latter stages of the century. Oratorios also retained their appeal, chamber music continued to be a feature of the homes of the rich or noble, choral and singing societies grew, as did amateur and professional musicianship, and the English nation's love of hymn-singing was undiminished. The Victorian period also produced women composers such as Agnes Zimmerman and Claribel, and even Queen Victoria applied herself to the piano. Meanwhile, more popular forms of British music began to flourish throughout the period. The comic or 'light' operas of William Gilbert and Arthur Sullivan, which inspired a series of musical comedies, were wildly successful, while brass bands, amateur choruses, folk songs and neighbourhood sing-songs were widespread. From the 1840s onwards, the working classes were entertained by the music of 'low' cabaret provided by tavern and music hall performances in towns throughout the country, as well as in London haunts such as Vauxhall Pleasure Gardens and Ranelagh.

Music hall entertainments combined ribald songs, burlesques, comic-sketches and small bits of theatre, many of which, originally at least, reflected working-class lives and travails. Yet because of its origins in the nation's often rambunctious inns, music hall never really lost its lowbrow associations with bawdy pleasures, indecent amounts to drink, unruly elements and prostitution. The class tensions between Britain's upper- and lower-class musical entertainments were in fact illustrated by the Peel government's passage of the Theatres Act in 1843, which prohibited music hall venues from staging 'serious' or legitimate theatre. As the century progressed, and particularly during the *fin de siècle* period, music hall then became associated with patriotism and British imperial belligerence, especially after G. H. Macdermot and G. W. Hunt's 'jingoistic' song, 'We don't want to fight, but by Jingo if we do . . . ', which appears to have been first sung in the London Pavilion (*c*.1878). The late Victorian period also produced a classical composer, Edward Elgar, whose *Enigma Variations* (1898–9) are thought to have finally imbued British music with a sense of tradition, even though Elgar is often described as more of a twentieth-century composer than a Victorian. Indeed, while the more tranquil moments of Elgar's music became associated with a certain shared memory or nostalgia for a pastoral England which was fast disappearing in the nineteenth century, they also became linked with stereotypical ideas about English modera-tion, temperance, gentleness and reserve. This was despite often bombastic performances of Elgar's own imperialistic composition, the deliberately immodest 'Pomp and Circumstance', and even though contemporaries such as Ralph Vaughan Williams accused Elgar's work of sounding German.

In the nineteenth century, the concept of music is bound up with all kinds of Victorian attitudes and anxieties. John Ruskin, for example, claimed that music was 'the first, the simplest, the most effective of all instruments of moral instruction', and in what was an already noisy London full of foreigners, Charles Dickens complained regularly about the din made by the city's large population of Italian organ-grinders. Similarly, in a discussion of one of Handel's oratorios on a visit to England in 1855, the German composer Wagner commented that the 'true spirit of English musical culture' – as with England's love of hymns – was 'bound up with the spirit of English Protestantism'. Handel wrote

about God's 'Chosen People' in the Bible, the Israelites, and it is no coincidence that many imperial Victorians regarded themselves in the same,
divinely elected, Protestant light. In terms of Protestantism itself, the
emphasis throughout the period in British music was very much on the
'self-control' of tonality and harmony, but also on the Protestant hymn
tradition, with its epigrammatic harmonies and sense of rhetorical
movement towards closure with 'feeling'. And yet, as if railing against
the idea of a distinctively 'English' music, the Victorian aesthete and
decadent Walter Pater wanted to disassociate the art from any such
external referent as 'nation', 'Protestantism', or worse, 'morality'. Pater
did concede that 'All art constantly aspires to the condition of music',
but this was part of his broader ideas about the purity of form and 'art
for art's sake'. Music, for Pater, was its own 'idea', a notion which was
similar to Wagner's concept of 'absolute music' – music, in other words,
which had no referent to the 'real' world outside of its own form. But
'absolute music' was itself part of Wagner's complex theory about the
way in which music evokes 'the individual will', which is at the same
time an expression of the 'universal will', and is therefore a peculiarly
British, Protestant and Victorian idea derived from the philosophy of utilitarianism.

No middle- or upper-class nineteenth-century home was complete
without a piano. In the domestic space the piano became an instrument
which was played more and more by women, and in Jane Austen's
novels and throughout Victorian literature there are many tricky incidents surrounding a woman at the piano. In Austen's *Pride and Prejudice*
(1813), for example, the piano becomes the site for vaguely romantic
encounters and rituals of courtship for the Bennett sisters, and in
Charles Dickens's *David Copperfield* (1850) Agnes Wickfield's accom-
plished tinkling seems to signify her suitability for engagement to the
novel's hero. Alternatively, in novels such as William Thackeray's *Vanity
Fair* (1847–8), the feisty figure of Becky Sharp declares that she wants to
take her skills on the piano out of the home and into the very public and
male spheres of capitalism and profit: 'Give me money, and I will teach
them [Becky's prospective students]', while an even more problematic
episode occurs around a piano in one of Charlotte Brontë's early pieces.
In Brontë's novelette, *Caroline Vernon* (1839), the pretty and much-
admired Caroline plonks out a tune which, although seemingly harmless
enough at first, proves to be full of the agony and violence of British
history. Her version of 'Jump Jim Crow', a white 'blackface' song, draws
a typically Brontëan analogy between the Victorian woman's enslavement to patriarchy – in this case Caroline Vernon's – and that of the
distant cries from slavery across the Atlantic. To the complaints of her

mother, who dislikes the piano, but seems to be aggravated by this tune in particular, Caroline answers with the musical 'voice' of 'Jim Crow' :

> A distant sound of music in a room below was heard – a piano very well touched . . . – 'Caroline! Caroline!' no answer except a brilliant bravura run down the keys of the Piano – 'Caroline!' was reiterated – 'give up playing this instant! . . . – a remarkably merry jig responded to her ladyship's objurgations . . . . 'I [Caroline] have only to play Jim Crow and then' & Jim Crow was played with due spirit & sprightliness. An open piano – & a sheet of music with a grinning capering nigger lithographed on the title-page . . . 'And ma' did fly – she never likes Jim Crow – '.

Here the tormented voice of the oppressed woman, Brontë's own, is projected through a musical accompaniment. But such a projection is only effected thanks to the work of a long-forgotten man called Thomas D. Rice. In 1828, Rice witnessed the song-and-dance routine of a Louisville slave owned by one 'Mr Crow', which he subsequently appropriated and set to a British tune. The violence of this appropriation, which corresponds with that of the history of slavery, is then captured, musically, by Brontë's discordant use of the term 'nigger', the flattest and most sombre note in the melody of her prose.

See also   *Contexts*: Nation, Other, Race; *Criticism*: Feminism.

Further Reading

da Sousa Correa, Delia, *George Eliot, Music and Victorian Culture* (Basingstoke and New York: Palgrave Macmillan, 2003).

Nation

The concept of nation is central to the way that the Victorians saw themselves and their place in the world. By the nineteenth century, Britain already had a long history of regarding itself as isolated and separate from other nations, and its construction of an island 'mentality' was underpinned by the nation's geographical position as a water-locked territory detached from mainland Europe. At the same time, however, the different ideas of nation and national identity within the British islands themselves had been fraught with political, socioeconomic and cultural conflicts, and these simmered throughout the Victorian period. The problems stemmed largely from Britain's centralized government in London and the history of English hegemony over the islands. Although

Wales, for example, had been formally assimilated by England as early 1536, Scotland only became part of the Act of Union in 1707. Ireland, a country subject to English colonialism for hundreds of years, was also integrated into the new 'United Kingdom' with the Act of 1801. The history of hostility between England and Ireland, which conservative statesman Benjamin Disraeli in 1844 described as the 'Irish Question', continued unresolved in British politics throughout the Victorian period, despite the efforts of the Gladstone administrations during the 'Home Rule' crisis in the 1880–90s. Irish nationalists and Fenians (the Irish Republican Brotherhood was established in 1858) also had to endure the long and steady imposition of Britain's, or rather England's, 'official' religion, Protestantism, although the majority of the Irish population were Catholics.

Since the Reformation, Britain's, and in particular England's, sense of itself as a nation had become inseparable from its sense of itself as a bastion of Protestantism. This sense of national identity, as historian Linda Colley has shown, was part of Britain's need to define itself against its great historical enemy, the Catholic French, an enmity which was still fresh in early and mid-Victorian minds after the Napoleonic Wars in 1815. Although, for example, in *England and the English* (1833), the writer Edward Bulwer Lytton reasoned with Talleyrand that in post-Napoleonic Europe, 'We [English] no longer hate the French', many Victorians remained cautious, not to say actively hostile. The Victorians may have lived in an age when any real threat of a French invasion no longer seemed possible, but for many reactionary Britons the French, especially, after events such as the revolution in 1789, the 'Reign of Terror' and the rise of Napoleon, were still seen as republican trouble-makers, as bloodthirsty, if ultimately weak (because beaten) warmongers, as well as sexual deviants and writers of salacious novels. Indeed, many commentators view the long nineteenth century (c.1815–1914) in Britain and the construction of nation as bookended by fears of invasion by foreigners – with the French at one end, and Germans at the other (c.1880s onwards). This is not to say that there was anything necessarily systematic about the Victorian construction of nation. As contemporary historian John Seeley put it, just as Britain acquired its empire through a state of 'absent-mindedness', so British nation building in the nineteenth century was often a shambolic process, albeit one with violent implications. Walter Bagehot, for example, in *The English Constitution* (1867), even claimed 'Englishness' was achieved 'almost without consciousness'.

The Great Exhibition of 1851 was the Victorian nation's showpiece of British industrial and imperial might. So grand, it seems, was Joseph

Paxton's glass and steel building that the *Morning Chronicle* was moved to write that, 'it is probable that no other people in the world could have achieved such a marvel of constructive skill'. The exhibits were arranged nation by nation, and Britain dominated the floor-space. Each display proclaimed the nation's industrial might, and the sense of strength, vigour and purpose which turned Victorian Britain into the most successful and powerful capitalist nation the world had ever seen. It is, moreover, such national bravado as that attached to the Great Exhibition that made many Protestant and imperial Britons feel justified in their assumed role as world leaders, and that led the then Archbishop of Canterbury to describe the English as God's 'Chosen People'. But if the Victorians' at once pious and secular construction of nation came to be largely middle-class in conception and practice, it is precisely at the interface between socioeconomic, cultural and religious ideas that this construction needs to be understood. The modern, albeit stereotypical idea of Englishness, is one based on classically Victorian ideas about reserve, moderation, temperance and individualism. But these ideas are themselves built on a history of Protestantism, which is also the history of capitalism. Crucially, many of Britain's early capitalists and entrepreneurs were strict Protestants, Protestantism being characterized, unlike Catholicism, by a more 'individualistic' relationship with God (the 'inner light') and the Bible. This individualism, combined with an ascetic (self-denying) lifestyle, enabled the early capitalists in Britain to create the nation's wealth and power by dint of what were, in this respect, essentially Protestant ethics: early capitalists saved their capital, moderated expenditure, and reinvested in better and more profitable business and economic interests, thereby creating greater wealth and so on. What became enshrined in English law as the English 'individual's rights to 'freedom' and 'property', by the mid-Victorian period, were then consolidated by the doctrine and practice of free trade, which became the economic and political rationale for Protestant 'individualism' in Britain.

All Victorian literature, in one way or another, is concerned with nation or national identity. But in a climate of increasingly assertive European nationalism and empire building, it is late nineteenth-century literature and culture which is most clearly imbued with a sense of patriotism and jingoism, especially that associated, for example, with Rudyard Kipling's 'Indian' novels or the musical compositions of Edward Elgar. Many popular novels of the period were also full of invasion and contamination motifs, such as H. Rider Haggard's *She* (1887), H. G. Wells's *The War of the Worlds* (1898) – in which Martians besiege Woking – and, most famously, Bram Stoker's *Dracula* (1897). The English novel had, since its inception, been the quintessential medium for reflecting on and constructing the English nation. By the Victorian period, consciously or otherwise, novelists had consequently inherited a long tradition of establishing ideas of Englishness against those of the foreign 'other', and particularly those represented by the French. The quintessentially 'English' spirit of Charles Dickens's novels, for example, is generally anti-French in mood and tenor, and Dickens's prejudices reached their apogee in *A Tale of Two Cities* (1859), a novel in which a revolutionary France full of blood and mad hags is compared unfavourably with a moderate England throughout. But the same goes for less widely read novels such as Charlotte Brontë's *The Professor* (1857), in which a stereotypically abstemious and sexless man, William Crimsworth ('I repressed all'), forges his sense of Englishness by way of a remorseless Francophobia and anti-Catholicism. Crimsworth moves to Belgium as teacher. There he ogles what he describes as his wantonly sensuous foreign pupils, avoids the amours of Mme Pelet, shelters from the 'showers' of 'Brabant saliva' created by a Flemish language he loathes, and criticizes the un-English moral 'laxity' and 'mere licentiousness' of Frenchmen such as M. Pelet. Brontë's novel combines these views with a complex critique of patriarchal Englishness – the ambiguities of which project a desire to be un-English, at times – which is underpinned throughout by the Protestant ethic and the spirit of capitalism which ultimately made the Victorian nation what it was, but which required the 'other' of Frenchness to define it.

See also *Contexts*: Domesticity, Empire and imperialism, Gothic, Orientalism, Other, Race, Religion, Slavery, War; *Texts*: Historical novel, Realist fiction; *Criticism*: Postcolonialism.

Further Reading

Herbert, Christopher, *Culture and Anomie: Ethnographic Imagination in the Nineteenth Century* (Chicago: Chicago University Press, 1991).

Orientalism

From the Renaissance period onwards, the Orientalists were largely British and French academics whose work it was to study the East. By the Victorian period, the 'discipline' of Orientalism included a range of European scholars, archivists, writers, travellers, explorers, missionaries, anthropologists and colonialists, all of whom contributed, in one way or another, to the establishment of a 'knowledge' of the Eastern cultures and languages which they came into contact with. Their work became particularly popular in the eighteenth and nineteenth centuries. It was typified, most notably, by monumental studies such as the

Description de L'Égypt, which was carried out by academics in Napoleon's entourage during his ill-fated expedition to Egypt in 1793, and by the French school of nineteenth-century Orientalist painters, which included Eugène Delacroix's portrait of a harem in *Women of Algiers in their Apartment* (1833).

Nowadays, the concept of 'Orientalism' has a far broader definition. It now defines the ways in which a 'knowledge' of the East is constructed both *by* and *for* the West. According to major theorists working in the field, especially Edward W. Said, Orientalism rests on the idea that throughout history the West has fundamentally misrepresented the East in order to define itself as the superior civilization. For Said, by its process of accumulating 'knowledge', the West came to dominate the East through its construction, for example, of alien Muslim cultures and 'characteristics' as other, and by making generalizations about Turkish, Indian or Chinese ways of life, such as the 'Asian sensibility' or the 'Hindoo's temperament'. In his groundbreaking book, *Orientalism* (1978), Said argued that the tensions and oppositions enshrined in language and culture between East and West, and particularly those which are represented through European cultural mediums such as English literature, are a fundamental part of the 'discourse' of Orientalism. Orientalism had, according to Said, immeasurable consequences for the modern world. It generated the mutual mistrust, conflict and violence that came to define relationships between East and West in the nineteenth century and beyond.

English literature has always been bound up in defining the concept of nationhood, in what it means to be British, or rather, English. But by that same process it has also been implicated in the project of Orientalism. Unsurprisingly, then, studies of Orientalism in Victorian literature, and those of the broader encounter between culture and imperialism they form part of, deal with the many difficult and complex portrayals of the Orient, its peoples, places and cultures, which characterize the texts. And indeed, given that India and China, especially, were British imperial and colonial spheres of interest throughout the nineteenth century, such portrayals have far-reaching implications. In the Victorian novel, most conspicuously, the East is frequently described as a distinctly different, irrational and 'other' space in relation to England. The literary Orient is an alluring place of mystery, enchantment, excitement, adventure and colour, but also one of sex, sensuality, and danger for Europeans. As Said puts it, 'the Orient was almost a European invention, and had been since antiquity a place of romance, exotic beings, haunting memories and landscapes, remarkable experiences', The West, he argued, identified itself as the complete antithesis of these representations. The resulting conflict between a familiar, rational Europe, and a strange, irrational Orient, is crucial to the development of Western notions about its identity and its inventions of the East, and such a conflict led Said to argue that Orientalism is 'a collective notion identifying Europeans ("us") against "non-Europeans" ("them")'.

Orientalism surfaces throughout Victorian literature, and there are a number of notorious representations. In one episode from Charlotte Brontë's *Villette* (1853), for example, Lucy Snowe comes across a sultry portrait of Cleopatra in a Brussels gallery, which the narrator describes as follows:

> larger ... than life ... a commodity of bulk ... extremely well-fed [with a] wealth of muscle [and] affluence of flesh. She lay half-reclined on a couch ... She had no business to lounge away the noon on a sofa. She ought likewise to have worn decent garments; a gown covering her properly, which was not the case ... Then, for the wretched untidiness surrounding her, there could be no excuse ....

Brontë's heroine combines all of the clichés associated with repressed Victorian women in the novel. Lucy Snowe's life is one of moral and sexual restraint, modesty, temperance, a 'snow'-like purity verging on prissiness, and dowdy grey dresses. She is, in fact, in many ways a caricature of a distinctly Protestant or English sense of order and propriety. However, her role in the text also functions by way of contrast to Brontë's many snide comments about Catholics, the French and the Belgians. Much like Cleopatra in the picture, the French and Belgians are generally described as wayward or sensuous throughout the novel and, intriguingly, Brontë mixes their image into her portrayals of the Orient, so that 'Frenchness' and 'the East' often appear interchangeable. As with the French and Belgian women, the representation of Cleopatra features as the complete antithesis to Lucy Snowe and the Englishness she represents. Put another way, Cleopatra is Lucy Snowe's absolute 'other', an Oriental figure of excess, exoticism, and some mystery, who in the portrait is vaguely sexy but also a bit repugnant, just as the Continental Europeans are in the novel.

Throughout classical history, Cleopatra has been represented as the dusky foreign beauty who seduced ancient Romans. Moreover, it is this eroticized image which has been handed down by Orientalist versions of the Cleopatra story ever since, most notably by famous plays such as Shakespeare's *Antony and Cleopatra* (c.1607–8), but also by Victorian novels such as *Villette*. Brontë suggests that, unlike Lucy Snowe, in this respect, Cleopatra lacks self-discipline, that she is lazy, voluptuous, indulgent, negligent, untidy, and uniquely fat. Cleopatra is therefore a figure marked by un-English images of disarray, which establishes tensions in the scene between the Englishwoman and the Egyptian, 'self' and 'other', Occident and Orient. However, on closer inspection, Brontë's depiction of Cleopatra appears to operate on another, more complex level. From this perspective, Cleopatra is also, perhaps, a projection of Lucy Snowe's own secret desires for a more un-English and sybaritic life of laxity and luxury, in which she might get undressed and loll about eating on sofas all day, in a sensuous manner, when all good Victorians – especially the men – are supposed to be working, bustling, being purposeful, and generally doing something worthwhile with their lives. In other words, while Cleopatra's sultry and slatternly ways throw Lucy's Englishness into relief, she is also a vision of Lucy's own repressed 'self', her Orientalized stranger whom she assumes she is 'not'. Cleopatra is, in this interpretation, the dark foreign double trapped within all that stuffy Englishness Lucy Snowe exemplifies, and her image entrances Lucy in the gallery. Part of what the concept of Orientalism enables critics and theorists to understand is, consequently, that which might otherwise seem a fairly insignificant episode in Brontë's novel. This is a momentary encounter between East and West, in a Brussels gallery, which actually contains all of the violence and desire of national and sexual politics endemic to the history of Orientalism.

See also *Contexts*: Empire and imperialism, Nation, Other, Race, Slavery; Criticism: Postcolonialism.

Further Reading

Kabbani, Rana, *Imperial Fictions: Europe's Myths of Orient* (London: Pandora, 1994).
Said, Edward W., *Orientalism: Western Conceptions of the Orient* (Harmondsworth: Penguin, 1995).

Other

The concept of the other, although central to any understanding of the Victorians, is not really a Victorian category at all. It is, rather, a modern theoretical term applied to the Victorians (and other periods) in various academic disciplines, and particularly literary theory. In its widest and most simplistic sense, the other refers to everyone and everything that the Victorians saw as different or 'other' to themselves. It is, in this respect, inextricable from the concept of 'self', in the same way that it is inseparable from Victorian anxieties about identity, race, and related problems such as class, gender and sexuality. Some Victorians, for example, regarded everyone outside of the British Isles as suspiciously 'other', particularly those with darker skins, foreign tongues, different cultures, religions, and generally strange ways. For others, even those closer to home, yet still 'not English' – the Welsh, the Scots and the Irish, were also often regarded as 'other'. By the same token, there persisted within England an all-pervasive Victorian hierarchy of otherness. This hierarchy placed the Victorian lower classes at the bottom, with their women members and those of the underclass even lower and more 'other', particularly prostitutes, criminals and lunatics. At the top were those men of the industrial and professional middle and upper classes, with their women below them although still above the lower classes. In other words, for the Victorians, the concept of the other comprises all those who do not conform to what became the dominant sense of an English 'self' in the period, those unlucky enough not be born, as commentator Catherine Hall succinctly puts it, 'white, male and middle class'.

The British, or rather English, sense of 'self' is bound up with those important categories which are nowadays stereotypically associated with 'the Victorians'. These include, but are not exhausted by, Protestantism, masculinity, heterosexuality, whiteness, rationality, sanity, moral and sexual temperance, propriety, industry, purpose, invention and endeavour. 'Other', as the contrast suggests, is represented by the antithesis of all those categories, meaning Catholicism (but also Hinduism or Islamicism), and Godlessness, foreignness, femininity, homosexuality, blackness, irrationality, madness, moral and sexual laxity, criminal deviance, lack of industry, lack of purpose, lack of invention or endeavour, and outright laziness, all of which constitute a threat to the integrity of Victorian ideas and attitudes. Indeed, it is in this manner that the Victorians invented numerous 'alien', foreign and un-British others which they could define themselves against. Their century was, in this respect, framed by fears of invasion by two great enemies: the Catholic, revolutionary and imperial French at the beginning of the century, and the industrial might and power of the newly unified Germans towards the end. At the same time, as Western Europeans, Victorian Britons came to establish their sense of 'self' against notions of Oriental 'otherness' and against the others they encountered in their colonies, or otherwise fought against, conquered and enslaved: Indians, Chinese, Africans, native Americans, native Australians, and so on.

The idea of the 'other' and its relationship to the 'self' has captivated the Western philosophical tradition for centuries. Early in the nineteenth century, for example, 30 years before Victoria's accession to the throne

in 1837, a giant of German philosophy, G. W. F Hegel, argued in his enor-
mously influential *The Philosophy of Mind* (1807) that the consciousness
of 'self' can exist only when and because it is acknowledged – or rather
recognized – by an 'other'. For Hegel, crucially, the two ('self' and
'other') are mutually dependent upon one another for each other's existence; their relationship is effectively one of enslavement, in which the
'self' strives to assert dominance over the subordinate 'other'. Hegel's
ideas in 'Lordship and Bondage' – a work which appeared in the same
year, 1807, in which Britain abolished the Atlantic slave trade – therefore
seeks to explicate the nature of power in human relationships. In terms
of understanding the Victorians, Hegel's important lesson is that,
throughout the century, the West undertook a haphazard process of self-
recognition, or rather mis-recognition, in which the idea of 'self' was
essentially made in the 'mirror' of 'otherness'. However, in line with
Hegel's theories, the concept of the 'other' is rendered more complex by
the fact that that which the Victorians invented as 'other' often only
amounted to a projection of anxieties and desires which proceeded from
the Victorian sense of 'self' in the first place. Such a notion of otherness
is one which, in the light of such interpretations, commentators such as
Jacques Lacan and Julia Kristeva have described as that unconscious
other or 'foreigner' within, or rather as that 'stranger within ourselves'.
At the level of Victorian ideas about themselves and their place in the
world, the 'other' is consequently that which is mistakenly perceived to
be not 'self', in a process which often places the 'self' in violent antagonism with its sense of the 'other'. The two concepts, 'other' and 'self',
are therefore ultimately bound up together in a mutually dependent
dialectic in which, as Hegel suggests, each requires the existence of the
other, at all times, in order to be in any way meaningful, even though,
as it turns out, time and again the Victorian 'self' can only describe itself
as that which it is 'not'.

Victorian literature is obsessed with others and images of otherness.
It was, though, pivotal to the process of representing or inventing both
the idea of Englishness and its others at the same time. One illuminating example of this process is the case of Podsnappery in Charles
Dickens's *Our Mutual Friend* (1865), Mr Podsnap being an emblem in
Dickens of the utmost Victorian and imperial hubris. Podsnap regards
the entire world outside his garden of England as not only 'other', but as
something of a blot on the globe: 'other countries . . . a mistake.' And
yet, perhaps, he can only measure his England, as suggested above,
against that which he perceives it is 'not': 'Not English!' Rather, he is
'inclined to be oratorical over the astonishing discovery he has made,
that Italy is *not* England' (my italics). For Podsnap, the entire world

seems to orbit around the British imperial sun which rises and sets in his own back yard. Indeed, apart from 'not' being Britain, other countries lack any shape, definition or meaning in his purview. In this sense, Podsnap represents the quintessential Dickens solipsist, one whose hollow sense of Englishness eventually gestures all 'otherness', including Britain's colonial territories, into nothingness: 'with his favourite right-arm flourish, he put the rest of Europe and the whole of Asia, Africa, and America nowhere'. But Podsnap is also the self-styled policeman of correctly spoken English in the novel. In one memorable incident, he can be found admonishing that most 'other' of others for the Victorians, a Frenchman, who intriguingly enough is taken to task for not being able to pronounce the word 'other' correctly. The vignette captures perfectly the way in which English, as the all-powerful language of Victorian imperialism, of Podsnappery itself, would one day conquer all 'others'. In the event, Podsnap's 'th' sounds seem to strike the 'foreign gentleman' with all of the bad breath of Englishness he can muster: '"We do not say Ozer; we say Other: the letters are 'T' and 'H'; You say Tay and Aish . . . "The sound is 'th' 'th!".' But what we must also note, of course, is that Dickens is critical of Podsnap, and that Victorian Britons could, at times, recognize their own limitations. If we looked more closely at *Our Mutual Friend*, on the other hand, we might well decide that, for all his superiority to Podsnap, Dickens cannot free himself of the standard British suspicion of the French other.

See also   *Contexts*: Class, Empire and imperialism, Gender, Gothic, Individualism, Madness, Nation, Orientalism, Race, Slavery; *Criticism*: Feminism, Postcolonialism, Poststructuralism, Psychoanalysis, Queer theory.

Further Reading

Bowen, John, *Other Dickens: Pickwick to Chuzzlewit* (Oxford: Oxford University Press, 2000).

Pre-Raphaelitism

The Pre-Raphaelites were a mid-nineteenth-century artistic and literary movement which railed against Victorian conventions and orthodoxies. The nucleus of the movement, the 'Pre-Raphaelite Brotherhood' (PRB), was so called because of its attempt to establish, or re-establish, the artistic styles and achievements which prevailed during the medieval period, and which preceded the life and work of Italian Renaissance painter Raphael (1483–1520). Raphael and his 'divine' classicism was often regarded by mainstream or more conservative Victorian academics and artists as the important model for all art, and this is part of what Pre-Raphaelitism rejected. With respect to the movement itself, its members, associates and followers, who first convened in 1848, included the three founding members, Dante Gabriel Rossetti, William Holman Hunt and John Everett Millais, along with others such as William Michael Rossetti, James Collinson, Frederick George Stephens, Ford Madox Brown, Thomas Woolner, Edward Burne-Jones and J. W. Waterhouse. Although it would all but disintegrate by the mid-1850s, after considerable bouts of internecine squabbling, Pre-Raphaelitism as an idea limped on until the end of the century, in various shapes and forms. Meanwhile, many of the artists, writers and critics associated with the movement had their views expounded in their own short-lived periodical, *The Germ* (1850).

Central to the Pre-Raphaelite ethos was, as *The Germ* put it early on, to 'enunciate the principles' of those who 'enforce a rigid adherence to the simplicity of Nature either in Art or Poetry'. To that end, one of the central tenets of the movement's artistic manifesto was the necessity of faithful and detailed representations of nature. Along with such loyalty, PRB paintings, especially, are characterized by their vividness, clarity, their often brilliant colour, their deep sense of moral and religious seriousness, and their preoccupation with medieval symbolism (Dante Rossetti, for example, became increasingly enamoured of Arthurian legends). Painters are also preoccupied with the representation of literary subjects, as found in Millais's interpretation of Keats in *Isabella* (1848–9), Shakespeare in *Ophelia* (1852), Tennyson in *Mariana* (1851), and J. W. Waterhouse's depiction of Tennyson's *Lady of Shalott* (1888).

The cross-over in Pre-Raphaelitism between art and literature also had a profound impact on other poets and writers who took up the cause, most notably Christina Rossetti, Algernon Swinburne, William Morris, Elizabeth Siddal, and George Meredith. As with the paintings, Pre-Raphaelite writing is a complex mixture of Victorian themes, obsessions, fears and anxieties. Concepts and figures such as realism, allegory, Gothicism, castles, fairies, goblins, ghosts, dreaminess, forbidden fruits, endangered women, and thoughtful-looking medieval damsels with rosebud lips all have a part to play. Thematically, for example, PRB verse negotiates the close proximity of life, love and death, as observable in Swinburne's poem, *The Triumph of Time* (1866): 'Come life, come death', and indeed, as with the paintings, a rich sense of medieval symbolism and sensuousness distinguishes Pre-Raphaelite poetry. Similarly, much of the poetry contains a deep and vibrant sense of colour and detail, as well as a dense layering of cryptic allusiveness. Criticized as the 'fleshly school of poetry' by Robert Buchanan in 1871, Pre-Raphaelite poets, like the painters, were also influenced by

Tennyson's medieval meditations and the work of Keats, as well as by other literary luminaries such as Shakespeare and Dante. But if the movement was criticized heavily from its inception, it also found an admirer early on in the pre-eminent art critic and moralist of the day, John Ruskin. In a letter to *The Times* of 14 May 1851, Ruskin praised the Pre-Raphaelites' 'fidelity to a certain order of truth', which for him meant a faithful rendering of nature and an indefatigable attention to detail.

The Pre-Raphaelite exuberance in colour and sensuality was deemed to be vulgar by those Victorians with more conservative ideas about art and its role in society. Paradoxically, however, reactions to the movement are complex because PRB ideas were often just as 'serious' or 'realistic', in the strictly Victorian senses of the terms, as those held by the movement's detractors. In paintings such as Millais's *Christ in the House of His Parents* (1849), for example, Joseph's carpenter's room – with its plain people, simple clean lines, slightly ugly Mary and a very average and earthy-looking young Jesus at its centrepiece – seems to have been regarded as not abstract or sacred and respectful enough for such an elevated subject. In an article in *Household Words* called 'Old Lamps for New Ones' (1850), indeed, even otherwise progressively minded Victorians such as Charles Dickens took umbrage at the painting. Dickens described Millais's depiction of Jesus' home, 'Pre-raphaelly considered', as 'mean, odious, repulsive, and revolting', and Millais's Christ himself as a loathsome 'blubbering, red-headed boy, in a bed-gown'. Millais's work was full, for Dickens, of the 'vilest' 'ugliness', with its 'snuffy old woman', 'dirty drunkards' and 'two almost naked carpenters', and for these reasons, Dickens goes on, it was lower and more decadent than a 'cabaret in France, or the lowest gin-shop in England'.

Other contemporary criticisms of Pre-Raphaelite work are just as instructive. As a letter to *The Times* dated 7 May 1851 testifies, one anonymous writer was appalled by the PRB's 'contempt for perspective . . . aversion to beauty in every shape . . . and a singular devotion to . . . seeking out, every excess of sharpness and deformity . . . and caricature'. In those epithets, 'ugliness' and 'excess', in fact, lay one of the PRB's major offences against Victorian notions of propriety and their Keatsian respect for the 'beauty' of 'truth' and 'reality'. An editorial in *The Times* further described the PRB as 'morbid' and 'absurd', while the influential periodical *Athenaeum* (1850) saw 'Abruptness, singularity, uncouthness', as well as 'faults in shade', 'eccentricity', 'affectation', and perhaps worst of all, 'insincerity', everywhere in its art. Oddly, then, the Pre-Raphaelites seem to have offended Victorian good taste by being at once too 'realistic' in their 'fidelity to nature' and too distinctively pre-industrial and nostalgic, and hence un-Victorian in that way.

Pre-Raphaelite writers such as William Morris, Elizabeth Siddal and Algernon Swinburne translated Pre-Raphaelite ideas directly into their verse. Their poetry is also full of romanticized, sleepy-looking medieval women in dreamy and often ghostly settings, with rosebud, yearning lips, mournful eyes, long necks, white smooth skin, luscious hair, and an overall air of the *femme fatale*. William Morris's sensuous 'Praise of My Lady' (1856), for example, foregrounds the typical Pre-Raphaelite attention to full-blooded yet uncontented lips, such as those found in Dante Rossetti's portrait of *Proserpine* (1873): 'Her full lips being made to kiss / Curled up and pensive each one is', and, like the reddened split in Proserpine's fruit, 'Her lips are parted longingly'. In Algernon Swinburne's equally rich and sensuous verse, such as 'Rondel' (1866), the numerous images of kissed lips and hair have more explicitly erotic connotations. But although Swinburne's words are moist with sibilance throughout – 'Kissing her hair I sat against her feet . . . / Sleep were not sweeter than her face to me' – his poem ends on a typically morbid note of Pre-Raphaelite ambiguity and the raised eyebrow of a question mark: 'Unless, perhaps, white death had kissed me there / Kissing her hair?' Swinburne's dark erotics become most pronounced in 'The Triumph of Time' (1866), in which the narrator's desires for the death-like embrace of the sea is once more depicted through the wetness of lips, as well as by the fall and swell of waves that move beneath his kisses like a body: 'My lips will feast on the foam of thy lips / I shall rise with thy rising, with thee subside'.

The Pre-Raphaelite obsession with moribund desires and tempting lips is not, however, restricted to male writers. In Elizabeth Siddal's dreamy and deathly verse, lips become both the site of passion and the membranes through which the yearnings of a repressed woman might find their escape. 'A Year and a Day' (*c*.1855–9), for instance, expresses a fairly simple desire to regain a lost lover's lips: 'Slow hours that make a day / Since I could take my first dear love / And kiss him the old way'. 'Dead Love' (*c*.1855–9), on the other hand, as its title suggests, again brings together a more complex set of Pre-Raphaelite images about the deathly allure of love and desire, in which the 'fairest words on truest lips / Pass on and surely die'. In 'Love and Hate' (*c*. 1855–9), a 'false' lover is admonished in the very first line, by way of reference to lips – 'Ope not thy lips, thou foolish one' – and in the 'closed lips' which are the Victorian woman-poet's living death of 'Speechless' (*c*.1855–9), Siddal passionately desires the return of a lover who might have saved her from the tomb of her silent needs, but who apparently can hear her no more: 'But words come slowly one by one / From frozen lips shut still and dumb'.

See also   *Contexts*: Decadence ad Aestheticism, Body, Death, Gender, Sex and sexuality; *Texts*: Poetry; *Criticism*: Psychoanalysis.

Further Reading

Sambrook, James (ed.), *Pre-Raphaelitism: A Collection of Critical Essays* (Chicago, IL: Chicago University Press, 1974).

Race

In 1862, the Scottish anatomist Robert Knox claimed in *The Races of Man* that 'Race is everything: literature, science, art, – in a word, civilization depends on it'. Victorian anxieties about race, however, a product of centuries of British involvement in slavery and imperialism, were largely of their own conception. This conception was, in turn, both partly constructed and reaffirmed by the rise of the biological sciences, by discourses of anthropology and Orientalism, and especially by the sinister theories which grew out of 'scientific racism'. By the end of the century, most Victorians assumed that the Anglo-Saxon race was the biologically 'natural' superior to other races, and theories about the dominant 'Aryan' or 'Nordic' races, for example, found countless advocates in the period. Some of the more infamous were those of Arthur de Gobineau in his work on the hierarchy of racial inequalities in *Essai sur l'inegalité des races humaines* (1853–5), although similar ideas were being discussed in Britain in Charles Hamilton Smith's *The Natural History of the Human Species* and Knox's work discussed above. In 1844, in his *Two Lectures on the Natural History of the Caucasian and Negro Races*, the slave-owner and 'scientist' Josiah C. Nott deduced that the black race was more stupid and more bestial than the white race, because 'The head [and 'brain'] of the Negro is smaller by a full tenth', and because the 'concave visage' of 'the Negro' 'gives them an Apish character'.

Nott's work, as with that of those such as Francis Galton, Max Nordau and Cesare Lombroso later in the century, was indebted to the pseudo-science of 'Phrenology' popular in the 1820s and 1830s. The phrenologists interpreted bumps in human skulls as indices to racial identity. Their research, and that of a similar ilk, was responsible for establishing the numerous 'sciences' of skull measurement otherwise known as craniology or the 'cephalic index'. But other deeply rooted anxieties about the purity of race or the threat of cross-racial contamination (miscegenation) also prevailed throughout the Victorian period. They were taken to a lower level, perhaps, by the various misapplications of Charles Darwin's theories of evolution and 'natural selection' in *On the*

Origin of Species (1859) and *Descent of Man* (1871), and especially by what Herbert Spencer called, in the light of these theories, 'the survival of the fittest'. The term 'eugenics' was also first used in 1883 by a Victorian, the explorer, 'private' scientist, and skull-reader, Francis Galton. It was Galton who proposed that, in spite of Darwin's ideas about the 'chance' element in natural selection, a selective process of breeding would eventually remove the danger posed by hybrid and hence 'inferior' races altogether, thereby ensuring the 'survival' of those superior races deemed to be most 'fit'. Only one year later, in 1884, during the last great phase of British nation and empire building, and after Victorian racial ideology had received fresh stimulation from violent conflicts in the colonies such as the Indian Mutiny (1857) and the Morant Bay Rebellion in Jamaica (1865), leading reference works such as the *Encyclopaedia Britannica* could still make claims such as that typified by the following: 'No full-blooded Negro has ever been distinguished as a man of science, a poet, or as an artist, and the fundamental equality claimed for him by ignorant philanthropists is belied by the whole history of the race.'

The *Encyclopaedia Britannica* was, in fact, a source of authority that encapsulated Victorian ideas about race throughout the nineteenth century. In 1810, one of its entries described 'people of African descent' in terms that read as a modern inventory of racist assumptions: 'Vices the most notorious seem to be the portion of this unhappy race; idleness, treachery, revenge, cruelty, impudence, stealing, lying, profanity, debauchery, nastiness, and intemperance.' It is clear, moreover, that many eminent Victorians held similarly open and hostile ideas about race, and the idea of the inherent laziness of the black 'race' was particularly intransigent. In his notorious, albeit oddly satirical and unnervingly jocular, 'Occasional Discourse on the Nigger Question' (1849), Thomas Carlyle discussed what he called 'idle' 'Negroes' in the West Indies, who lazed about all day with their 'ears in pumpkins'. As in the *Encyclopaedia Britannica*, Carlyle's 'Discourse' is full of clichés about the black other. For Carlyle, along with his 'ugliness, idleness, rebellion' and 'foolishness', the 'Negro is a swift, supple fellow; a merry-hearted, grinning, dancing, singing, affectionate kind of creature, with a great deal of melody and amenability in his composition'. Although Carlyle was explicitly against a return to slavery (abolished in the British colonies in 1833–4), he does, at the same time, bewail the decline of Britain's plantation colonies with their 'ruined sugar estates', and the concomitant rise of the 'idle black man'. According to Carlyle, it was the laws of 'Fact and Nature', as well as the 'law of Heaven', which decreed that the 'Demerara Nigger' must be 'compelled' to 'work', because the 'Black gentleman', unlike the 'white' man (who should also be made to 'work'), is 'useful in God's creation *only* as a servant' (my italics). Put another way, for Carlyle, after slavery Britain had to find 'slavery' by other means, such as paid work, for a black race whose members would, whatever they did, become part of the myth of the idle and disruptive other in British racial consciousness.

It is along such racist lines that, in 1865, in response to the Morant Bay Rebellion in Jamaica, Victorian writers such as the poet Alfred Lord Tennyson suggested to liberal statesman William Gladstone that Britons 'are too tender to the savage'. Indeed, Tennyson's rhetoric, like that of Nott and Carlyle (and many others), also contained a refrain which draws, in visual rhymes, upon the slavery-era idea which described the black races as animals: 'Niggers are tigers, niggers are tigers'. Similarly, a few years later, the novelist Anthony Trollope, in the account of his travels he provided in *Australia* (1873), prophesized that it was 'the fate' of the Australian Aboriginal black race 'to be abolished'. Trollope's vision was, as it turns out, fulfilled in territories such as Tasmania, in which the systematic extermination of the island's Aboriginal population by British colonialists had all but eliminated them from the island by the turn of the century. Elsewhere, the frequently offhand racism of supposedly more liberal and progressive Victorian novelists and humourists is also illuminating. In his essay, 'The Noble Savage' (1853), for example, Charles Dickens opines that 'I have not the least belief in the Noble Savage . . . I call a savage a something highly desirable to be civilised off the face of the earth.'

Other writers expressed their views on race in terms which frequently slipped across categories of 'race' and 'nation'. This led Charles Kingsley, for instance, author of *Alton Locke* (1850) and The *Water Babies* (1863), to 'racialize' those other nationalities closer to home such as the Irish, whom Kingsley described on a visit to Sligo in 1861 as 'white chimpanzees'. It is in this way that the Irish poor and those of the Fenian uprisings were simianized (made monkey-like), much in the way that Britons simianized black races throughout the nineteenth century. A series of Punch cartoons about the 'British Lion and the Irish Monkey' (1848) led the way, along these lines, as did the writings of journalist Henry Mayhew, who was disturbed by the 'low foreheads and long bulging upper lips' displayed by the Irishmen he encountered. Similarly, in *Chartism* (1839), Thomas Carlyle wrote that the 'Irish National character is degraded, disordered . . . Immethodic, headlong, violent, mendacious', a low mess of 'rags and laughing savagery'. Yet the idea of race in the Victorian period is complex because it came to signify everyone and everything considered to be devoid of strictly Anglo-

Saxon, or rather English, 'characteristics' and 'colour'. Along, then, with their 'racialization' of the Irish, this amounted to the Victorians' racialization of everyone including Indians, Africans, West Indians, Orientals and the French, but also Jews, Catholics, Muslims, the lower classes, criminals, lunatics and women.

The concept of race and the process of racial 'othering' finds countless examples in Victorian literature. Wilkie Collins's *The Moonstone* (1868), for example, is a story which centres around the theft of a huge and valuable 'Hindoo diamond' (the Moonstone), which was stolen by English forces from an Indian shrine in the storming of the 'Palace of Seringapatam' in 1799. In England, as the plot unfurls in a rapid series of events, this sublime piece of imperial plunder is then stolen again from Rachel Verinder, who had been presented with the diamond as a birthday present. Among those immediately suspected of the theft are, tellingly, a trio of 'strolling' Indian jugglers and, as this brief outline suggests, the novel is revealing because it is steeped in such racial and imperial tensions. India is portrayed throughout the text as a place of mystery, sensuousness and exoticism, a country of romance, curses, 'magic' and 'hocus-pocus'. Alongside his anxieties about the 'English foundation' beneath all that 'foreign varnish' – and in what amounts to conspicuous pieces of Orientalism – Collins's Indians are further described in excessive terms. At each stage of the novel they can be found either 'lurking' or being 'rogueish' and 'heathenish'; they are endowed with 'tigerish quickness' and 'snaky' ways, and they are all either 'fanatically devoted' Hindus or 'lawless Mohammedan(s)' who endanger prim and ordered Britain with the threat of 'wild places'. On the other hand, and somewhat intriguingly, Collins's novel also deconstructs its own Victorian assumptions about race. It is, for example, Herncastle himself, the English soldier who stole the Moonstone from India, and not the Indians, who is described as bearing 'a dash of the savage' at 'the taking of Seringapatam' in which he murdered the Indians guarding the jewel. At the end of the novel, it also becomes apparent that the jewel was stolen from Rachel Verinder, not by the Indian jugglers (who prove to be high-caste Brahmins in disguise on a quest to recover the diamond), but by another 'cruel', 'thieving' – and to use another one of the *Encyclopaedia Britannica*'s terms from its entry on the 'Negro race' – 'treacherous' Englishman, Godfrey Ablewhite, who is subsequently murdered because of his involvement with the jewel. According to Collins, 'crime brings its own fatality with it', hence Ablewhite's death. However, the real mystery remains the extent to which his work is haunted by Victorian anxieties about race, some of which he invents. In a story in which the Moonstone becomes a synecdoche for Britain's 'theft 'of India, India being widely known as Britain's 'jewel' in the imperial 'crown', this is the same theft which generated many of the racial anxieties which underpin his novel in the first place.

See also *Contexts*: Class, Empire and imperialism, Evolution, Gothic, Music, Nation, Orientalism, Other, Slavery; *Criticism*: Postcolonialism, Psychoanalysis.

Further Reading

West, Shearer, *The Victorians and Race* (Aldershot: Scolar Press, 1996).

Reform

The issue of reform in the Victorian period demands to be read in terms of the three parliamentary Reform Acts of 1832, 1867 and 1884–5. In 1831, only around 5 per cent of the adult male population of Britain were entitled to vote, and the great Reform Acts eventually paved the way for greater democracy in Britain. The first act of 1832 was perceived by many reformers to be inadequate, because it extended the vote only to those adult males whose property was worth £10 or more in annual rent (£2 if the landowner lived in the country). Benjamin Disraeli's second act of 1867 extended the franchise further – to all men who rented or owned property in urban areas – and this increased the electorate by around a million. William Gladstone's third act of 1884–5 then gave the vote to Britain's rural as well as urban populations, so that by the end of the century almost 30 per cent of the adult male population was enfranchised (women would not get the vote until 1917).The first reform act, especially, did not appease the growing Victorian working classes, many of whom in the 1830s and 1840s were either unemployed or underpaid, hungry or disenchanted (or all of these at the same time), as well as disenfranchised. By the late 1830s, however, these same working classes had become better organized, and out of increasing worker and union activities there came increasing calls for reform. In the same year as the Tolpuddle Martyrs controversy (1834), Robert Owen's ill-fated Grand National Consolidated Trades Union was formed, and the London Working Men's and Radical Associations came about in 1836. Meanwhile, the Anti-Corn Law League was founded in 1836, as were the various movements which agitated against the Poor Law (Amendment) Act of 1834, a law which effectively intensified the terrors of the 'Workhouse' system condemned in Charles Dickens's *Oliver Twist* (1837). In 1838, the Chartist movement was born, partly out of decades of working-class discontent, but also in response to the insufficient reforms or 'betrayal' of 1832. The Chartists aimed, above all, for democratic reform in the shape of universal male suffrage, but later their aims merged with calls for better living conditions and more progressive economic and social reforms in general.

Chartism eventually became a nationwide movement. It was initially made up of middle-class and working-class activists, although successive disappointments and internal disagreements between moderates and radicals led to its eventual domination by the working class. The Chartist petitions was represented at parliament in 1839 by William Lovett's 'People's Charter', a document in which a list of signatures was appended to a six-point manifesto. The petition was rejected three times by government, in 1839, 1842 (despite over three million signatories) and 1848. Public disorder frequently followed the rejection of Chartist demands, and some activists, such as the flamboyant Feargus O'Connor, were arrested for causing trouble. Others were transported, and in 1839 22 Chartist demonstrators in Newport, South Wales, were shot dead for rioting. Social and economic unrest also led, in 1842, to a series of miners', mill- and factory-workers' strikes led by Chartist, trade unionist and other reformist agitators. In 1848, a year after the passage of the 'Ten Hours' Factory Act, and the same year that saw both the revolutionary 'springtime of the European peoples' and some of the worst excesses of the Irish Famine, the Chartist petition was all but ridiculed in parliament for what proved to be the last time.

By 1858, the last year in which activists convened at a national level, Chartism had virtually ceased to be an effective force for reform. Its spirit lingered, however, in the mid-Victorian decades and beyond, and in the working-class movements and trade unions which came to prominence in the second half of the century, most notably the Reform League, which was established in London in 1865. For many conservative Victorians, the idea of reform and radical Chartism was all too often equated with notions of 'mob' rule, French 'revolutionary' terror, and anarchy. In 1848, writing in the *Examiner*, even progressives and reformers such as Charles Dickens claimed 'not to have the least sympathy with physical-force Chartism'. Other novelists, such as Charles Kingsley – despite, at one stage, expressing solidarity with the Chartists – and Elizabeth Gaskell depicted working-class reformers, rioters and Chartists alike, as either ill-educated or childish. Similarly, in her *Passages from the Life of a Radical* (1840), written at the height of reformist and Chartist agitation, George Eliot argued that one night of temperance, restraint, 'mercy', 'rational conversation', and being kind to 'families' and 'children', was worth more to the individual than any amount of 'Radical or Chartist meetings' put together. Furthermore, Chartist reformers, the more zealous of whom went under the famous contemporary slogan, 'peaceably if we can, forcibly if we must', were accused by reactionary Victorian commentators, even by their own activists and sympathizers, of 'Jacobinism', although they were generally portrayed as hopeless romantics. The 'sage of Chelsea', Thomas Carlyle, in his treatise *Chartism* (1839), went as far as to describe the movement as 'Delirious'. Carlyle talked of the 'madness of discontent' Chartism provoked, its anti-individualism, and the need to restore 'sanity' to the unhappy 'mass'. Indeed, his fear of the more violent elements of the 'mob', of 'Chartism with its pikes' and 'Glasgow thuggery', displayed deeply rooted ruling-class anxieties concerning the working class, whose unruly tendencies Carlyle aligned with those of the French: 'These Chartisms, Radicalisms, Reform Bill, Tithe Bill, and infinite other discrepancy . . . are *our* French Revolution.'

Victorian literature is full of ruling-class anxieties about reform and working-class rebellion. George Eliot's *Felix Holt, The Radical* (1866), for example – a novel written just before the passage of the Second Reform Act in 1867 but set at the time of the industrial tensions of 1832 – has a committed reformer as its centrepiece. Felix Holt signifies his militant working-class presence in the novel from the moment he is introduced, when in 'loud abrupt tones', if somewhat anti-climatically, he announces to Mr Lyon that, 'I thank Heaven I am not a mouse to have a nose that takes note of wax or tallow'. In Charles Kingsley's *Alton Locke* (1850), the eponymous hero falls in with radical Chartists, who eventually inspire him to take the gentler route of reformist poetry. In reality, in fact, such working-class and reformist poetry thrived in the Victorian period, and Chartist verse in particular was regularly published in the Chartist newspaper *Northern Star*. Much of this poetry, as in the typically anonymous, 'The Judges are Going to Jail' (1840), is ribald and celebratory doggerel: 'Hurrah for the masses / The lawyers are asses'. Some, such as the 'Chartists and Liberty' (1841), is optimistic about reform – 'Yes! the morning is awakening / When the Charter must be won' – while others, such as 'The Patriot's Grave' (1843), are more belligerent – 'There is blood on the earth – "tis the blood of the brave'.

Reformist poetry also ranges from the elevated and Godly, as in 'A.W.'s' 'To the Sons of Toil' (1841) – 'Ye sons of men give ear awhile / And listen to my prayer' – 'R.M.B's 'Nursery Rhymes' (1840) – 'Little Jack R-ss-ll sat on his bustle / Counting his sal-a-ry' – to the distinctly morbid, as in Thomas Cooper's 'The Purgatory of Suicides' (1853) – 'We'll toil no more – to win a pauper's doom! . . . Big with fear and darkness of the tomb'. Others still formed part of the 'factory slavery' debate which preoccupied the early Victorians. In one, 'The Slaves' Address to British Females' (1838), 'A.L' appeals on behalf of West Indian and

American slaves – 'Natives of a land of glory / Daughters of the good and brave / Hear the injured Negroes' story / Hear and help the fetter'd Slave!' Another, 'The Black and the White Slave' (1840), suggests that the privations and oppressions endured by the 'factory' classes are akin to the miseries of slavery itself: 'I had a dream of slavery / A vision of the night'.

See also   *Contexts*: Law; *Texts*: Historical novel, Social-problem novel; *Criticism*: Marxism.

Further Reading

Dennis, Barbara and Skilton, David (eds), *Reform and Intellectual Debate in Victorian England* (London: Croom Helm, 1987).

Religion

Religion underpins many of the attitudes and anxieties associated with the Victorians. Statistically, apart from dips such as that revealed by the 1851 census, there was no real decline in church attendance figures until the 1890s, and the Bible became cheaper and more widely available to everyone in the period. Churchgoers were recruited from the largely Anglican middle and upper classes (the 'Tory party at prayer'), but also from a large proportion of the working classes; and folk religions remained popular in remote areas of Britain. Along with soldiering, medicine and law, the Church remained one of the major career options for Victorian gentlemen. By Victoria's death in 1901, there were also almost 5000 women preachers in Britain. In 1829, Wellington's government passed the Catholic Emancipation Edict, which enabled Catholics to take up seats in parliament, other state offices and places at university, for the first time since 1688. Although the edict was supposed to cultivate greater religious tolerance, it also renewed ancient hostilities between Protestants and Catholics. It led, for example, to a 'Catholic Revival' throughout the United Kingdom, louder appeals for political and religious independence from the predominantly Catholic Irish, and the Anglican–Catholic pretensions of the 'Oxford Movement' (established in Oxford University c.1833).

The 'movement' was to some extent a reaction against the Grey administration's Reform Act of 1832, part of which called for greater state involvement in ecclesiastical matters. Its members called for less state interference in the church, a return to deeper religiosity, and renewed respect for clerical authority (especially bishops), ritual and doctrine. The Protestant establishment, in turn, responded to the Catholic Revival with a wave of anti-Catholicism and the rise of evangelism. At the same time, the official freedoms created by the edict also consolidated the 'Broad Church' movement, otherwise known as the 'latitudinarians', the aim of which was greater religious tolerance *in toto*. Abroad, the Victorians celebrated Dr Livingstone's missionary work in central Africa (*c.*1850–73), where he called for 'Christianity, Commerce and Civilization', and the colonial endeavours of General Gordon against Sudanese Muslims during the relief of British forces in Khartoum (1885). After the violence of the Indian Mutiny in 1857, there was also renewed missionary activity in Britain's Indian empire, and Colenso, the Bishop of Natal, translated the Bible into Zulu for Africans in that part of the continent.

At home, there were growing disputes over the authority of the King James Bible (the Revised Text appeared in 1881–5), and constant quarrels between the Anglican Church and non-conformists such as Unitarians, Methodists, Presbyterians, Baptists and Quakers. It was, in fact, the fragmentation within the dominant Protestant faith, rather than the onset of doubt, which explained why organizations such as the National Secular Society (1870) had few adherents, and why fewer Victorians still committed themselves to atheism. It was, nonetheless, a Victorian, Thomas Huxley, who in 1869 first used the term 'agnostic' to define those unwilling either to deny or confirm the existence of God. Agnosticism most accurately describes the uncertainty which crept into Victorian ideas about religion as the century wore on.

In 1843, Karl Marx famously described religion as the 'opium' of the people, in a work called *Contribution to the Critique of Hegelian Philosophy of Law* (1844). For Marx, the church served ruling-class ideology by persuading the oppressed classes that their lowly status in society is divinely ordained and thus unchangeable. Philanthropic and religiously minded groups such as the Christian Socialists (formed around 1848) did attempt to lessen the privations of the working classes by creating a more co-operative society based on Christian virtues. Their efforts went in vain, however, due to the gathering momentum of free-trade capitalism in the period, and the ideology of individualism it brought with it. Similarly, along with its emphasis on moral, economic and sexual reserve, the British Protestant faith demanded its own form of 'individualism' from its adherents, especially in terms of its stress on the individual's relationship to the authority of the Bible and his or her recognition of their 'inner light'. Victorians did, on the one hand, seek comfort in the rites and rituals associated with religious observance throughout the century. On the other hand, any sense of stability and 'meaning' that religion provided became vulnerable to more secular and scientific ideas as the century wore on. Following the ground breaking work of British geologist Charles Lyell in *Principles of Geology* (1831–3), and in particular Charles Darwin in *On the Origin of Species* (1859), Victorian faith in fundamental principles such as 'creation', the idea of Christian time, and ultimately the existence of God, were shaken. In short, Lyell and Darwin showed that the evolution of life on earth long antedated the biblical account of creation, which Christian fundamentalists pinpointed to around 4004 BC. Nature, without God's benign direction, was increasingly seen by some commentators to be as pitiless a force as it was purposeless and chaotic. The evolutionary sciences foreshadowed, in this respect, the slow decline of faith in the period and the long retreat from the Christian 'truth' of things, a process which would culminate in Frederich Nietzsche's notorious claim in *The Gay Science* (1882) that 'God is dead'.

Victorian literature is haunted by what the literary critic J. Hillis Miller called the 'disappearance of God'. One novelist, William Thackeray, even satirically described his own work, *Vanity Fair* (1847), as 'a set of people living without God in the world'. In *Barnaby Rudge* (1841), Charles Dickens dispenses with the fine distinctions between the major British religions in his account of the anti-Catholic Gordon riots of 1780, in a question that performs a sort of Godless flippancy all of its own: 'What a pity it is you're a Catholic! Why couldn't you be a Protestant . . . '. Another novelist, George Eliot, claimed that 'God is inconceivable, immortality is unbelievable', and published her translation of D. F. Strauss's controversial *Life of Jesus* in 1846, a work which cast doubt on the accuracy of the Gospels, while some years later in *Jude the Obscure* (1894–5), Thomas Hardy described the vacuum left when 'religion has passed away'. The 'passing' of religion is also lamented by Matthew Arnold's poem 'Dover Beach' (1867), in which the ebb and flow of the 'the sea of faith' contains a 'melancholy, long withdrawing roar', and such literal and metaphorical 'wavering' is further invoked in Alfred Lord Tennyson's *In Memoriam* (1850): 'I falter where I firmly trod . . . / That slope through darkness up to God'. Tennyson's elegy also contains his famous question – 'Are God and Nature then at strife . . . ?' – as well as more paradoxical lines which encapsulate the narrator's newfound faith in scepticism: 'There lives more faith in honest doubt / Believe me, than in half the creeds'.

Victorian novels are equally rich in such paradoxes, but they are also full of satires on piety, hypocrisy, and disreputable clerics. The chaplain Mr Slope in Anthony Trollope's *Barchester Towers* (1857), for example, is as 'greasey' and conniving as he is lusty and ill-fated, a man who can 'stoop to fawn, and stoop low indeed' in his desire for the material and secular gains which the bishopric of Barchester would bestow upon him.

Such worldly desires are also illustrated by Dickens's *Dombey and Son* (1848). This novel, with the Dombey family business and its dabblings in the West Indian colonies at its centre, deals not so much with the disappearance as the displacement of God, a shift in consciousness deftly performed by Dickens's play upon biblical language and 'meanings': 'Common abbreviations took new meanings in his [Dombey's] eyes, and had sole reference to them. A.D. had no concern with anno Domini, but stood for anno Dombei – and Son'. The 'earth', as Dickens goes on, was made for Dombey and Son 'to trade in', and his emphasis on their business ventures parodies the Victorians' faith in themselves as God-like leaders of world civilization. Such a faith hastened the disappearance of God by moving capitalism to the centre of the Victorian universe, so that where there was once a divine partnership, 'God and Son', there was now only men and money.

See also   *Contexts*: Death, Education, Evolution, Gothic, Science; *Texts*: Children's literature, Historical novel; *Criticism*: Deconstruction, Postmodernism, Poststructuralism.

Further Reading

Wheeler, Michael, *Heaven, Hell, and the Victorians* (Cambridge: Cambridge University Press, 1994).

Science

The term 'scientist' was first coined by a nineteenth-century geologist, William Whewell, and the Victorians made huge advances in science throughout this period. Although a clearly underwhelmed Thomas Carlyle wrote in *Sartor Resartus* (1833–4) that all science showed was that 'the Creation of a World is little more mysterious than the cooking of a dumpling', science came to dominate the Victorian consciousness to such an extent that other writers, such as George Henry Lewes, were moved to claim that 'science is penetrating everywhere'. The story of Victorian science is partly one of its middle-class professionalization and specialization, and partly one of its emergence as a force for authority over all knowledge. Various organizations sprang up with the aim of promoting science as a serious occupational and academic discipline: the British Association of the Advancement of Science (established 1831), the Geological Survey (established 1835) and the Laboratory of the Government Chemist (established 1842). At the same time, London's Natural History Museum (established 1873–81), the British Museum (established 1824–47) and the Museum of Practical Geology (established 1851) made science more readily available to a increasingly fascinated population, and Prince Albert himself joined the Geological Society of London in 1849. Albert was also behind the Great Exhibition (1851), which showed off British prowess in science, industry and technology to the world, and he argued repeatedly for science education right up until his death, in 1861.

Scientific ideas and debates were also made more accessible by cheap publications such as the *Penny Cyclopaedia*. Otherwise, there were a range of periodicals in circulation, including James Knowles's *Nineteenth Century*, Chambers's *Cyclopaedia*, the *Encylopaedia Britannica*, the *Edinburgh Review*, the *Quarterly Review*, and in particular the journal *Nature*, which first appeared in 1869, but which tended to have a more scholarly readership. The Victorians made headway in all of the major 'natural' sciences: biology, physics, chemistry, geology, and astronomy; they branched off into 'social' sciences such as anthropology, sociology and psychology; and they dabbled in crackpot sciences such as phrenology, the reading of bumps on the skull; craniology, which became associated with the dubious assumptions of 'scientific racism'; and Havelock Ellis's infamous sexology. They displayed, in fact, a mania for 'ologies' which Charles Dickens parodies in *Hard Times* (1854) as the fact-obsessed pursuit of 'somethingological' undertaken by the Gradgrinds. The nation's engineering and technological achievements, such as Joseph Bazalgette's sewage system in London (*c.*1850s), were all underpinned by scientific endeavours, as were Britain's heavy industries such as coal, iron and steel. Scientific know-how further enabled the Victorians to make advances in transport and communications systems, especially in the railways. The Morse Code system was operable by 1840, submarine telegraphic cables were laid in the 1850s across the English Channel and the Atlantic, and long-distance telephones were in use by the late 1890s.

Groundbreaking scientific ideas inevitably led to a vast epistemological turn in the Victorian consciousness. Charles Lyell's widely read *Principles of Geology* (1831–3), for example, confirmed that the Earth was far more ancient than hitherto believed, and it undermined the idea of biblical time in which Christians held that God created the earth around 4004 BC. It is in this respect that the Victorian sciences slowly discredited the earlier 'scientific' tradition of 'natural theology', the champions of which, such as William Buckland in *Geology and Mineralogy Considered with Reference to Natural Theology* (1837), maintained that 'No reasonable man can doubt that all the phenomena of the physical world derive their origin from God.' Yet the secularity and despair heralded by the new scientific age was to an unprecedented degree compounded by the momentous publication of Charles Darwin's theories of evolution in *On the Origin of Species* (1859), which would eventually change the way that Victorians perceived themselves entirely. Darwin subjected human beings to the same scientific scrutiny he applied to pigeons. Like Lyell, he showed that the origins of humankind, and its destiny, were no longer in the hands of God, and that humanity, like all species, was vulnerable to the essentially random process of 'natural selection'. Nature, in the Darwinian epoch, came to be seen as essentially capricious, amoral, potentially cruel and ruthless, but worst of all, indifferent to who or what it let survive. In terms of what 'Darwin's Bulldog' and popularizer T. H. Huxley described as 'the severe truthfulness of science', Darwin's work was at the vanguard of Victorian scientific achievement. To many, however, his new 'truths' were unpalatable, because they envisioned only a Godless world full of meaningless struggle and chaos.

In Thomas Hardy's *A Pair of Blue Eyes* (1873), the amateur geologist Henry Knight finds himself, at one point, in something of a Darwinian nightmare. As an indifferent coastal cliff suddenly subsides beneath his feet, he is forced to contemplate his feeling of smallness in a pitiless natural world. Amid Knight's sense of his own insignificance, as Hardy writes, the 'dignity of man' is all but ignored by the 'immense lapses of time' which the earth's formation contains. Elsewhere, in the genre of Victorian science fiction, scientific developments open up whole new worlds of possibilities for Victorians, although, as with the case of Henry Knight, it also portends anxieties about that future. Futuristic writings were published throughout the Victorian period, such as Robert Folkestone Williams's *Eureka, a Prophesy* [sic] *of the Future* (1837), Hermann Lang's *The Air Battle* (1859) and Frenchman Jules Verne's popular *Journey to the Centre of the Earth* (1864). But many of the more popular writings appeared towards the latter stages of the nineteenth century, in the decades more closely associated with Victorian anxieties about sexual and racial contamination, genetics, moral degeneration, decadence, class, national identity, empire and the threat of invasion by foreigners. In Robert Louis Stevenson's *The Strange Case of Dr Jekyll and Mr Hyde* (1886) and H. G. Wells's *The Island of Dr Moreau* (1896), for example, the title characters illustrate the disastrous consequences which might occur when the chemical and biological sciences are misused: Dr Jekyll takes 'the powders' and 'the blood-red liquor' in the phial, and is transformed into the mad and bad Mr Hyde, while Dr Moreau has evolutionist fantasies about transforming animals into humans, which lead him to create 'Swine Woman', 'Leopard Man', 'Ape-man', even 'St Bernard Dog Man'.

In Wells's *The Time Machine* (1895), set in the year 802701, the possibility of manipulating, not to say escaping, Darwin's logic of evolutionary time, is again evoked. In this novel, Wells debates the idea of humankind's regression to monkeys, which finds the narrator suggesting that evolution had become 'split' along 'lines of social stratification': 'gradually the truth dawned on me: that Man had not remained one species, but had differentiated into two distinct animals'. These 'species' in the novel are an 'ape-like' subterranean working class, the Morlocks, and a decadent upper-class, the Eloi, who dwell above ground, and Wells's language is full of social-Darwinian terminology such as mankind's ability to 'adapt' to and 'survive' by dint of its 'triumph over nature'. Other *fin de siècle* writings, such as Walter Besant's *The Revolt of Man* (1882), deal with the crisis over the emergent 'New Woman' in Victorian society, by fantasizing a world taken over by women, and in *The War of the Worlds* (1898), H. G. Wells's allegory of the terrifying potentialities unleashed by science, Britain is invaded by technologically superior Martians, somewhere near Woking, although his work also foreshadows the imminent European and imperial crises with which Britain became embroiled. Intriguingly, though, Wells's Martians – 'one of the gravest dangers that ever threatened the human race' – are eventually overthrown, not by British scientific or defensive capabilities, but by their own susceptibility to the 'natural selection' of human 'bacteria'. They are vanquished, it seems, by the evolution of everyday British germs which Victorian science also sought to overcome.

See also *Contexts*: Disease, Evolution, Religion, Transport; *Criticism*: Deconstruction, Postmodernism.

Further Reading

Young, Robert, *Darwin's Metaphor: Nature's Place in Victorian Culture* (Cambridge: Cambridge University Press, 1985).

Sex and Sexuality

Despite being one of the more formidable clichés attached to the period, Victorian anxieties about sex are well documented, especially by contemporary writers and commentators. According to 'eccentric' physicians such as William Acton in *The Functions and Disorders of the Reproductive Organs* (1857), for example, 'much mischief would happen' to sexually incontinent young men whose wanton ways produced only 'weakly, sickly children, that can with difficulty be reared'. In contrast, as Acton went on, notoriously, the 'majority of women are not very much troubled with sexual feeling of any kind' at all and, as he concludes, 'the best mothers, wives and managers of households know little or nothing of sexual indulgences'.

The Victorian period does, in fact, begin and end in sexual scandal. In 1836, one year before Victoria's accession to the throne, prime minister Lord Melbourne was accused of adultery by the husband of writer Caroline Norton, and in 1895, Oscar Wilde was tried and prosecuted for homosexuality. There is also evidence that the Victorians indulged in a variety of sexual peccadilloes throughout the century. A huge underground of graphic pornography was available. Sado-masochist activity was popular, as was paedophilia; there were unprecedented prostitution and child prostitution rates, an array of virulent sexual diseases, and in 1888 *My Secret Life* was published, which in 11 volumes detailed the shadowy 'Walter's' sexual encounters with around 1200 women, many of whom were prostitutes. Public anxiety about 'fallen' women such as prostitutes, adulterers and the generally unchaste also reached its height in the period. In 1857, the journalist Henry Mayhew estimated that there were probably around 80,000 prostitutes in London alone. Records further indicate that these 'Swindling Sals', 'Chousing Bets' and 'Lushing Loos' – or 'bunters' or 'gays' as they were also known in early Victorian slang – might earn anything between £4 and a relatively lucrative £35 per week.

Charles Dickens recommended that prostitutes should be segregated from society or 'go abroad'. In the 1840s he and his rich philanthropist friend Angela Burdett-Coutts commissioned a home for 'fallen' women, Urania House, with the aim of reforming bad women into good wives and mothers. Following further public alarm about the spread of syphilis and gonorrhoea in the armed services, the Contagious Diseases Acts of 1864, 1866 and 1869 (dismantled in 1886) gave rise to the detainment and medical inspection of prostitutes suspected of carrying such diseases. Brothels remained widespread throughout London, however, and Oscar Wilde was associated with one particularly infamous house for 'renters', a Westminster homosexual or 'Molly House', during his trial. In 1885, ten years before Wilde's conviction (1895), the Labouchère Amendment outlawed 'the commission by any male person of any act of gross indecency with another male person', making sodomy punishable by two years' hard labour. Up until 1861, in fact, such acts were still a capital offence. Amid widespread concern in the period about the so-called 'white slave trade', the broader Criminal Law Amendment Act (1885), of which the Labouchère Amendment was a part, also aimed at the protection of 'Women and Girls' from prostitution, by raising the age of consent from 13 to 16.

The idea of the 'repressive hypothesis' concerning Victorian attitudes to sex and sexuality has long been discredited. Most notably in his influential *The History of Sexuality* (1976), the French historian Michel Foucault argued that far from being simply repressed or 'silent' on the subject of sex, Victorian society was preoccupied with 'speaking' about it, to the extent that it spoke with 'immense verbosity' on the subject, or 'verbosely of its own silence'. For Foucault, sexuality became a 'discourse' which was heavily implicated in the rise of middle-class professionalization, knowledge and power, especially in terms of the study of medicine, and the emergence of 'Sexology' in the 1890s is only the most obvious example of this discourse. Although lesbianism was hardly recognized at all by the Victorians as a classification, medical or otherwise, the concepts of heterosexual and homosexual were also largely late nineteenth-century distinctions. The *Oxford English Dictionary*, for instance, points out that the term 'homosexual' was first coined around 1892. In the event, the Victorians defined 'heterosexual' as 'natural' or 'normal', 'homosexual' as 'unnatural' or 'abnormal'. But they also drew parallels between their outward concern with moral, physical or sexual reserve and the notion of economic 'saving' and restraint. It is no coincidence, therefore, that a popular Victorian euphemism for orgasm was 'to spend'. Acton, for example, talks at one point about the 'importance of the fluid semen, which young men would lavishly expend'.

The idea of an 'economic' body is also linked to Victorian ideas about self-control, asceticism, purpose, industry and, above all, 'productiveness'. Neither masturbators nor homosexuals, in this respect, use semen in a 'purposeful' or 'productive' manner. At least part of the contempt the Victorians had, as Acton proposed, for those who enjoy such individual and non-utilitarian pleasures – masturbation was called the 'solitary vice' – seems to have been that they 'misspent' or 'squandered' their semen, and this would mean, ultimately, that they failed to reproduce other Britons to help in the nation's factories or fight its imperial wars. Yet it would take the revolutionary ideas of Sigmund Freud and the discourse of psychoanalysis towards the end of the century to posit sex and sexuality as the roots of Western civilization and its discontents. For Freud, who described homosexuals as 'inverts', Western society was only civilized, where at all, because its sexual appetites and neuroses were generally well-disciplined, and because the chaos of its desires were repressed.

It is not surprising that images of sexual congress are conspicuously absent in the major works of Victorian literature. The novels of Charles Dickens and Elizabeth Gaskell, for example, or the poetry of Alfred Lord Tennyson and Malcolm Arnold, are not really the places to look for frisky bed-hopping antics or exuberantly detailed frolics in the hay. On the other hand, later Victorian novelists such as G. W. M Reynolds did write erotic prose for a predominantly working-class readership, the Pre-Raphaelites became notorious for their 'fleshy' verse, and the racy 'sensation' novels of the 1860s, associated with Wilkie Collins and Mary Elizabeth Braddon, contained a sexual frisson all of their own. Similarly, other popular women writers of the day, such as George Eliot or the Brontë sisters, are famous for narrating the lives of sexualized, albeit repressed, women. Moreover, when sexual desire is re-routed through metaphors and codes – as it is in the writings of these women – it becomes all the more explicit in the novels, as Foucault suggests, *because* of its professed repudiation and silence. In Charlotte Brontë's *Jane Eyre* (1847), the dowdy heroine's anxieties about her sexual short-comings are initially projected onto her principal rival for Mr Rochester in the novel, the frippet Blanche Ingram, who is 'showy . . . not genuine', but worst of all sexy. Brontë's darker and more bestial desires are then played out by Jane Eyre's 'dark' colonial 'double' in the novel, the 'madwoman' Bertha Mason, Rochester's wife who is brought back from Jamaica and imprisoned as the exotic 'tigress' and 'wild beast or fiend in yonder side-den'. Later in the century, other, more violent incidents of sexual desire in Victorian literature include the rape scene in Thomas Hardy's *Tess of the D'Urbervilles* (1891). This seems to occur, as if to underline the problem of sex and sexuality in Victorian discourse, in the silent or rather 'invisible' space between Hardy's paragraphs. Although the scene is typically metaphorical in its reticence – 'the coarse appropriates the finer thus' – it speaks volumes about Victorian anxieties relating to sex. Its violence inaugurates Tess's 'fall' at the hands of an exploitative upper-class man, Alec D'Urberville, and eventually her death by hanging for the vengeful murder of her antagonist. Three years after the publication of *Tess*, in another Hardy story full of sexual tension based on class problems, *Jude the Obscure* (1894–5), Arabella Donn throws a dead pig's penis (the 'pizzle') at Jude Fawley's ear, as an emblem of the woman's animal – and eventually disruptive and fatal – working-class lust.

See also   *Contexts*: Body, Disease, Gender; *Texts*: Poetry, Sensation fiction; *Criticism*: Feminism, Psychoanalysis, Queer theory.

Further Reading

Armstrong, Nancy, *Desire and Domestic Fiction: A Political History of the Novel* (New York: Oxford University Press, 1987).

Slavery

The British Atlantic slave trade, which began with the voyages of Captain John Hawkins c.1562, was finally abolished in 1807. Slavery itself, however, was only abolished in the British colonies in 1833–4, three years before Victoria's accession to the throne. It continued in America until after the Civil War in 1865 (by 1860, a quarter of all American families in the southern states owned a slave), in French colonies until c.1848, Dutch colonies until c.1863, and in former European colonies such as Cuba (c.1886) and Brazil (c.1888). By that time, although figures vary, between 12 and 20 million slaves had been taken from their homes in Africa and shipped across the Atlantic to the Americas and the West Indies. There they were either transformed into domestic slaves or were worked to death on the plantation systems, picking a range of crops including tobacco, indigo, cotton, and most lucratively for the European market, sugar. After emancipation in 1833–4, the British government paid out £20 million in compensation to the slave holders for the loss of their slaves. It also put in place the invidious 'apprentice' or 'indenture labour' system, which effectively kept slaves bonded to their former masters for another four years, and until the system was repealed in 1838. In 1840, the World Anti-Slavery Convention first met in London. It was set up in order to deal with the continuation of slavery throughout the world, and oversaw, for example, the implementation of two Anglo-Zanzibar treaties (1840, 1871) which outlawed Arab slave traders working in the Middle East and Africa. Even though other major European slaving nations such as France, Portugal and Spain had abolished their Atlantic slave trades by 1840 (France in 1815, at the behest of the British), Britain's Anti-Slave Trade squadrons continued to patrol the Atlantic looking for pirate slave ships, particularly those of the Portuguese, who were smuggling slaves to countries such as Brazil.

Slavery created huge profits for the European empires. At the same time, with its brutal history of kidnappings in Africa, the horrors of the Middle Passage (the voyage of the slave ships across the Atlantic between Africa and the 'New World'), branding, whipping, 'breaking in', beating, and rape, slavery also went on to underpin Western civilization's idea of itself as superior. As the writer Toni Morrison put it in an interview with Paul Gilroy, the violence of slavery 'broke' the 'world in half', dividing it along racial lines between whites and blacks. The idea that the system of slavery grew out of racism, however, is something which has long been disputed. Marxist commentators such as Eric Williams, for example, argued in *Capitalism and Slavery* (1944) that slavery and racism were 'basically an economic phenomenon', and that, as he goes on, 'Slavery was not born of racism: rather, racism was the consequence of slavery.' Whichever came first, one of the major results of slavery was that it commodified the slave's body. As an integral part of the rise of European capitalism, slave merchants bought and sold human beings like any other capitalist object, turning slaves into complete possessions of their owners and masters.

It is also revealing that British calls for the abolition of slavery from the late eighteenth century onwards coincided with the rise of industrial capitalism in Britain. Despite claims made by William Wilberforce and others that the system of slavery was contrary to the West's enlightened and egalitarian values, slavery was, as other commentators pointed out, only dismantled when it was deemed to have become unprofitable, or when there was a sufficient working class – those who endured 'white slavery' – to take its place. Furthermore, philosophers and theorists have grappled with the idea of slavery for centuries. According, most notably, to the German philosopher G. W. F Hegel in *The Phenomenology of Mind* (1807), writing in the same year in which the British abolished the Atlantic slave trade, master and slave, or rather 'lord' and 'bondsmen', become inseparable from one another in a dialectical relationship. For Hegel, the relationship exists only because it is one of mutual recognition which constructs the 'self-consciousness' of both and renders them dependent on one another. In the twentieth century, the Martiniquan anti-colonialist and psychiatrist Frantz Fanon, in *Black Skin, White Masks* (1952), refined Hegel's basic point in the specific context of slavery and colonialism, as a 'neurotic orientation'. He surmised from this that the black man is 'enslaved by his inferiority, the white man enslaved by his superiority'.

There are many uncomfortable references to slavery in Victorian literature. Slaves feature, for example, in works as diverse as the maritime novels of Captain Frederick Marryat, such as *Mr Midshipman Easy* (1836), in which the emphasis is on forgetting the slave trade – 'Can he [Mesty, the freed slave] forget the horrors of slavery?' – and in less obvious places such as the novels of Charlotte Brontë. In Brontë's *The Professor* (written 1846, published 1857), slavery is a metaphor for domestic oppressions. William Crimsworth describes himself as springing 'from my bed with other slaves' and Brontë writes that 'if a wife's nature loathes that of the man she is wedded to, marriage must be slavery'. Such patriarchal oppressions resurface in *Jane Eyre* (1847), a novel haunted by a spectre of slavery from the British former colony of Jamaica. Jane Eyre describes herself at one point as 'a slave or victim', and her engagement to Rochester is full of metaphors of bondage and enslavement, in which jewellery performs the role of slave fetters and chains: 'I'll [Rochester] just – figuratively speaking – attach you to a chain like this' . . . and I will clasp the bracelets on these fine wrists, and load these fairy-like fingers with rings'. The question of slavery in other Victorian novels, such as William Thackeray's *The Newcomes* (1853), on the other hand, receives only lip-service and a set of tokenistic remarks, in respect of a 'black footman (for the lashings of whose brethren she [Mrs Newcome] felt an unaffected pity)'. Similarly, Thackeray's reluctance to articulate slavery reappears in *The Virginians* (1857–9). In this novel, which is partly set in a North American slave state, the narrator points out, somewhat too conveniently, that 'the question of slavery was not born at the time of which we write', even though slavery was very much an issue in the America of 1857 when the novel was published. Indeed, the guilt, anxiety and desire to forget that such reticence implies also seems to have affected another major novelist, Charles Dickens. Although in his miscellaneous writings Dickens was broadly sympathetic towards slaves, as testified by his letters – 'But I want to help the wretched slave' – his fiction is often less forthcoming and far more equivocal on the subject. As part of the Victorians' long-running 'factory slavery' debate, for example, and as a precursor to what Dickens would later describe in *Bleak House* (1853) as 'telescopic philanthropy', Mr Tickle in *Sketches by Boz* (1836–7) complains that 'a large number of most excellent persons and great statesman could see, with the naked eye, most marvellous horrors on West India plantations, while they could discern nothing whatever in the interior of Manchester cotton mills'. Elsewhere in the novels, in *Dombey and Son* (1848), the servant figure of Susan Nipper describes herself as a 'black slave and mulotter', Major Bagstock mistreats a characteristically 'silent' slave figure throughout, and in *Oliver Twist* (1837) Monks's murky and ultimately unspeakable history in the slave colonies finds him emerging from an 'estate in the West Indies' and returned in disgrace to some vague 'part of the New World'. Even in *Martin Chuzzlewit* (1843), a novel which contains a fairly detailed episode in America and a broadly progressive discourse on slavery, Dickens's 'silences' on the issue remain, as John Bowen in *Other Dickens* (2000) has pointed out, more 'eloquent than words'. Such a silence can be heard most memorably in the novel when Mark Tapley regales a slave figure with a well-known British song of slavery and empire, 'Rule Britannia', in which he withdraws his breath at the climatic moment: 'where Britons generally are supposed to declare . . . that they never, never, never'.

See also *Contexts*: Empire and imperialism, Nation, Other, Race; *Criticism*: Postcolonialism, Psychoanalysis.

Further Reading

Bowen, John, *Other Dickens: Pickwick to Chuzzlewit* (Oxford: Oxford University Press, 2000).
Ring, Betty J. and Plasa, Carl (eds), *The Discourse of Slavery: Aphra Behn to Toni Morrison* (London and New York: Routledge, 1994).

Transport

For much of the nineteenth century, British transport was still largely horse-powered. Horses pulled the many Hackney cabs, hansom carriages and omnibuses, and The London General Omnibus Company, which was established in 1855, carried passengers around town for about a penny a mile. The Victorians did, on the other hand, make great advances in all modes of transport. The first motorized bus appeared c.1899, the first unreliable cars were in use by the rich towards the end of the century, and by the 1840s steamships had reduced the voyage from London to Calcutta from several months to six weeks. Tramways were in operation in many British cities by the 1860s, and the 'bone-shaker' or 'penny farthing' bicycles were seen on Britain's notoriously bad roads by the 1870s. Meanwhile, the roads themselves were only really improved after the 1870s thanks to the revolutionary ideas of John Loudon Macadam. Macadam ensured quicker and better transport along the nation's roads after they had been 'macadamized'; that is, built from a layering system of flattened broken stones which would eventually be 'tarmacked', the process of adding 'tar' to stones in 'macadamization'.

It was, however, the railways, especially in the 1840s, that best exemplified Victorian achievements in transport engineering and technology. The railways, with their robust new bridges and viaducts, led not only to the speedier transport of goods and peoples between Britain's industrial centres, but to greater communications in general, along with better travel for those seeking holiday entertainments and popular one-day 'excursions' to growing seaside resorts such as Brighton. Britain's first railway was up and running between Liverpool and Manchester in 1830 (trains reaching speeds of 28 mph); the Great Western Railway between London and Bristol was constructed by Isambard Kingdom Brunel in 1844; and the London Underground system, which was begun in 1854, opened with the Metropolitan line in 1863. Come the turn of the century, Britain was covered with a network of railway lines which John Ruskin described as the nation's 'iron veins', and which it was the perilous and often fatal task of the many navigators to build. By the mid-1840s, the new railroads had already begun to replace Britain's canal system, although abroad, in 1874, Britain's acquisition of Ferdinand de Lesseps's Suez Canal (completed in 1861) made British access to its Eastern trade routes and Indian empire easier and more secure. Most Victorians seem to have taken to the trains with alacrity, even though the Duke of Wellington disliked them and called them 'steam elephants'. Famously, Prince Albert took his first train ride in 1839, followed by Victoria herself in 1842, who travelled on the line between Slough and Paddington and found the experience 'charming'. Looking back on the period just after Victoria's death in 1901, H. G. Wells commented that if there was one image which would characterize the nineteenth century most it would be 'a steam engine running upon a railway'.

The 'Victorian age' has became synonymous with the 'Railway Age', and for some commentators the terms are interchangeable. Trains heralded the modern world of iron, steam and speed, the noisy world of Victorian industry and purpose, but they also symbolized progress and power. The railways increasingly connected the nation's rural and urban areas, and brought the British population into contact with one another on platforms and carriages throughout the country. Their timetables also forced the Victorians to restructure and regulate British time. Before the national railway system, local times differed in Britain from region to region. In 1841, for example, according to the Great Western Timetable, London time was 14 minutes ahead of Somerset time. In order to secure a more efficient national railways network, this meant that Somerset time had to be converted to Greenwich time, a change which became emblematic of the way in which the Victorians tried to regulate and re-construct British society as a whole. In what amounts to a further reflection of the Victorian order of things, trains were then divided into first-, second-, and third-class coaches, so that the railway system effectively became a microcosm of Victorian ideas about hierarchy and class.

Despite Victoria's 'charming' journey and the Victorians' love of travel in general, railways and trains are often portrayed negatively in Victorian literature. Even towards the end of the century, when Britain's railway system had been established for almost half a century, Thomas Hardy in *Tess of the D'Urbervilles* (1891) described trains, with their 'fitful white streak of stream', as marking a curious intrusion of 'feelers' upon his rural Wessex, and as a series of noisy metal probes which 'denoted intermittent moments of contact between their [the inhabitants of Wessex's] secluded world and modern life'. Hardy also described a distinctly out-of-place 'engine-man' in the novel, who with his 'strange northern accent' serves 'fire and smoke' in order to tow the 'threshing-machine' from 'farm to farm'. The man is, as Hardy has it, consequently, 'in the agricultural world, but not of it'. Even though Charles Dickens's apprehensions about the railway age of 'fire and smoke' are under-standable, given that he was involved in a serious railway accident at

Staplehurst in 1865, five years before his death, his mid-century novel *Dombey and Son* (1848) contains one of the most famous railway incidents in Victorian literature. In this novel, Dickens discusses the upheaval wreaked by the laying of the new London to Birmingham line through Staggs's Gardens, in Camden Town, as a figure of absolute chaos:

> The first shock of a great earthquake had, just at that period, rent the whole neighbourhood to its centre . . . Houses were knocked down; streets broken through and stopped . . . Everywhere were bridges that led nowhere; thoroughfares that were wholly impassable . . . carcasses of ragged tenements, and fragments of unfinished walls and arches, and piles of scaffolding, and wildernesses of bricks . . .

For Dickens, the new terror of the trains encapsulated the way in which the modern world was encroaching upon the idyll of pastoral England, where 'Stags' might have once roamed in their 'gardens'. As he goes on, 'Staggs's Gardens was regarded by its population as a sacred grove not to be withered by Railroads'. Later in the novel, indeed, Dickens provides an even more hellish and ultimately fatal representation of trains. Hours before his demise, the villainous Carker becomes 'haunted' by a series of approaching trains which Dickens describes as 'monsters', 'fiery devil[s]' with 'red eyes, and a fierce fire, dropping burning coals'. When Carker's pursuer, Mr Dombey, finally catches up with him in a Parisian railway station, Carker is so shocked he falls onto the lines, and the oncoming train kills him instantly:

> He . . . knew in a moment that the rush was come [he] was beaten down, caught up, and whirled away upon a jagged mill, that spun him round and round, and struck him limb from limb, and licked his stream of life up with its fiery heat, and cast his mutilated fragments in the air.

Before closing the scene, Dickens lingers on the description of Carker's remains on the railway lines, just as he does the 'carcasses' of Staggs's Gardens' tenements. He then finishes on a funereal pun which underlines the indifferent way in which the train and the age of modernity it heralds had come to overwhelm and destroy its human makers: 'recovered from a swoon, he [Dombey] saw them bringing from a distance something covered, that lay heavy and still, upon a board, between four men, and saw that others drove some dogs away that sniffed upon the road, and soaked his blood up, with a train of ashes'.

See also   *Contexts*: Industry, Travel.

Further Reading

Shivelbusch, Wolfgang, *The Railway Age: The Industrialization of Time and Space in the Nineteenth Century* (Berkeley, CA: University of California Press, 1987).

Travel

After the restrictions imposed by the Napoleonic Wars, the early decades of the nineteenth century gave rise to the first great age of travel. 'Grand Tours' of Europe, for example, were revived, and they continued to be popular with wealthy Victorians. The tour was a cultural odyssey, of sorts, that frequently climaxed in Italy, a country in which the traveller would get to cultivate his or her knowledge of the classical heritage of Western civilization and its Renaissance splendour. Along with revolutionary developments for travellers in the trains or the steamships, the first full decade of Victoria's reign also saw the rise of the package holiday. Thomas Cook established his travel organization in 1845, and tourist guides such as the 'Baedekers' or Mariana Starke's *Guide for Travellers on the Continent* (1832) became increasingly popular. Other favourite European destinations for Victorian travellers included Switzerland, with its supposedly health-giving spas, and skiing holidays to the Alps became fashionable from the 1890s onwards.

Victorians also went off on voyages of discovery and exploration, and many more left Britain for commercial, scientific and colonial reasons. It was during his travels to South America in 1831–6, for example, that Charles Darwin first recorded his groundbreaking findings in the *Voyage of the Beagle* (1839), while the explorer John Franklin made three ill-fated attempts at finding the Northwest Passage to the east between the Atlantic and Pacific oceans. The last of these attempts resulted in Franklin's mysterious disappearance in 1847, and his demise was thought by many, including Charles Dickens, to have been at the hands of Innuit cannibals. Another famous Victorian explorer, Richard Burton, travelled incognito to the forbidden city of Mecca and recorded his experiences in pursuit of the elusive source of the Nile in Africa; and Charles Doughty attempted to elevate his *Travels in Arabia Deserta* (1888) to literary status. Others, such as Richard Sturt and the tragic 'Burke and Wills' travelled extensively in Australia (the latter pair dying on their return through the centre of that continent), while the celebrated missionary David Livingstone is frequently credited with the 'discovery' of African natural wonders such as the Victoria Falls. In terms of the burgeoning genre of 'travel literature' in the period, many titles were published, including Frances Trollope's *Domestic Manners of the Americans* (1832), George Borrow's *The Zincali, or an account of the Gipsies in Spain* (1841), Richard Ford's influential *Handbook for Travellers in Spain* (1845), and Mary Kingsley's *Travels in West Africa* (1897). The most famous of Victorian women travellers was Isabella Bird, who wrote morally improving accounts of her journeys from the Americas to the Far East in works such as *A Lady's Life in the Rocky Mountains* (1879).

The Victorians were fascinated by exotic lands and cultures, and it is no coincidence that the era of travel and travel literature coincides with the age of empire. British travellers, from casual holidaymakers and sightseers to a range of colonialists, explorers, Orientalists, missionaries, archaeologists and scientists, all played their part in constructing the idea of foreign lands and cultures for the British people. For some contemporary commentators, however, the idea of travel, and the very notion of being itinerant and thus somehow slightly unstable, was perceived as a threat to the integrity of Englishness. There were particular anxieties, for example, over the fate of women travellers, whom it was thought might be contaminated by their sojourns abroad. In *Handbook for Travellers in Southern Italy* (1858), John Murray cautions that English women on their travels are susceptible to foreign men, and that those who marry foreigners should 'forfeit their nationality' altogether. Such fears for the imperilled woman abroad were only intensified in the violent context of the British Empire, and especially during the Indian Mutiny (1857), in which many Englishwomen were thought to have been 'raped' by Indians, a belief which led to bloody reprisals on both sides of the conflict.

Many Victorian novelists also recorded their travels abroad. Although in *American Notes* (1842), for example, Charles Dickens can be found moaning his way across America, in *Pictures of Italy* (1846) he was clearly more impressed with that country, while later in the century, Robert Louis Stevenson wrote numerous accounts of his travels in France and the west coast of America in *An Inland Voyage* (1878), *Travels with a Donkey in the Cevennes* (1879) and *The Silverado Squatters* (1883). In terms of fiction, fantasies of time travel and exploration were equally popular, especially Jules Verne's *Journey to the Centre of the Earth* (1864) and *Around the World in Eighty Days* (1873–4), with its quirky English hero Phileas Fogg, and H. G. Wells's *The Time Machine* (1895). Many other characters in more 'domestic' Victorian novels also disappear on their travels, where they seem either to find their fortune or to perish. In Dickens's *Little Dorrit* (1857) for example, the Dorrits embark on a Grand Tour around Europe, Arthur Clennam has been on mysterious business in China, the Barnacles are 'all over the world', as are the Merdles, and even the beleaguered figure of Tattycoram is described as being 'a greater traveller in course of time than Captain Cook'. Elsewhere, in Elizabeth Gaskell's *Cranford* (1851), the gamester Poor Peter becomes a sailor and then is 'ordered off to India'; Joseph Sedley makes his fortune in India as 'collector of Boggley Wollah' in William Thackeray's *Vanity Fair* (1847); in George Eliot's *Felix Holt* (1866), Harold Transome goes mysteriously 'silent' while working for the Embassy in Turkey; and in Thomas Hardy's *Tess of the D'Urbervilles* (1891), Angel Clare travels to Brazil for a spell after Tess reveals her ruin. Similarly, in Arthur Conan Doyle's first Sherlock Holmes story, 'A Study in Scarlet' (1887), the first thing that Holmes deduces is that Watson has just returned from his travels, and has been stationed with the British army in the East: 'You have been in Afghanistan, I perceive.'

Representations of travel in Eliot's *Middlemarch* (1872) are also illuminating. During her honeymoon in Italy with her unromantic husband Mr Casaubon, Dorothea Brooke 'finds' herself, metaphysically speaking, in the ruins and relics of ancient Rome. Despite having been reared on 'English and Swiss Puritanism' and 'fed' a diet of 'meagre Protestant histories', Dorothea seems impressed by the 'thrust' of that 'Imperial and Papal' city. It is, indeed, on her travels in Italy, and specifically amid the 'stupendous fragmentariness' of Rome, that she fully realizes the miseries, oppressions and 'dream-like strangeness of her bridal life' with Casaubon. In Rome, 'the city of visible history', Dorothea begins to sense the burden of her own history bearing down on her, a weight construed in terms of patriarchal oppression. Her anxieties are then projected onto the ancient history which surrounds and envelops her like the loveless marriage itself: 'She had been led through the best galleries, had been taken to the chief points of view, had been shown the greatest ruins and the most glorious churches, and she had ended by oftenest choosing to drive out to the Campagna where she could feel alone with the earth and sky.' Dorothea, as Eliot writes, remained haunted by the 'vastness of St Peter's' forever. But her travels to Italy also inspire her to leave 'manmade' Rome behind, so that when she communes with nature in the Campagna she is really communing with her own sense of self. It is also during her time in Italy – a frequently romanticized, not to say eroticized country in Victorian consciousness – that her pivotal affair with Will Ladislaw blossoms. Ladislaw, conveniently enough as it turns out, is a poor but attractive painter who travels a lot across Europe himself, in a Byronic manner, complaining about German art: 'I travelled from Frankfort'. Although the couple had met briefly in England, their forbidden desires for each other begin, it seems, on their travels, in the romance of other worlds.

See also *Contexts*: Empire and imperialism, Orientalism, Transport; *Criticism*: Postcolonialism.

Further Reading

Franey, Laura, *Victorian Travel Writing and Imperial Violence: British Writing of Africa, 1855–1902* (Basingstoke: Palgrave Macmillan, 2004).

Violence

Violence was endemic to Victorian Britain. Statistics show high rates of violent crimes throughout the period, including street robbery, murder and rape, and newspapers took relish in grisly cases such as the garrotting panic of the 1860s or the 'Ripper' murders in Whitechapel of 1888, during the so-called 'autumn of terror'. Violence against immigrant populations was also a prominent feature of the period, especially against Britain's Irish, Jewish, Italian, German and Chinese communities. British aggression against the Irish, in particular, has a long history steeped in British colonialism in Ireland and centuries of anti-Catholicism, and Victorian images of the Irish depict them as a backward nation full of drunken fighters and troublemakers. Following the Irish Famine of the 1840s, figures from 1861 show that Irish immigration to Britain had more than doubled to over 800,000. As a result, immigrants who made their way to Britain's major cities and industrial centres were then forced to compete with the natives for scarce resources and jobs. Although the Catholic Emancipation Act (1829) relaxed the laws on Britain's Catholic population, anti-Irish/Catholic tensions simmered and violent incidents broke out throughout the country. They peaked in areas such as Liverpool (c.1830s–40s), Stockport (1852), London and Chesterfield (1862), Wolverhampton (1858), Birmingham (1867), Lancashire (1868) and Tredegar, South Wales (1882). In 1868, the Irish newspaper *The Nation* was driven, in response, to report that 'Nowhere can our countrymen consider themselves safe from English mob violence.'

Sporadic disturbances and 'mob' violence were, at the same time, largely the result of working-class unrest aroused by economic hardship and hunger. Violent incidents took place in agricultural and urban areas throughout the period, involving a series of industrial disputes around mills, mines and factories. Meanwhile, reformist and Chartist violence in the name of electoral and economic change was largely confined to two significant outbreaks: 1830–2 and 1839–43. During the 'Rebecca Riots' in South Wales in 1839, for example, 22 Chartist demonstrators were shot dead in Newport. It was such violence that prompted contemporary commentators, such as Thomas Carlyle in *Chartism* (1840), to condemn the working classes and the 'Glasgow Thugs' with their 'brickbats, cheap pikes, . . . rusty pistols, vitriol-bottle and match-box'. On the other hand, following disturbances in London's Hyde Park, a slightly more sympathetic Matthew Arnold, in *Anarchy and Authority* (1868), wrote that even though the 'Hyde Park rough' desires to 'break(s) down the Park railings', he is 'only following an Englishman's impulse to do as he likes', a freedom enshrined, as Arnold suggests, by the British constitution. Successive Victorian governments and local authorities attempted to counteract public violence, with some success – at first with the use of militias, and then, after Robert Peel's establishment of the Metropolitan Police Force in 1829, through the nation's growing police constabularies. A taste for violence was, however, always present in Victorian society. It was apparent, for example, even in such ephemeral cultural products as the infamous 'penny dreadful' magazines and novels. Otherwise known as 'bloods', these publications, such as the *Weekly Magazine* (*c.*1840s) and George Reynolds's grim *Mysteries of London* (a novel issued weekly for a penny a copy between 1841 and 1856), carried true but sensationalized stories of violence, blood and murder, some of which recounted the vicious lives of highwaymen, and some of which dealt with fictional characters, such as Sweeney Todd, the 'Barber of Fleet Street' who murdered his customers.

The historical records and archives do not, however, account for all of the violence meted out by Victorian society itself. This is the 'concealed' violence of what one recent commentator, Jeremy Tambling, describes as the violence of the Victorian 'modern state'. The apparatus of violence, in this respect, was manifest in Victorian systems of surveillance, discipline and punishment. It operated in the 'spectacle' of public whippings (which were still legal until 1862), the hangings (for murderers and traitors only, 1824–9), the transportation of felons to the colonies, the prisons, the ragged schools, the workhouses, the hospitals, the asylums, the child-labour systems, and the inspections of prostitutes for disease. The violence ingrained, moreover, in the very fabric of Victorian society, is equally visible in the discourses of class, patriarchy, law, politics, economics, sexuality, nation, race and empire, in the Victorian ideology of individualism and the integrity of the 'self'. There is also that violence of the English language or the imperial 'mother tongue' to take into consideration, and thus the violence of Victorian literature itself, which reflected and to an extent constructed Victorian ideas and attitudes, and their representation throughout the modern world.

Victorian literature can be construed as violent on many levels. In the most literal sense, Charles Dickens's work, for example, is full of violent characters and incidents: murderers, housebreakers, rioters, ruffians, street-scrappers, fighters, wife-beaters, child-beaters, menacing strangers, explosive lunatics, drownings and hangings. Even in Dickens's early, more light-hearted works, such as *The Pickwick Papers* (1836–7), Sam Weller can be found attacking Mr Pickwick with a combination of punches to the 'nose' and 'chest' when they first meet, before setting about the others in Pickwick's entourage. Furthermore, throughout the novels there is a host of eccentric but suddenly violent episodes such as the Smallweeds' cushion-throwing or Krook's 'spontaneous combustion' in *Bleak House* (1853), Krook also being a bitter fleecer of kittens before his death. Dickens's simultaneous attraction towards and repulsion from other forms of violence, on the other hand, such as whipping, is often overlooked. Nonetheless, as part of his critique of the ubiquitous violence of disciplinary methods in Victorian society, Dickens can be found brandishing the whip throughout his work, and almost every novel contains at least one image of whipping. In *Oliver Twist* (1837), the orphan's various oppressors think he needs to be flogged out of his idleness: 'They'll never do anything with him, without stripes and bruises', and the violence in the novel between 'low' men and women is taken to extremes when the prostitute Nancy is pistol-whipped to death by Sikes. In *Nicholas Nickleby* (1838–9), Squeers at Dotheboys Hall, one of literature's more notorious figures of bad Victorian schooling and violence against children, compares himself to 'A slave driver in the West Indies' and uses his 'strong, supple, wax-ended' cane to whip his schoolboy 'blacks'. Amid the violence of the anti-Catholic 'Riots of '80' in *Barnaby Rudge* (1841), a novel which mirrors the Chartist violence of the early 1840s in which it was published, it is supposed, at one point, that Barnaby's idiocy and all the Victorian anxieties about madness he embodies might be remedied by the whip: 'There's nothing like flogging to cure that disorder', and in *Martin Chuzzlewit* (1843), an embittered coachman gives Jonas Chuzzlewit a 'cut with his whip, and bids him get out for a surly dog'. In *Great Expectations* (1861), Pip glumly recalls the almost everyday violence of Victorian family life in the shape of Mrs Joe's 'tickler' – a 'wax-ended piece of cane, worn smooth by collision with my tickled frame' – and in Dickens's last unfinished novel, *The Mystery of Edwin Drood* (1870), the account of whipping briefly looks out again to the wider historical and global context in which the Victorians were embroiled, with further intimations of colonial violence: 'Before coming to England [Neville Landless] had caused to be whipped to death sundry 'Natives' ... vaguely supposed in Cloisterham to be always black'. That the violence of the Dickens world reflects the violence of Victorian Britain is well known. That such violence is partly the reflex of

Britain's involvement in the violence of empire, that extraordinary history upon which British 'greatness' and superiority was built, is something with which scholars of Victorian literature have become increasingly preoccupied.

See also   *Contexts*: Body, Crime and punishment, Death, Gothic, Madness, Nation, Other, Race, Slavery; *Texts*: Crime fiction, Drama, Historical novel, Penny dreadfuls, Sensation fiction; *Criticism*: Deconstruction, Feminism, Marxism, Postcolonialism, Queer theory.

Further Reading

Tambling, Jeremy, *Dickens, Violence and the Modern State: Dreams of the Scaffold* (Basingstoke: Macmillan Press, 1995).

War

Victorian armies were largely embroiled in the defence of Britain's imperial interests. They fought in only one major European war between 1815 and 1914, in the Crimea (1853–6), but even this had imperial dimensions. The war allied Britain, France, Turkey and, in 1855, Sardinia, against Russia. British involvement was largely aimed at the protection of its colonial routes from the Mediterranean to India against Russian expansionism south into the Ottoman Empire, and allied successes eventually forced the Russians to retreat. Elsewhere, British forces were involved in a series of military campaigns, as well as brinkmanships, scrapes, skirmishes and outright wars in almost every year of Victoria's reign. These included the first 'buffer' wars in Afghanistan to preserve the borders of India in 1838–42; the Opium Wars with China in 1839–42 and 1856–60; the Sikh Wars in 1845–6 and 1848–9; the Indian Sepoy Mutiny in 1857; the Maori Wars in New Zealand c.1863–72; the suppression of the Morant Bay Rebellion in Jamaica in 1865; the Ashanti Wars in West Africa (1873–4); the second Afghan War (1878–80); the Zulu Wars in South Africa in 1879; the first Anglo-Boer War (1880–1); the Egyptian War (1882); the crushing of the Mahdist regime at the Battle of Omdurman in Sudan (1898), and the second phase of Boer Wars in South Africa (1899–1902). The last three conflicts were part of British campaigns in the so-called 'scramble for Africa' in the last quarter of the century, the last major period of British and European imperialism. Tactically and strategically speaking, the wars of movement associated with the Napoleonic wars (1800–15) began to give way to wars of attrition in the nineteenth century. Warfare became characterized by heavier and heavier artillery, larger-scale mobilization and trench warfare. At the same time, the Victorians also made significant advances in weaponry, such as the replacement of the slow and clumsy flintlock muskets by rifle muskets, while early machine guns were in use by 1870. Despite various recruitment initiatives, however, the British army in the Victorian period remained drastically undermanned. It was also under-trained, old-fashioned, riven by quarrels in high command, and undermined by feeble leadership. Such problems partly accounted for why the British war machine struggled as it did in the early decades of Victoria's reign, particularly against formidable enemies such as Russia. They also account for why it was so poorly equipped and ill-prepared for conflicts towards the end of the century, especially the notoriously protracted Boer Wars.

Soldiering became an increasingly professionalized career in the period, and the British army, like Victorian society as a whole, was full of class tensions. The officer ranks were still largely recruited from Britain's middle and aristocratic classes, and this process conferred a gentlemanly status on the officer in civilian life. Common soldiers and sailors, on the other hand, continued to be enlisted from the lower echelons of Victorian society, particularly from the class of unemployed or unskilled labourers. Some of these new recruits were then, for about a shilling a day, deployed against the disaffected and often rebellious working classes themselves. By the early to mid-Victorian period, soldiering had begun to lose much of its romanticized and gentlemanly lustre, and a career in the lower ranks of the army was deemed at best unglamorous, at worst, a vocation for degenerates. Due to poor resources and inadequate barrack accommodation, soldiers also suffered from terrible sanitary conditions. They endured numerous illnesses and complaints, and syphilis and gonorrhoea were rampant. When Britain's military shortcomings were famously exposed during the Crimean War, proposals for reform were led by popular figures such as nurse-cum-military-critic Florence Nightingale, and conditions for serviceman gradually improved as the century wore on.

Given the worldwide scope of British belligerence in the nineteenth century, one might assume that war would be a significant feature of Victorian literature. However, this is not really the case. There were, on the one hand, the militaristic novels of lesser-known Victorian writers such as Charles Lever, whose work in the 1830s and 1840s is steeped in the tradition of post-Napoleonic British triumphalism. There were also heroic and glorified paeans to the brave dead of the Crimean War, such as that exemplified by Alfred Lord Tennysons's popular poem, 'The Charge of the Light Brigade' (1854) – 'Their's not to reason why / Their's but to do and die' – and there was an extensive fictional response to anxieties about imperial crises such as the Indian Mutiny, including

James Grant's *First Love, Last Love* (1868) and Philip Meadows Taylor's *Seeta* (1872). Similarly, there were the numerous duels and old-fashioned militaristic codes of honour and duty found in the novels of the inappropriately named William 'Makepeace' Thackeray, whose work is full of war references, particularly to the Seven Years War (1756–63) in *Barry Lyndon* (1852), the Battle of Waterloo (1815) in *Vanity Fair* (1847), and the American War of Independence (1775–83) in *The Virginians* (1857).

Mostly, though, as recent commentators have pointed out, Britain's wars are hardly referred to at all in many of the major works of Victorian literature. The novels of the 1850s, for instance, which are overshadowed by the Crimean War, are, with the exception of bellicose tales such as Charles Kingsley's *Westward Ho!* (1855) – a projection of the Crimean War onto the Elizabethan context of war against the Spanish – more concerned with domestic and social crises. Other mid-Victorian literary luminaries appear to all but ignore Britain's wars. During the rise of classic realist British fiction in the period, for example, authors seemed to have been preoccupied with the concerns of individuals, rather than the wider national context of war, and this is testified by titles such as Charlotte Brontë's *Jane Eyre* (1847), Elizabeth Gaskell's *Mary Barton* (1848), Charles Dickens's *David Copperfield* (1850), and George Eliot's *Adam Bede* (1859). Nonetheless, the spectre of war haunts the domestic and social focus of such works on numerous conscious and unconscious levels. Dickens's *Little Dorrit* (1857), for instance, which was first published in the immediate aftermath of the Crimean War, does not allude to that war directly. Yet Dickens's satire on 'how not to do it' in the novel is often read as a critique of Britain's inability to prosecute that war effectively, while the presence of the second 'Opium War' (1856–60) between Britain and China in the novel goes completely unspoken, being, as it is, perhaps, another violent part of the text's colonial unconscious.

But if early Victorian literature is generally reticent about Britain's wars, this yields to an increasing garrulity on the subject towards the later decades of the century. In the period associated with Britain's imperial campaigns in Africa, the age of jingoism, and the writings of Rudyard Kipling, in particular, images of war become prominent. As if to underline this point, although the sexy and alluring soldier figure of Jane Austen's novels (*c*.1811–18), for example, went into decline with the emergence of the Victorians, later in the century he is revived somewhat. In Thomas Hardy's portrayal of Sergeant Troy in *Far from the Madding Crowd* (1874) Troy first appears as a rogueish but sexy seducer and he enters the pastoral world of the novel complete with all the swagger, swashbuckling clothes, flashing blades, gallantry, charm and sheer impetuosity of earlier incarnations. Troy is, however, also a disruptive and somewhat menacing figure in the novel, who lies 'to all women like a Cretan'. He is, furthermore, at once 'middle-class' and a 'common soldier', whose uncertain status in society leaves him as a character, as Hardy puts it, marked by 'idiosyncrasy and vicissitude'. After mistreating Bathsheba Everdene throughout the story, Troy is eventually shot in a farmhouse. He dies in a distinctly unheroic and ignominious manner, at the hands of a mere civilian, Farmer Boldwood.

It is, indeed, as if there was an unspoken declaration in the period that the domain of Victorian literature was the domestic arena. It is there that manly individuals such as Troy and Boldwood assert their authority, rather than in the international domain of war. At the same time, Boldwood's singular act of violence underlines that contradiction which is central to the period and its literature: behind the civilized façade of the Victorian gentleman there lies, time and again, a less peaceful and more alarming reality. In this respect, although the concept of war is not integral to the domestic focus of *Far from the Madding Crowd*, the under-lying violence of Hardy's novel, with its climactic death of a soldier and the warlike nature of Victorian Englishness it suggests, ultimately provides an important perspective on this contradiction.

See also *Contexts*: Empire and imperialism, Nation, Violence; *Texts*: Historical novel; *Criticism*: New historicism/Cultural materialism, Psychoanalysis.

Further Reading

Peck, John, *War, the Army, and Victorian Literature* (Basingstoke: Macmillan, 1998).

2 Texts: Themes, Issues, Concepts

Introduction

Victorian literature is most distinctly characterized by the rise to prominence of the novel. Whereas the preceding Romantic age (*c.*1789–1830) was dominated by poetry, it was during the course of the nineteenth century that poetry was, perhaps for the first time in English literary history, eclipsed by the novel as the most popular form. As can be imagined, the historical and cultural contexts behind the novel's rise are many and complex. In a period which saw increasing urbanization, industrialism and calls for reform, Britain was in a state of transition. It underwent rapid socioeconomic and political upheaval, witnessed the encroachment of scientific rationalism into all walks of life, and experienced a crisis of religious faith. The novel, it is clear, proved to be the form best suited for reflecting the sheer enormity and complexity of the Victorian experience. Time and again in the intellectual and cultural debates of the period there is anxiety that the confusions brought about by an industrial-capitalist society will overwhelm the individual. In 1849, this led the poet and educationist Matthew Arnold to describe his fear of being 'prevailed over by the world's multitudinousness'. In the face of such uncertainties, the Victorian novel, with its neat expositions, complications and resolutions, and the manner in which the logic of its narrative so often engineers a happy ending, provided some sort of structure for Victorians. It established, in other words, a semblance of order and consolation against the chaos and contradictions of a changing world.

Other significant changes were taking place in nineteenth-century literature and culture. In the preceeding century, for example, it was estimated that more novels were being written and read by women than men. The situation became such that some contemporary commentators (mostly men) wrote off the novel as an upstart form suitably 'light' and jejune for women, whose passive lives required a sedentary pastime to keep them occupied. Yet by the 1830s–40s, as Victorianism was getting into its stride, and when novelists increasingly turned their attention to the industrial and political issues facing Victorian Britain, the novel form became both more respectable and, unsurprisingly, male-dominated. Although, statistically, more women wrote novels in the Victorian period than ever before, and notwithstanding the hugely successful careers of the Brontë sisters, Elizabeth Gaskell and George Eliot, to name only the most obvious, the majority of novels which reached publication were by men. Such an imbalance inevitably underlined the patriarchal structure of Victorian society. It also, moreover, determined the ideological shape of the novel. At the same time, Victorian fiction was monopolized by several male-dominated publishing houses, and some of the major businesses remain formidable concerns today: Macmillan, Smith and Elder, Bentleys, Chapman and Hall, Blackwood (publisher of best-sellers such as George Eliot), Bradbury and Evans, and Longmans. As the first of its kind, Mudie's Select Library (founded in 1842), expanded quickly, working on a subscription and loan basis. At a guinea-a-year per reader, one volume at a time, it made novels more cheaply available to a broad social spectrum, and especially to an increasingly educated, and aspirational, Victorian middle class.

Such factual matters are easy to catalogue. It is, however, a lot more difficult to summarize the nature of Victorian fiction. The Victorian period encompasses around three-quarters of the nineteenth century. As a result, there is no single or easily definable characteristic of the Victorian novel, apart from a sense of the development of realism and a focus on the integrity of the individual. Indeed, the novelist Henry James in a famous discussion of the almost promiscuous variety and openness of the novel form, declared it to be made up of 'loose baggy monsters'. Most commentators do, on the other hand, agree that Victorian fiction, as we have come to know it, has some of its origins in the early works of Charles Dickens. From the beginnings of Victoria's reign, and before they were collected into single-volume or 'triple-decker' editions, the majority of novels were published in serial form. Dickens's *The Pickwick Papers* (1836–7) was issued in 20 monthly instalments between April 1836 and November 1837, and then as a complete volume later in 1837, neatly enough during the first year of Victoria's reign. Although not a novel as such, *The Pickwick Papers* has all the vibrancy and energy associated with the Victorians, and it was this work which helped establish the lucrative 'cliff-hanger' motif of Victorian fiction. The transition to the novel as a distinct form with a discernible 'Victorian' theme and structure, however, is widely thought to be that performed by Dickens's immediate follow-up, the enduringly successful *Oliver Twist* (1837). Whereas *The Pickwick Papers* have an episodic and picaresque, rather shambolic structure, and a generally lighthearted and unsentimental tone reminiscent of eighteenth-century novels, *Oliver Twist* – itself reminiscent of the earlier 'Newgate prison' genre – is a strikingly different combination of menace and mawkishness which came to typify the Victorian *bildungsroman* ('education' novel). The novel comprises a broadly linear narrative structured around Oliver's famous rags-to-riches story. It has the order and inevitability, that is to say, of wretched beginnings and implausible happy endings. Although not without Dickens's inimitable comic touches, unlike *The Pickwick Papers* the text is dark with Dickens's indictment of the cruelties meted out by the infamous Poor Law (1834) and workhouse systems. Its mixture of fact, fiction and socially aware narrator, as it turned out, in many ways set the tone for the Victorian novel. In the first great age of reform, it suggested that the novel was a medium not just for political protest and reflection, but for real and lasting change.

As suggested above, the history of the Victorian novel is also partly the history of realism, and it is such doubleness that partly explains why the uniquely grotesque and Gothic elements of a novel such as *Oliver Twist* also need to be understood as part of the social realism germinating in the many 'industrial' or 'social problem' novels which dominated the early years of Victoria's reign. In response to the upheavals of the 1830s–50s, and particularly the economic and social crises of the 'hungry forties', a series of novels-cum-indictments of the brutalities and inequalities of Victorian society began to appear. Titles included Frances Trollope's *Michael Armstrong, The Factory Boy* (1840), Benjamin Disraeli's *Sybil, or Two Nations* (1845), Elizabeth Gaskell's *Mary Barton* (1848), Charlotte Brontë's *Shirley* (1849), Charles Kingsley's *Alton Locke* (1850) and Dickens's *Hard Times* (1854). These works all viewed what Thomas Carlyle called the 'Condition of England' from an emergent and increasingly unified middle-class perspective. They reflected the fact that the first great age of industrial capitalism had turned Victorian society into a class system dominated by a new industrial and professional middle class, one which controlled both the means of production and consequently what Karl Marx called 'ruling class ideas'. It is, more to the point, middle-class ideas and values, a middle-class system of representing 'reality', which we have come to understand as quintessentially 'Victorian', and it is this reality which stamped itself on the development of the English novel. That these ideas and values are themselves dominated by an overarching preoccupation with the individual, and that this preoccupation is, in turn, the product of the first great epoch of free-trade economics and its ideology of 'individual' competition, is also reflected in the array of popular novels from the period that take an individual hero as their title: *Oliver Twist* (1837), *Barry Lyndon* (1844), *Jane Eyre* (1847), *Adam Bede* (1859), *David Copperfield* (1850), *Daniel Deronda* (1876), *Tess of the D'Urbervilles* (1891), *Jude the Obscure* (1895), to name only a few. But even some of the successful novels with more abstract titles and satirical subtitles, such as William Thackeray's *Vanity Fair* (1847) – 'A Novel without a Hero' – acknowledge the period's obsession with the heroic individual.

This is not to say that individuals in Victorian novels do not vastly differ or become complicated by the novelist's broader vision of everyone and everything, because they do. Take, for example, the differences between Dickens's individual heroes and those of George Eliot. Dickens's comic and often highly eccentric individuals, generally his more peripheral characters such as Mrs Gamp in *Martin Chuzzlewit* (1843–4) or the pillow-throwing Smallweed family in *Bleak House* (1853), were described even by his contemporary critics as 'flat'. That is to say, Dickens's characters do not develop as individuals or grow through time in the novels, as such, but remain static. Neither do they appear to have any lasting sense of inner subjectivity or 'individual' depth. This is largely because Dickens tends to describe his characters in terms of their individual and timeless surface qualities, such as their clothes and prominent physical features, rather than the complexities of their minds. Mr Micawber in *David Copperfield*, for example, has a head described as bald as 'an egg', but he is not a particularly profound or reflective individual, so much as a symbol of misguided optimism. Similarly, most of Dickens's major heroes – Oliver Twist, Nicholas Nickleby, Martin Chuzzlewit, David Copperfield, Pip Pirrip, are quite wooden and interchangeable heroes, more like social types, if anything, than individuals. They are generally of good, wholesome, rather bland dispositions, and they are all destined, as essentially middle-class heroes, to emerge from difficult circumstances into the bourgeois comforts of money or marriage, or both. The notorious mystery of Oliver Twist's plummy middle-class voice, for example, signifies his essentially good middle-classness from the outset: 'Please, sir, I want some more.' As Dickens has it, the orphaned Oliver grows up in a workhouse with other waifs and strays. He then consorts with an assortment of London ruffians: chimney-sweeps, pickpockets, fences, housebreakers and prostitutes. How, then, as critics of the novel have asked, does he go through life with his perfect diction intact, and not end up sounding a bit like the Artful Dodger: 'I'm an Englishman, an't I? where are my priwileges?' The answer, it seems, has already been suggested above, and it lies in Oliver's innate 'purity' as a fated middle-class hero.

George Eliot's novels, on the other hand, are associated with a more coherent, less compromised, notion of Victorian realism. To a greater extent than those of Dickens, Eliot's many heroes and heroines lead highly stylized 'individual' existences. Although, like Dickens, Eliot does read the surface features of her individuals as indices to their minds, her work also continually probes the deepest thoughts and inner motivations of her protagonists. Her heroes and heroines are all, in this respect, ascribed some sense of a coherent or developing 'inner' self; they are not flat, as in Dickens's novels, but 'rounded', and generally complex individuals that 'begin' somewhere and 'arrive' somewhere else, albeit not always happily. Eliot's women are especially distinctive and individualistic. Even if some are showy and superficial at first, they all tend to succumb to some form of inward-looking profundity. Such is the case, at any rate, with the following heroines and their stories: the vain and selfish Hetty Sorrel in *Adam Bede* (1859), who gets seduced by the wrong man and becomes an accused infanticide; the audacious but ultimately ill-fated Maggie Tulliver in *The Mill on the Floss* (1860); the refined but often frivolous Esther in *Felix Holt* (1866), who falls in love with Felix in a remarkable volte-face which marks her middle-class capacity for reflection and change; the idealist and essentially good Dorothea Brooke in *Middlemarch* (1872), who eventually marries the right man and secures a reasonably romantic and happy denouement; and the assertive and self-centred Gwendolen Harleth in *Daniel Deronda* (1876), who is initially caught up in a disastrous marriage to a bad man, Henleigh Grandcourt, from which she is freed by the fluke of his drowning in Italy. Generally confused by, or in conflict with, the patriarchal codes of society at the start of the novels, Eliot's women either conform to social 'realities' or remain at variance with them by the end; either way, it is their tales of individual growth and development which are foregrounded in the novels. That the novels also appear to take a panoramic perspective on the sociopolitical and economic realities facing Victorian Britain, that their scope and depth enable Eliot to assume a God-like knowledge of everyone and everything, only underlines what remains the essentially middle-class versions of the realities they depict. Such a perspective enables Eliot to speak both with the collective moral 'voice' of Victorian society and in the intimate tone of a knowing individual – the narrator – confiding to another 'individual' – the reader – about the fraught lives of all the various individuals concerned. As a result, the social and political concerns of the novels are always, one way or another, understood from the perspective of individuals, or in terms of the way they impact on individuals.

The struggle of the individual to accommodate his or her self to society is the most prominent theme in fiction throughout the period.

Even towards the end of the century, for example, in the far more pessimistic outlook of Thomas Hardy's novels, Hardy repeatedly draws attention to a series of conflicts in which individuals are embroiled: town and countryside, upper class and lower class, man and woman, faith and faithlessness. Hardy's novels all appeared in the aftermath of Darwin's theories of evolution in *On the Origin of Species* (1859), and time and again his work reflects on the anxieties provoked by the Victorians' consciousness that they lived in a potentially Godless and Darwinian world. His series of doomed individuals all seem condemned, therefore, to the complex and contradictory mix of uncertainty and fatal survivalism these anxieties created: Tess Durbeyfield in *Tess of the D'Urbervilles* (1891), for example, is raped and hanged, and Jude Fawley in *Jude the Obscure* (1895) marries badly and dies penniless in a hovel. These are individuals who are continually at the mercy of both a natural order and a society which are as ruthlessly competitive as they are cold and indifferent.

The *fin-de-siècle* sense of world-weary cynicism and dissatisfaction with Victorian attitudes and values signified by Hardy's novels is not peculiar to his work. It is also central to George Gissing's novels of struggle and survival, such as *New Grub Street* (1891), which was published in the same year as *Tess of the D'Urbervilles*, and in the more decadent milieu of Oscar Wilde's only novel *The Picture of Dorian Gray* (1891), with its fading aristocrats and overarching sense of fatigue. Later Victorian novels also tend to reflect more consciously on Britain's expanding world role. In the context of the 'Scramble for Africa' campaigns and especially the Boer Wars (1880–1, 1899–1902), and in a climate of increasing concern about questions of nationalism and empire leading up to Victoria's death in 1901, a number of novels were published with a colonial or imperial theme. Popular titles included H. Rider Haggard's *King Solomon's Mines* (1886) and *She* (1887), both set in Africa, and Rudyard Kipling's *The Jungle Book* (1894), set in India. Joseph Conrad's brace of novels, *The Nigger of the 'Narcissus'* (1897), set between Bombay and London, and *Heart of Darkness* (1902) , set in Africa, were equally popular. Although this broader historical picture is important to bear in mind, some recent commentators, such as Daniel Bivona, have dispensed altogether with what he calls the 'invisible wall' in Victorian studies between the 'domestic novel' and the 'imperial novel'. It is, indeed, with this in mind that we must recognize that Victorian fiction throughout the period is both *of* and *about* Britain and its empire, at all times.

• • •

Much like the novel, Victorian poetry is marked by the fragmentary nature of its themes and preoccupations, and there is no quintessential 'Victorian poem'. Like the novels, though, much of the poetry of the period is also concerned with examining the individual's sense of uncertainty and doubt in the face of a complex and chaotic world, as illustrated by a famous line from Alfred Lord Tennyson's *In Memoriam* (1850): 'I falter where I firmly trod'. Other poems deal with far less grandiose themes. Some, as in the realist novel, subject the minutiae of everyday life and a range of seemingly mundane objects and events to the poet's scrutiny. Objects such as soap, snow, dead dogs, onions, tobacco and chairs all feature in Victorian poems. Similarly, as with Eliot's novels, Tennyson's *In Memoriam* – a poem ostensibly about the death of his friend Arthur Hallam – appears to deal with everyone and everything at once. Its daunting length, in fact, like the Victorian novel, makes it seem stretched in an audacious attempt to accommodate the sheer volume and scale of Victorian experience. In a revealing comment on this point, Tennyson himself remarked of his contemporary Robert Browning: 'His new poem has 15,000 lines: there's copiousness!' But Tennyson was a fine one to talk, and his popular poems, such as *In Memoriam* (1850), *Maud* (1855) and *Idylls of the King* (1859), are massive.

Tennyson was the third and most revered of Victoria's four poet laureates, and he remains very much the dominant figure in Victorian poetry. Indeed, his appointment to the laureateship in 1850 followed the tenure of two fading Romantics, Robert Southey (1813–43) and William Wordsworth (1843–50), neither of whom appears to have achieved much in the way of establishing 'Victorian poetry' as a unique literary idiom. Wordsworth, arguably the greatest of the Romantic poets, had all but fallen silent by this time, although his demise seems to have given an added lustre to the rise of Tennyson. After Tennyson's death in 1892, the much ridiculed and widely unloved Alfred Austin assumed the laureateship, but only after the position was left vacant for four years while everyone mourned Tennyson. As part of his office, Austin wrote an ill-advised ode celebrating Britain's disastrous 'Jameson Raid' (1895–6) in South Africa, and a poem to commemorate the Queen's Jubilee in 1897, which only Victoria herself seems to have liked. A stinging critic of other poets himself, one of Austin's peers, W. B. Yeats, would later accuse him of being a mere 'monger of platitudes'.

Other Victorian poets, however, were frequently great innovators in terms of both the content and the form of their poetry. The dramatic monologue form, for example, is full of experiments with multiple subjectivities and emotional extremes. In Robert Browning's

'Porphyria's Lover' (1836), there is a disturbing mix of the sensuous and the sinister, in which the narrator lingers on the eroticized body of a murdered woman:

A thing to do, and all her hair
In one long yellow string I wound
Three times her little throat around
And strangled her.

As with the novel, there also emerged a diverse array of poetic themes and obsessions throughout the period. Victorian poets wanted, it seems, to discuss everything: industrialism, Chartism, radicalism, slavery, morality, immorality, love, war, satire, religion, atheism, agnosticism, decadence, aestheticism. There were, furthermore, a raft of poetic movements that came and went in the century, such as 'New Woman' poetry, working-class poetry, protest poetry, the socialist poetry associated with William Morris of the early 1890s and the imperialist verse of Rudyard Kipling in the same period. The many classic poetic forms were equally in abundance in the Victorian period, any list of which must comprise elegies, sonnets, ballads, hymns, pastorals, lyrics and odes. These were all extremely popular, as were the more eccentric and absurdist ideas and forms such as those used by Edward Lear in the *Book of Nonsense* (1846).

The Pre-Raphaelite Brotherhood (PRB) was another major artistic movement in the period, the poets of which were described by contemporaries as the 'fleshly school'. As one of the most influential and radical movements in poetry and art of the mid-Victorian period, the work of the PRB is characterized by its fealty to nature, its preoccupation with medievalism, and its fetish for sensuous, rose-lipped, tragic-looking women. Some it was so controversial, in fact, that due to Victorian rules about censorship it was all but excluded from one of the most popular contemporary anthologies of poetry, *The Golden Treasury of the Best Songs and Lyrical Poems in the English Language* (1861), a publication which also censored many other poems perceived to be in any way lurid or degenerate, such as those composed by the many poor and working-class poets who scribbled away throughout the century. Needless to say, most of those Victorian poets who did achieve fame and success, even publication, were drawn, as with the novelists, from the middle or upper echelons of Victorian society. Most of these, inevitably, were men.

• • •

As with its poetry, Victorian drama is generally given rather short shrift and is often treated as something of a less important genre in the period, and the single entry on drama in this section (as with the entry on poetry) is not in any way intended to repeat this marginalization. Rather, it is designed in such a way as to provide as full and detailed a discussion as possible, in the space permitted, of the changes and developments within nineteenth-century drama, while suggesting ways in which the reader might pursue his or her research further. For now, it is sufficient to point out that by far the most popular form of Victorian drama was melodrama. Melodrama, typically, was full of simplistic moral allegories, overdrawn good characters and unambiguous villains, and, like the majority of Victorian novels, it tended to reflect the dominant middle-class order of things. However, the many farces, pantomimes and burlesques also associated with the period often parodied middle-class values and attitudes, and especially its sacred institutions such as marriage.

Equally popular in the period were theatrical productions including social comedies and early adaptations of 'social problem' or 'industrial' novels. These ranged from John Walker's *The Factory Lad* (1832) and Douglas Jerrold's sister piece, *The Factory Girl* (1832), to Gilbert and Sullivan's light and comic 'Savoy Operas' of the 1880s such as *The Mikado* (1885), as well as later plays which dealt, like the novels, with the controversy surrounding the rise of the 'New Woman'. Critics seem to agree that although a night at the theatre was extremely popular with all classes in Victorian society (everyone from costermongers to Queen Victoria attended regularly), the only major developments in the thematic and structural aspects of nineteenth-century drama came towards the end of the century. Such developments emerged, most notably, in the controversial plays of Norwegian playwright Henrik Ibsen such as *A Doll's House* (1879), and in those of an Irishman, George Bernard Shaw, with works such as *Mrs Warren's Profession* (1894). These were more complex 'social problem' plays than the Victorians were generally used to, and they were, more importantly perhaps, full of unconventional 'new' women. The rhetoric of Shaw's plays, for example, champions the lower classes of society and the plight of women, and *Mrs Warren's Profession* deals with the always thorny problem of prostitution. Indeed, as with the novels and poems of the day, such plays draw much of their dramatic tension from contrasts between the ordered world of the stage itself, with its acts, scenes and stage directions, and the chaos and complexities of the lives they dramatize.

The decadent 1890s was also the period in which Oscar Wilde's plays dominated the London stage. Wilde's witty and urbane social comedies

generally pivot on guilty secrets of a sexual nature, and his famous paradoxes and epigrams became notorious for the way in which they repeatedly inverted Victorian norms and attitudes: 'I can resist everything
except temptation'. The same goes for his linguistic 'plays' upon words,
within 'plays', which have been interpreted as radical linguistic inversions of his homosexual 'inversions': 'Work is the curse of the drinking
classes'. In addition, there was the very real drama being played out in
Wilde's colourful life as the nation's most widely known aesthete and
homosexual, with his green carnations and lurid double existence as a
married man with children. His private life did, in fact, come to overshadow his literary career, and it eventually led to his downfall. During
a time when sodomy was still heavily punished by Victorian law, Wilde
was sentenced in 1895 to two years in prison for crimes 'against nature'.
He died, a broken man, in Paris in 1900, one year before Victoria died.

The following section attempts to capture some of the diversity,
energy and complexity of Victorian literature. While not being exhaus-
tive, it provides entries on many of the more (and less) well-known
genres and sub-genres, such as Children's Literature, Sensation Fiction
and Social-Problem Novels, as well as one on what contemporaries
considered to be lower or more degraded publications, Penny Dreadfuls.
'Non-fictional Prose' offers an introduction to another equally diverse
and complex set of writings in the period. This entry includes discussions of the work of the many religious, scientific and political commentators and essayists who appeared in the period (including authors such
as Benjamin Disraeli, who wrote as both politician and novelist). It also
discusses the range of periodical publications which became increasingly available and popular as the century progressed, including week-
lies, quarterlies, reviews, the rise of the daily papers, and the many
magazines mass-marketed for the masses.

Children's Literature

The Victorian age from the 1860s onwards is widely thought to be the
first 'Golden Age' of children's literature. With the expansion of literacy
in the period and the development of more sophisticated print and
publishing technologies, the Victorian readership increased, as did the
sheer number of books available for children. Child literacy was further
encouraged after the Education Act (1870) had made free elementary
education compulsory. While children's books became more and more
lavishly illustrated, by the 1850s they had also begun to offer children
pleasures beyond moral and religious instruction, although typically
Victorian controversies over the 'purpose' of children's literature

lingered throughout the century. Under the ever-watchful eye of the Religious Tract Society, for example, an organization which published 'improving' children's books, the censorship of more 'disreputable' children's books continued apace. In the mean time, influential commentators such as John Ruskin in his essay, 'Fairy Stories' (1868), began to voice fears that some children's literature, particularly that of an overly didactic nature, might actually disturb what he called 'the sweet peace of youth'.

Children's literature is dominated by adult writers and publishers, and it is the genre in which the power relationship between text and reader is at its most pronounced. Literature for children consequently had an ideological influence on its readership early on, and it was central to the cultivation of Victorian ideas and attitudes. Nonetheless, the genre is as complex and varied as changing ideas about childhood itself in the period. Popular late works such as Hilaire Belloc's *A Bad Child's Book of Beasts* (1896), for example, continued to caution against the perils of disobeying figures of authority, especially parents, and being naughty in general. Other works, on the other hand, while still part of the Victorian cult of domesticity and family, such as fairy tales, with their countless bad parents and even worse step-parents, are full of rebellions against authority figures. There was also considerable dispute throughout the century, in both children's literature and society in general, over whether or not children were inherently good or inherently bad. In stern and moribund early-century children's books such as Mary Martha Sherwood's *The History of the Fairchild Family* (1818), the narrator brooks little disagreement on this issue from the outset: 'All children are by nature evil'. But the Victorians also inherited and then modified a more Romantic conception of childhood, which perceived children in now familiar terms as innocent, pure, vulnerable, and so on. As the century wore on, childhood came to represent humanity in its most natural and prelapsarian, that is to say unfallen and unerotic, state; it began to embody a nostalgia for humanity's youth in all its wild but uncorrupt, and by extension preindustrial, glory, after which adulthood became something of a fall. This growing ideology of 'natural' innocence is suggested by two contemporary reviews of the state of children's literature. In 1844, Elizabeth Rigby claimed that the 'secret' of the good children's book lies, like the children themselves, in its being more 'true to nature', whereas Charles Dickens, in his article, 'Frauds on the Fairies' (1853), argued that 'In an utilitarian age' fairy tales need to be preserved because of 'their usefulness' to society, but above all for their 'simplicity, and purity, and innocent extravagance'.

A series of forms and sub-genres such as fairy tales, folklore, fables, nursery rhymes and legends were all popular with children throughout the nineteenth century. Similarly, landmark texts such as *Robinson Crusoe* (1719) and *The Arabian Nights* (first translated into English *c.*1704–17) continued to be widely read, the former providing many children with their first colonial allegory, the latter offering them their first impressions of the East. Significant early works of Victorian children's literature included Catherine Sinclair's *Holiday House* (1839), with its gentle critiques of conventional morality and slightly bad children, and the famous fairy tales of the Brothers Grimm and Hans Christian Andersen which were already in translation by 1823 and 1846, respectively. By mid-century, many 'adult'-oriented Victorian writers and novelists had begun writing children's literature. Titles included John Ruskin's *The King of the Golden River* (1850), William Makepeace Thackeray's burlesque fairy tale of Christmas, *The Rose and the Ring* (1855), and Christina Rossetti's sensuous and ambiguous fairy-tale poem, *Goblin Market* (1862). Charles Kingsley's *The Water Babies* (1863) combined fantasy with a critique of the very realistic plight of chimney sweeps, as well as introducing sisters with allegorical names such as Mrs Doasyouwouldbedoneby and Mrs Bedonebyasyoudid, and towards the end of the century, Oscar Wilde published his sentimental fairy stories, *The Happy Prince and Other Tales* (1888). Around mid-century, a major change of tone to a more nonsensical, slightly anarchic children's literature was indicated by the publication of Edward Lear's popular limerick collection, *Book of Nonsense*, in 1846, while other works of the period parodied the dryness and cautionary nature of the morality and sentimental tales, such as Heinrich Hoffman's *Struwwelpeter* (translated 1848).

For many critics, however, the 1860s remain the 'Golden Age' of children's literature, the decade of Lewis Carroll's *Alice's Adventures in Wonderland* (1865). The publication of the *Alice* tales was momentous largely because they seem to have heralded the most significant retreat from Victorian realities into ever-deeper realms of fantasy and nonsense. In Wonderland, Carroll presented an alternative and quite literally 'underground' Victorian society. His nether world was nonsensical, illogical, irrational, unrealistic, chaotic, and because of this either fundamentally un-Victorian or quintessentially Victorian, depending on one's standpoint, in its overarching picture of a world full of mad and purposeless individuals. Carroll's stories are marked by an underlying struggle for meaning and a mischievous questioning of Victorian moral certainties in which the 'truths' of the adult world are no longer secure. They are, in this respect, products of an age of scientific scepticism, the evolutionary ideas of Charles Darwin and what at least one commentator has described as the 'disappearance of God'. Elsewhere, the period also gave rise to the essentially conservative and ethical 'schooldays novel', such as Thomas Hughes's influential *Tom Brown's Schooldays* (1857), and sentimental 'good girl' books such as Charlotte Yonge's *The Daisy Chain* (1856), Maria Elizabeth Charlesworth's *The Rambles of a Rat* (1857), and the American Louisa May Alcott's *Little Women* (1868), which was slightly more critical about the nineteenth-century role assigned to young women. Also popular were Anna Sewell's soppy *Black Beauty* (1877), Frances Hodgson Burnett's fairy tale of class relations, *Little Lord Fauntleroy* (1886), and poetry such as Robert Louis Stevenson's *A Child's Garden of Verses* (1885).

Towards the end of the period, when British society had become more and more imbued with a culture of imperialism, jingoism and racism (the 'Golliwog' caricatures first appeared around 1895), a series of masculine and heroic adventure stories for boys also began to flourish. Popular titles included the prolific G. A. Henty's *The Young Buglers* (1880) and *St George for England* (1885), and Rudyard Kipling's empire tales for children, *The Jungle Book* (1894) and *Kim* (1901). 'Robinsonnades' (adventure stories and colonial allegories in the vein of Robinson Crusoe) were also still popular, such as Robert Louis Stevenson's *Treasure Island* (1883) and R. M. Ballantyne's earlier *The Coral Island* (1857), while the maritime adventures of Captain Marryat's *Masterman Ready* (1841-2) remained perennial favourites. Wholesome and hearty magazines for boys also thrived in the period, such as the unequivocally-named, if short-lived, *Boys of the Empire* (established 1888), as did a series of comics and publications such as the *Boy's Own Magazine* (established 1855). For girls, typically, there was the sister section to the *Boy's Own Paper* (1879) (published in the same issue), the distinctly unadventurous and unheroic *Girl's Own Paper* (established 1880), which was produced by the Religious Tract Society and full of household advice and needlework tips. Other notable children's authors of the later period published their most famous work in the early twentieth century, and consequently their values and attitudes were rooted in both late Victorianism and the new century. These include Beatrix Potter, whose first successful story, *The Tale of Peter Rabbit*, was begun in the early 1890s and published in the year of Victoria's death, Kenneth Grahame's hugely successful allegory of class and gender anxieties, *Wind in the Willows* (1908); and J. M. Barrie's equally popular fantasy about never growing up, *Peter Pan* (1911), which was first performed as a play in 1904.

See also *Contexts*: Childhood, Family: *Texts*: Penny dreadfuls: *Criticism*: Feminism, Marxism, Psychoanalysis, Structuralism.

Further Reading

Hunt, Peter, *An Introduction to Children's Literature* (Oxford and New York: Oxford University Press, 1994).

Kutzer, Daphne M., *Empire's Children: Empire and Imperialism in Classic British Children's Books* (New York: Garland, 2000).

Crime Fiction

The rise of crime fiction in the nineteenth century coincided with the development of Britain as a modern police state. Robert Peel's Metropolitan Police Act (1829) put a visible police force on the nation's streets for the first time in the 1830s, in the first decade of Victoria's reign; the establishment of a plain-clothes Detective Office in 1842 led to 800 police detectives around the country by the 1880s and the increasing respectability of the detective as 'professional'; and by 1878 there was a CID unit in New Scotland Yard. Victorian crime fiction consequently grew out of a modern bureaucratic state and a culture of discipline and surveillance. Its roots lie partly in the infamous 'Newgate prison' novels, which themselves grew out of a climate of radicalism, reform and Chartist disorder in the late 1820s–30s. These novels took their inspiration, however, not so much from the notorious London prison itself as *The Newgate Calendar* (1773), otherwise known as the *Malefactor's Bloody Register*, a publication which gave romanticized and often sensational accounts of true eighteenth-century crimes and criminals. Popular works in this sub-genre included Edward Bulwer Lytton's *Paul Clifford* (1830), in which the title hero becomes a highwayman, and two of William Harrison Ainsworth's novels, both of which also have a 'highwayman' theme. Ainsworth's *Rookwood* (1834) deals with Dick Turpin, and *Jack Sheppard* (1839), which was thought to have influenced the murderer of Lord William Russell in 1840, was criticized for its romantic sympathy for the criminal. A more famous work which is equally full of crime and villainy (and early policemen), Charles Dickens's *Oliver Twist* (1837), was also partly influenced by the 'Newgate novel', and indeed Fagin spends his last nights within the 'dreadful walls of Newgate' itself. But Dickens was at pains to point out in the preface to *Oliver Twist* that works such as *Paul Clifford* had no 'bearing' on his own, and critics have argued that this is presumably because they were deemed to be 'low' literature. Equally frowned upon, but popular, was the life of crime and violence portrayed by some of the period's newspapers, magazines and 'penny dreadfuls', such as G. W. M. Reynolds's long-running *Mysteries of London* (1845–55). This series, as with the Newgate novels, comprised largely sensationalized stories of horrific true crime.

There was plenty of controversy in the period over whether or not the subject matter of crime fiction debased its readership. In 1837, for example, Lord Melbourne told Queen Victoria herself that he thought *Oliver Twist* was 'low'. But just as policemen and detectives became more visible and respectable in society, so crime fiction became more acceptable and popular as a genre. In a culture of growing anxieties about crime, the detective figure steadily became an increasingly middle-class hero of order and resolution. Preoccupied as they were with finding observable truths, like scientists and doctors, detectives had the authority to solve life's mysteries and restore meaning where 'meaning' was absent. The narrative logic of most Victorian crime fiction is, in this respect, structured around a movement from enigma to resolution, in terms of the discovery of the crime, the disclosure of the 'true identity' of the criminal, and so on. There would, of course, be little point to crime fiction if the perpetrator was revealed on the second page. What such logic contrives, though, is a happy ending in which the laws of society eventually overcome the disruptive desires of the individual criminal. In other words, the ideological form of crime fiction necessitates a denouement which is always a solution, always a restoration of the Victorian order of things. Crime fiction thrills by revealing the facts slowly. In doing so, it cultivates the reader's desire for meaning, in which the trail of clues left by the work yield to the satisfying closure of truth.

Victorian crime fiction developed from a focus on the criminal in the early nineteenth century, to an increasing concentration on the detective. A private sleuth of sorts called Mr Nadgett emerges, for example, in Dickens's *Martin Chuzzlewit* (1843), and Inspector Bucket in *Bleak House* (1853) is often credited with being the first proper detective in Victorian fiction. Other commentators claim that the first modern detective story proper, however, is American Edgar Allen Poe's *The Murders in the Rue Morgue* (1841), with its detective C. Auguste Dupin and his 'peculiar analytic ability'. Even Arthur Conan Doyle acknowledges Poe's influence on that most legendary and well-loved of Victorian detectives, Sherlock Holmes. As Dr Watson puts it, in the first Holmes story, *A Study in Scarlet* (1887): 'It is simple enough as you explain it [Holmes had just deduced, on their first meeting, that Dr Watson has been away in Afghanistan]. You remind me of Edgar Allan Poe's Dupin.' Otherwise, Wilkie Collins's *The Moonstone* (1868), with its story of the theft of a priceless Indian diamond and the subsequent investigations of Sergeant Cuff, is widely regarded as being the first English detective novel, and as the century progressed Andrew Forrester published the first female detective novel, *The Female Detective* (1864). This book, along with others such as W. Stephens Hayward's *The Experiences of a Lady Detective* (1864), published in the same year, seems also to have anticipated the 'New Woman' fiction of the later period.

From the 1870s onwards, crime fiction became increasingly popular, and it seems to have left its murkier origins in the criminal-centred 'Newgate novels' far behind. By the 1880s, the man who would become Britain's most famous detective ever was at once a charismatic individual, a cultured intellectual, a scholar of criminology with a complex, vaguely bohemian status, and a violin player who took cocaine while mulling over his mysteries. In the omniscient figure of Sherlock Holmes, in fact, the shift of focus in nineteenth-century crime fiction from criminal to detective became complete, and the last decades of the period are dominated by Arthur Conan Doyle's pipe-smoking legend. Doyle was not modest about his achievements, either in the Holmes stories or in real life. When, for example, Holmes first appears in *A Study in Scarlet* (1887), he immediately attacks his popular, notably French, literary predecessors, as if trumpeting his own rise to prominence as the all-conquering English hero of the genre. Poe's Dupin, for example, is written off as 'showy and superficial', while Émile Gaboriau's Lecoq – another detective thought to have been influenced by Dupin – is little more than a 'miserable bungler'. That such a well-loved individual as Sherlock Holmes, in an age of individualism, could sell as many books as Doyle did, from *The Adventures of Sherlock* Holmes (1892) onwards, and that the rise of crime fiction in general would become so lucrative in the period, is summed up in Doyle's memoirs. There he discusses the marketable allure of individualism and crime: 'It struck me that a single character running through a series, if it only engaged the attention of the reader, would bind that reader to that particular magazine.' Furthermore, in a period which also saw the emergence of dubious sciences such as Havelock Ellis's 'criminal anthropology', or more reputable ones such as forensics, Holmes brings the century to a close as a reassuring figure who combines detective ingenuity with a somewhat awe-inspiring knowledge of the sciences. Holmes's methods are essentially those of a doctor who administers to society's ills. He ensures that the business of detecting crime becomes – in Doyle's own words – an 'exact science' in which, time after time, order is restored.

See also *Contexts*: Crime and punishment, Law, Violence; *Texts*: Penny dreadfuls, Sensation fiction; *Criticism*: Poststructuralism.

Further Reading

Knight, Stephen, *Crime Fiction: Detection, Death, Diversity* (Basingstoke: Palgrave Macmillan, 2004).

Worthington, Heather, *The Rise of the Detective in Early Nineteenth-Century Popular Fiction* (Basingstoke: Palgrave Macmillan, 2005).

Drama

In 1879, Matthew Arnold claimed that 'In England . . . we have no modern drama at all'. And, yet, Victorian drama flourished. Some 3000 playwrights emerged in the period (only a fraction of whom were women), a variety of different performances were on offer, and nights at the theatre were extremely popular with people from all classes. Queen Victoria was an avid theatre-goer herself, and she bestowed her valuable patronage on many plays, even though in 1855 she was accused by a famous actor of the day, Charles Keane, of enjoying 'farce and rubbish better than the high class drama'.

Unlike those of the Regency and earlier periods, and despite some rowdy elements, audiences at Victorian theatres generally seem to have been less unruly in the period, and the Victorians are widely credited with ensuring that a 'night at the play' became respectable entertainment. The London theatres of the 1860s were still, however, somewhat grubby affairs, and one critic, John Holingshead, said they reeked of 'escaped gas, orange peel' and 'tom-cats', while another smelled nightly of 'fish'. Similarly, complaints about 'disreputable' productions were received from the various moral and religious quarters of Victorian society. Many patrons continued to take umbrage at the prostitutes who worked the foyers and forecourts of the West End theatre district, especially Drury Lane, Covent Garden and the Haymarket, and Victorian actresses were often treated with the same contempt by public opinion as prostitutes. Even the architecture of British theatres in the nineteenth century reflected and upheld Victorian preoccupations with status and class. With their all too visible hierarchy of boxes, galleries and pits, theatres were designed in such a way that upper-class patrons did not have to mingle with those in the cheap seats, and the Victorians were obsessed with ascertaining which social class attended which kind of play.

Drama was also at the mercy of economic booms and slumps in the period. However, although many theatres suffered irreparable financial loss and closure as a result of depressions, the theatre did gradually became more prosperous as the century wore on. After the hardships of the 'hungry forties', by the 1860s British theatre building underwent something of a renaissance. By 1899, there were over 60 theatres in London alone, with over 200 or so more scattered throughout the country, and the new railways brought patrons in from the provinces to swell the already large city audiences. Throughout the period, productions were at the mercy of the Lord Chamberlain, a man who, thanks to the work of his Examiner of Plays, would issue licences and censor plays considered unsuitable or radical in any way. Otherwise, early on in Victoria's reign, important legislation such as the Theatre Regulation Act of 1843 enabled all theatres, for the first time, to perform what was then deemed to be 'legitimate' or 'spoken' drama, such as tragedy and comedy. Better stage technologies, meanwhile, also became available to Victorian playwrights and performers. Particular innovations were the replacement of candlelight with gaslight and the first use of limelight. The Victorians were, indeed, exuberant stage designers. Many performances were decorated with lavish sets and props, including boats and shipwrecks for the 'nautical' melodramas, or volcanoes for 'natural disaster' melodramas, and there was often a menagerie of animals on hand. Such embellishments served the Victorian audience's lust for action and spectacle, and created as much an atmosphere of 'reality' on stage as possible.

That Victorian drama was, in the main, preoccupied with portraying 'reality', was problematic for some contemporary dramatists. In the 'Decay of Lying' (1889), a piece of writing that bemoans the ascendancy of Victorian realism and the triumph of 'truth' in general, Oscar Wilde criticized what he perceived to be the dreariness of that most enduring and popular form of Victorian theatre, melodrama: 'And yet how wearisome the plays are. They do not [even] succeed in producing that impression of reality at which they own . . . '. Frequently subversive, Wilde, as with many aesthetic writers and intellectuals, argued that melodrama, in particular, and drama, in general, like all art, should not be reduced to the function of faithfully representing 'reality'. As he maintains in 'The Decay of Lying', 'the object of art is not simple truth but complex beauty', which underlines his point that drama should serve no purpose – social, ethical or otherwise – other than the glory of its own fleeting splendour. Nowadays, however, and despite Wilde's efforts, a large proportion of Victorian drama is construed as essentially a conservative sop to middle-class 'truths' and 'reality'. It is with this point in mind that it becomes easier to understand the radical significance of Wilde's ideas, which, by attacking Victorian attitudes to the role of art, were essentially an attack on the Victorian order of things itself. Although, for example, the fairly straightforward escapism provided by Victorian melodrama was hardly 'realistic' in the mundane or everyday sense, being full, as it was, of vivid emotions, adventure, sensation, violence, last-minute reprieves, volcanoes, Gothic set-pieces and supernatural settings, it also consisted of chaste women, spotless heroes, and class allegories of wicked aristocrats abusing the virtuous poor, where complications are resolved by clear and simplistic moral resolutions. Some productions, on the other hand, lampooned Victorian marital restrictions. Pantomimes railed against the idea of authority; burlesques offered parodies and satires on contemporary moralities; and comedies and farces indulged in chaotic social problems of sexual desire and class. Nonetheless, come the final curtain, most Victorian audiences went home with their dramas sweetened by happy endings, in which a 'realistic' order was generally restored with considerable pathos and sentiment.

Victorian drama is diverse and voluminous. It comprises a range of genres, including the ever-popular melodramas, serious or 'problem' theatre, comedy, renderings of Shakespeare, dramatic readings of Alfred Lord Tennyson's poetry, adaptations of the work of famous novelists such as Walter Scott and Charles Dickens, pantomime, farce, burlesque, extravaganzas, harlequinades, opera and music hall. Victorian drama embraces repertory theatre, touring companies, itinerant troops or 'strollers', booth theatres, as well as companies which took their performances across the world and into the empire. Particularly popular plays included Douglas Jerrold's nautical melodrama, *Black-Ey'd Susan* (1829), social comedies such as Edward Bulwer Lytton's *Money* (1840), the prolific Dion Boucicault's *The Corsican Brothers* (1852), John Maddison Morton's hugely successful farce *Box and Cox* (1847), and Tom Taylor's *The Ticket of Leave Man* (1863). There were also performances of 'social problem' or 'industrial' plays, such as John Walker's *The Factory Lad* (1832) and Jerrold's *The Factory Girl* (1832), Sheridan Knowles's 'family' dramas such as *The Daughter* (1836), Westland Marston's poetic drama, *The Patrician's Daughter* (1842), and Robert Browny's complex and unsuccessful historical dramas such as *Strafford* (1837) and *A Blot in the 'Scutcheon* (1843). By the mid-1860s, there were a range of largely reactionary middle-class comedies treading the boards, such as H. J. Byron's *The Lancashire Lass, or Tempted, Tried, and True* (1867) and Thomas Robertson's *Society* (1865). Gilbert and Sullivan's light and satirical 'Savoy Operas', including *Iolanthe* (1882) *The Mikado* (1885) and *The Gondolier* (1889), achieved massive runs towards the end of the period, and W. S. Gilbert even found time to compose mildly subversive and ironic 'fairy' comedies such as *The Palace of Truth* (1870) and *Engaged* (1877).

The *fin de siècle* period also gave rise to the hugely successful high-society comedies of Oscar Wilde. Wilde's most popular plays, *Lady Windermere's Fan* (1892), *A Woman of No Importance* (1893), *An Ideal Husband* (1895) and *The Importance of Being Earnest* (1895), all pivot on guilty secrets and indiscretions, generally of a sexual nature, and many commentators have interpreted Wilde's witty epigrams and paradoxes as subverting Victorian attitudes. His sensuous and bloody *Salomé* (1894), on the other hand, in which Salomé desires to kiss the severed head of Jokanaan, was deemed to have gone too far, and the play was refused a licence by the Lord Chamberlain. Around the same time, there were other popular plays in circulation, some more controversial than others, including Henry Arthur Jones's *Saint and Sinners* (1884), his melodrama, *The Dancing Girl* (1891), Arthur Wing Pinero's farces and satirical comedies such as *Trelawny of the 'Wells'* (1898), and his serious 'social' plays about the 'New Woman', *Lady Bountiful* (1891) and *The Second Mrs Tanqueray* (1893). Indeed, in response to anxieties about women's rights and the rise of the so-called 'New Woman' in the period, numerous other plays sprang up, such as Elizabeth Robins's *Alan's Wife* (1893) and Sidney Grundy's unambiguously named comedy, *The New Woman* (1894). By the 1880s, the revolutionary influence of Norwegian playwright Henrik Ibsen proved to be the turning point in Victorian drama. In plays such as *A Doll's House* (1879), *Ghosts* (1881) and *Hedda Gabler* (1890), which were construed by many British critics at the time as morally dubious, often degenerate, Ibsen had composed avant-garde tragedies of modern domestic life which were full of unconventional women and resistant to happy endings. Another late-century playwright whose work was heavily indebted to Ibsen's, George Bernard Shaw, also wrote witty and subversive 'social problem' plays, such as *Widowers' Houses* (1892), *The Devil's Disciple* (1897) and *Mrs Warren's Profession* (1898). These, however, with their manifesto-like prefaces, were frequently censored by the Victorians, and Shaw's 'socialist' dramas only achieved real recognition in the early Edwardian period. By way of response to his censure, Shaw criticized Victorian drama for its lack of a basis in social reality, and he lambasted the social order in general for its oppression of the lower classes and women. It is in this respect that his plays look forward, in various complex ways, to the changing moral and social attitudes which heralded the new century.

See also   *Contexts*: Decadence and aestheticism.

Further Reading

Booth, Michael R., *Theatre in the Victorian Age* (Cambridge: Cambridge University Press, 1991).

Historical Novel

Defining the Victorian historical novel is more problematic than might be thought, and the term should be approached with caution. George

Eliot's *Middlemarch* (1872), for example, is not recognized as being a 'historical novel' as such, even though it is set some 40 years prior to the novel's publication, during the passage of the important first Reform Bill (1832). Equally, Charlotte Brontë's *Shirley* (1849) is generally described as an 'industrial novel', rather than an 'historical novel', despite the fact that it is also set several decades back during the Luddite Riots (1811–12). Nonetheless, the Victorian historical novel did evolve as a fairly distinct, if somewhat multifarious, genre, which dealt with major historical events that were often, but by no means exclusively, set centuries before the publication of the novel. The major characteristics of the genre were established early on in the nineteenth century. Irish novelist Maria Edgeworth's account of eighteenth-century Ireland in *Castle Rackrent* (1800) is often credited with being the first historical novel, although her work came to be overshadowed by the wildly popular and influential work of Scottish writer, Walter Scott. Scott's action-packed romances, including *Waverley* (1814) set in the Jacobite Rebellions of 1745, *Rob Roy* (1817) set just before the Jacobite Rebellions with a Scottish clansman as the title hero, and *Ivanhoe* (1819) set in the crusades, spawned countless Victorian imitators. Later novelists relished Scott's historical sweep and the derring-do of his heroes, as well as his tendency, on a formal level, to provide neat narrative resolutions to the chaos of history. It is thought, altogether, that over a thousand historical novels were written in the nineteenth century (although they were not all published or very successful). Combined, they cover just about every period of history from the first century onwards. Many contemporary critics seem, however, to have been somewhat underwhelmed by the genre, while others working in the publishing business quietly admitted that some of the stories were both less lucrative and less riveting than they might have been. A writer in *The Saturday Review* (1858), for example, claimed that 'The objection to historical romance is that so few men are fit to write it', and in one incident, Anthony Trollope was taken to one side by his publishers, before they accepted his manuscript of *The Three Clerks* (1857), and asked, 'I hope it's not historical Mr Trollope?'

The historical novel blurs fiction into history, and vice versa, in a period in which the distinctions between the two concepts were unstable. Indeed, as if to underline this point, Oscar Wilde described Thomas Carlyle's popular historical work, *A History of the French Revolution* (1837), as 'the greatest novel of the nineteenth century'. The implications of Wilde's seemingly paradoxical, albeit playful comment, are twofold: they draw attention to the historical nature of fiction writing and, less obviously but more controversially perhaps, the fictional

nature of history writing. That the Victorians shared a complex relationship to history is also evidenced by the fact the historical novels themselves were and are frequently read as allegories of the Victorian
present. The historical upheavals and major events they depict reflect on
the fact that the Victorians presided over huge historical transformations
themselves, namely the end of the agricultural age and the rise of industrial modernity. Yet for such a forward-looking nation – one described in
1834 by contemporary historian Thomas Babington Macaulay as being
bound to a 'history of progress' – this begs the question: why is it that
the Victorians were so obsessed with turning over the past in the first
place? At least part of the answer lies in the Victorians' obsession with
class and national identity. At the same time, for example, that Britain
was becoming increasingly dominated by middle-class ideologies, their
preoccupation with the mediaeval and Gothic periods intensified. Many
earlier historical novels of the nineteenth century, in this respect, such
as Scott's *Ivanhoe*, evoke nostalgia for a lost, preindustrial world of
knights, maidens and servants, in which one's social-economic and
sexual status, indeed the whole balance of power in British society, were
more easily defined. Others re-enact a British history which was full of
blood and mayhem, especially in terms of the nation's many wars with
the Catholic French and Spanish.

The violent memory of historical novels had important sociopolitical
and cultural implications. Most obviously, it helped create and consolidate a unified sense of a largely Protestant British nation which had
defined itself for centuries – largely against the French and Spanish – as
a pragmatic nation of fighters, doers and triumphant heroes. Similarly,
the historical novelist's attempt to excavate 'timeless' truths about
Britishness from the past, in an age haunted by ideas about evolution
and crises of religious faith, points to the Victorians' desire to restore
faith in themselves as the rational, if rarely peaceful, historically
ordained leaders of world civilization. It is in this way that the anxieties
of the past recorded by historical novels had such an important bearing
on the anxieties of the present. Historical novels enabled the Victorians
to look forward by looking back, so that the past remained an
inescapable fact of the present. In doing so, the presentness of the past
invoked by the novels endowed the Victorians with the substance of
historical meaning and the legitimacy provided by a collective national
memory.

The historical novel is a complex and hybrid form made up of various
genres: Gothic, romance, satire, tragedy, farce, melodrama, realism, to
name only some. Early titles included G. P. R. James's *Henry Masterton:
Or, The Adventures of a Young Cavalier* (1832), set during England's

bloody Civil War, and Harrison Ainsworth's Gothic 'Newgate prison' novels about eighteenth-century criminals such as *Jack Sheppard* (1839), although Ainsworth also wrote Tudor escapades, such as *The Tower of London* (1840) and *Windsor Castle* (1843). Later in the century, he further revived Scott's Jacobite tales, with uncomplex titles such as *The Good Old Times: the Story of the Manchester Rebels of the Fatal '45* (1873), as did Robert Louis Stevenson, more successfully, in *Kidnapped* (1886) and *The Master of Ballantrae* (1889). Other early writers such as Edward Bulwer Lytton delved even further back in history to the ancient Roman Empire. In books such as *The Last Days of Pompeii* (1834), Bulwer Lytton attempted work of dense and epic proportions that he thought was appropriate for a modern British Empire, before turning to the rise and fall of other Britons in *The Last of the Barons* (1843) and *Harold, the Last of the Saxon Kings* (1848). A much later work, Walter Pater's *Marius the Epicurean* (1885), also returned to the Romans, but this 'philosophical romance' is more of an indulgent, and somewhat controversial, *fin de siècle* essay in aestheticism and decadence.

Many popular Victorian novelists also tried their hands at historical novels. Anthony Trollope, for example, set *La Vendée* (1850) in the aftermath of the French Revolution, as did Charles Dickens in *A Tale of Two Cities* (1859), although Dickens's novel is often interpreted as a response to the violence of empire carried out in the Indian Mutiny of 1857 as well. Dickens also projected the violence of the 1830s–40s Chartist troubles back into his earlier historical novel, *Barnaby Rudge* (1841), another cautionary tale which deals with the anti-Catholic 'Gordon' riots of 1780, and indeed both of his historical novels portray contemporary anxieties towards the working classes and the ever-present threat of mob violence. Elizabeth Gaskell's *Sylvia's Lovers* (1863), on the other hand, is a Napoleonic romance haunted by the press-gang; Renaissance Florence is the setting for George Eliot's *Romola* (1862–3); and William Makepeace Thackeray's ironic and unheroic *Barry Lyndon* (1852) is set in the Seven Years War (1756–63), during a series of conflicts between the major European powers in Europe and the colonies. Elsewhere in Thackeray's oeuvre, *Henry Esmond* (1852) is set in the Glorious Revolution (1688), against the backdrop of the Battle of the Boyne (1690) and the War of the Spanish Succession (1701–13), and *Vanity Fair* (1847) features the Battle of Waterloo (1815). Charles Reade's bizarre story of a man who proves to be the father of Erasmus, *The Cloister and the Hearth* (1861), was hugely popular, as were R. D. Blackmore's pro-Catholic account of an heroic late-seventeenth-century farmer caught up in a romance which crossed class boundaries, *Lorna Doone* (1869), and Thomas Hardy's Napeoleonic *The Trumpet Major* (1882), another provincial history concerned with the impact of historical events on everyday British lives.

In response to the Catholic Emancipation Edict of 1829, which exacerbated religious tensions in a predominantly Protestant Victorian Britain, another sub-genre of historical novels arose. Titles here include, most notably, John Newman's pro-Catholic allegory, *Callista* (1856), set in third-century North Africa, and an anti-Catholic antagonist to Newman's work, Charles Kingsley's *Hypatia* (1853), set in fifth-century Egypt during the last phase of the Roman Empire. The first Catholic Archbishop of Westminster's novel, *Fabiola: a Tale of the Catacombs* (1854), proved, however, to be successful across Britain's religious divides, as did William Hale White's later tale of religious dissent, *The Revolution in Tanner's Lane* (1887). Meanwhile, another of Kingsley's forays into historical fiction, *Westward Ho!* (1855), projects Britain's involvement in the Crimean War (1854–6) back onto the Elizabethan wars against the Catholic Spanish, while another still, *Hereward the Wake* (1866), is a romance which recounts the life of a Lincolnshire man who went up against William the Conqueror in 1060. Also significant are the 'Indian empire' historical novels of Philip Meadows Taylor, such as *Confessions of a Thug* (1839) and *Ralph Darnell* (1865), the latter being a fictional account of Robert Clive and the East India Company's expansion across India.

See also   *Contexts*: Empire and imperialism, Nation, Slavery, War; *Texts*: Crime fiction, Penny dreadfuls; *Criticism*: Deconstruction, Feminism, Marxism, New historicism/Cultural materialism.

Further Reading

Rance, Nicholas, *The Historical Novel and Popular Politics in Nineteenth-Century England* (London: Vision Press, 1975).

Sanders, Andrew, *The Victorian Historical Novel, 1840–1880* (Basingstoke: Macmillan, 1978).

Mid-Victorian Novel

The mid-Victorian period, sometimes described as the 'Victorian Noon-Time', was very productive for Victorian novelists. By the late 1840s to the early 1860s, those writers whose names would become synonymous with the age – Charles Dickens, the Brontë sisters, William Thackeray and George Eliot – were flourishing, novels were becoming ever more desirable commodities, and, thanks to the rise in literacy rates, more and more people were reading them. In 1870, Anthony Trollope even declared that 'We have become a novel-reading people'. But why did the Victorian novel peak, as many commentators argue it did, in this period? At least one of the reasons was developments in the publishing industry itself. This was the age of the rotary steam press, mechanical printing, and the serialization or part-issue of novels, all of which ensured that the needs of mass production and an increasingly consumerist society could be served more efficiently. At the same time, the growth of circulating libraries was also instrumental. Apart from the expensive subscription libraries and the 'mechanics' institutes', there were no public lending libraries in Britain until around mid-century, after which organizations such as Charles Mudie's 'guinea-a-volume' empire (established in 1842) sprang up everywhere.

The most significant reason, however, for the sheer quantity of novels published in the mid-Victorian years is the fact that they grew up in response to an historical period of unprecedented change and upheaval in the so-called 'hungry forties'. This period saw the intensification of the so-called 'Condition of England' crisis, which involved a series of socioeconomic problems and industrial crises: the expansion of free trade after the repeal of the Corn Laws in 1846, Chartist agitations for reform (late 1830s–40s), the Irish famine (c.1845–51), the railway boom (1840s), and a series of European-wide revolutions (1848). It is also no coincidence that revolutionary works such as Karl Marx and Frederich Engels's *Communist Manifesto* (1848) also appeared in the period. Furthermore, by the 1850s, following the celebration of British world supremacy in the Great Exhibition (1851) and the illusion of more prosperous times it promised, the Victorians became increasingly preoccupied with crises outside of the domestic context, in particular the Crimean War (1854–6) and a notorious conflict in empire, the Indian Mutiny (1857).

Central to the rise of Victorian ideology is the idea of individualism, and such an ideology is consolidated in mid-Victorian novels. This was the age of the Victorian *Bildungsroman* – the 'education' or 'formation' novel – in which the 'individual' is shaped in his or her journey from childhood to maturity. Through the structure of narrative, the *Bildungsroman* performs an attempt to construct a coherent sense of identity or self against the adversities of life. Such a 'journey' is integral, for example, to two of the period's most famous novels of the genre, Charlotte Brontë's *Jane Eyre* (1847) and Charles Dickens's *David Copperfield* (1850) – in the latter David Copperfield wonders early on whether or not he will become 'the hero of [his] own life'. Both novels, however, begin in childhood misery and end with adult success, which in these stories amounts to marriage, and both suggest that the individual hero or heroine will learn, progress and, ultimately, prevail. Yet despite the emphasis in the novels on tensions between the individual (both are written from the first-person perspective) and society, such tensions also reflect on the broader social-economic and political problems facing most Victorians. By the mid-Victorian period, the novel had become the medium most suited to reflect, often at great length (*David Copperfield* runs to over 800 pages), on the complexities and sheer energy of Victorian life in an increasingly urbanized and industrial society. As a result, the triumph of prose fiction seems to have met the 'prosaic' needs of 'modern' living, and there was genuine belief in the efficacy of novels to promote socioeconomic and political reform. Having said that, it is also not by chance that the novel, which by mid-century had become the dominant literary form in Victorian Britain, had also become the perfect form for representing the growing dominance of bourgeois ideas and attitudes. The rise of the novel and the rise of the Victorian middle classes were, in other words, inseparable; more than being simply coterminous events, they were part of the same process. With the novel's increasing focus on the day-to-day problems facing the individual, on 'reality', the notion that the novel is merely a window through which to view the 'real' world had become, by the mid-Victorian period, little more than a bourgeois illusion of what constitutes reality and 'realist fiction' in the first place.

It has been estimated that during Victoria's reign (1837–1901) over 42,000 novels were published, and the mid-century years between 1847 and 1851 were especially prolific. Titles from this period include Charlotte Brontë's *Jane Eyre* (1847), Emily Brontë's *Wuthering Heights* (1847), Benjamin Disraeli's *Tancred* (1847), Anthony Trollope's *The Macdermots of Ballycloran* (1848), William Thackeray's *Vanity Fair* (1847), Dickens's *Dombey and Son* (1848) and *David Copperfield* (1850), Elizabeth Gaskell's *Mary Barton* (1848), Anne Brontë's *Tenant of Wildfell Hall* (1848) and Charles Kingsley's *Alton Locke* (1850), not to mention landmark poetical works such as Alfred Lord Tennyson's *In Memoriam* (1850) and William Wordsworth's last version of *The Prelude* (1850). The novels in those four to five years alone cover the full range of Victorian issues and sub-genres. These include what to do with the working classes in Gaskell's 'industrial novel', and the problem of Chartism in Kingsley's, the Gothic romance of Emily Brontë's *Wuthering Heights*, and the woman's journey from bondage to freedom in Charlotte Brontë's *Jane Eyre*. They also include satires such as Thackeray's 'Novel without a Hero', *Vanity Fair* (1847), and the growing preoccupation with family, capitalism and empire, in Dickens's *Dombey and Son*.

In an age of religious uncertainty, there were also a number of historico-religious novels published in the period. These include John Henry Newman's *Loss and* Gain (1848), James Anthony Froude's *The Nemesis of Faith* (1849), but also Gaskell's *Ruth* (1853), which was also a social-problem novel, and Charlotte M. Yonge's popular *The Heir of Radclyffe* (1853). More straightforwardly historical novels, such as Charles Kingsley's *Westward Ho!* (1855) – a thinly disguised call to arms for the war in the Crimea – were also best-sellers. More importantly, perhaps, a novel such as Brontë's *Jane Eyre* was deemed subversive, and not a little outrageous, in the mid-Victorian period; that it reflects on many of the social, cultural and political upheavals of its day is exemplified by Elizabeth Rigby's critique of the work in the *Quarterly Review* (1848). In this piece, Rigby argues that Brontë's novel is 'stamped with a coarseness of language and laxity of tone which have certainly no excuse'. Jane Eyre is then described as an emblem of 'pedantry, stupidity, or gross vulgarity', while the text as a whole is condemned as fundamentally 'anti-Christian', 'unrealistic', and, mistakenly as it turns out, written by a 'man': 'We deny that *he* has succeeded . . . in making the story plausible.' Rigby's conclusion also contains what is her most telling criticism of all, one which only underlines the radical nature, in its day, of this most influential of mid-Victorian novels, even if modern-day critics see in Brontë's attitudes towards the British Empire and the working class a more deeply engrained conservatism: 'We do not hesitate to say that the tone of mind and thought which has overthrown authority and violated every code human and divine abroad and fostered Chartism and rebellion at home, is the same which has also written *Jane Eyre*' (italics added).

See also *Contexts*: Class, Evolution, Individualism; *Texts*: Realist fiction, Social-problem novel; *Criticism*: Deconstruction, Feminism, Marxism, Poststructuralism, Structuralism.

Further Reading

Skilton, David (ed.), *The Early and Mid-Victorian Novel* (London and New York: Routledge, 1993).

Non-fictional Prose

It is important to appreciate the significance of non-fictional prose in the Victorian period. The Victorians wrote copiously on everything and everyone: religion, science, economics, politics, philosophy, race, sexuality, art and culture. In an age that pre-dates the specialization of the twentieth and twenty-first centuries, many Victorians were polymaths, with two of the great statesmen and politicians of the age – the

Conservative Benjamin Disraeli, and the Liberal William Ewart Gladstone – illustrating the point well. Both men, for example, had sufficient time, and a compulsion, to read and write extensively. Both men also had huge libraries. Gladstone commented on just about every subject imaginable, from classical literary studies to politics, in works such as *Studies in Homer and the Homeric Age* (1858) and *Bulgarian Horrors and the Question of the East* (1876). Disraeli, on the other hand, although he also wrote non-fictional prose, is best known for his novels. Before becoming prime minister in 1868 (he entered parliament in 1837), Disraeli was already a hugely successful novelist, sealing his popularity with his 'hungry forties' 'social problem' trilogy, *Coningsby* (1844), *Sybil* (1845) and *Tancred* (1847). Earlier than this, however, he had published non-fictional political writings, such as *A Vindication of the English Constitution* (1835) and *The Spirit of Whiggism* (1836), which he continued writing throughout his life.

If there is one subject that could be said to have preoccupied non-fictional prose writers of the Victorian period, it is religion, a topic that the devout Gladstone returned to again and again. In an increasingly rational and secular Britain, the crisis of Victorian faith deepened in the course of the nineteenth century, and the religious debates it inspired intensified in the wake of controversial events such as the Catholic Emancipation Edict of 1829. The edict, which was supposed to end centuries of Catholic persecution by Protestants, actually worsened Protestant–Catholic rivalries in what remained a predominantly Protestant (Church of England) nation, leading to a series of voluminous writings and treatises on the crisis of faith in general. The most notable pieces were those produced by the so-called Oxford Tractarian Movement (established *c.*1833). This group of academic clerics called for a return to a more spiritual view of life in an industrial – and therefore implicitly misguided – society, that demanded greater respect for traditional religious observances and the authority of bishops. They also, in the face of increasing state interference in church matters and Britain's transition towards scientific and capitalist modernity in general, appealed for the doctrine of 'absolute faith'. The movement, which included the illustrious likes of Edward Pusey and John Keble among its members, was led by John Henry Newman. Like many Victorians, Newman was a resourceful intellectual who tried his hand at non-fictional and literary writings, especially devotional poetry. In addition to his substantial contribution to the Oxford Movement's non-fictional works, most notably the hugely influential *Tracts for the Times*, published from 1833 onwards and running to around 90 separate issues, his *Lyrica Apostolica* appeared in 1836, and *The Dream of Gerontius* was published in 1865.

Newman criticized Christian doctrine throughout his writings, and especially in the tracts. In *Tract XC* (1841), the most inflammatory, he argued that certain Protestant/Anglican articles of faith – namely the Thirty-nine Articles of doctrine, which since 1571 had been regarded as dogma by the Church of England – had a strongly Roman Catholic dimension. In 1845, his beliefs led him to make a scandalous conversion to Roman Catholicism, a move which both estranged him from his colleagues in the movement and ensured that his writings became subject to censure. Around the same time, other major Victorians such as the novelist George Eliot were also producing radical non-fictional prose writings on sensitive religious matters. Most notably, Eliot published her translation of D. F. Strauss's *Life of Jesus* in 1846. This proved to be another controversial piece of work, but one that moved in an opposite direction to that chosen by Newman, in that it undermined Christianity by casting doubt on the 'true' word of the Gospels.

The anxieties about religion that characterize the nineteenth century also have to be seen in relation to developments in scientific thinking in the period. It is not surprising, in this respect, that scientific ideas and debates constitute another prominent feature of Victorian non-fictional prose. Unlike in our own day, however, much of Victorian scientific writing was both directed at and accessible to a broad spectrum of the literate public. There was, for example (to draw on the most obvious and ground-breaking publication), the appearance of Charles Darwin's theory of evolution in *On the Origin of Species* in 1859. Darwin's ideas about 'natural variation' magnified the element of chance and the threat of godlessness in a climate of growing religious doubt. They had an immeasurable impact on the Victorian consciousness, largely because they undermined Christian notions of time and, by extension, the entire history of life on earth. By contradicting the biblical story of Creationism, Darwin's writings eventually altered the way that the Victorians regarded their position in the universe forever, at the same time that they sharpened their sense of themselves as a 'species' made for social and economic competitiveness and survival. But there were other important commentators – social scientists rather than scientists in the more traditional sense – whose non-fictional writings would, inadvertently or otherwise, help erode the idea of Christian faith and the notion of spirituality in the period. The full impact and implications of Karl Marx's political and economic writings would be felt most obviously in the twentieth century. Yet his revolutionary ideas about the 'material' and essentially Godless – because 'man made' – history of class struggle appeared in the mid-nineteenth-century period, in works such as *The Communist Manifesto* (1848) and *Capital*, the first volume of which was published in 1867.

Of equal significance were the writings of social and political commentators such as the leading utilitarian thinker of the day, John Stuart Mill. Mill discussed the rights of the individual in his most famous work, *On Liberty* (1859); and in *On the Subjection of Women* (1869); a piece published when the 'Woman Question' was gathering momentum in the last third of the century, he expounded his belief that 'the legal subordination of one sex to the other – is wrong in itself, and now one of the chief hindrances to human improvement'. On a lighter note, in the same year as both Darwin's *On the Origin of Species* and *On Liberty*, another hugely successful work of 'self-improvement' non-fiction was published, Samuel Smiles's celebration of individual achievement, *Self-Help* (1859). This book is one of a flurry of similarly didactic, middle-class guides on how to live correctly and properly that grew up in response to a nineteenth-century world of change and upheaval, and which testified to the advance of middle-class values and attitudes in the period. Another, published two years later, is Isabella Beeton's *Book of Household Management* (1861). This book, a dazzling compendium on the virtues of domesticity and household maintenance, good manners and social etiquette, tells us a great deal about the age that needed such a book. Mrs Beeton combines her guidance on housekeeping with forth-right opinions on wifely modesty, chastity, family routine, correct gender roles, and how to 'keep' a husband. She supplements these with a series of recipes and trenchant appeals to eat 'economically, tastefully and well', and more mysterious tips for mothers, such as those on how to 'bleed' one's children.

In a sense, Beeton's work reflects the age. However, there are other prose writers from the period who are best remembered as commenta-tors on the more chaotic world that the Victorians had brought into exis-tence. Their equivalent today could be said to be the newspaper columnist, but the comparison does not even begin to suggest just how significant, influential – and perhaps most of all, necessary – these social, political and artistic pundits and philosophers were in the Victorian era. Amongst a virtually inexhaustible list of names, any such list must include, to name only some of the most famous, the 'Sage of Chelsea', Thomas Carlyle, John Ruskin, Matthew Arnold and Thomas Babington Macaulay. Carlyle wrote on everything, from the so-called 'Condition of England Question' and problems of reform in *Chartism* (1839) and *Past and Present* (1843), to mob violence in *A History of the French Revolution* (1837) (an odd mix of historical and polemical prose-poetry). He also held forth on God, the work ethic, hypocrisy, morality, the right to vote, and the idea of the hero. On the topics of race and slavery, he used his most notorious piece, 'Occasional Discourse on the

Nigger Question' (1849), to describe what he saw as essentially 'likeable' but lazy 'blacks', the 'ugliness, idleness, and rebelliousness' of whom he thought formed the majority of workers on former British slave plantations in the West Indies. Carlyle also found time to produce literary biographies of German giants, such as Johan Schiller, in *The London Magazine* (1823-4), as well as two volumes of biography on *Oliver Cromwell* (1845), and six volumes on *Frederick the Great* (1858-65).

John Ruskin wrote hugely influential criticisms of art and architecture, and, like Carlyle, he was also preoccupied with sociopolitical and ethical questions. As with his contemporary, indeed, there was no real division between Ruskin's aesthetic and social concerns. His most notable works include his massive *Modern Painters* (published between 1843 and 1860), which demonstrated his admiration of the Romantic painter J. M. W. Turner, *The Seven Lamps of Architecture* (1849) and *The Stones of Venice* (1851-3). In a long career (blighted towards the end by mental instability), Ruskin's complex ideas and opinions changed and often contradicted themselves. In what now appears, however, to be a fairly typical Victorian attitude, he argued – fairly consistently – that the 'function' of art was to be faithful to nature and reality, as opposed, that is, to creating impressions or idealizations of reality. Art, in other words, had a duty to be 'truthful'. Such links between art, culture and the general well-being of society are also evident in the writings of the poet and educationist Matthew Arnold, who also wrote a series of speculative and satirical non-fictional and critical books. In these, Arnold debated a range of topics, including the function of literary criticism, tensions between high and low culture, class and religion; of particular note are *On Translating Homer* (1861), *Essays on Criticism* (1865), *God and the Bible* (1875), and the piece which he is most famous for, *Culture and Anarchy* (1869). Like Ruskin, Arnold thought that art should have a 'function'. He argued that it should inspire the individual to greater things, while dignifying him or her in the process. In short, his basic thesis in *Culture and Anarchy* is that 'man' will dwindle into 'anarchy' without the 'sweetness and light', or rather the socially and morally stabilizing effects, of 'culture'. Lastly, with Gladstone and Disraeli, Thomas Babington Macaulay, another of the Victorian sages, achieved early success as a parliamentarian. Yet in a typically versatile career, he was also a barrister, a 'Whiggish' historian, a critic, a reviewer and a colonial administrator, a post which found him promoting the virtues of an 'English' education in British imperial India. Such diverse roles fed into a series of his reviews and pamphlets published in a collection called *Essays Contributed to the Edinburgh Review, Critical and Historical* (1843). In these writings, Macaulay outlined his influential 'Whiggish', that is to say, liberal ideas, which now sound like quintessentially Victorian appeals for 'gradual' political 'evolution' and (peaceful) 'progress'. Equally popular and successful were his four volumes of *History of England* (1849, 1855), although he died in 1859 before this huge work was completed.

A consideration of what the Victorians wrote needs to be complemented by an awareness of how their ideas and attitudes came to the attention of the public. There were important developments in nineteenth-century publishing in terms of the way that non-fictional prose was distributed and received. Broadly speaking, a vast assortment of periodicals appeared throughout the period – quarterlies, weekly and daily papers, magazines, 'penny dreadfuls' and broadsides, which contained all manner of news, sociopolitical commentary, histories, diaries, statistics, poems, travel writings, scientific commentaries, pieces of literature, literary reviews and works of satire. *The Illustrated London News*, for example, which in its early days was often concerned with discussing the many problems facing the Victorian poor, began publication in 1842, and the *Daily Telegraph* was first issued in 1848. There was also a series of cheap and popular (and often scurrilous) magazines for the masses in circulation, often at a cost of two pence or less. These, most notably the penny dreadfuls, dealt with various acts of murder and mayhem (especially the activities of highwaymen), while the 'broadsides' – single sheets of news recounting outrageous deeds of true crime and suicide, along with autopsy reports and prayers for the dead – were equally controversial. Meanwhile, the ever-popular satirical publication, *Punch*, was founded in 1841, and best-selling novelists such as Charles Dickens found an outlet for his journalism and miscellaneous writings (and those of others), as editor of two consecutive weekly publications, *Household Words* (1850–9) and *All the Year Round* (1859–70), to which he was also the major contributor.

Among numerous publications of a similar ilk, there were two major highbrow periodicals in the period. The fairly moderate, Whig-supporting *Edinburgh Review*, which numbered Gladstone, Carlyle and Macaulay amongst its contributors, was founded in 1802, and the more savagely Tory-supporting and influential *Quarterly Review* was established in 1809. The *Quarterly Review* was, in fact, formed largely in response to the more liberal tone of the *Edinburgh Review*. Literary reviews and criticism were an integral feature of both journals, and the *Quarterly Review* delivered particularly hostile attacks on reformers and radicals such as the Romantic poet John Keats and the novelist Charles Dickens, although it also ravaged progressive statesmen and rival essayists such as Macaulay. In a notorious issue of 1848, for example, the *Quarterly*

Review's Elizabeth Rigby set about Charlotte Brontë's novel *Jane Eyre* (1847), accusing the book as a whole of being 'stamped with a coarseness of language and laxity of tone which have certainly no excuse', and its heroine in particular as a symbol of 'pedantry, stupidity, or gross vulgarity'.

Much of the non-fictional prose of the period, especially the work of the sages such as Carlyle, Ruskin and Arnold, set itself apart from the vulgar, capitalist spirit of the age. Paradoxically, on the other hand, many publications, non-fiction or otherwise, were also used as advertising space for the many products made increasingly available by Victorian commerce. Preceding each instalment of Charles Dickens's *Nicholas Nickleby* (1838–9), for example – a work of fiction with a decidedly 'factual' agenda of sociopolitical and educational reform – are advertisements for a range of consumables, including other books. Items on offer include non-fictional prose works such as Lieutenant Lecount and Thomas Roscoe's 'A History and Description of the London and Birmingham Railway', and J. Paxton's now little-known 'Practical Treatise on the Cultivation of the Dahlia'. But these advertisements, published in 'The Nickleby Advertiser', sit side-by-side with promotions for 'Frank's Great Hat Store' (on Regent Street), Benjamin Edgington, 'Tent Manufacturer', and an assortment of products, including 'Ede's Marking Ink', 'Chapman's Improved Gloves', 'Brett's Improved Brandy' (sold by the gallon), 'Dickins' Celebrated British Tooth Powder', and 'Beatson's Ringworm Lotion'. Such products, to our ears, might sound absurd. They do, nonetheless, reflect the bustling, enterprising spirit of the age, and it was this age of innovation and change that every non-fictional writer was attempting to get the measure of. Curiously, and strikingly, however, it is in the monthly instalments of novels such as *Nicholas Nickleby* that we glimpse both the urge to comment on the state of society and the presence, in the form of the advertisements, of this extraordinary new society.

See also *Contexts*: Class, Economics, Individualism, Industry, Race, Reform, Religion, Science, Sex and sexuality; *Texts*: Crime fiction, Historical novel, Penny dreadfuls, Realist fiction, Sensation fiction; *Criticism*: Introduction, Feminism, Marxism, Psychoanalysis.

Further Reading

Le Quesne, A. L. (ed.), *Victorian Thinkers: Carlyle, Ruskin, Arnold, Morris* (Oxford: Oxford University Press, 1993).

Turner, Frank M., *Contesting Cultural Authority: Essays in Victorian Intellectual Life* (Cambridge: Cambridge University Press, 1993).

Penny Dreadfuls

The term 'penny dreadful' is thought to have been first coined around 1874. It refers to a series of sensationalized magazine or newspaper publications, published for most of the century, that dwelt on villainy and violence, were issued in 'penny' parts or other cheap periodicals, had a wide circulation, and were hugely successful. Although a derogatory term, the Victorians seem to have relished such tags as 'dreadful'. Penny dreadfuls were known as 'bloods' in the earlier part of the century, and 'penny horribles' at other stages. Similarly, the particularly 'dreadful' works published by Charles Fox or George Emmet were described by journalists as 'penny packets of poison', a 'penny stinker' was a poor man's cigar, and a 'shilling shocker' was a later variety of the penny dreadful. The precursor to the dreadfuls was *The Terrific Register*. This publication thrived in the mid-1820s, largely due to its numerous stories of crime, disease and the dismemberment of villains. In the 1840s, the penny *Weekly Magazine* emerged, which, despite a taste for gory true stories, was a slightly more respectable publication. Alongside longer-established publications such as *The Newgate Calendar* (*c.*1773), penny dreadfuls nourished the Victorian appetite for crime fiction. At only a penny a copy, they offered a weekly diet of affordable real-life and fictional accounts of murder and mystery for adults, many with brutal and bloodthirsty woodcuts, although from the 1860s many more were aimed at children.

The popularity of the dreadfuls with the working classes goes beyond the escapist excitement of adventure and gore they provided. When, for example, Lewis Carroll's *Alice in Wonderland* (1865) was first published, it retailed at six shillings, which at around a third of an average working-class Victorian's weekly wage was unthinkable. The dreadfuls, on the other hand, were often all that poorer families and their children could afford. Indeed, it has been shown that even those children who could not afford a penny a week read second-hand copies or they received them from the many clubs which distributed them around the country. Such, in fact, was the increasing popularity and notoriety of the dreadfuls with children that, by way of counter-offensive, the Religious Tract Society began publishing its more corrective magazine, *The Boy's Own Paper*, from 1879. The publication's 'sound and healthy reading' offered adventurous and sporty – but also far more wholesome – tales and advice for young boys. In the well-named Dr Stables's column, for instance, the writer dispensed weekly advice such as 'Take a cold tub, sir!', if boys were troubled at all by 'nervousness', an often-used euphemism for masturbation in the period. For girls, there was the even weedier sister publication, *The Girl's Own Paper* (1880), which, despite its needlework tips and guidance 'in moral and domestic virtues', proved not to be so popular. The leading campaigner against the dreadfuls was Alfred Harmsworth, who in the late decades of the century used his jingoistic publications for boys, such as *Marvel* (1893), *Union Jack* (1894) and *Pluck* (1894), expressly to 'Suppress Bad Books for Boys'. Unfortunately, for Harmsworth, he was widely scorned for producing little more than penny packets of 'poison' himself. His publications, many of which were even cheaper than the dreadfuls, were frequently thought to have been written by the same 'scoundrels' and 'miserable beer-swilling wretches' he condemned. Harmsworth was later accused, in fact, by A. A. Milne, of destroying the 'penny dreadful' only to make way for the 'ha'penny dreadfuller'.

The popularity of the penny dreadfuls points towards a typically Victorian paradox: the attractiveness of that which is repulsive. But the fact that such 'trashy' publications were enjoyed largely, but not exclusively, by the poorer members of society, and especially by children and adolescents, is significant because it underlines Victorian anxieties about class. Largely because, it seems, the dreadfuls were thought to glamourize crime and encourage bad behaviour, many figures of authority such as magistrates, clergymen, teachers and 'reputable' journalists became concerned about their influence on the nation's 'dangerous' lower orders and the perceived threat of the 'mob'. Contemporary commentator Edward Salmon, in *Juvenile Literature As It Is*, for example, complained that the dreadfuls would result in the 'moral and material ruin of the working-class'. Meanwhile, an anonymous writer in the *Quarterly Review* described the low publications of Charles Fox and others as the 'Literature of rascaldom', which recruits 'scapegraces and ne'er-do-wells' for the nation's 'prisons', 'reformatories' and 'Colonies'. Much of the criticism was rooted in the fact that many penny dreadful criminals, especially the ever-popular highwaymen, were not really straightforward or unambiguous villains. Some even attained a sort of Robin Hood status in publications such as the suitably named Edward Viles's 'Dick Turpin' tales, in which the highwayman is portrayed as morally superior to the upper classes he terrorizes and robs.

Penny dreadfuls provided a lowbrow counterpoint to the rise to prominence of 'serious' or highbrow Victorian literature. The most popular titles included George Reynolds's best-selling, long-running serial, *The Mysteries of London* (1841–56), which dealt with everything from murder to adultery, and Gothic pot-boilers such as Thomas Rymer's *Varney the Vampire, or the Feast of Blood* (1846–7). Although there were also anonymous works published, such as *The Dance of Death: or, The Hangman's Plot. A Thrilling Romance of the Two Cities*

(1865–6), and others such as Viles's highwayman tale, *Black Bess; or, the Knight of the Road* (1867–9), which were equally popular, the anonymous and grisly, *May Turpin, The Queen of the Road: A Romance* (1864), was less so. Thomas Prest's *The String of Pearls, or, the Barber of Fleet Street* (1850–2), was perhaps the most dreadful of all penny dreadfuls. Prest's fictional story recounts Sweeney Todd's life as an unpredictable barber, who slits the throats of his customers and chops up their bodies for 'delightful, gushing gravy pies'. A little later, the Aldine Publishing Company began publishing versions of the American equivalent of the dreadfuls, the 'dime novels', with their equally violent stories of outlaws, trappers, rustlers, frontiersman and cowboys, such as *Buffalo Bill* (1869) and *Deadwood Dick's Head Off* (1894).

For children the publication of 'dreadfuls' came to be dominated in the 1860s by Edwin John Brett, who emerged from vaguely subversive origins in the Chartist movement to produce lurid tales of pirates, highwaymen and crime in London, such as *Black Rollo, the Pirate* (1864–5) and *Red Ralph* (1865–6). Brett was also behind the long-running and slightly more respectable, *The Boys of England* (1866–99), the aim of which was to 'enthral' its young readership with yet more tales about manly adventure involving pirates and smugglers, although it also contained 'useful' information about work opportunities for the nation's working-class youth. The publication, with its self-explanatory subtitle, 'A Young Gentleman's Journal of Sport, Travel, Fun and Instruction', had a massive readership, and seems to have peaked around 1871 with over a quarter of a million copies sold. Towards the close of the century, in fact, if sales figures are anything to go by, the more scurrilous dreadfuls seem to have lost out in the market to such increasingly popular boys' magazines, most of which appeased their readership's hunger for bravery and heroism, in an increasing climate of nationalism and empire, without 'degrading' the nation's youth. This was certainly the case with another one of Brett's less dreadful periodicals, the fleetingly popular and full-colour *Boys of the Empire*, which was published from 1888 to 1893, and again from 1901 to 1906, following Britain's involvement in the Boer Wars (1899–1902).

See also *Contexts*: Crime and punishment, Law, Sex and sexuality, Violence; *Texts*: Children's literature, Crime fiction, Sensation fiction.

Further Reading

Penny Dreadfuls and Comics (London: Victoria and Albert Museum, 1983), foreword by Roy Strong, introduction by Kevin Carpenter.

Poetry

Victorian poetry is as complex and dynamic as the society from which it emerged. Despite the formation of certain poetic schools or movements in the period, the poetry of the day left neither a homogenous legacy nor a set of easily definable themes and characteristics. A mid-century discussion of poetry by the poet Matthew Arnold, in his preface to *Poems* (1853), is illuminating on this point: 'The confusion of the present time is great, the multitude of different voices counselling different things bewildering.' Such confusion did not, however, prevent Arnold from attempting, in the same piece, to define Victorian poetry as preoccupied with 'the dialogue of the mind with itself'. Nonetheless, over eight decades, the sheer range and scope of Victorian poetry is enormous. It does, in fact, encompass everything: neo-Rromantic verse, social-problem or 'industrial' verse, working-class verse, 'New Woman' verse, decadent verse, satirical verse, moral and amoral verse, sacred and secular verse, as well as love poetry, war poetry, imperial poetry and nonsense poetry. Victorian poetry looks at once forwards, backwards and directly, often most critically, at its own age. It is, in this respect, both sceptical and affirmative, hopeful and regretful, often within the same poem. Such a period of socioeconomic and political change and uncertainty is in fact glimpsed in the appointments to Poet Laureate. When Victoria acceded to the throne, the ageing Romantic and conservative Robert Southey was laureate (from 1813–43). Southey, a man who once told Charlotte Brontë that poetry was not really a women's 'business', was then succeeded by the even more ageing and conservative William Wordsworth (1843–50). At Wordsworth's death in 1850, Elizabeth Barrett Browning, a respected woman poet, was considered by some to be a suitable laureate for a ruling Queen, but as it turned out it was another man, Alfred Lord Tennyson (1850–92), who was eventually appointed. Tennyson's work, which is marked by its tense confrontation with the past, the present and the future, would come to overshadow the Victorian period. At his death in 1892, he was succeeded by Alfred Austin (1892–1913), a poet who made the mistake of criticizing his peers (especially Tennyson), only to be much ridiculed and parodied himself, largely for writing shallow and platitudinous poetry.

Much contemporary criticism of Victorian poetry is in fact instructive, and especially that of Austin. In a society notorious for its patriarchal culture based on the division of gender and sexual roles, Austin, in *The Poetry of the Period* (1870), tried to define the differences between 'masculine' and 'feminine' writing. Austin accused 'Mr Tennyson's compositions', for example, of being 'feminine'. For Austin, whose own poetry would form part of the late-Victorian ethos of masculine imperi-

alism, Tennyson's poetry exemplified 'the feminine, narrow, domesticated, timorous temper of the times'. According to Austin, works such
as 'The Charge of the Light Brigade' (1854) betrayed a fear of the 'glorious bloody thick of the fight', and worse, a 'feminine' predilection for the
passivity of 'still life'. In similar ways, other successful and progressive
women poets such as Elizabeth Barrett Browning were accused by male
critics, such as Edmund Gosse in *Critical Kit-Kats* (1896), of being 'hysterical', a poet of unpoetic 'tirades' which are accompanied by a 'sort of
scream'. That such a 'scream' might be Browning's poetic response to
the violence inflicted on women by Victorian patriarchy is typically
absent from Gosse's criticisms. Otherwise, such was the sense of confusion and change wrought by the impact of the modern Victorian world
that, in 1849, Arnold was famously moved to describe the age as fundamentally 'unpoetical'. But Arnold's comments were, partly at least, a
response to the rise to pre-eminence of prose in the period, and in
particular the growing prestige of the novel, in which Victorian 'realism'
became the dominant literary form and the distinctions between poetry
and prose became ever more pronounced. As a result, whereas the
novel came to be regarded as the most suitable medium for reflecting
the new urban and industrial 'reality' the Victorians were building, much
of Victorian poetry came to be perceived as inadequate.

The poetry of the early nineteenth century also came under regular
attacks from utilitarian philosophers, many of whose ideas eventually
had a profound influence on mainstream opinion. Exponents of utilitarian arguments tended to favour only those forms of art and culture
which were 'realistically' useful to, and productive for, the greatest
number of people in society. Consequently, in a period in which the
social and moral function of poetry had become increasingly less certain
(hence the rise to prominence of the 'social' and 'moral' novels), intellectuals such as the utilitarians sat about debating what poetry was 'for'.
Initial discussions were framed around the philosopher Jeremy
Bentham's claims in *The Rationale of Reward* (1825). In this work,
Bentham argued that if the children's game of 'push-pin', for example,
gave more 'pleasure' to more people, then it '[was] more valuable than'
either 'the arts and sciences of music and poetry' put together. That is to
say, according to Bentham, music and poetry were essentially nonutili-
tarian and thus un-democratic entertainments which were 'only relished
by the few'. For Bentham and his followers such entertainments served
no broader public purpose or social 'point' whatsoever. A few years
later, like-minded philosophers such as John Stuart Mill expanded the
terms of the debate about poetry by questioning the limits of 'sensation'
and 'truth' in essays such as 'What is Poetry?' (1833). For Mill, that

poetry which was not 'truthful' was ultimately 'not poetry at all'. In the writings of other Victorian sages, on the other hand, such as Thomas Carlyle's *The Hero as Poet* (1840), the role of poet is eulogized as that of a brave visionary, an individual genius who reveals the 'secret mystery' of life to those uninitiated. This is despite the fact that, as Carlyle also pointed out in oddly utilitarian terms himself, Tennyson's poetry more often than not 'wants a task'. Indeed, in a post-Romantic age in which the mythology of the poet was under constant scrutiny, the significance of poetry to the Victorians should not be underestimated. An older Arnold even went so far as to argue, in *Study of Poetry* (1880), that in the scientific, Darwinian epoch in which Victorians lived, people would increasingly turn to poetry 'to interpret life for us, to console us, to sustain us'. Poetry would, in this respect, offer Victorians nothing less than a new religion which would console them in the face of a disappearing God.

The Victorians were also innovators in poetic form. One of their major achievements, for example, the dramatic monologue, was in development as early as the 1830s–40s. Though varied and experimental, dramatic monologues are characterized by the writer's disassociation from the speaking subject(s) of the poem. As a result, many of the poems appear to be grappling, amongst other things, with the psychological uncertainties of the 'self' which arise from their own proliferation of 'voices'. Such ambiguities often led to monologues of madness, desire, menacing passions, moral conflict, and tensions between men and women, and some poems, particularly those of Robert Browning, contain deeply unpleasant subject matter. In 'Porphyria's Lover' (1836) and 'My Last Duchess' (1842), Browning's narrators linger on images of murdered, sensual women, where 'all smiles stopped together', while in Tennyson's 'Ulysses' (1842), a typically ambiguous narrator desires a 'newer world' before the 'Death' which 'closes all'. Other poems of the early period, such as the working-class Ebenezer Eliot's popular *Corn Law Rhymes* (1831), were often no less dark or violent. With its protest for free trade and assault on the government's policy on corn, a policy which led to high prices for bread and starving Victorians, Eliot's poetry was more explicitly concerned with the 'Condition of England' question, as was the all-encompassing, ten-book poetry of Thomas Cooper's Chartist, *The Purgatory of Suicides: A Prison Rhyme* (1845). The early to mid-period also gave rise to the long, exuberant and often psychotic poetic-dramas of the so-called 'Spasmodic' school (much of which was influenced by Browning's dramatic monologues). Works in this subgenre included Richard Bailey's *Festus* (1839), Sydney Dobel's *Balder* (1854), in which Balder murders his wife rather than let her succumb to madness, and Alexander Smith's *Life Drama* (1853). The period also produced the utmost in frivolous and solemn verse, in the publication, respectively, of Edward Lear's *Book of Nonsense* (1845) and Tennyson's massive elegy, *In Memoriam* (1850). Tennyson's poem is a lament both for the passing of an individual (Tennyson's friend Arthur Hallam) and for the passage of time. It is also a poem of faith and doubt, seemingly about everyone and everything.

There were, furthermore, a series of diverse and often very long sequence poems published throughout the century. These include Coventry Patmore's notorious celebration of marriage and domestic virtue, *The Angel in the House* (1854–61); Tennyson's historical reflections on the legends of King Arthur and the state of modern Britain in *Idylls of the King* (c.1857–85); Robert Browning's self-proclaimed 'Epic of Psychology', *The Ring and the Book* (1868–9); and Elizabeth Barrett Browning's 'novel in verse', *Aurora Leigh* (1856), with its critique of women's unequal status in society, prostitution, and calls to forget the past in favour of engaging with 'this live, throbbing age'. The 1860s then saw the publication of George Meredith's critique of sentimental Victorian love, *Modern Love* (1862), Christina Rossetti's sensuous and highly ambiguous fairy-tale poem, *Goblin Market* (1862), the deeply religious John Newman's response to the age of science and Darwin, *The Dream of Gerontius* (1865), and the extremely controversial, because decadent, work of Algernon Charles Swinburne in *Poems and Ballads* (1866). As part of the Pre-Raphaelite Brotherhood (PRB) movement, Dante Gabriel Rossetti's equally controversial *Poems* appeared in 1870, while in *The Contemporary Review* (1871) Robert Buchanan famously criticized this movement as the 'fleshly school of poetry'. In particular, Buchanan was appalled by the PRB's 'nasty' attention to the body (in particular the lips) and what he perceived to be its 'erotic dimensions'. At the same time, while the 1870s also saw the publication of Gerard Manley Hopkins's energetic and revolutionary rhythms in *The Wreck of the Deutschland* (1875–6) and Robert Browning's *Dramatic Idylls* (1879), towards the end of the century, Swinburne's poetry, with its decadent French influences, continued to offend mainstream Victorian tastes. Austin, for example, thought that Swinburne's verse was even 'less' masculine than Tennyson's, while Swinburne himself, like other aesthetes, raged against the idea that poetry should contain any 'masculine' or 'moral lesson' at all. Swinburne's views were part of the 'art for art's sake' movement of the period, the aesthetic and decadent manifesto of which contained the crucial point that art should be free from being socially useful ('utilitarian') in any way. Arch-aesthete Walter Pater, for example, claimed in *Renaissance* (1873) that all 'art', including poetry, 'aspires to the condition of music', and that the enjoyment of poetry lies purely in the ephemeral pleasures it affords. Typically diverse until the end, however, later Victorian poetry also includes William Morris's radically minded *Chants for Socialists* (1891), the nationalist and imperialistic bravura of Rudyard Kipling's *Barrack Room Ballads* (1892), the emergence of modernism in W. B. Yeats's *The Wandering of Oisin and Other Poems* (1889), Thomas Hardy's ruralism in *Wessex Poems and Other Verses* (1898), and Oscar Wilde's indictment of an essentially punitive Victorian society in *The Ballad of Reading Gaol* (1898).

See also   *Contexts*: Decadence and aestheticism, Pre-Raphaelitism; *Criticism*: Feminism, Marxism, Poststructuralism, Psychoanalysis.

Further Reading

Armstrong, Isobel, *Victorian Poetry: Poetry, Poetics and Politics* (London and New York: Routledge, 1993).

Realist Fiction

The concept of realism became increasing currency in the 1850s, when realist fiction rose to prominence. At its most simple level, realist fiction reduces the distance between literature and life so that it imitates 'reality'. As George Eliot, one of the major exponents of realist fiction, commented, in an essay published in the *Westminister Review* (1856), 'Art is the nearest thing to life'. George Henry Lewes (Eliot's lover), in an article for the *Fortnightly Review* (1866), also championed the virtues of realist art, largely because for him it offered 'truthful' representations of society, although he added the crucial point that in realism, 'the commonplace is raised into art'. Realism, for Lewes, was that art which elevated the ordinary, the mundane, the minutiae of everyday life and familiar things, and this was the very milieu, in fact, in which Victorian realist fiction flourished. Given its accumulation of 'realistic' descriptions and detail, its capacity to name and map out time and space as if it mirrored reality, realist fiction emerged as part of a culture obsessed with the truths and realities of an increasingly scientific and secular world. Realist fiction is, in this respect, the literary counterpart of Victorian empirical achievements in science and technology, which grounded British culture in a more rational Darwinian world of observable facts and 'truths'; in the idea, more precisely, that the world was essentially knowable and classifiable. The assumption which underlay the rise of Victorian realist fiction was, in this respect, that there was a 'new' reality which needed to be reflected and understood, one in which an often anonymous and all-knowing, God-like narrator would attempt to give order and meaning to Victorian realities.

Realist fiction is centrally concerned with the antagonism between individuals and society. It is preoccupied with character, with the development of individual self-consciousness, and with the idea of an 'inner self'. Yet, as modern commentators frequently point out, it is no coincidence that the Victorian age of literary realism – with its focus on individual and 'human' relationships – is also the first great age of modern capitalism – with its ideologies of liberal 'humanism' and the freedom of the 'individual' – all of which were enshrined in the economic system of 'free trade'. According to Marxist critics, for example, realist Victorian literature was written largely by and for the dominant middle class. It therefore embodies middle-class ideologies and values, so that the very discourse of 'realism' it provides is really a middle-class adaptation of 'reality' from the outset. But, more than just imitating or reflecting reality, some critics have argued that realist fiction actually constructs that reality. Its effect, therefore, however inadvertent or unconscious, is to pass this 'reality' off as the true or 'natural' order of things, even though, as Catherine Belsey in *Critical Practice* (1980) warns, 'realism' in fiction can only ever be 'plausible', '*not real*' (italics in original). Victorian realism is that literature which, as other commentators such as George Levine point out, represents a 'middling condition', one of a mythically bourgeois English restraint and moderation, which 'defines itself against the excesses, both stylistic and narrative, of various kinds of romantic, exotic, or sensational literatures'.

Levine's definitions of realism are not necessarily secure, however. As feminist critics have shown, Charlotte Brontë's *Jane Eyre* (1847), is, for example, a novel very much grounded in the 'realities' of patriarchal oppression and the desire to escape that oppression. But the text is also an intricate combination of realism and realism's supposedly greatest antagonist, romance. At the same time, the work is haunted by the Gothic presence of the Jamaican Creole Bertha Mason, and the very 'real' history of Britain's involvement in slavery and empire she represents. Furthermore, the arguments amongst contemporary writers about what constituted realist fiction are, as ever, as instructive as they are politically charged, especially because many of them can only define 'realism' by that which it is not. George Eliot, for example, in the same essay quoted above, argued that Charles Dickens was too 'humorous and external' a writer, to be 'realistic', and that he was even 'transcendent in his unreality'. For Eliot, Dickens's fiction lacked any real psychological depth, and it was therefore incapable of probing the 'real' inner life of his characters. In a similar manner, E. M. Forster complained that

Dickens's characters were 'flat'; that is, he thought that they were fixed in time, unable to develop or change, while a like-minded Henry James, in a review of Dickens's *Our Mutual Friend* (1865) for *The Nation* (1865), argued that Dickens remained 'the greatest of superficial novelists' because of this tendancy. On the other hand, in a *Spectator* article entitled 'The Genius of Dickens' (1870), Richard Holt Hutton described Dickens's failure to construct convincing 'ordinary' characters such as Nicholas Nickleby and David Copperfield as indicative not so much of his shortcomings as a realist, but of his genius for the grotesque, concluding that, 'A realist as regards human nature, he never was at all.'

If, however, as these criticisms suggest, realistic fiction is concerned with psychological 'depth', it nonetheless has many permutations. The 'realism' of the 1840s embraces, for example, the 'social problem' or 'Condition of England' novel, such as Benjamin Disraeli's *Sybil, or the Two Nations* (1845), Elizabeth Gaskell's *Mary Barton* (1848) and the 'industrial' realism of Charlotte Brontë's *Shirley* (1849), which, following the 'romance' of *Jane Eyre* and as if to underline its realist credentials, proclaims itself to be as 'unromantic as Monday morning'. The period also encompasses the satirical, 'unheroic' and often highly self-conscious 'realism' of William Makepeace Thackeray's novels, such as *Vanity Fair* (1847), which contemporary critic Elizabeth Rigby described as a 'literal photograph of the manners and habits of the nineteenth century'.

The religious problems and politics of Anthony Trollope's defiantly unromantic 'Barsetshire' novels are another part of the richness and complexity of realist fiction in the period. From *The Warden* (1856) to *The Last Chronicle of Barset* (1867), Trollope's work presents itself as true reflections of life in an English Cathedral community. However, its satires on corruption, greed, embezzlement and careerism lack, for example, the close examination of subjectivity and human 'truths' provided by the 'classic realist' novels of George Eliot. In Eliot's work, time and again, the assurances once offered by the 'meanings' and 'truths' of 'Christian doctrine' are dismissed. In their place, a spiritual enlightenment is sought in everyday 'human' realities, as they are for Maggie Tulliver in *The Mill on the Floss* (1860): 'No dream-world would satisfy her now. She wanted some explanation of this hard, real life.' Indeed, by the time of *Middlemarch* (1872), Eliot's work had begun to construct both a 'realistic' account of social transitions in a provincial English setting and a panoramic view on Victorian society in its entirety.

In the later period, there was also the more cynical and humourist realist fictions found in George Meredith's scandalous *The Ordeal of Richard Feverel* (1859) or in the marital intrigues of *The Egoist* (1879).

Similarly, while the tense Anglo-American relationships and moral and sexual equivocations of Henry James's *The Portrait of a Lady* (1881) ensured that the writer's work would prove to be as controversial as it was popular, James's works pointed towards modernist realist fiction. And by that time, as recent critics such as Elizabeth Deeds Ermath point out, the Victorian consensus on 'rationalism' was beginning to fall apart. On the other hand, the later period is also characterized by the 'naturalistic' realism of working-class poverty and despair in George Gissing's *The Nether World* (1889), George Moore's 'Pottery' novel, *A Mummer's Wife* (1885), and two of Thomas Hardy's novels, *Tess of the D'Urbervilles* (1891) and *Jude the Obscure* (1895), in which the burden of reality frequently overcomes those individuals straining against it.

See also *Contexts*: Evolution, Individualism; *Texts*: Historical novel, Mid-Victorian novel, Social-problem novel; *Criticism*: Deconstruction, Feminism, Marxism, Poststructuralism.

Further Reading

Ermath, Elizabeth Deeds, *Realism and Consensus in the English Novel: Time, Space and Narrative* (Edinburgh: Edinburgh University Press, 1998).

Sensation Fiction

The Victorian sub-genre of sensation fiction had its heyday in the 1860s. It emerged in a decade of economic depression and social transformation, and was born of a generic instability which overlapped with Gothic fiction, crime fiction and melodrama, or rather 'sensation' theatre (after which the fiction was named). Sensation fiction is marked by tangled and often spicy plots, which are full of secrets, suspense, mystery, danger, chills, thrills, remarkable twists and frequently unbelievable coincidence. Its themes are seduction, bigamy, adultery, madness, lost identity, as well as wrongful incarceration, blackmail, poisonings, violence and murder. Much of the fiction grew up in response to true, albeit sensationalized and scandalous, criminal cases taken from gossipy newspaper reports (the sub-genre was known as the 'Newspaper novel' for a time). Its numerous incidents of wrongful imprisonment, for example, were partly based on a culture of anxiety about the government's pernicious lunacy laws. These laws were promulgated after statistics provided by the Lunacy Commission (established 1845) found soaring rates of insanity in the British population, and they led to a shocking spate of incarcerations of the sane in the 1850s.

The line between sanity and insanity was, indeed, a precarious one in the nineteenth century, and sensation fiction reflected – and to some degree exploited – the uncertainty and fear this created. It also exploited, as many Victorian authorities maintained, the idea that madness was derived from moral corruption, of which a mid-century article in *The Times* (1853) concedes: 'In strictness we are all mad when we give way to passion, to prejudice, to vice, to vanity.' Another important factor which underpinned sensation fiction was the mania surrounding divorce and bigamy trials, such as the long-running Yelverton case (began in 1857), incidents of true crime such as that of the poisoner Madeline Smith in 1857, and the case of Constance Kent in 1860, the 16–year-old 'child' alleged to have stabbed her brother. When reforms in divorce law, such as the Matrimonial Causes Act (1857), gave women divorcées slightly better property rights, and allowed them to divorce adulterous husbands on the grounds of violence, incest and bestiality, their impact on the moral crises of the day was also registered by sensation fiction.

Although largely written by middle-class authors, sensation fiction was generally thought to be of a low and scurrilous nature. With its indulgence in forbidden pleasures and hint of salacious Frenchness, many thought it degraded its readership, which was largely made up of women. Henry Mansel in the *Quarterly Review* (1863), for example, described the sub-genre as 'preaching to the nerves', and as a crass form which was essentially populist 'trash' that nourished the 'cravings of a diseased appetite'. Mansel also worried about the influence of the many 'railway stalls' on sensation literature. This most 'modern' of novels, it turned out, was frequently being bought for 'sensational' journeys on the equally modern transport provided by the train, in which the juddering and jolts administered to the body 'electrif[ied] the nerves' along with the books. That sensation fiction preyed on the 'sensations' of the body, giving goose-bumps – what *Punch* in 1863 called 'Making the Flesh Creep' – as well as producing sweats, sudden frights, heightened blood pressure, and worse still, sexual stimulation, is also significant. This, it seems, was fiction for the body, and anxieties about the body were a timeless Victorian bugbear. Sensation fiction was provocative and controversial because it contained unconventional, highly physical and often sexually adventurous women. Far from simply reinscribing the 'angel in the house' role assigned to women by Victorian patriarchy, the novels suggested that middle- and upper-class women led furtive but impassioned lives in which they were no longer simply the victims of men, but their antagonists. It is in this respect that, time and again, women in sensation fiction break up the cherished Victorian institution of the family; women flee the home, have illicit desires and exciting relationships, they lie, steal, murder and they are generally spectacularly bad mothers. That the same fiction is so often set in the most mundane and middle-class of family environments is equally illuminating. In an article for *Nation* (1865), Henry James argued that the sensation novelist's greatest achievement was to show 'those most mysterious of mysteries, the mysteries that are at our own doors'. Sensation fiction revealed, in other words, the sensation of everyday things, those hair-raising moments which lurked within the dreary walls of Victorian domestic realism; it illuminated a bourgeois world which was haunted by its own desires. Far from relying on Gothic set-pieces such as the haunted foreign castle, ruined abbey or derelict graveyard for its thrills, however, sensation fiction suggested that terror began at home.

Sensation fiction was often published in cliff-hanging serial form. It also sold, it need hardly be pointed out, sensationally, and readers were gripped by what Anthony Trollope described as the 'all plot', 'no character', drive of its narratives. Generally recognized as the first true sensation novel, Wilkie Collins's *The Woman in White* (1860) has everything: spine-tingling set-pieces, lunatic asylums, mysterious doubles, a titled woman beset by aristocratic villains, a slightly boring bourgeois hero, Walter Hartright, and a series of unreliable narrators, all of whom read the clues to the identity of the 'woman in white' differently, and so contribute to the overall frisson of sensation and mystery Collins creates. Ellen Price Wood's *East Lynne* (1861) was the first major piece of 'bigamy' sensation fiction published by a woman, and one of the nineteenth-century's biggest single sellers. A somewhat reactionary novel, which with its repentant bad mother ultimately reaffirms the domestic ideal of the middle-class marriage, Wood's story follows Lady Isabel's adultery, elopement and desertion of her children, her disfigurement in a train accident, and subsequent return to the family home disguised as a governess. Of a similar ilk was Mary Elizabeth Braddon's racy and hugely popular *Lady Audley's Secret* (1862), which appeared in the year after Wood's novel. In this work, the adulterous heroine deserts her children, commits arson, is thought to have murdered her first husband (she pushes him down a well), is suspected of madness, and placed in an asylum. Braddon's follow-up, *Aurora Floyd* (1863), contains yet another bigamous heroine, who absconds with her father's groom and takes eight husbands in all. Equally successful in that year was Charles Reade's didactic, but violent, *Hard Cash* (1863), which deals with the wrongful imprisonment of the sane, as does Joseph Sheridan Le Fanu's *The Rose and the Key* (1871), although Le Fanu also wrote the chiller, *Uncle Silas* (1864). Meanwhile, a series of unconventional heroines were also portrayed in Rhoda Broughton's *Not Wisely but Too Well* (1867) and *Cometh Up as a Flower* (1867), while other writers not best remembered for their work in this sub-genre, such as Charles Dickens, also became associated with sensation fiction. Three of Dickens's novels, his Gothic and grotesque *Oliver Twist* (1837), his secretive and labyrinthine *Bleak House* (1853), and his sensationally unfinished tale of suspected murder and disappearance, *The Mystery of Edwin Drood* (1870), were all influential in this respect. Even arch-realists such as Anthony Trollope in *The Eustace Diamonds* (1872) and George Eliot in *Felix Holt* (1866), a novel which contains adultery and an illegitimate child, dabbled in sensation fiction, as did Thomas Hardy. Hardy's first published novel, *Desperate Remedies* (1871), contains blackmail, murder, secrets and a suggestion of bigamy, while his tales of seduction, rape and illegitimate offspring, in novels such as *Tess of the D'Urbervilles* (1891) were also considered sensational at the time.

See also   *Contexts*: Body, Consumerism, Crime and punishment, Disease, Gothic, Sex and sexuality, Violence; *Texts*: Crime fiction, Penny dreadfuls; *Criticism*: Deconstruction, Feminism, Marxism, Poststructuralism, Psychoanalysis.

Further Reading

Bourne Taylor, Jenny, *In the Secret Theatre of Home: Wilkie Collins, Sensation Narrative, and Nineteenth-Century Psychology* (London and New York: Routledge, 1988).
Wynne, Deborah, *The Sensation Novel and the Victorian Family Magazine* (Basingstoke: Palgrave, 2001).

Social-problem Novel

'Social-problem novel' is a twentieth-century category, one that covers a range of Victorian fictions, but generally those published in the decades between the late 1830s and the 1860s. Loosely defined, it refers to those novels characterized by their focus on the social, political, economic and industrial problems facing early to mid-Victorian Britain in the wake of the Industrial Revolution. Although the term is often used interchangeably with other designations such as the 'Condition of England novel', or the slightly more specific 'industrial novel', social-problem novels arose in response to the transition of British society from a cottage- and agriculture-based economy to that of a factory- and industry-based economy. The books subsequently confronted a number of problems and issues associated with these upheavals: the miseries of crowded urban and industrial centres, unemployment and deprivation in the 'hungry forties', the exploitation and abuse of workers by employers, working-class unrest, and calls for electoral and political reform made by movements such as Chartism (*c*.1830s–40s). As a sub-genre, the social-problem novel set a precedent for English literature, precisely because it had an explicit political agenda. Most social-problem novels are socially, morally and religiously instructive; they aim to provoke debate and ultimately economic and political reform in the public arena. To that end, many of the novels draw upon contemporary newspaper and parliamentary reports and statistics to ground their stories in the suitably Victorian rhetoric of 'reality', although such factual data often sit uncomfortably with 'fictional' elements such as romance, adventure, tragedy and murder. Despite exceptions, some of which are discussed below, the sub-genre of social-problem novels seems to have been in decline by the 1860s, and this was attributable to a number of factors. With the onset of the Crimean War (1854–6) and crises in empire such as the Indian Mutiny (1857), many Victorians shifted their focus from Britain's domestic problems onto those in the international context. Other factors, such as the Factory Acts of the 1840s–50s and especially the Ten Hours Act (1847), which reduced the number of hours worked by women and children to ten, lessened some of the worst exploitations and hardships in Britain's factories and industries. Later in the century, Disraeli's second Reform Bill of 1867 expanded the British electorate, if only to men who rented or owned property in urban areas, and this further eased some of the problems underpinning calls for reform.

There are numerous contradictions inherent to social-problem novels. Most novels, for example, appear to advocate change and reform while at the same time being profoundly conservative. Put another way, social-problem novels question the Victorian order of things, but this does not mean that they necessarily advocate radical change – hence anxieties displayed in a large proportion of the texts towards the threat of working-class 'mob' violence. Part of the problem with the novels, it seems, is that they largely involve middle-class authors recounting the lives of working-class people, to the extent that the political difficulties they raise lie within the texts themselves. At the same time that Elizabeth Gaskell's work, for instance, is broadly sympathetic to the problems facing the poor, her novel *Mary Barton: A Tale of Manchester Life* (1848) also moves, somewhat voyeuristically, through the miserable and squalid lives associated with the nation's industrial heartlands. Gaskell lingers in the interiors of working-class hovels, on starving men and women with their dead or dying children, and she focuses on the despairing and eventually murderous figure of John Barton. But she also describes the 'uneducated' masses represented by Barton as 'Frankenstein', a fairly common Victorian metaphor for a disenchanted and 'monstrous' working class which might rise in rebellion against its makers – the Victorian industrialist and capitalist classes: 'The people rise up to life; they irritate us, they terrify us, and we become their enemies'. Consequently, whilst Gaskell's novel sought to expose social problems and injustices, it also draws attention to the conflicts between the classes which created them. Effectively, her work constructs a discourse of the working class against which the upper echelons of Victorian society, including Gaskell herself, could define themselves as superior.

Social-problem novels tend to be full of the ideological tensions and complexities suggested by Gaskell's novel. Charles Dickens's *Oliver Twist* (1837), for example, was written to promote more progressive reforms. This famous novel deals with the changes in society wrought by the Poor Law Amendment Act (1834), the miseries of the workhouse system and its abuses of children, and an urban criminal underclass full of pickpockets, burglars and prostitutes. Yet Oliver prevails, it seems, only because the narrative logic of his journey from rags to riches demands a happy ending, and because the reader senses that he is an essentially good, middle-class hero from the outset, one who speaks with a Home Counties accent which is miraculously untouched by its scrape with London's thieves and women of easy morals. Other social-problem novels focus more directly on the exploitation of factory workers, and titles within this sub-division include Frances Trollope's *Michael Armstrong: The Factory Boy* (1839), Charlotte Tonna's *Helen Fleetwood* (1839) and Paul Pimlico's *The Factory Girl* (1849). One, Charles Kingsley's *Alton Locke* (1850), follows the life of a man who is a working-class taylor, poet and Chartist sympathizer all at once. Another, Benjamin Disraeli's *Sybil: or the Two Nations* (1845), dissects a range of social problems: industrial strife, working-class abuse, the excesses of wealthy 'Lords' and 'Ladies', the noble Charles Egremont's sympathy for the 'low' radicalism of Chartist agitations for reform, and a broader analysis of a society which has become divided into 'two nations' along class lines, 'the Rich and the Poor'. Indeed, by the 1850s, the sheer size and scope of some social-problem novels, such as Dickens's *Bleak House* (1853) and *Little Dorrit* (1857), enabled them to provide a critique of just about every Victorian problem imaginable, social or otherwise, from the wretched lives of crossing-sweepers to the spectre of empire.

Other social-problem novels from the mid-century onwards reveal what are often slight but perceptible shifts in their ideological emphases. Although Dickens's indictment of a society obsessed with education and 'facts' in *Hard Times* (1854) is arguably an exception, 'industrial' novels such as Charlotte Brontë's *Shirley* (1849) and Gaskell's *North and South* (1855), tend to contain more sympathetic portrayals of employers, factory owners and industrialists, anf this is particularly the case with the romantically desirable Moore brothers in Brontë's novel. Later social-problem novels, however, such as George Eliot's *Felix Holt: The Radical* (1866) and Anthony Trollope's *The Way We Live Now* (1874–5), seem to provide just as broad an analysis of Victorian society and its ills as those of Dickens. Towards the last decades of the century, another diverse crop of social-problem novels, such as George Gissing's *Workers in the Dawn* (1880) and *The Nether World* (1889), William Morris's *News From Nowhere* (1891), or those which comprise the so-called 'New Woman' fiction, including Sarah Grand's *Heavenly Twins* (1893) and Grant Allen's *The Woman Who Did* (1895), also found an audience. Such novels blended their discussions of the social problems facing the lower classes with an increasing emphasis on women. To that end, much of their rhetoric called for more radical solutions, which would have been anathema to earlier writers like Disraeli, Gaskell, Kingsley and Dickens.

See also *Contexts*: Cities and urbanization, Evolution, Industry, Nation; *Texts*: Mid-Victorian novel, Realist fiction; *Criticism*: Deconstruction, Feminism, Marxism, Poststructuralism, Structuralism.

Further Reading

Gallagher, Catherine, *The Industrial Reformation of English Fiction: Social Discourse and Narrative Form, 1832–1867* (University of Chicago Press, IL: Chicago and London, 1985).
Guy, Josephine, *The Victorian Social-Problem Novel* (Basingstoke: Macmillan, 1996).

3 Criticism: Approaches, Theory, Practice

Introduction

Critical approaches to Victorian literature have changed dramatically over the years. During the nineteenth century itself, with the growth of English literature as an institutional discipline (the first chair in English Literature was established at the University of London in 1829), literary criticism steadily became more professionalized, respectable and scholarly. Nowadays, much of Victorian criticism itself is dismissed as an intellectual curiosity. It is, however, important to listen to how Victorian critics received the literature of the day. From there, one is in a better position to observe the trajectory of criticism and theory towards the twenty-first century, especially as many modern approaches grew up largely in response to the intransigence of Victorian ideas and attitudes. Victorian literary critics were preoccupied with a number of issues and problems, one of which was their anxiety about whether or not the text achieved a true or faithful representation of reality. In an age of utilitarianism and unprecedented industrial production, many critics took the idea that literature imitated life for granted, and that, by holding a mirror up to society, it had a 'useful', because productive, sociopolitical function. It is this attitude that convinced Victorian writers like Charles Dickens that novels such as *Oliver Twist* (1837) had a socially ameliorative function, which, because it exposed the socioeconomic and political injustices endemic to Victorian society, was capable of producing change in 'reality'. But the Victorians were also obsessed with poring over the biographical and psychological details of the author, and their reverence for past greats helped turn Shakespeare, most obviously, into the national icon of Englishness he became.

Victorian criticism was also largely evaluative. Reviewers and commentators established criteria for 'good' and 'bad' literature based on a series of questions which they asked of texts time and again, and which often pivoted on the problem of realism: Is it truthful? Is it useful? Is it didactic ('instructive', particularly in a moral sense)? In what way is it productive? Will it have an improving or deleterious effect on the reader, particularly those deemed more susceptible to its influence, such as the young, women and the working class? What does it say about the nature of the individual? And to what extent does it reflect on the eternal truths of the human condition? As such questions suggest, literary criticism, was a serious business for the Victorians. But it was not without its moments of levity. In a review of the American poet Walt Whitman, for example, one anonymous critic in 1856 said that Whitman was 'as unacquainted with art as a hog is with mathematics'. As for the specific role of the Victorian critic, the emphasis was very much on detachment and objectivity. In his *Essays in Criticism* (1865) the influential critic and poet Matthew Arnold argued for the critic's 'disinterestedness'. Yet Arnold's own, extraordinarily lyrical estimation of the Romantic poet Shelley undermines this claim, suggesting that criticism is never impartial. Arnold's attempt to disarm the radical and self-proclaimed 'legislator[s] of mankind' as an 'ineffectual angel, beating in the void his luminous wings in vain', clearly says more about the critic than the poet.

Neither criticism nor literature, as modern critical approaches have shown, are ever 'disinterested'. Both are implicated within the ideological constructs of the day, and as a result the relationship between critic and text has profound implications. When Victorian critics divided novels into 'serious' novels or escapist 'romances', for example, their attempt to maintain a hierarchy of intellectually 'worthy' literature is all too visible. As suggested above, literary realism became the dominant form in the period, and contemporary observers tended to measure the success with which the author provided a 'true' reflection of society as indicative of its aesthetic merit. Similarly, the extent to which the author provided a sufficiently profound meditation on the human condition also depended on whether or not the critic's own outlook on life was confirmed, and such a confirmation became the point at which a critical consensus on the relationship between literature and 'reality' was reached. Furthermore, the idea that literature should be mimetic of 'real life' and everyday experience preoccupied the majority of contemporary commentators. Many Victorian writers of realist novels, such as Anthony Trollope and George Eliot, were also literary critics (some even reviewed their own books), and they were all, in one way or another, anxious about the critical status of realism, as were other writers and poets. In 1858 George Henry Lewes wrote that art should always be 'a representation of reality', and the novelist Edward Bulwer Lytton wrote in 1862 that the author of novels 'must be as thoroughly in earnest as if he were the narrator of facts'. The peculiarly Victorian emphasis here on the 'actual' and the 'factual' – on that which is physically 'out there' – should not be taken lightly. It captures the spirit of scientific rationalism, empirical enquiry and, in more subtle ways, the ideology of industrial capitalism which underpinned the Victorian ethos. By insisting that the gap between literature and reality, fiction and fact, is effectively non-existent, Victorian critics presumed that a natural and 'common-sense' meaning was produced by literature. It followed that the meaning of the text was easily inferred because it was as clear and 'present' to language as it was tangible or 'thing-like', in the same way that any other material object was produced by Victorian industry.

The critical preoccupation with reality, fact and empiricism, with that which is 'present', drove the Victorian ethos, and implicit in Victorian criticism was the idea that the meaning of literature was simply 'there' for the critic to reach into language and 'touch'. Such an idea has long since passed into everyday English metaphors. Consider phrases, for example, such as 'grasping the meaning' or 'getting hold of the sense'. Both suggest that the abstract relationship between language and meaning is a tactile one and that meaning can, as it were, be held in the hands. That these metaphors are the legacy of Victorianism, however, and that they are derived from the world's first industrial-capitalist society, which commodified everything including meaning, should not be forgotten in the attempt to understand both Victorian and modern critical approaches to literature. Another comment made by Matthew Arnold, whose work so often appears to be a barometer of conventional opinion, underlines the way in which the Victorians regarded 'reality' as a clear and 'visible' 'object'. In his essay 'The Function of Criticism at the Present Time', from *Culture and Anarchy*' (1869), Arnold defended the importance of criticism, and by extension the Victorian ethos in its entirety, in his point that the 'critical effort' in all 'branches of knowledge', from 'theology' to 'science', is to 'see the object as it *really* is' (my italics).

It was only after the 1860s that the 'realist' and 'objective' consensus on criticism and literature met with any serious challenge. When it did, it came largely from the decadent and aesthetic writers associated with the 'art for art's sake' movement. These included Algernon Swinburne, Walter Pater, and, most famously, the Oscar Wilde circle in the 1880s–90s. The aesthetes condemned the idea that literature should be 'useful' and 'realistic' in any way, or that it should contain a 'moral purpose'. Wilde thought art should be 'impressionistic', if anything, and, in his controversial preface to *The Picture of Dorian Gray* (1891), he proclaimed that 'All art is quite useless'. A rejection of Victorian critical approaches, and particularly those of Arnold, can also be heard in Wilde's remarks in his 1891 essay, 'The Critic as Artist', in which he argues that in practice the critic loses any 'disinterestedness' altogether and becomes, to all intents and purposes, as important and commend-able as the 'artist'. 'Anybody', according to Wilde, 'can write a three-volume novel'. Not everybody, on the other hand, can be as 'cultivated' and 'creative' as the 'critic'. Wilde also inverted the Arnoldian idea of seeing objects as they 'really' are, and some of his comments on this point have a strikingly modern tone: 'the primary aim of the critics is to see the object as in itself it really is not'. Modern critical approaches, as we shall see, also tend to interpret the text in terms of that which it could not be conscious of itself, or rather, in terms of that which it might regard itself as 'not' but which in effect it 'becomes' in the work of crit-icism. The task of the modern critic is, therefore, to paraphrase Wilde in his discussion of the Mona Lisa, to decode those 'secrets' of Victorian literature which, 'in truth, it knows nothing' about at all.

Most Victorian critical approaches were not nearly as progressive as Wilde's, however. Women writers, for example, such as the Brontë sisters and George Eliot, were up against the prejudices of a patriarchal society and a largely male-dominated literary arena, the critics of which often took a dim view of the intellectual 'deficiencies' of women. In response, many women authors were forced to take masculine *noms de plumes* in order to be taken seriously and get published. Mary Ann Evans, for instance, was George Eliot's pseudonym, and Currer Bell was the slightly more androgynous name taken by Charlotte Brontë. Brontë always claimed that she had a 'vague impression' that women writers would be 'looked on with prejudice' by critics, and this was confirmed after she had sent the poet laureate, Robert Southey, some of her poetry in 1837. Southey told Brontë, in no uncertain terms, that literature was not the 'business' of a women's 'life', and that she should return to her 'proper duties'. Although by modern standards Brontë's fiction might seem mild and even conservative, it is indicative of the way that approaches to Victorian literature have changed that her story of an oppressed governess in *Jane Eyre* (1847) was rejected as downright 'immoral' by some contemporary critics. If such a criticism again says more about the patriarchal codes underlying Victorian society than it does about Brontë's novel, it remained the dominant one until the advent of feminist criticism in the late twentieth century. At the same time, George Eliot was often a waspish critic of other women novelists herself, particularly those whom she thought wrote frivolous and romantic trash about swooning 'ladies' and conniving aristocrats. She ridiculed the clichés of such fiction in her unambiguously titled article for the *Westminster Review* in 1856, 'Silly Novels by Lady Novelists'. Eliot was, it should be remembered, part of the burgeoning Victorian middle classes. That her work lambasts the aristocracy consequently says more, perhaps about her own investment in the bourgeois ideas and attitudes with which her realist fiction came to be implicated than it does about novel writing.

Contemporary critical approaches to literature were also affected by the formation of the literary canon, and Matthew Arnold's opinions on this point are again representative. Arnold argued that there was a standard, or rather, to use his quintessentially Victorian term, 'class' of 'truly excellent' texts which were unsurpassed in their 'poetic quality' and aesthetic worth. The trouble, typically, was how this 'quality' was to be assessed, although it usually meant the celebration of those such as Shakespeare, the period's own leading poet, Alfred Lord Tennyson, and other writers not perceived to be subversive or degenerate in any way. One of the major factors which determined the canonization of acceptable texts was in fact forced on contemporary criticism by the early library and distribution businesses, including W. H. Smith's and Charles Mudie's Lending Library. From 1842, Mudie acted as a sort of moral guardian over which works of literature were stocked and made available to the Victorian public. These were almost exclusively those titles Mudie considered to uphold Victorian attitudes and values. Such were his powers of censorship and eventually his control of the book market, in fact, that he could often make or break an aspiring writer's career quicker than a negative review.

The Victorians were responsible for creating the male-dominated canon of 'quality' Romantic poetry, for example. This consisted of Blake, Wordsworth, Coleridge, Byron, Shelley and Keats, and it still exists in some intellectual quarters today. It was, however, in the twentieth century that the canon of English literature was formed in influential critical works such as Cambridge critic F. R. Leavis's *The Great Tradition* (1948). Like the Victorians, Leavis looked for and found in texts a timeless and coherent quality of humanistic enquiry and realism which was quintessentially 'English', especially in the novels of Jane Austen, George Eliot, Henry James and Joseph Conrad, whom he called 'The great English novelists'. It is revealing, as this list suggests, that all four of Leavis's 'greats' were nineteenth-century writers – the last three being Victorians – especially because it was the Victorians who invented the study of 'English literature' in the first place. In conspicuously Victorian tones, Leavis included George Eliot in his canon for the 'moral seriousness' of her novels, for an 'interest in human nature that made her a great psychologist', and for the formal 'originality' and complexity of her work. He initially snubbed the most popular and successful Victorian writer, Charles Dickens, as a 'genius' who was hampered by being a 'great entertainer'. Dickens was then reinstated in Leavis's *Dickens the Novelist*

(1970), when the critic reread *Hard Times* (1854) as a decent enough 'moral fable'. Other Victorian writers, like Emily Brontë, 'the genius, of course', but not, significantly, her more prolific and successful sister, Charlotte, enjoyed some recognition in an endnote to Leavis's work, whereas Thomas Hardy was largely written off as 'gauche and heavy'.

As with those of the Victorians, Leavis's criticisms need to be situated in their historical and cultural contexts. *The Great Tradition* appeared in 1948, soon after the upheavals of the Second World War (1939–45), and the work appears to gain much of its critical impetus from the need to re-establish some sense of order and structure over an institution, English Literature, which was widely considered to be important to the national sense of history and identity. But Leavis and his acolytes, as shown above, only really compounded what Victorian critics had already begun. Indeed, long before the Second World War, the institution of English literature had begun to fulfil a significant social and national function in Victorian society. With the growing impact of scientific achievements on Victorian consciousness throughout the nineteenth century, and partic-ularly after individual landmarks such as Charles Darwin's theory of evolution in *On the Origin of Species* (1859), many Victorians became increasingly uncertain about their status on Earth in God's great scheme of things. And, as modern commentators such as Terry Eagleton in *Literary Theory* (1983) have argued, this is the same historical context in which English Literature rose to prominence. When the 'social "cement"' of 'religion' in Victorian society, in other words, began to crumble, 'English', as an educational discipline promoting English culture and national identity, began to replace it. From this perspective, Victorian literature reinvigorated the culture of Englishness, at the same time that it lent some sense of certainty and cohesion to a modern society marked by crisis and change. In the nineteenth century, literature had started to carry what Eagleton calls an 'ideological burden'. Its task was to bring Englishness back together in the next great phase of European national-ism, from the jingoism and imperialism of the last decades of Victoria's reign, through to the First World War (1914–18), and right up to the reconstruction of national identity provided by the critical reign of the Leavis circle after the Second World War.

• • •

These days, much of the traditional, or rather anti-theoretical, literary criticism associated with the Victorians and the Leavis circle is referred to, often in a hostile manner, as 'liberal humanism'. The hostility arises from a number of factors, but largely because such criticism, as suggested above, is based on assessing the unity and cohesiveness of the Victorian text, and its representation of timeless and universal 'human' truths about what is perceived to be an essentially unchanging, and equally cohesive, 'human' nature. Modern criticism, at least the majority of more progressive criticism from the 1950s onwards, tends to be less reverent towards these literary and critical shibboleths. It is not preoccupied with concepts such as 'humanism' and 'realism' as such; rather, it stresses the cultural politics of literature which made such ideologies of humanism and realism possible. In terms of its approach to the liberal, capitalist age of the Victorians, modern criticism is especially interested in the way that texts construct, rather than just reflect, the integrity of the individual and the category of human subjectivity. This is not, however, to say that modern criticism is a cold fish that does not care about 'humanity'. On the contrary, modern criticism seeks to understand how a concept such as the 'human subject' came to be implicated in Western ideologies of capitalism and its preoccupation with the 'free-thinking', individual 'self'. In this respect, the questions for modern criticism are rarely, if ever, 'What does this text say about individual truths?', 'Is this literature like reality?', or 'Is it factual and truthful?' In a nutshell, the questions it asks include, 'How do these individual truths come about?', 'Whose "reality", exactly, with its "facts" and "truths" are we supposed to be living in?' Neither do modern critics waste time sitting about discussing which piece of Victorian literature is better than the next; nor are they seduced by the bleak 'liberal humanist' assumption that 'great' English literature makes us better human beings. Such evaluative approaches are, needless to say, oddly Victorian and Leavisite in tenor, and, more importantly, they tend to remove the politics from what is the fundamentally political nature of Victorian literature.

Modern critical approaches are, nevertheless, better understood when other liberal humanist positions are clarified. The critical approach of Q. D. Leavis, for example, which differed in significant respects from that of her husband, was to locate a single or 'correct' meaning in Victorian literary works, and by that to ascribe to texts a coherence and unity which modern critics reject. Such an approach is suggested by the declarative and, to modern ears perhaps, rather pompous tone of one of the titles of her essays in *Dickens the Novelist*, which she co-authored with her husband: 'How We Must Read *Great Expectations*'. Revealingly, it is in the preface to this book that the Leavises set the critical tone of their anti-theoretical approach to the Victorians, at the turn of the 1970s when modern theory was gathering momentum: 'The Marxizing and other ideologically slanted interpretations of Dickens's achievement were comparatively harmless and are now a dead letter'. Here, the reactionary, but no less 'ideologically-slanted' tone of Leavis's own criticism is, disingenuously enough, all-too clear. In the essay on *Great Expectations*, Leavis goes on to drain Dickens's work of any suggestion of class antagonism, recommending that, instead, 'what is required' is substantiation that Dickens's novel is a 'great novel,' which is 'engaged in discussing, by exemplifying, profound and basic realities of human experience.' If Leavis's 'liberal humanism' is not clear enough from this quotation, one can certainly detect the way she encodes it into in her points about Dickens's writing being, above all, 'always sympathetically human', and that it contains a 'homogeneous tone'. Modern critical approaches grew up precisely in reaction to the kind of approach taken by the Leavises. In short, whereas Leavis perceives a 'homogeneous tone' in the Victorian text, which is as singular and unified as the 'human' individuals it discusses, modern critics tend to see a radical 'heterogeneity' in all texts; they perceive a series of multiple voices which mark both the fragmentary nature of human experience and, because of these voices, a degree of self-doubt or self-criticism within the text itself. Such tensions are particularly prevalent within important Victorian novels themselves, such as Dickens's *David Copperfield* (1850) and Eliot's *Middlemarch* (1872), which seem at once to construct the ideas and values which underpin Victorian middle-class humanism, and take them apart.

The rise of the Leavis circle did, however, mark a substantial change in the direction of critical practice. Its approach, which emphasized close readings of the texts over biographical contexts or literary and cultural history, was revolutionary for its day, and it was largely this emphasis which separated its approach from Victorian approaches. The work of the Leavises became, in this respect, part of the other influential, early twentieth-century critical movements, such as the 'practical criticism' associated with I. A. Richards in 1920s–40s Britain, and the 'new criticism' associated with Americans such as John Ransome in the same period. These approaches were also more text-focused and less author-based than their Victorian predecessors. More so than Leavis's work, which tended to lapse into paraphrase, the 'new' critics began to place greater emphasis on closer readings of the words on the page themselves, and they treated each text as a self-sufficient and discreet artefact to the exclusion of its historical and theoretical contexts. In important works such as Richards's *Practical Criticism* (1929) and Ransome's *The New Criticism* (1941), the authors set out to undermine centuries of vague critical assumptions about texts, and the crude evaluations about the relationship between art and life they led to, especially those left to posterity by the Victorians. They approached literature, from all periods, in such a way as to understand the complexities, ambiguities and ironies it contained, and many of their methods remain influential today.

The most significant break with traditional humanist criticism was the emergence in France of structuralism in the 1950s. Structuralism was more than just a literary or critical movement, but broadly speaking, leading structuralist thinkers such as the anthropologist Claude Lévi-Strauss and the semiotician cum literary critic Roland Barthes argued that what was important were the 'structures' of sign systems which constitute human experience, not just the experience or the behaviour itself. Structuralists see a world of signs in which 'everything signifies', from the structures of myth and tradition which underpin human behaviour in Lévi-Strauss's work, to the patterns of images and metaphors which make up literary language in the work of Barthes. Structuralist literary theorists also tend to emphasize the structures which link individual texts together, rather than their specific differences, and the problem of language is central to their thought. As with poststructuralism (discussed below), it is structuralism's preoccupation with language, in fact, which marks its indebtedness to the influential, early twentieth-century work of Swiss linguist Ferdinand de Saussure. In his *Course in General Linguistics* (1916), Saussure founded a revolutionary theory of the 'structure' of language, one which is made up from a system of signs. His work was based on the idea that the structural relationship between the signifier (the sound-image or the word) and the signified (the concept, the meaning) is an arbitrary and therefore 'unnatural' social construct, albeit one which, crucially, constructs our 'ideas' about the world.

Saussure held that language is a system of differences in which each signifier is definable, not by the 'presence' of meaning contained in the signifier, but by each signifier's 'difference' from another. The signifier 'duck', for example, is only definable by its difference in language from 'luck' or 'ruck', not by any reference to the feathered, semi-aquatic species of bird that its signified conjures up. Saussure's theories of language proved to be momentous for modern literary and theoretical approaches, particularly for their emphasis on the social 'constructedness' of meaning, and especially for poststructuralism, which grew up in the 1960s partly alongside, but also in reaction to structuralism. Poststructuralism took Saussure's ideas further and applied them to the problematic ways in which readers make meaning from texts. But whereas structuralist approaches stressed that the underlying structures of sign systems used language, in a Saussurean manner, to 'construct' the meaning of human or social 'reality', poststructualist criticism works from the premise that it is impossible for any text to have any secure or unified meaning at all, precisely because texts are made from the complex and ambiguous material of language.

Unlike the more 'unifying' approaches taken by the Victorians or the Leavises, and to some extent the structuralists, poststructuralism stresses the fragmentary nature of texts, and the multiple meanings they unleash. In his groundbreaking work, *Of Grammatology* (1967), one of the founding poststructuralist thinkers, Jacques Derrida, contradicted Saussure's point about the inseparable, albeit socially constructed, relationship between signifier and signified in language. Instead, what Derrida saw in language was an endless movement or 'sliding' of meaning from one signifier to the next, the result being that no signifier could refer to a world 'outside' itself at all, only to other signifiers in a system in which, as he puts it, 'there has never been anything but writing'.

In the Derridean perspective, the signifier is essentially empty of meaning at all times. Due to each signifier's 'difference' from all other signifiers, the signifier is built on a fundamental 'absence' to which Saussure and, as Derrida argues, Western society in general, have attributed a 'presence'. One way of appreciating the significance of Derrida's position is to recall the way in which Victorian criticism took for granted the 'presence' of a 'tangible' meaning in 'realist' fiction. Derrida's work, the work of deconstruction (a term often used interchangeably with poststructuralism), is broadly definable, if at all, as a critique of the West's preoccupation with the notion of 'presence'. And it is this preoccupation with 'presence', with the thingness of things or with reification (making things 'thing-like') which, for many modern critics of Victorian culture and its commodified society, defined both the nature of Victorian realism and the urge of conventional criticism to 'grasp' the singular and unified 'meaning' of realism. In the poststructualist perspective, the structuralist consensus about the 'presence' of underlying 'structures' begins to break down. For postructuralists, because the relationship between signifier and signified is predicated on 'absence', on 'nothing' rather than 'something', texts are seen to be fundamentally unstable and their meanings undecideable. Texts therefore contain numerous voices and release various contradictory meanings and interpretations, which are forever undoing, for example, what Q. D. Leavis called the 'homogeneous tone' of Dickens's *Great Expectations*.

Similar ideas to those of Derrida and the poststructuralists had already been put forward in the influential work of Russian critic Mikhail Bakhtin. In the 1930s–40s, Bakhtin divided texts into either 'monologic' texts, the more 'unified' product of one authorial voice, or dialogic texts, the product of multiple voices ('polyphony'), which tend to contradict each other and clash. Bakhtin was, however, like Derrida and his followers later in the century, critical of linguists such as Saussure and his own predecessors in the 'Formalist' school of pre-revolutionary and 1920s Russia. First and foremost, Bakhtin was suspicious of the Formalist tendency to concentrate on individual linguistic 'devices', the 'formal' properties and structures of the text such as syntax, metre, rhyme, narrative and so on, at the expense of the sociopolitical contexts or 'content' of literature. Similar criticisms, although for different reasons, would also be levelled at some of the more extreme structural, post-structural, and deconstructive approaches which were to follow in the wake of his work. Bakhtin's ideas were also influential on the post-structuralist Julia Kristeva's notion of 'intertextuality', which appeared in the mid-1960s. Intertextuality is another important critical concept which refers to the way that the many 'voices' of all texts haunt each other and are in constant dialogue with each other across time, either with or, to paraphrase Roland Barthes, without quotation marks.

As with Victorian and Leavisite approaches, modern criticism also needs to be situated in its social and historical contexts. It is no coincidence, for example, that the most important sea changes in literary and critical theory were gathering apace during the 1960s, in a period which has become associated in Western consciousness with a time of social, sexual and cultural revolution. By the late 1960s, structuralist approaches were gradually giving way to those of postructuralism, and, like structuralism, most of these approaches emanated from mid-1960s France. The immeasurable impact on modern criticism made by philosophers, psychoanalysts, literary critics and historians of ideas, especially that of Derrida, Kristeva, Barthes and Michel Foucault respectively, is nowadays widely acknowledged, albeit still hotly disputed and controversial. Much of the work of these complex and very different writers performed, in fact, the transition between structuralism and poststructuralism, and some pointed towards the age of postmodernism which is supposed to define the current social and critical epoch. In 1968, for example, in the aftermath of strikes in France, student rebellions, civil rights protests around the world, and the crisis of the war in Vietnam, Barthes and Foucault embarked on an important literary debate about what Barthes called the 'birth of the reader' and the 'death of the author'. The debate was based around a concept which has come to be known in literary theory as the 'intentional fallacy', which alerts readers and critics to the dangers (fallacies) of attributing the singular meaning of a text to the 'intention' of the author, and which, as we have seen, was largely a Victorian and Leavisite preoccupation. Just to give a flavour of the argument between Barthes and Foucault (a fuller discussion is provided in the entry on Poststructuralism in this section), Barthes argued in 'The Death of the Author' (1968) that in Western society the role of 'the author' exerts a tyranny over meaning and truth akin to that of 'God', and that to 'give a text an Author is to impose a limit on that text'. Foucault countered this argument by suggesting, in 'What is an Author?' (1969), that because of its very centrality to the history of Western capitalist 'individualism', the author should be allowed to participate in the 'proliferation' of meanings emitted by the text, and that not to do so would be an injustice to both the text and history. Yet despite their differences, Barthes' and Foucault's approaches to this complex problem were broadly similar, in that they both took 'language', which is what literature 'is', as both the fundamental problem and the basis of critical enquiry. Unlike in Victorian and Leavisite criticisms, their debate underlines the point that, in modern theory language is always the first and most formidable impasse, from which all other problems and issues extend. Subsequently, although the problem for modern critical approaches remains what Victorian literature 'says', what the author had in mind is less important than the idea that, as Barthes put it long ago in 'The Death of the Author', it is 'language which speaks, not the author'.

• • •

Most of the major critical and theoretical approaches to Victorian literature, which either preceded or grew out of the advent of poststructualism, are dealt with in this section. I have not gone into them in any detail here, or explained their differences, because that seemed best left for each separate entry. At this juncture, it is sufficient to point out that deconstruction, feminism, Marxism, new historicism, cultural materialism, postcolonialism, postmodernism, poststructuralism, psychoanalysis, queer theory and structuralism, are all fundamentally concerned with the nature and distribution of power in society, and the various complex ways in which, in mediums such as Victorian literature, that power is represented or rather ideologically constructed and performed. To take just one critical approach for now, feminist criticism, for example, which came to prominence in the 1970s, revolutionized the approach to major Victorian writers such as George Eliot and Thomas Hardy. At the same time, it rescued others, such as Charlotte Brontë, as a prototypical feminist writer from her exile from Leavis's 'Great Tradition'. Thomas Hardy, for instance, in the feminist purview, is no longer regarded as the rather quaint-sounding 'Grand Old Man of English Letters' or as England's 'rural annalist' *par excellence*, a role ascribed to him in more orthodox, liberal humanist, generally male-dominated criticism. Feminism has repeatedly subjected Hardy's novels (and those of other Victorians) to the kind of scrutiny which has ensured that they are now seen as both part of, and critical of, the dominant Victorian ideologies which underpin them, those pertaining especially, but not exclusively, to problems of class, race, gender and sexuality.

As with the other sections, what follows is in alphabetical order. For the sake of chronological clarity, however, it might be easier for the reader to read the entry on 'Structuralism' before the entry on 'Poststructuralism', because, as the concepts suggest, and as shown above, the latter positions itself against the former. On the other hand, each entry is discrete, and can be understood on its own terms, although again the reader's understanding of structuralism will be strengthened by reading 'Poststructuralism', and vice versa. Likewise, a reading of 'Deconstruction', being part of the umbrella term. 'Poststructuralism', will inform the understanding of 'Poststructuralism'; 'Postmodernism' might better be understood with some grasp of 'Poststructuralism', and so on. A point about one entry does require further clarification. I have combined the essay on 'New Historicism' in this section, a critical movement largely of American orientation, with that on 'Cultural Materialism', largely of British orientation, not to ride roughshod over the important distinctions between the two, but for the sake of time and space to show their important similarities. Indeed, modern works which want to stress the distinctions between the two concepts and their critical approaches also find themselves linking the two in one volume, as witnessed in two recent publications, Kiernan Ryan's edited *New Historicism and Cultural Materialism: A Reader* (1996), and John Brannigan's *New Historicism and Cultural Materialism* (1998), both of which are highly recommended.

Although most of the theories and criticisms discussed in this section are very much separate entities in their own right, many effectively combine in the work of criticism. To illustrate this point, recently, when asked by a suspicious-looking student in front of a large Critical Theory group what my precise position was, on literature and life in general, I found myself replying that my own work on the Victorians involves what can only be described, in no particular order, and not quite so clearly, as 'Poststructuralist Marxist Psychoanalytic Deconstructive New Historicist Cultural Materialist Feminist Postcolonialism', although it is also in sympathy with Queer Theory, Structuralism, and just about every other broadly progressive 'ism' one might think of. This is not to say that I was frightened of 'sticking my neck out', as it were (at least I do not think so), or that many of these approaches are not antagonistic towards each other, because they are. My response was more a sort of ungainly tribute to the influence of one of the other major concepts that finds an entry in this section, 'Postmodernism'. Postmodernism appears to permit one to draw upon the innumerable ideas and political implications of all the other critical approaches, embracing both their radical heterogeneity, their endless contradictions, and their combined usefulness in tackling something as equally massive and diverse as Victorian literature. There are, that is to say, merits in all of the theories and approaches discussed in what follows, although that, perhaps, is for the reader to decide.

Deconstruction

Deconstruction grew out of the social and intellectual ferment of 1960s France, and its theories and ideas are closely associated with the work of Jacques Derrida. Derrida's work began, broadly speaking, as a critique of the Western philosophical tradition, and particularly metaphysics, the branch of philosophy concerned with the nature of being and what exists. His most basic, but complex and far-reaching point, is that Western consciousness is predicated upon a rationalism which, in turn, bases itself on an illusion of 'presence' created by rhetorical constructions in language. From this premise, Derrida questioned the West's wider preoccupation with locating the 'presence' of a stable and unified truth or 'meaning' about the world, which he called the 'transcendental signified'. In doing so, he questioned, or rather, he deconstructed, Western civilization in its entirety. The transcendental signified, for Derrida and his followers, was throughout Western history supplied by the all-truthful, all-'meaningful', authority figures of God and religion, but also by other authorities preoccupied with the meaning of things, such as science and philosophy.

With the Victorians' own obsession with the presence of 'meaning', itself the legacy of the rationalist and scientific methods they inherited from the Enlightenment, it is not surprising that the nineteenth century has proven good hunting ground for deconstructors. The Victorians looked for a stable meaning everywhere: in God, science, history, in their work ethic, in industry, capitalism, in the integrity of the individual, in the commodity, in their Empire, and in their literature, particularly in literary 'realism'. What deconstruction has shown – to the Victorians and to their literary critics – is that the nature of 'meaning' is fundamentally unstable. Meaning, as Derrida has argued, is 'absent' in the signifier (the word, the sound-image); it is the result of 'differences' created by an endlessly shifting and deferred system of signs. No single or determined meaning in the text, for Derrida, can be arrived at securely, only an endless plurality of conflicting and undecideable meanings which society selects from and endows with the 'presence' of 'truth'. Derrida's controversial idea (which concludes these points) that language does not refer to anything or anyone outside of its own system of signs, is what underpinned his notorious claim in *Of Grammatology* (1967), that *'Il n'y a rien hors du texte'* ('there is nothing outside the text'). It is this claim, perhaps more than any other, which led to criticisms from some feminist and Marxist commentators that deconstruction removes texts from their historical and socioeconomic contexts, and that it is consequently 'anti-humanist'. Understandably though, with its focus on language, deconstruction has had a massive influence on literary studies. Where they are united at all, as suggested above, deconstructionists dispute that there is any singular or unified meaning in the text, only a series of multiple voices, significations, absences, silences, impasses, many of which overlap, blend, clash with and contradict each other. The work of deconstruction consequently involves what Barbara Johnson calls the complex and 'careful teasing out of warring forces of signification within the text', or what Steven Connor describes as an unpicking of the text's 'internal arguments'.

Notoriously hard to define, deconstruction as a critical practice does in fact have one defining characteristic: it reads, and it reads closely. Yet as one of the more misunderstood terms in literary theory, a common misconception is that deconstruction is about 'destruction'. On the contrary, leading thinkers such as Derrida have maintained throughout their writings that deconstruction is ultimately concerned with 'construction', or rather reconstruction. Put another way, deconstruction is about perpetual disruption and change, but its aims are ultimately positive and 'constructive'. The deconstruction of a work of Victorian literature involves an approach which in practice is closer to the Greek etymological roots of 'analysis', which connotes 'setting free'. The deconstructive critic sets meanings 'free', in a sense, by undoing or dismantling the text, by deconstructing the text to see how it works. But the deconstructive critic also explores the ways in which the text is already falling apart from within (self-deconstructing) because the text is made, as shown above, from the fragile material of language. Part of the point of deconstructing Victorian literature is to remain sensitive to the text's 'constructedness' in language, and by that the constructedness of the ideas, attitudes, ideologies, meanings, individuals, universal human 'truths', realities, 'facts', obsessions with the 'presence' of things, and so on, it gives rise to. When these ideas are shown to be 'constructs' of language, of culture and society, and not therefore 'natural' or 'inevitable', it follows that they can be deconstructed and then 're-constructed'.

To demonstrate this point more fully, Derrida set about deconstructing what he calls in *Of Grammatology* the 'violent hierarchy' of binary oppositions constructed by language, a dualist system of thinking which, he argues, underpins Western consciousness. Starting from the seemingly harmless opposition between speech and writing, Derrida showed that historically speech has always been endowed with greater prestige in the West than writing (what he called the West's 'phonocentrism' or 'logocentricism'). Speech, he argued, is perceived to be 'present' or emanating from the 'inside' of individuals, and consequently it is thought to be physically or rather 'naturally' closer to the inner sense of 'self'. Writing, on the other hand, is perceived to be learned, cultural, unnatural, and therefore something 'outside' of the individual and less 'present' or integral to the 'self'. For Derrida, however, speech and writing are both essentially constructs of language; neither is more naturally nor intrinsically superior to the other, and both achieve only that status which culture and society confer on them. Derridean deconstruction is significant for modern critics of Victorian literature because its approach can then be applied to the other fundamental binary oppositions in Western culture, most of which may have more obviously profound – because more obviously 'violent' – implications for society: man/woman, native/foreign, master/slave, self/other, soul/body, good/evil, fact/fiction, sane/mad. In these oppositions, it is quite easy to see that the first term in each has historically been granted greater prestige, or rather has always been dominant in Western society, over the subordinate or oppressed second term. But what Derrida and deconstruction have shown, crucially, is that each term in the opposition depends on the other for meaning, so that the two in effect constitute each other. Each term, that is, such as 'man', can only define itself by that 'other' which it thinks it is not, 'woman'. 'Man' is, as a result, continually haunted by the 'presence' of that which it perceives to be 'absent', 'woman', but which actually gives it its 'meaning' and status. Likewise, 'masters' need 'slaves' in order to be masters, 'good' is unknowable without the knowledge of 'evil', 'fact' requires the untruth of 'fiction' to distinguish itself, 'sanity' means nothing without the definition of 'madness', and so on.

One way to begin deconstructing Victorian literature is, then, to locate the 'violent hierarchy' of binary oppositions in language that literature is based upon. The man and woman dyad in Victorian culture is especially revealing and useful in this respect, because it gave rise to a subset of equally violent oppositions which are also rooted in questions of gender and sexuality throughout the period. One of these oppositions is what feminist critic Penny Boumelha has called the 'virgin' and 'whore' dichotomy in Victorian culture. In Thomas Hardy's *Tess of the D'Urbervilles* (1891), for example, the 'maiden' Tess becomes a 'fallen' woman in the eyes of Wessex society after her rape and impregnation by Alec D'Urberville. Without a middle or third ground in language/ consciousness with which to rescue her from the violence of the binary opposition, the narrative logic of Tess's transgression in the text from 'virgin' to 'whore' effectively means she is destined to lose her child, scandalize her lover Angel Clare, and murder her assailant, for which she is eventually hanged. Other Victorian texts, in this manner, might be deconstructed by analysing the violent hierarchy of their organizing binary oppositions. These might include the tensions between 'fact' and 'imagination' ('the robber fancy') of Charles Dickens's *Hard Times* (1854), the Protestant 'rationality' and 'Gothic romance' of Charlotte Brontë's *Jane Eyre* (1847), the 'us' versus 'them' of Benjamin Disraeli's 'Two Nations' (the working and middle/upper classes) in *Sybil* (1845), and the 'real' versus the 'unreal', the 'fleshy' versus the 'ghostly' – the 'presence' versus the 'absence' – in Henry James's chiller *The Turn of the Screw* (1898).

The violence of another binary opposition, white/black, is also significant. In Western consciousness, 'white' has always had positive associations, denoting goodness, purity, clarity, light, enlightenment, intelligence, beauty, and cleanliness. 'Black', on the other hand, has consistently been associated with the opposite of whiteness: badness, darkness, evil, irrationality, stupidity, inferiority, ugliness and dirt. It is not hard to see from this opposition why deconstructive postcolonial critics have used it to undo the discourses of race and nationalism which underpinned Britain's history of slavery and empire, and which culminated in the Victorian period. The black/white opposition haunts nineteenth-century literature throughout the period. It forms, for example, part of what Edward W. Said calls the 'shadowy presence' of empire in the works of Jane Austen, Charles Dickens and George Eliot, only to become more pronounced in the Anglo/Indian tensions of Rudyard Kipling's imperialistic work in *Barrack-Room Ballads* (1892) and *The Jungle Book* (1894), or in the novels of Joseph Conrad, such as *Heart of Darkness* (1902).

The problem with binary oppositions is that, as Derrida warned in *Positions* (1972), 'the hierarchy of oppositions always re-establishes itself'. Consequently, the black/white opposition, as with that between man/woman or virgin/whore, is always resettling and making its violent 'presence' felt in culture and society. It is in this respect that deconstruction is forever. Deconstruction is not, as Derrida says, something you simply choose to do on a fine afternoon. Deconstruction calls for a non-binary or non-dualistic consciousness which does not simply reverse the terms in the binary opposition, by making, say, 'blackness' superior to 'whiteness', or 'woman' superior to 'man', but which thinks and practises outside of the violence of such hierarchies, at all times. Furthermore, as Derrida has argued, even '"Everyday language" is not neutral or innocent. It is the language of Western metaphysics'. It follows that the language of Victorian literature, and especially the 'everyday' illusion laid down by its classic 'realism', was integral to Western consciousness and, consequently, to the spread of Western culture and 'civilization' around the world. For deconstructors, what happens in a work of realist literature such as George Eliot's *Middlemarch* (1872), is that the text creates the illusion of 'presence' through its reflections on 'reality', place, character, voice, identity, through its accumulation of realistic detail, and through its emphasis on substantial and coherent individuals with 'real' inner feelings. Such texts also establish the illusion that the author uses the work to communicate a single 'message' or meaning to the reader – what Derrida calls the 'single mission' – which he or she can then easily 'grasp' or hold in the hands, in the age of the commodity, like the 'presence' of something 'thing-like'.

But 'realism' can only, as deconstructive critics maintain, offer an approximation or a 'construction' of 'real' Victorian life, which is precisely what makes the realist text, to use Catherine Belsey's useful phrase, 'available for *deconstruction*' (italics in original). It is part of the illusion, and for feminist and Marxist deconstructors, patriarchy's bourgeois-capitalist illusion, created by Victorian realist texts, that the ideas and attitudes they present are unimpeachable because 'real', where real connotes natural, truthful, authentic, worthy, obvious, commonsense, meaningful, 'present' in language, and so on. Deconstruction undoes the 'realist' text, all texts, by revealing the series of absences and silences which punctuate them, and by saying that which the text cannot say about the anxieties and neuroses upon which it is built. By locating the text's contradictions in the violence of its binary oppositions, deconstruction holds liberal humanist illusions up for the ideological and discursive constructions that they are. Working from the basic premise that Western civilization's obsession with obtaining the 'presence' of a fixed and God-like meaning of everyone and everything is precisely the problem, the deconstructive critic shows that this problem is endemic to Victorian literature. Ultimately, that Victorian literature yearned for the one true 'meaning' of everyone and everything is unquestionable. What deconstruction has questioned, however, is the extent to which such yearning is itself a construct of language laid down by Western metaphysics, and whether or not the space for reconstruction and change lies in deconstructing the Victorians.

See also   *Contexts*: Empire and imperialism, Individualism, Religion, Science; *Texts*: Mid-Victorian novel, Realist fiction; *Criticism*: Feminism, Marxism, Postcolonialism, Postmodernism, Poststructuralism, Structuralism.

Further Reading

Connor, Steven, 'Deconstructing *Hard Times*', in *New Casebooks: David Copperfield and Hard Times*, ed. John Peck (Basingstoke: Macmillan, 1995)
Derrida, Jacques, *Positions* (London: Athlone Press, 1972).

Feminism

Feminism helped expose the fundamentally patriarchal and oppressive nature of Victorian society. Its critics and commentators have repeatedly shown the ways in which women were oppressed by men in all walks of life, both private and public, and they have drawn attention to the ways in which patriarchal ideology confined most women to the private spheres of domesticity and motherhood. This is not to say that Victorian women were not actively pursuing changes to their position themselves, because they were. In Britain, the term 'feminism' only really became common from around the mid-1890s onwards. The 'woman question', however, had been debated vigorously from at least as early as the late eighteenth century onwards. Important publications of the period included Mary Wollstonecraft's *Vindication of the Rights of Woman* (1792), which equated marriage with 'slavery', and two years before Victoria's accession in 1837, Harriet Martineau's critique of patriarchal attitudes appeared in *Society in America* (1835). Later in the period, liberal Victorian men produced essays on the plight of women as well. In *The Subjection of Women* (1867), for example, John Stuart Mill argued that the 'legal subordination of one sex to the other – is wrong in itself'.

Much Victorian literature also has a feminist impulse. Elizabeth Barrett Browning's verse novel *Aurora Leigh* (1857), for example, contains a critique of the unequal divisions in society between men and women, and the work is often held up as a prototypical piece of feminism. Otherwise, popular novels such as Elizabeth Gaskell's defence of a 'fallen women', *Ruth* (1853), and George Eliot's *The Mill on the Floss* (1860), albeit not expressly feminist fictions, are nonetheless intellectually serious works which deal with abused or disillusioned women who strain against the role that patriarchy has bestowed on them. From the mid-century onwards, women's groups such as the Langham Place Circle sprang up everywhere, as did the publication of such progressive women's journals as the *English-woman's Review* (1866). The women's associations called for women's greater access to work and education, for more equality in divorce and legal rights, and, above all, for the right to vote. By 1870, women had gained slightly better rights over property, earnings and divorce, although they were not enfranchised until 1918, and then not fully until 1928. The suffrage movement (established *c.*1866) gathered pace in the latter stages of the century, and in the 1880s–90s the 'votes for women' campaign had become the dominant issue for Victorian feminists. In the same period, the cult of the 'New Woman' was entering its heyday. Its calls for the greater independence of women were reflected in the plays of Henrik Ibsen and George Bernard Shaw, and in best-selling novels such as Grant Allen's *The Woman Who Did* (1895), although this work contained another 'fallen woman' story that was rejected by contemporary feminists on the grounds of its patriarchal tone and underlying contempt for women.

Nowadays, feminism combines various critical approaches and schools of thought. There are moderate and radical feminists, Marxist, postmodernist and postcolonialist feminists, 'Queer' theorist feminists (lesbian and gay theorists), and Freudian feminists. Following the rise of the women's movement in the late 1960s–70s, landmark critical texts began to appear. Kate Millett's *Sexual Politics* (1969) contains a radical approach in which literature written by men is firmly implicated within the history of patriarchal ideology, and Germaine Greer's *The Female Eunuch* (1970), although not primarily concerned with literary criticism, is a major critique of male fantasies about women. Twentieth-century French feminist theory has also had a major influence on British feminists. Some of its ideas have, in fact, become central to modern feminist theory, beginning with Simone de Beauvoir's assault on the idea of the 'natural' woman and her theories about the social constructedness of gender in the *The Second Sex* (1949), which are encapsulated in her phrase, '*On ne naît pas femme, on le devient*' (One is not born a woman, one becomes one). Other important ideas include those of psychoanalytic critic Julia Kristeva, who in 1974 both ridiculed feminism for being women's 'last religion', and claimed that 'Woman can never be defined', least of all by men. Hélène Cixous's notion of '*écriture féminine*' (women's writing) has also had a lasting impact. In her postulation that men's dominance over language is at the root of patriarchal oppression, Cixous's thesis in *The Newly Born Woman* (1975) is that women can only be freed from men by finding an essentially feminine or 'bi-sexual' way of writing, in which a new woman will emerge from a 'language' of her own. Cixous calls for a 'boundless' prose, a writing of the body which runs 'away with syntax' and consequently 'away' from the order and authority imposed by the grammar of patriarchy, which she sees as essentially 'phallocentric' ('penis-centred').

Intriguingly, Cixous's ideas are similar to those of Virginia Woolf in *A Room of One's Own* (1929). In this work, Woolf, an early twentieth-century feminist, accuses a prototypical Victorian feminist, Charlotte Brontë, of writing a 'man's sentence' full of stereotypically masculine energy and purpose, which is 'badly adapted for women'. Woolf further appealed for a 'woman-manly or man-womanly' mode of writing, one which undoes the violent opposition between men/women upon which, as Cixous argues, patriarchal oppression is based. Modern feminists have also attacked the institution of English literature itself, largely because it is also thought to be a patriarchal construct dominated by 'dead white men'. For some feminists, such as Eva Figes, for example, 'English literature' is a man-made institution that has served male interests throughout history, just as 'women' throughout history were effectively 'man-made' for the same purpose. The idea that English literature, especially Victorian literature, played an important role in disseminating patriarchal attitudes and oppressing women has indeed become central to feminist criticism and theory, while the relationship between text, institution and ideology has been neatly summed up by Toril Moi's memorable phrase, *Sexual/Textual Politics* (1985). And yet, as suggested above, far from just illuminating this role, feminism has shown that literature was influential in the re-invention or construction of women in Victorian discourse. Other critics, meanwhile, such as Elaine Showalter, have called for a concept known as 'gynocriticism', a criticism that is focused solely on women's writing and culture and on unearthing hitherto unknown women's work, to the complete exclusion of men.

By the 1980s, feminist literary and critical theory had revolutionized approaches to Victorian culture and society, although these approaches came with their own problems and complexities. Take, for example, a famous Victorian poem written by a man, Alfred Lord Tennyson's 'The Princess' (1847). On the surface, this poem contains what appears to be a quite straightforward acknowledgement of the sexual politics of the day. On closer inspection, however, there is something faintly critical and ironic about the lines Tennyson gives to the king, especially given their broader narrative context and the insistent quirkiness of their metre: 'Man to command, woman to obey / All else confusion'. Alternatively, Coventry Patmore's popular verse sequence, *The Angel in the House* (1854–6), provides what appears to be a fairly unapologetic (and distinctly unironic) celebration of the Victorian woman's role as meek and gentle virgin of the domestic sphere: 'Yet it is my chosen task / To sing her worth as Maid and Wife'.

There are, on the other hand, more unconscious patriarchal ideologies at work in Victorian literature, which have led some feminist critics to point towards the limitations of feminist theory itself. When Charlotte Brontë's hugely successful *Jane Eyre* (1847) was published, for instance, in the same year as Tennyson's poem, it was treated as a controversial, impassioned, and for some, 'distasteful' piece of proto-feminist writing. Brontë tells the story of a dowdy and repressed yet resourceful and resistant governess, Jane Eyre, whose restricted life under patriarchy is indicated by the novel's opening line – 'There was no possibility of taking a walk that day' – although our heroine does eventually find fortune and 'freedom', of a sort, in romantic love and marriage to Mr Rochester: 'Reader, I married him.' In order to situate this novel in its modern critical context, one of the twentieth-century's most influential feminist approaches to Brontë's work was that undertaken in Sandra Gilbert and Susan Gubar's *The Madwoman in the Attic* (1979). This study was a groundbreaking approach to what was perceived to be the radical 'feminine imagination' of numerous Victorian works written by women. Significantly, however, recent commentators have criticized Gilbert and Gubar's approach to Brontë's novel on its own terms, largely because, for some, it favours a Western-oriented, middle-class woman's reading of Victorian ideologies.

For feminist scholars rereading Victorian fiction from a postcolonial perspective, Gilbert and Gubar's work amounts to a feminist appropriation of Brontë's text, one which, while foregrounding the plight of lower middle-class women like Jane Eyre, actually marginalizes that of other women in the novel. In short, such critics have tended to focus on the figure of Bertha Mason. Bertha is the Jamaican Creole first wife of Mr Rochester and Brontë's disturbing representative of empire and slavery in the novel. According to many postcolonial critics, Gilbert and Gubar's critique reduces the role of Bertha in the novel to a mere 'dark double' of the great white heroine, Jane Eyre, so that Bertha has no real subjectivity or identity of her own in the text, a process which, on both critical and conceptual levels, replicates Brontë's own 'doubling' of the women. The point of such criticisms is not simply to undermine or do away with the significance of Gilbert and Gubar's approach, which was revolutionary for its time, so much as to show that there are other important debates surrounding the question of women in the sexual/textual politics of the Victorian period. A postcolonial feminist's reading of *Jane Eyre* is equally sensitive in this respect to the complex layering of oppressions in nineteenth-century patriarchal ideology. But it also connects these oppressions to the wider implications of the role of Victorian literature in British colonial history. With this in mind, such an approach is, if anything, more rigorously feminist than that of Gilbert and Gubar's. In the broader cause of feminism, it ensures that the beleaguered voices of other women in Victorian literature are not consigned to the same silence of history to which Bertha Mason seemed condemned.

See also *Contexts*: Body, Class, Clothing, Disease, Education, Family, Food and famine, Gaze, Gender, Madness, Music, Other, Sex and sexuality, Slavery, Violence: *Texts*: Poetry, Realist fiction, Sensation fiction, Social-problem novel.

Further Reading

David, Deirdre, *Intellectual Women and Victorian Patriarchy: Harriet Martineau, Elizabeth Barrett Browning, George Eliot* (Ithaca, NY: Cornell University Press, 1987).
Eagleton, Mary (ed.), *Feminist Literary Theory: A Reader* (Oxford: Blackwell, 1986).

Marxism

Karl Marx was German, but it is easy to forget that he was to all intents and purposes a Victorian himself. After leaving mainland Europe for England in 1849, Marx spent much of his time burrowing away in the British Library, from where he saw London, in his own words, as a 'convenient vantage-point for the observation of bourgeois society'. Many of his revolutionary ideas and theories were consequently shaped by what he saw around him in Victorian Britain. In 1848, Marx and Frederick Engels published their groundbreaking *Manifesto of the Communist Party*, following upheavals caused by a series of European-wide revolutions in that year. The basic argument of the manifesto is well known, and its terminology has become central to the intellectual vocabulary of the modern world. Marx and Engels set the tone in the work's famous opening line: 'A spectre is haunting Europe – the spectre of communism'. From there, they proceed to their main thesis: 'The history of all hitherto existing society is the history of class struggle' – a 'struggle' which they argue is based on 'the antagonism of oppressing and oppressed classes'. The manifesto's closing exhortation for the working classes to 'UNITE', because they 'have nothing to lose but their chains', ensured that the text has gone down in history as nothing less than a revolutionary call to arms.

Marx saw history as divided into four crucial stages: tribal, communal, feudal, capitalist. With the Victorian 'capitalist' stage after the Industrial Revolution, the class system comprised the industrial bourgeois or middle classes (which owned and controlled the 'means of production'), and the working classes, which sold their labour to the owner classes. For Marx, each historical stage contains a process of tension and resolution (technically known as 'thesis, antithesis, synthesis'), which entraps human beings 'independent of their will'. Indeed, as Marx and Engels argued in the manifesto, the owner classes become, in effect, their own 'gravediggers' to the extent that the antagonist nature of the capitalist system 'forged the weapons that bring death to itself', and 'called into existence the men who are to wield those weapons' against it – 'the modern working class – the proletarians'. Capitalism, according to Marx, was ultimately the most vital historical stage because it created its own 'solution', communism, which would also be the end of the class system. By the late twentieth century, however, and especially after the disintegration of the Soviet Bloc in 1989, Marxism was becoming discredited for its failure to work, even though Marxists frequently point out that the communism of the revolutionary states which led to Stalinist Russia and Maoist China were not the types of communism Marx had in mind.

The practice and philosophy of Marxism has come to share a complex and often fractious relationship with literary, critical and cultural theory. Most notably, postmodernist critics accuse Marxism of attempting to provide a far too broad and all-encompassing 'Grand Narrative' of history and everything. They have argued that the reduction of history made by classic or 'vulgar' Marxism to the class tensions created by the economic system fails to account for other factors such as gender, sexuality, nation and race, and the multiple stories of oppression and resistance these have generated. For such critics, Marxism overlooks the crucial question of 'difference', by constructing the idea of a society based on an overly simplistic opposition between 'us' (the oppressed classes) and 'them' (the oppressing classes) which all but silences the exploitation of others.

Marx famously applied his theory of historical 'materialism' in order to turn the 'idealist' ideas of another giant of German philosophy, G. W. F. Hegel (1770–1831), on their 'head'. Marx was suspicious of abstract theories based on what he called in *Contribution to a Critique of Political Economy* (1859), a 'general theory of the human mind'. He argued, controversially, that 'men' were not made in the realm of 'ideas' but in 'real' or 'material' historical relationships between 'men', which were grounded in the economic system. In a famous formulation, he further maintained that 'men' are not constructed from what is 'inside', but by the 'material conditions of life' which constructs them from 'outside': 'it is not the consciousness of men that determines their being but, on the contrary, their social being that determines their consciousness'.

Marx's epistemological turn (a turn in the theory of knowledge) represented a major break with the metaphysical philosophies of mind that had dominated Western thought for centuries. It broke, most clearly, with René Descartes's influential formulation in *Discourses* (1637–9), otherwise known as the *Cogito*: 'I think, therefore I am'. In short, Descartes's point was that he could doubt the external existence of 'material' things (contrary to Marx's theories), but not that he was a 'thinking' being who could have such 'doubts'. His conclusion, encapsulated in the *Cogito*, has underpinned the notion of liberal humanism and its idea of the individual's inner 'subjectivity' ever since. It helped give shape, and more importantly the illusion of substance, to the 'ruling class ideas' which Marx described in *The German Ideology* (1846): 'The ideas of the ruling class are in every epoch the ruling ideas, i.e. the class which is the ruling *material* force of society, is at the same time its ruling *intellectual* force'. This emergent ruling 'force' in the Victorian age was the industrialist and bourgeois-professional classes, and it is their 'Cartesian', liberal humanist 'ideology' of 'free-thinking individualism' that Marxists became primarily concerned with exposing and challenging.

Marx argued that society is divided into an economic 'infrastructure' (base), and a 'superstructure' , which is the realm of culture and ideas incorporating law, politics, education, religion, literature and so on. But crucially for Marx, and his more unswerving supporters, the economic infrastructure of society ultimately determines what happens in the superstructure. As a result, and although late-1960s Marxists such as Louis Althusser argued that the 'superstructure' does enjoy a degree of 'relative autonomy' from the economic base, according to classic Marxist theory Victorian literature became central to the middle-class 'system of representations' – the 'ideology' of middle-class 'realities' – it at once reflected and constructed. Marx claimed in *The German Ideology* that 'during the dominance of the bourgeoisie the concepts freedom, equality, etc.' become dominant. But such concepts, Marxists have argued, became so central to Victorian ideologies of free-trade capitalism and individualism that they assumed the tone of 'universality' and 'common sense'. Moreover, for later Marxists such as Althusser, 'individuals' in Western society are constructed by the extraordinarily prosaic or rather everyday nature of ideology, in a process which Althusser called 'interpellation'. 'Interpellation' refers to the form of 'calling in' by culture and society which solicits the individual to accept as 'real', 'true' or 'natural', society's 'system of representations'. And this 'calling in' invites him or her to participate in ruling-class ideology by way of their own 'free-will' as 'equal' individuals. It enlists, in other words, their consent to an illusion of 'freedom' and 'equality' which is precisely the aim of capitalist ideology.

Marxist critical approaches have been hugely influential on Victorian studies. They are, however, no longer reducible to worthy essays in 'spotting' the oppressed lower classes in texts, of which there are countless examples throughout the period, from Charles Dickens's Nancy in *Oliver Twist* (1837) to Thomas Hardy's Arabella Weir in *Jude the Obscure* (1895). More sophisticated Marxist theory probes Victorian literature for the subtler means by which the structure of ruling-class ideologies is both reproduced and resisted. Terry Eagleton's Marxist study of the Brontë sisters, for example, *Myths of Power* (1975), interprets the class tensions in the novels against the turbulent backdrop of industrial and agricultural crises in the area of Yorkshire in which they lived. The Brontës wrote during a period of upheaval in which the landed gentry were yielding power to an industrial bourgeoisie, and at a time when both classes were anxious about an increasingly well-organized and militant working class. But Eagleton does not merely detect a simple 'us' versus 'them' dialectic in the broadly middle-class ideologies of the Brontë canon. He argues, instead, that the conflicting voices in Charlotte Brontë's work strike a 'balance or fusion of blunt bourgeois rationality and flamboyant Romanticism . . . passionate rebellion and cautious conformity'. Eagleton concedes that the Brontës' novels are in some ways complicit with an ideology of 'bourgeois rationality'. Yet those attributes which he imputes to Charlotte Brontë's heroines, 'rebellion' and 'conformity', are also suggestive of an intricate relationship between the plight of bourgeois women and the Victorian working class, both groups being relatively powerless in society and sharing complex anxieties about subversion and change.

In *The English Novel from Dickens to Lawrence* (1970), Raymond Williams takes a far broader Marxist view of the rise of the Victorian novel. He situates the long build-up of class tensions in Victorian Britain's 'hungry forties' in terms of what he calls the new 'exploration of community' in the period, that constructed by the flowering of novels in the 'twenty months' between 1847 and 1848: '*Dombey and Son, Wuthering Heights, Vanity Fair, Jane Eyre, Mary Barton, Tancred, Town and Country, The Tenant of Wildfell Hall*'. For Williams, these novels initiated a new and potentially destructive 'historical consciousness' that was formed at that time, and which grew out of class antagonisms endemic to an industrial-capitalist society. Elsewhere, in studies such as *Alfred Tennyson* (1986), Alan Sinfield takes a vastly different approach to what he describes as 'middle-class' appropriations of the Victorian poet's work. These have, he argues, positioned Tennyson's poetry in terms of offering bourgeois 'universal human truths' centred on a tortured 'individual', and he aims to relocate the poems firmly within the complex 'structures of power and ideology' which prevailed at the time.

A similar approach is that taken by modern Marxist readings of classic Victorian realist novels, especially following Catherine Belsey's critique of George Eliot's *Middlemarch* (1872). In *Critical Practice* (1980), Belsey argues that Eliot's novel offers the reader a bourgeois 'realist' position from which to see an illusory 'inside' of Eliot's heroine. Eliot's Dorothea Brooke is described as a modern 'individual' with a rampant 'imagination', who is always 'inwardly debating' and eager to 'know the truths of life'. After some 800 pages full of conflict and heartbreak, Dorothea eventually marries the right man (Will Ladislaw). Belsey's point is that the effect of such a typically Victorian resolution is that it enables fiction to offer the reader a reassuring closure to the contradictions in 'reality'. The novel climaxes by celebrating Dorothea's 'individual' triumph against an oppressive 'community': 'a young and noble impulse struggling against the conditions of an imperfect social state'. But even at the end of her story, as Belsey maintains, the reader is being quietly 'interpellated' into the 'system of representations' made by Eliot's middle-class ideology of realism. Constructed by the text as another intimate 'individual' (like Dorothea and the narrator), the reader is clearly invited to collude with the text's universalizing mode of address: '*We* insignificant people . . . the Dorothea whose story *we* know . . . things are not so ill with *you* and *me*' [my italics]. However, as Eliot also suggests, even this high-Victorian piece of bourgeois realism makes some concessions to Marx's idea about the 'social' determination of the individual, and this is why Victorian literature remains so complex for Marxist critics: 'For there is no creature whose inward being is so strong that it is not greatly determined by what lies outside it.'

See also   *Contexts*: Class, Clothing, Economics, Empire and imperialism, Individualism, Industry; *Texts*: Historical novel, Mid-Victorian novel, Realist fiction, Social-problem novel; *Criticism*: Deconstruction, Feminism, New historicism/Cultural materialism, Postcolonialism, Poststructuralism, Structuralism.

Further Reading

Sinfield, Alan, *Alfred Tennyson* (Oxford: Basil Blackwell, 1986).
Eagleton, Terry, *Myths of Power: A Marxist Study of the Brontës* (Basingstoke: Macmillan, 1975).

New Historicism/Cultural Materialism

'New Historicism' is a relatively new concept, first used in its current sense by American critic Stephen Greenblatt in1982. It emerged partly in response to what it perceived to be the unhistorical or rather ahistorical

'New Critic' and deconstructive approaches to literature, and its aim is to resituate texts back in their historical contexts. The same goes for 'Cultural Materialism'. Cultural materialism is a British concept largely associated with the work of Jonathan Dollimore, Alan Sinfield and (originally) Raymond Williams. Williams first used the term in *Marxism and Literature* (1977), in which he makes the important point that 'we cannot separate literature and art from other kinds of social practice'. As the title of his book suggests, cultural materialism is a more heavily Marxist-influenced approach than New Historicism. Indeed, some cultural materialists have accused some new historicists of ignoring the 'material' nature of class oppressions in history and culture. But what is more interesting is the similarities between the two movements, rather than their differences. Adherents of both approaches have, for example, been swift to counteract claims that their work represents any systematic or unified theory at all, and that it is rather a set of 'preoccupations', or what Greenblatt calls a 'practice rather than a doctrine'. New historicists and cultural materialists recognize, for instance, that texts are not inert but active parts of the historical and cultural formation in which they were produced. They also recognize that historical materials such as Victorian literature are subjective, and that any critical rereading of the relationship between literature and history is equally subjective. The way in which texts are interpreted, in other words, is contingent upon the historical context of the reader and interpreter, who brings his or her own 'present' to bear on the 'past' of the text. That both movements share an interest in what some critics from both schools call the 'return to history', and others the 'textuality of history', in which the past is a complex 'text' to be read, is paramount. A slightly more forward-looking dimension, perhaps (especially for cultural materialists) is to be found in what Kiernan Ryan succinctly describes as the 'debate about how and why literature should be restored to the past in order to make it count in the present'.

Both movements are primarily concerned with the nature of power in history. Together, they explore the way in which texts either interact with or subvert society's power structures, and they examine the relationship between the violence of the text and the violence of the state. It is in this respect that many of their ideas are derived from the work of French historian Michel Foucault, whose theories about the historical discourses of sexuality, discipline and madness in Western societies were preoccupied with the nature of power and resistance. Foucault disrupted the idea of a progressively linear or coherent account of history constructed by liberal humanist (and some Marxist) historians. He argued that history is made up of a series of resistances, ruptures, conflicts and contradictions. Most new historicists (and some cultural materialists) also, along Foucault's lines, reject grand narratives of history. In what Greenblatt and Catherine Gallagher, in *Practising New Historicism* (2000), call the 'fascination with the particular', time and again their work emphasizes the local rather than the global story, the smaller, but no less significant historical moment over the larger historical picture, or the minutia rather than the mass. As such, their approach, like Foucault's, is characterized by its focus on disruption and difference, but also on incident, episode, anecdote, on overlooked cultural sources and artefacts, and on newly recovered documents such as travel writings or penal, medical and legal documents. As Greenblatt puts it in 'Towards a Poetics of Culture' (1990), the new historicist critic watches history not so much for the visible picture, but for the submerged or 'hidden places of negotiation and exchange'.

New historicist approaches are also heavily influenced by what anthropologist Clifford Geertz called 'thick description', which is effectively a method of close reading that stresses critical attention to detail. In *The Interpretation of Cultures* (1973), Geertz underlined what would become the centrality of 'culture' to new historicist and cultural materialist ideas about the individual and the 'self', with his point that there is 'no such thing as a human nature independent of culture'. It is with such historical detail and close reading in mind that critics from both schools resist the often clumsy periodization foisted on history by some literary critics, who do so to seek out the underlying patterns in a given period such as 'the Victorian'. It is also why new historicist and cultural materialist critics refuse to extract literature from other important contexts such as anthropology, politics, economics, the sciences, all of which they regard as 'texts' which are in constant circulation together. At the same time, both movements reject the distinctions between authentic art and inauthentic art, high art and low art, the 'literary' text and the 'non-literary' text, seeing these categories, like everything else in history, as constructed by society's dominant socioeconomic and cultural forces. With their emphasis on 'crisis not consensus', this sort of approach has led some critics to question the English canon of 'great' English writers such as Shakespeare and Austen, in what H. Aram Veeser describes as 'canon-bashing'. The canon is held up as a construct of the institution of English Literature, a product of ideological motivations which developed in historical contexts that either deliberately, or unconsciously, suppressed or excluded other voices and texts, those for example by working-class writers, women writers, black writers, homosexual writers, those who did not necessarily conform to the 'universal human truths' attributed to a 'genius' such as

Shakespeare. Typically, new historicists and cultural materialists are more interested in the underlying, albeit fractured, historical discourses which helped such 'geniuses' attain that level of cultural and intellectual cachet in society.

Critics from both schools frequently approach Victorian literature from unusual or unexpected angles. Greenblatt and Gallagher, for example, read George Eliot's *Daniel Deronda* (1876) against what they envisage as the nineteenth-century's guiding 'metaphor of the author as whore'. From this perspective, they situate anxieties towards best-selling Victorian women writers in terms of similar anxieties towards prostitutes and Jews, both forming part of Eliot's novel. For the Victorians, prostitutes, money-lending Jews and popular women authors were all, in a sense, 'prostitutes' to the Victorian marketplace, and consequently they occupied a negative – and somewhat dark – status in Victorian consciousness. Such groups were all considered guilty of making money without actually producing anything tangible or worthwhile, and Eliot herself described 'authorship' as essentially a 'bread winning profession', as mercenary, in that respect, as prostitution. Nancy Armstrong's approach to Victorian novels in *Desire and Domestic Fiction* (1987) is also characteristic. Her thesis begins by attributing the violent opening of the novels of 1847–8 to what is essentially a discourse of discipline and punishment in Victorian society, which is observable in the order represented by 'the factory, prison, and schoolroom' and a discourse which is at root, for Armstrong, a sexual oppression. In novels such as Emily Brontë's *Wuthering Heights* (Hindley's violent treatment of Heathcliff), Thackeray's *Vanity Fair* (Becky Sharpe's brusque dismissal by Joseph Sedley) and Charlotte Brontë's *Jane Eyre* (the young Jane's incarceration in the 'red-room' after being bullied by the 'slave-driver' John Reed), the oppressions of a wider society, as Armstrong shows, are repeatedly visited upon individuals: 'Four hands were immediately laid upon me [Jane Eyre], and I was borne upstairs'.

Armstrong also uncovers the history of sexual tensions and the subversive desires of women which are embedded within these novels. To do so, she draws upon contemporary sources such as journalist Henry Mayhew's influential *London and Labour Poor* (1862) to make her point about the effective 'criminalization' of lusty Victorian women. The problems stem, Armstrong argues, from Mayhew's voyeuristic obsession with reporting London prostitutes, whose careers were perceived as a major cause of crime in Victorian society, and the standard by which the correct and incorrect behaviour of all women was judged. The violence of Victorian attitudes to prostitution, and to women in general, all of whom, as Mayhew puts it, use their 'charms for immoral purposes', is exhibited throughout Victorian literature, but perhaps most notoriously by Sikes's murder of the 'good-hearted' prostitute Nancy, in Dickens's *Oliver Twist* (1837). Although, as Armstrong maintains, Dickens's sympathies lie with Nancy, the important point is that this figure of bad sexuality must, it seems, die (she is pistol-whipped to death), so that the novel can restore order by way of 'cleansing' it of prostitution. Armstrong's critical strategy, in other words, is to embed the seemingly marginal but disruptive history of prostitution within the sexual and textual anxieties underpinning the period.

In John Brannigan's cultural materialist interpretation of Alfred Tennyson's poetry, there is a similar approach to that taken by Armstrong. Brannigan hears in the poet laureate's work more subversive or 'dissident' voices than those which have hitherto been acknowledged by more conservative critics and commentators. Such critics, he argues, tend to have positioned Tennyson as a reactionary and imperialist mythologizer of national unity, in which his 'Ulysses', for example, dreams of expanding across 'that untravell'd world', and where his *Idylls of the King (c.*1833–74) 'link attractive Arthurian legend to the realities of power in Victorian Britain'. But Brannigan, like Armstrong, is also interested in the disruptive sexual politics of Tennyson's work, in what he calls the elements of 'male femininity' and gay love in *In Memoriam* (1850), which subvert the masculine-imperialist codes of the day.

In contrast to both Armstrong's and Brannigan's work, and by adopting what might seem a far more flippant approach in 'The Potato in the Materialist Imagination' (2000), Gallagher and Greenblatt base their critique of the Victorian culture of materialism on the seemingly innocuous history of the potato. They begin, characteristically, with a modern anecdote about former American Vice-President Dan Quayle's famous missspelling of 'potato' (Quayle added an extra 'e'). They proceed, from this, to a discussion of the great potato 'debate' of late eighteenth-century and early nineteenth-century Britain, over whether or not potatoes were a more suitable (because cheaper) staple diet than bread for the working classes. From there, they analyse the cultural significance of the potato as the stigmatised food of the peasantry in the period, in particular the Irish peasantry, and from there to a wider discussion of the Irish Famine (c.1845–52), English attitudes towards the Irish as inferior foreigners, and the legacy of the British Empire in Ireland.

Intriguingly, Gallagher and Greenblatt do not make the link to Victorian literature explicit in this piece. New historicist and cultural materialist critics can, however, draw on their insights to explore the tensions and anxieties surrounding the issues they discuss, and the manner in which they surface in Victorian literature, themselves. Charlotte Brontë's *Shirley* (1849), for example, features a stereotypically militant, and rather savage, shillelagh-wielding Irishman called Malone. As a 'native', as Brontë puts it, of the 'land of shamrock and potatoes', Malone's telling first words in the novel are 'More bread!'. That famine and hunger are central to the novel, and that they are embedded in the colonial unconscious of Brontë's language, is underlined by the fact that 'Malone' is an anagram of 'no meal'.

See also *Contexts*: Class, Clothing, Drugs, Madness, Music, Race, Religion, Transport, Violence; *Texts*: Crime fiction, Sensation fiction; *Criticism*: Marxism, Postcolonialism, Psychoanalysis, Queer theory.

Further Reading

Gallagher, Catherine and Greenblatt, Stephen, *Practicing New Historicism* (Chicago and London: The University of Chicago Press, 2000).

Ryan, Kiernan, *New Historicism and Cultural Materialism: A Reader* (London: Edward Arnold, 1996).

Postcolonialism

Postcolonial theories and approaches are primarily concerned with the history and legacy of colonialism and empire. Nowadays, they comprise a complex and interdisciplinary set of ideas and practices, including literary studies, economic theory, political science, sociology, anthropology, ethnology, and philosophy. In Western academies, postcolonialism is derived from an equally diverse assortment of Marxist, feminist, post-structuralist, postmodernist and psychoanalytic theories. At its broadest level, it is a critique of the colonial and imperial dominance of European culture around the world, and many of its theories and ideas have filtered into current debates on what some postcolonialists describe as the latest phase of Western imperialism: globalization. But postcolonialism is also about resistance to the dominance of Western imperialism, both throughout history and in the modern world. Many critics and commentators are intent on giving 'voice' to those voices hitherto rendered silent in colonial and postcolonial societies and texts. They listen, for example, to what leading postcolonial critic, Homi K. Bhabha, calls 'the discourses of "minorities" within the geopolitical divisions of east and west, north and south'. By doing so, they aim to recover the histories of those 'peoples without a history'.

Bhabha's points underline the complexities of postcolonialism. In modern debates, the 'postcolonial' has become, as suggested above, a concept which covers a combination of historical processes, psychological conditions, practices, texts, moments of resistance, violence and a number of critical theories and questions which emerged – largely in Western academic institutions – in the 1970s. The term also refers to the politics, societies, cultures and experiences of those indigenous populations living in the many countries scattered around the world which were formerly European 'colonies' or imperial territories. These countries include parts of the near and Middle East, India, Africa, Australia, South America, North America, Canada, the West Indies and Ireland. At the same time, because former European centres of colonialism and empire such as Britain and France contain large immigrant (and now native) populations from their former colonies, they are also regarded as 'postcolonial' societies, even though these countries retain 'nominal' colonies around the world.

To complicate things further, many critics express dissatisfaction with 'postcolonialism' as the 'umbrella' term for such a wide and disparate field. Elleke Boehmer, for example, argues that the term is dangerously reductive. It is reductive, she points out, because it suggests that the chaos of history and the violence of colonialism are divisible into neat and linear stages: precolonialism, colonialism, and postcolonialism, which belie the legacy of colonial problems left in those countries still very much affected by them. Indeed, it is in this way that many postcolonial critics, some of whom like Boehmer are influenced by postmodernist ideas, reject the imposition of the West's 'grand narrative' of history on the rest of the world. Such critics demand a more sensitive approach to the fact that the histories of slavery, colonialism and immigration led to the displacement of millions of people over hundreds of years, and that the result is a vast and heterogeneous array of postcolonial peoples and cultures living around the globe. Moreover, the impact of such multicultural difference and dislocation has led to what are now recognized as the key concepts in postcolonialism. These are, amongst others, displacement, diaspora, marginality, nationalism, race, identity, hybridity, ambivalence, silence, violence and voice.

Postcolonialism has encouraged a radical reappraisal of English literature. In groundbreaking studies such as *Orientalism* (1978) and *Culture and Imperialism* (1993), Edward Said began from the premise that English literature has played a vital role in reflecting, and to some extent 'inventing', both British colonialist attitudes and the lands they conquered. As Said argues in *Orientalism*: 'the Orient was almost a European invention, and had been since antiquity a place of romance, exotic beings, haunting memories and landscapes, remarkable experiences'. Building on Said's insights, Padmini Mongi maintains in

Contemporary Postcolonial Theory (1996), that it was English literature, in fact, which 'laid the groundwork for and buttressed the structures of imperialism'. In other words, at the same time that Victorian literature represented colonized territories and peoples as at once inferior and slightly menacing to its English readership, it participated in the construction of Englishness as an 'imagined community' *against* those it colonized. For Said, who worked from insights into language provided by poststructural theory, Western imperialism was predicated on a series of binary oppositions which underpinned Victorian conscious-ness, the violent hierarchy of which imprisoned the foreign and the colo-nized in an interminable logic of dualistic thought and practice: self/ other, us/them, West/East, European/non-European, centre/periphery, white/black, rational/irrational, civilized/uncivilized, colonizer/ colonized, and so on. Basing itself on such oppositions, English litera-ture became, in this respect, a very physical and aggressive part of British imperialist expansions around the globe.

Cultural imperialism partly explains why the works of Shakespeare, for example, made their way onto the curricula of Indian education authorities in the age of British expansionism. As postcolonial critics such as Gauri Viswanathan have shown, it was in countries like India that Shakespeare, an icon of Englishness, became what she describes as one of Britain's cultural 'masks of conquest'. In a more light-hearted and ironic, but ultimately no less serious manner, such 'masks' led the writer C. L. R. James in *Beyond a Boundary* (1963) to point out the relationships between cricket and the novels of Charles Dickens in British cultural imperialism in the West Indies, and their combined influence on his life as a boy growing up in early twentieth-century Trinidad: '"The Pickwick Papers", my father would say, taking up the book. "By Charles Dickens. A great book my boy. Read it".' Understandably, then, because it repre-sented the last great age of British imperialism, the Victorian period has proven fertile ground for postcolonial critics and scholars. For some critics, such as Daniel Bivona and Carl Plasa, the idea that the literature of the age is haunted by images of empire, by what Said calls the empire's 'shadowy presence', has become central. It has even led them to what they describe as the 'colonial unconscious' of the text, which, as the Freudian terminology suggests, refers to an endless cycle of repres-sion, guilt, anxiety and trauma, which points to the violent memory of colonialism and its return in Victorian literature.

There are many complex and contrasting postcolonial approaches to Victorian literature, and all forms and genres have come under scrutiny. In the novels of the so-called 'Condition of England' genre, for instance, such as Benjamin Disraeli's *Sybil* (1845), Charles Egremont regrets that he could not get out to 'New Zealand'. But his regrets feature in a text which otherwise deals with Britain's colonial history, and the wealth it created, in a typically brief and off-hand manner, to the extent that it effectively goes 'silent' or rather unnoticed in the novel: 'A couple of centuries ago, a Turkey merchant was the great creator of wealth; the West Indian Planter followed him. In the middle of the last century appeared the Nabob'('nabobs' were colonialists who returned to Britain after amassing a fortune in the colonies). On the other hand, there is also Disraeli's vignette of John Warren in the novel. Warren is a nabob who resolves the 'mysterious' disappearance of rice in 'Hindostan' only because, unsurprisingly as it turns out in the light of Victorian colonial attitudes, the Indians are deemed to be incapable of looking after themselves. Conversely, William Thackeray's *Vanity Fair* (1847) – in which characters devour Indian curries – has received plenty of recent 'postcolonial' treatment, and Thackeray quite consciously packs Captain Dobbin's regiment off to the Burmese War (1824–6). However, as in Disraeli's work, Thackeray's text is typically vague and uneasy with the other imperial details concerning 'Miss Swartz', the mysterious 'Black Princess' or 'mulatto girl', of which hearsay and gossip suggest that her 'father was a German Jew – a slave owner they say – connected with the Cannibal Islands in some way or other'. In *The Newcomes* (1853), Thackeray's violent discourse on colonialism also seems fairly unambiguous. Captain Newcome, for example, is an Indian Army officer: Sedley makes his fortune in the intriguingly named 'Boggley Wallah'; and everyone is bedevilled by the sinister Bengali figure, Rummon Loll, a lecherous and obsequious conman who pretends to be an Indian prince.

Nevertheless, some postcolonial critics have pointed out that the inscription of India in *The Newcomes* still only forms part of what Thackeray describes as the 'mystery of Eastern Existence'. As a result, the empire is still very much background noise to the novel's preoccupation with England and English ways. The same goes for the work of other major Victorian writers such as Charles Dickens and the Brontës, in which all too often the discourse on colonialism only seems significant in terms of the light it throws on domestic oppressions. At the same time, however, Susan Meyer in *Imperialism at Home* (1996) has recently complicated this discourse on its own terms. In her postcolonial work, Meyer interprets an unconventional and somewhat rebellious literary heroine, George Eliot's Maggie Tulliver in *The Mill on the Floss* (1860), in the light of 'hardening' racial attitudes after the imperial crisis of the Indian Mutiny (1857), which occurred just three years before the novel's publication, and in which many Britons and Indians were slaughtered.

As part of the text's historical reflex to this crisis, argues Meyer, Eliot describes the 'mutinous' Maggie as having a 'mulatter' or 'gypsy' 'brown skin', in images of the body which find her repeatedly linked to those of wild natives and rebellious colonial 'savages' in Victorian consciousness. But such a conceptual slippage, for Meyer, only underlines her point that Eliot's primary concern in the text is not so much with the effect of British imperialism around the world, as with imperialism's 'effect on the British'.

It is along these lines, in fact, that Victorian literature raises a series of complex questions for postcolonial critics. One, for example, would be why, in Thomas Hardy's *Tess of the D'Urbervilles* (1891), does Angel Clare disappear to Brazil for a spell, after Tess has revealed to him her 'fall' at the hands of Alec D'Urberville? At the start of the novel, Hardy suggests that the vaguely subversive Angel is cultivating his farming skills with 'a view either to the colonies, or the tenure of a home-farm, possibly in the Americas'. Although, it should be stressed, Brazil was not a British colony (it was part of the Portuguese empire), it is nevertheless the exotic otherness of this country in the Victorian imagination that leads Angel to contemplate life in a 'country of contrasting scenes and notions and habits', as a place where his love for Tess might flourish once more away from Victorian attitudes and repressions. As Hardy has it in the novel, Brazil turns out to be anything but a place of romance and sexual reawakening; it is, on the contrary, a land of 'sad' experiences, which age Angel a 'dozen' years and where he contracts a nasty illness. Hardy's Brazil is a 'desperate' resort for British colonialists and emigrants, a land in which it is suitable to offload – as in the history of British colonialism itself – the nation's undesirable citizens with their undesirable behaviour. Indeed, in line with Tess's sexual 'indiscretion', back in England Angel had himself 'plunged into eight-and-forty-hours dissipation with a stranger'. Although the reasons why, exactly, Hardy chose Brazil for Angel's exile remain uncertain, for postcolonial critics of Victorian literature it is precisely those shadowy and hostile silences which are significant.

See also   *Contexts*: Empire and imperialism, Evolution, Nation, Orientalism, Other, Race, Slavery, War; *Texts*: Historical fiction; Poetry, Realist fiction; *Criticism*: Deconstruction, New historicism/Cultural materialism, Poststructuralism.

Further Reading

Mongia, Padmini, *Contemporary Postcolonial Theory: A Reader* (London: Edward Arnold, 1996).

Said, Edward, *Culture and Imperialism* (New York: Vintage, 1994).

Postmodernism

Postmodernism refers to the West's economic, intellectual and cultural formations in the latter half of the twentieth century. It denotes the latest period of Western history, 'postmodernity', and the many fragmented or multicultural lifestyles and attitudes the period has given rise to, 'postmodernist'. A typically (and for its adherents necessarily) difficult term to define, postmodernism has become something of a catch-all term. Much like poststructuralism or postcolonialism, it emerged in the intellectual debates of the 1960s–70s, and nowadays it covers a range of ideas and theories, as well as numerous cultures, artefacts, texts, and artistic, literary and architectural practices. As the prefix 'post' suggests, postmodernism is thought to be a reaction to the preceding age of 'modernism'. It is supposed to mark a break from the various artistic and cultural movements which developed in the decades between the late-Victorian period (c.1890) and the first half of the twentieth century (c.1939). Such periodization is, however, notoriously insecure. Postmodern scholars are forever contesting the dates which supposedly separate historical periods, and they continually disagree over the ideas or attitudes which distinguish them. At the same time, 'modernism' is distinguished from the broader historical term, 'modernity'. Most commentators date the so-called 'modern world' to c.1600 in Western societies, and more specifically to the earliest developments of capitalism and empire building during the Renaissance.

That problems of time and periodization are integral to debates about postmodernism has long been acknowledged by postmodern thinkers. In *The Postmodern Condition* (1979), for example, Jean-François Lyotard asks a difficult question, to which he supplies a difficult response: 'What is, then, the postmodern? . . . It is undoubtedly part of the modern'. But he goes on to add the crucial point that, 'All that has been received, if only yesterday . . . must be suspected', and that it is this 'suspicion' which is the postmodern 'condition' . More pragmatic Marxist postmodern critics, on the other hand, such as Frederic Jameson, have argued that 'postmodernism' represents 'the cultural logic of late capitalism' (1991). Jameson stresses that the 'task' of postmodernism, in this respect, is to find new practices, 'social and mental habits', which can meet the 'new global division of labour ("multinational capitalism")'. Another critic, Francis Fukuyama, situates postmodernism in relation to the decline of communism after 1989, and hence the decline of the last great antagonist of capitalism. In *The End of History and the Last Man* (1992), Fukuyama notoriously argued that the decline of communism indicated the 'possibility that History itself might be at an end'. For Fukuyama, in other words, nothing will change and history will 'end', as such, because in the late twentieth century there is only one 'competitor standing in the ring . . . : liberal democracy'.

For the Victorians, however, 'history' was only just, as it were, beginning. It was they who rewrote history in the nineteenth century, by reinventing Britishness and by positioning themselves at the forefront of world capitalism with an empire which has had an immeasurable impact on the globalized world of postmodernity. But where postmodern ideas are even more useful in understanding the Victorians is on the crucial question of 'grand narratives'. Grand narratives, which some postmodernists call 'metanarratives', refer to those large Western 'stories' of everyone and everything which claim to have an authority over meaning, truth and the 'grand' course of history. Indeed, to use Lyotard's own words on this point: 'Simplifying to the extreme, I define *postmodern* as incredulity toward metanarratives'. In what he goes on to describe as the 'breaking up' of 'grand narratives', Lyotard and other postmodernists reject the authority over meaning held by the discourse of science in the modern world, and specifically the West's Enlightenment project of rationalist and 'positivist' progress (what Lyotard calls the 'Enlightenment narrative'). Their approach consequently questions the history of capitalism and liberal humanism which grew out of the rationalist spirit, with its assumptions about 'realism', individualism, and the coherent, stable and free-thinking self.

Some postmodernists also question historically based theories such as Marxism. They argue that Marxism, at least 'vulgar' or classic Marxism, which bases all history on class struggles and on changes in the economic infrastructure of society, is reductive. As with the discourse of science, in the postmodern perspective Marxism is thought to offer only another grand narrative of humankind's linear progress through time towards a happy ending, one which can only foresee capitalism's self-destruction at the hands of a revolutionary working class and the inevitability of communism. The Marxist vision fails, for postmodernists, to take account of differences or contradictions throughout history. It subsumes other forms of oppression in society – especially those with a racial, sexual and gender dimension – within the classic Marxist dialectic between 'us' (the working class) and 'them' (the dominant class). In the postmodern lens, it was during the Victorian period, in particular, that the metanarratives of capitalism and patriarchy truly established themselves. Likewise, it was the Victorians, for postmodernists, who consolidated the dominance of other metanarratives in society, such as science and racism, even compressing these two into one: 'scientific racism'.

But in what ways can literature be understood in the light of postmodernism? Postmodern novels and poems, for instance, certainly of recent periods, tend to be unconventional and experimental. They are characterized by a sense of fragmentation, self-consciousness and self-referentiality, and they dwell on ambiguity, irony and pastiche. They also take delight in linguistic playfulness and a relish in relativity which, as suggested above, marks a rejection of the dominant truths, meanings and notions of 'reality' which make up the grand narratives constructed by the Victorians. And yet where, exactly, is Victorian literature in all this? Although Victorian writers were also the literary innovators of their time, their *Bildungsromans* or 'education' novels such as *Oliver Twist* (1837), *David Copperfield* (1850) and *Jane Eyre* (1847) have all come under heavy criticism from postmodernists. Such novels tend, for example, to contain a fairly straightforward logic of complication and resolution (childhood misery to adult happy endings) which moves steadily through time like history. That such novels also tend to construct a grand narrative of 'realism', which involves the 'coming to age' of the individual 'middle-class hero', has led some postmodern critics to suggest that Victorians took literature in a reactionary or regressive direction. As with poststructuralists, postmodernists are suspicious of 'consensus' thinking in every shape and form. Such a suspicion is aroused largely because the notion of 'consensus' does what Lyotard calls 'violence' to the radical ambiguity and play of language. But just because most Victorian novels do not, in this respect, appear 'postmodern' as such – even applying the term to the Victorians sounds anachronistic – this does not mean that they cannot be read with postmodern approaches and objectives in mind. That is, as with decon-structive approaches, the aim of postmodernism is partly to locate the points of contradiction in texts and partly to embrace their potentially subversive complexities, that chorus of 'different' voices which, by undermining the idea of a singular and unified 'voice' would, at the same time, undermine the Victorian grand narrative of everyone and everything. Such a critical manoeuvre is at heart a sort of interpretative freedom from the order and rationalism imposed by the Victorians, but one which also recognizes, implicitly, that the meanings of the text are contingent upon the interpreter's own time and place in history.

For the postmodern reader, Victorian texts comprise a potentially endless interplay of relative meanings and interpretations, some of which are more anchored in history than others. By the same token, some texts parade their own ironies, parodies and sense of relativity more self-consciously than others, while others seem hermetically enclosed within their own linguistic universes. Take, for example, Lewis Carroll's *Alice in Wonderland* (1865). Carroll's work lingers repeatedly –

and quite consciously – on what Lyotard describes as the 'pleasure' and 'invention' of 'language games'. In Wonderland, however paradoxically, the sheer nonsense of such games at once parodies Victorian certainties and 'realities', and underscores their authority, so that in one incident in the text the authority of teachers is underscored even while it is ridiculed: '"We went to school in the sea. The master was an old Turtle – we used to call him Tortoise" . . . "Why"? . . . Alice asked. "We called him Tortoise because he taught us," replied the Mock Turtle angrily. Really you are very dull.'

Another way of approaching Victorian literature is to observe how recent novels have reread Victorian literature from postmodern perspectives, in such a manner as to encourage a reinterpretation of Victorian ideas and attitudes. Jean Rhys's *Wide Sargasso Sea* (1966), for example, is a prequel to Charlotte Brontë's *Jane Eyre* (1847). What Rhys's work does, in effect, is to bring what recent critics describe as the 'colonial unconscious' of Brontë's novel to the foreground for the reader, by way of recounting the married life of the Creole Bertha Mason and Mr Rochester, in Jamaica, before Bertha is dragged back to England. Rhys consequently moves the history of slavery in Brontë's text, out from the margins of the novel, and into the centre, in order to tell, as it were, its silent story of empire. In a similar, but more playful manner, John Fowles in *The French Lieutenant's Woman* (1969), set in 1867, provides a series of parodies and postmodern 'imitations' of the Victorians and their novels. Fowles situates his own present, 1960s Britain, within the past. This enables his protagonists, Charles Smithson and Sarah Woodruff, to have explicit and hence un-Victorian – in the fictional sense – sex, with the added detail of premature ejaculation ('precisely ninety seconds'). In a series of characteristically self-conscious manoeuvres, Fowles even places himself, as novelist, on a train in the 1867 of the novel, and his work is full of digressions in time, 'postmodern' literary theories, and 1960s debates about Victorian novels, such as Roland Barthes's ideas in 1968 about 'the death of the author' and the 'birth of the reader'.

More recently, the Australian novelist Peter Carey's *Jack Maggs* (1997), along the same lines as Rhys's novel, has given another voice to the silent empire of Victorian fiction. But Carey's novel, like Fowles's, also has a more playful and highly self-conscious 'Dickins of a time' with the novels of Charles Dickens, particularly *Great Expectations* (1861). As with Rhys's Bertha Mason, Carey foregrounds the hitherto marginalized colonial figure, Maggs (Dickens's Magwitch). Maggs is transported to the Australian colonies, and then returns to England to pursue Henry Phipps (Dickens's Pip), but not before accruing a mysterious fortune in Australia which made Phipps's 'Great Expectations', and Dickens's original story, possible. Indeed, as in Dickens's novel – 'I [Pip] saw the shadow of no parting from her [Estella]' – Carey finishes off his story ambiguously, and the significance of its colonial dimension is left unresolved. To confuse things further, Carey adds a playful disclaimer to the front of his work, one which at once points towards the primacy of fiction and the fiction of fact in his novel. His words in many ways underline the Lyotardian 'suspicion' and irreverence of postmodernism to everything which has gone before, in this case Dickens, the Victorians and the violence of the British Empire, a topic on which it was clearly in Victorian interests to keep quiet about: 'The author willingly admits to having once or twice stretched history to suit his own fictional ends.'

See also *Criticism*: Deconstruction, Marxism, Poststruturalism, Queer theory.

Further Reading

Jaffe, Audrey, 'Modern and Postmodern Theories of Prose Fiction', in *A Companion to the Victorian Novel*, ed. Patrick Brantlinger and William B. Thesing (Oxford: Blackwell, 2002).

Lyotard, Jean-François, *The Postmodern Condition: A Report on Knowledge* (Manchester: Manchester University Press, 1979).

Poststructuralism

Poststructuralism developed in France in the 1960s and early 1970s, partly in response to structuralism. As a concept, it is now associated with a range of theories and approaches covered in this book, especially deconstruction, a term with which it is often used interchangeably. In short, poststructuralists reject the entire way of thinking which has shaped Western history since the Enlightenment. In *Of Grammatology* (1966), founding thinker Jacques Derrida set about deconstructing the West's obsession with what he described as the 'presence' of a 'transcendental signified'. Derrida questioned the basis for the rationalist pursuit of a single meaning or truth. Crucially, however, he also recognized that the question of language is central to, not to say constitutive of, this pursuit. The origins of poststructuralist literary criticism lie, in many ways, in Derrida's undoing of what seems to be an insignificant binary opposition in language between speech and writing, but which he called a 'violent hierarchy'. In *Of Grammatology*, Derrida argued that in Western societies speech has been dominant over writing in this hierarchy, because the voice is considered to be physically closer to individual consciousness. As a result of this assumption, Western societies took it for granted that speech is the most 'natural' reflection of that inner consciousness, a reflection which, more importantly, endowed that consciousness with the prestige of 'presence'. But Derrida maintained that the hierarchy between speech and writing, far from being a 'natural' or 'inevitable' development, is an entirely linguistic and hence cultural construct. For Derrida and other poststructuralists, moreover, the same argument can be applied to all other binary oppositions which underpin Western consciousness: men/women, self/other, soul/body, black/white, native/foreigner, sane/mad, fact/fiction, and so on.

Poststructuralists also reject the structuralist emphasis on the underlying structures of language and signification in texts. Their approach on this point proceeds largely from Derrida's complex argument in *Of Grammatology* that language, being made up of a system of self-referential signs with no external referent, in which meaning is not 'present' in the signifier, but 'absent', indicates that 'There is nothing outside the text'. Language, according to Derrida, is a self-enclosed system in which each signifier is only recognizable by its difference from another, not by what it signifies outside the system. As a result of this difference, language and meaning are fundamentally unstable. For poststructuralists, texts, literature, only 'mean' anything at all because they have the 'presence' of meaning grafted onto them by society. The assumption in the West, they point out, has always been that language is a mere window to the world of real and 'present' things, in which the relationship between signifier (word, sound-image) and signified (concept, meaning) is 'natural', obvious, commonsense, not worthy of discussion. Poststructuralism challenges this assumption, positing language as precisely the point of contradiction, and such an approach partly explains why poststructuralist literary critics seem more concerned with 'how' the text means rather than 'what' the text means. Consequently, their recognition of the fundamental 'absence' in the signifier, the 'absence' in language as in the human subject, leads them to explore the 'absences' and 'silences' which punctuate the text.

A common misconception about poststructuralism is that it leads to a world in which texts 'mean' nothing at all, and that ultimately human life itself is meaningless. On the contrary, for poststructuralists, life, like the text, is full of meanings; both are, if anything, far too 'meaningful'. The stress, however, is very much on that 's' in 'meanings'. In *Positions* (1972), Derrida called the letter 's' 'the disseminating letter par excellence', because it signifies the sense of plurality and indeterminacy of meanings that he sees everywhere in texts. It is in this respect that poststructuralists talk of 'meanings', not 'meaning', 'truths', not 'truth', 'voices', not 'voice', 'ideologies', not 'ideology', and so on. There are, however, limits to this insight, which should become obvious when the question of 'meanings' is applied directly to English literature. To para-phrase the modern cultural theorist Terry Eagleton in the context of the Victorians, Charles Dickens's *Oliver Twist* (1837), for example, 'means' lots of things, but it is hardly likely to be about 'Manchester United' foot-ball club. Neither, in this sense, is Alfred Lord Tennyson's *In Memoriam* (1850), whatever way one approaches it, really a poem about the sexual behaviour of giraffes, nor Emily Brontë's Gothic masterpiece, *Wuthering Heights* (1847), a book about woodwork.

A more useful way to understand poststructuralist debates is to listen to an important dialogue that occurred in the turbid intellectual milieu of France in 1968–9 between two major thinkers, Roland Barthes and Michel Foucault, at a time when students were proclaiming revolution in Paris. In his influential essay, 'The Death of the Author' (1968), Barthes made a number of controversial points. He claimed, for example, that it is 'language which speaks, not the author'; that the reader in effect 'rewrites' the book in the act of interpretation; and that ultimately 'the birth of the reader must be at the cost of the death of the author'. Barthes referred to the role of the author as akin to that of 'God'. To resist the 'authority' of the author is, he maintained, akin to resisting the 'author-ity' on meaning provided by God, but also that supplied by other 'author-ities' such as science. Intriguingly, the term 'author' derives from the Latin for 'originate', and Barthes deconstructed the ways in which the 'origins' of meaning came about in texts: 'We know now that a text is not a line of words releasing a single "theological" meaning (the "message" of the Author-God) but a multi-dimensional space in which a variety of writings, none of them original, blend and clash. The text is a tissue of quotations drawn from the innumerable centres of culture.'

Barthes's ideas about the author were challenged by Michel Foucault in 'What Is an Author?' (1969). In this piece, Foucault identified the rise of the 'notion of author' with the historical process of 'individualization' in Western societies. Similar to Barthes, he argued that to fetishize the author's 'single message' is to 'limit' the 'dangerous proliferation of significations' in the text. For Foucault, the anxieties in society towards multiple and hence potentially revolutionary meanings ensured the more stable notion of the 'single message' gets invested in 'the author': 'The author is therefore the ideological figure by which one marks the manner in which we fear the proliferation of meaning.' Also, according to Foucault, just as 'authorship' is associated with the 'ownership' of property in modern capitalism, to fix meaning is to foist 'ownership' on it, to make 'property' of its 'presence', like any commodity in consumerist societies. In positioning himself against Barthes's ideas, Foucault further stressed, however, that the author needs to be 'resurrected', as it were, if only to participate amongst the many diverse systems of significations and meanings unleashed by the text.

The debate between the two theorists becomes even more complex and illuminating in terms of the question of individualism in language, and the problem of the speaking 'I'. Typically, Foucault situates the rise of the 'I' in terms of Western capitalist ideologies, which celebrate the 'individual' author and the rise of 'individual' geniuses in the modern epoch such as Shakespeare or Dickens. These names, for Foucault, took on an aura in society and culture which surpassed the significance of their writings. Barthes, on the other hand, held that the authorial 'I' is embedded within language itself: 'Linguistically, the author is never more than the instance writing, just as *I* is nothing *other than* the instance saying *I*: language knows a "subject",' not a "person". The 'I', for Barthes, is a figure of language, but the image of its 'presence' in language bestows on it an immeasurable prestige in society. The 'I' is a grammatical construction of language which everyone can share; everyone, in other words, can speak and write and hence be an individual 'I'. But that 'I' is both 'subject' of, and, for some poststructuralists, subject 'to', other forms of language, in which the idea of the individual is also constructed, ideologically, by important cultural agents such as literature.

How does one approach Victorian literature as a poststructuralist critic? One way, amongst many, is to reconsider Barthes's points about each text being a 'tissue of quotations', derived from the many 'centres of culture', none of which is 'original'. When viewed through the poststructural lens, all texts are, in one way or another, references to each other, either with, or, as Barthes puts it, without 'quotation marks'. Another key concept, in this respect, which was first coined by Julia Kristeva *c*.1966, 'intertextuality', describes this process perfectly. Kristeva's point was that each text, as a mosaic of quotations, is an 'absorption and transformation of another', and it is this mode of appropriation and modification which marks the interdependency of all texts. Kristeva's ideas can be extended to the 'intertextual' nature of any number of ideas and anxieties which gripped Victorian consciousness, one of which, in the context of the British Empire, was cannibalism. Dickens's novels, for example, are full of references to people eating each other, and not just in terms of dark and savage island races. The Englishman Magwitch in *Great Expectations* (1861), for instance, returns illegally from exile in the Australian colonies, but he does so with certain cannibalistic appetites which are most memorably captured when he eyes Pip's 'plump' cheeks in the graveyard: 'Darn Me, if I couldn't eat 'em'. Magwitch, it appears, has brought back to England a renewed hunger and wildness imbued with his encounter in the colonies and the hint of his liaison with 'blackfellas'. The point, however, is that Dickens appears to have known very well that the myth of cannibalism his work draws on, time and again, is part of an intertextual inheritance which had echoed down through English literature. Dickens himself learned about cannibalism from what is widely recognized as the 'first' novel in English literature, Daniel Defoe's *Robinson Crusoe* (1719), a colonial allegory full of English fears of being eaten by black men: 'I [Crusoe] had heard the people of the Caribbean were cannibals'. Dickens even acknowledged as much in his comments in a piece called 'The Lost Arctic Voyagers'(1854), in which he discusses Sir John Franklin's ill-fated expedition to the Arctic Circle to find the elusive Northwest Passage. Franklin's entourage disappeared and many Victorians thought they were eaten by Inuktitut fisherman, but Dickens's thoughts keep turning back to Defoe: 'Our general impressions on the subject [are] – very often derived, we have no doubt, from Robinson Crusoe'.

The intertextual dimensions of cannibalism have also been explored in the period after the age of Dickens and the Victorians, in postcolonial encounters or rather postmodern rewritings of *Robinson Crusoe* such as J. M. Coetzee's *Foe* (1986). In this novel, the narrator composes letters to the author (Daniel 'Foe'), in which the linguistic or rather textual construction of cannibalism, not to mention its lucrative potential for authors like Defoe, is continually underlined: 'I forgot you are a writer who knows above all how many words can be sucked from a cannibal feast . . . It is all a matter of words and the number of words, is it not?' Cannibalism is a fiction of empire, a sensationalized 'matter of words' handed down through literature, from Defoe, to Dickens, to Coetzee, who subverts it, and so on. Its myth, in other words, exceeded and became more violent in its implications than any episodes of actual cannibalism witnessed by explorers, anthropologists or colonialists, throughout history. Ultimately, cannibalism is just one important concept which marks Victorian consciousness as an 'intertextual' consciousness. But the very textuality of its formation – and its ghostly resurrection in the works of those such as Dickens – underlies the violence of the binary oppositions, civilized/savage, white/black, self/other, English/foreign, on which the Victorians based their rationalist and superior ideas of themselves. Indeed, cannibalism is one of the many points at which, to end on one of Barthes's most striking formulations, 'Life never does more than imitate the book.'

See also *Criticism*: Deconstruction, Feminism, Marxism, New historicism/Cultural materialism, Postcolonialism, Postmodernism, Psychoanalysis, Queer theory, Structuralism.

Further Reading

Belsey, Catherine, *Poststructuralism: A Very Short Introduction* (Oxford: Oxford University Press, 2002).
Derrida, Jacques, *Positions* (London: The Athlone Press, 1972).

Psychoanalysis

Psychoanalytic theories and approaches are indebted to the late nineteenth-century and early twentieth-century ideas of Sigmund Freud. As with Marxism, in this respect, psychoanalysis grew up largely in response to the attitudes and anxieties of Victorian society. Classic Freudian psychoanalysis is structured around three key concepts: sexuality, repression and the unconscious. Freud's basic proposition was that the mind has a tripartite structure: a 'conscious' (superego), of conscious or waking thoughts; a 'preconscious' ('ego'), an anteroom full of buried but accessible thoughts; and the all-important 'unconscious' (the 'id'). His central argument was that repressed thoughts, desires and neuroses, many of which developed during the psychosexual experiences of childhood, are always seeking escape from the unconscious. In a series of writings collectively known as 'Papers on Metapsychology' (1915), Freud lucidly describes the concept of repression as a form of 'censorship': 'the essence of repression lies simply in turning something away, and keeping it at a distance, from the conscious'. For Freud, the unconscious and the conscious are bound together in a precarious state of 'delicate balancing'. Each pressures the other and maintains the tension which creates, in the most extreme cases, psychoses. In his paper, 'The Unconscious' (1915), Freud makes other important distinctions equally clear: 'Everything that is repressed must remain unconscious', and he 'rejects' terms such as 'subconscious' as confusing. Towards the end of his life, in *Civilization and Its Discontents* (1930), Freud went as far as arguing that Western civilization is only 'civilized', if at all, because it succeeds in repressing its desires and impulses.

In his crucial earlier work, *The Interpretation of Dreams* (1900), Freud suggested that repression is the mechanism which modifies the id's drives into 'latent states' (dormant but active), which find escape in what he called the 'wish-fulfilment' of dreams. Dreams, which Freud described as the 'royal road to the unconscious', were thought to displace the repressed impulses onto other symbols, images or metaphors, which explained their often bizarre nature. In works such as *The Psychopathology of Everyday Life* (1901), Freud turned his attention to those repressions which he referred to as 'slips of the tongue' and 'slips of the pen' (Freud gave them the more scientific-sounding name, 'parapraxes'), which in the twentieth century became known as the 'Freudian slip'. The importance of 'slips', for Freud, was that they betrayed unconscious desires or hostilities towards the person or thing mistakenly referred to. As he put it, 'distorting names is very often a form of insulting their owners . . . the changing of a name [is] an act of unconscious hostility', and, more precisely, 'even the most insignificant slip in writing can serve to express a dangerous secret meaning'. Freud's work becomes even more interesting for literary critics and theorists in the light of his other insights into what he called the 'misreading' of texts. These amount to an unconscious desire to repress 'meanings' which the individual cannot, for whatever unconscious reason, contemplate.

Psychoanalysis has received heavy criticism, particularly from feminist commentators. Freud based his all-important Oedipus Complex, most notably, on the psychosexual development of boys, and it is the patriarchal nature of psychoanalysis which feminists have rejected. Many critics in the 1960s–70s lambasted psychoanalysis for being a fundamentally misogynistic theory. For such critics, psychoanalysis, while being centred on male experience, is also based on Freud's erroneous assertions about the woman's 'sense of inferiority', due to her recognition as a young girl that she lacks a penis and undergoes 'penis envy'. The envy is only resolved, in classic psychoanalysis, when the woman transfers her desire for a penis onto the desire for a baby, which Freud po-facedly calls the 'penis-baby'. Such feminist objections to psychoanalysis have, however, themselves been objected to since by other feminists such as Juliet Mitchell. In *Psychoanalysis and Feminism* (1974), Mitchell attempts to rescue psychoanalysis as a useful feminist strategy for criticizing the way in which patriarchy works: 'psychoanalysis is not a recommendation *for* a patriarchal society, but an analysis *of* one' (italics in original). Meanwhile, psychoanalysis has remained controversial, largely because Freud was a radical reader of the image, of language, of the signifier, and because he audaciously called his methods 'scientific'. Freud says, for example, in *The Interpretation of Dreams*, that if one dreams of 'sticks' and 'snakes', this can be interpreted as anxieties about the penis (or lack of), and that if one dreams of spacious 'Rooms' or empty 'Cupboards', these are images of the vagina. For men, the vaginal images represent their unconscious desire to return to the mother's womb, and so back to that first painless and blissful state before the agony of life. This 'oceanic' condition was, for Freud, similar to the inanimate state of death, which explains why he later proclaimed that 'the aim of all life is death'.

A closer look at one of Freud's infamous case histories further demonstrates his radical method of reading signs, and hence the usefulness of his approaches for literary critics. In his study of Dora (c.1901), Freud found that this 19-year-old woman had developed an 'unconscious phantasy' about 'sexual intercourse (sucking at the male organ)'. But this 'phantasy', he concluded, was the return of repressed childhood neuroses from a time when she was a devoted 'thumb-sucker'. Indeed the thumb-sucking itself was merely, for Freud, a repetition of what he called an 'impression of sucking the mother's or nurse's breast'. Similarly, Freud's account of male sexuality is also based on the subject's desires for the mother, which are then re-routed onto other objects of desire when the boy is forced, because of the incest taboo in society, to resolve his Oedipus Complex. During the Oedipus Complex, which Freud called the 'nucleus of the neurosis', the boy develops an over-attachment to the mother, competes with his father for his mother's affections, and eventually yields to the threat of castration posed by the father's authority. According to Freud, Oedipus is the most vital stage in the boy's psychosexual development, and classic psycho-analysis is premised on the notion that, should the boy not resolve his Oedipus Complex, he endures a lifelong sense of loss and anxiety.

Another major development in psychoanalysis which has had a serious influence on literary theory was that made by French psychoanalyst Jacques Lacan. Lacan led a 'back to Freud' movement in the mid-twenti-eth century, but he challenged Freud by placing more emphasis on the role of language. His work was partly, and for literary critics most impor-tantly, based on structuralist ideas about what he described as the 'chain of signifiers' in language which has no reference outside of itself (to the signified, the meaning, the reality). He further suggested that the human subject, the 'I', is constructed by its entry into what he called the 'symbolic order' of the language system, which effectively constructs 'real' experi-ence as 'symbolic'. In *Écrits* (1977), Lacan made the crucial point that, far from being just the Freudian 'seat of the instincts', the 'unconscious' is both produced by and 'structured like a language', which operates as a play of images, signifiers, words, metaphors, much as it does in Freud's account of dreamwork. Indeed, for Lacan, 'dream-images' are 'to be taken only for their value as signifiers'. If one dreams, in other words, that one's mother has turned into a bear, this does not mean that the bear is necessarily important in whatever the dream signifies, or that the dreamer wants an actual bear for a mother. Quite obviously, the bear is a signifier which, if anything at all, signifies something else.

Lacan's arguments inverted Freud's idea that the unconscious precedes language. For Lacan, the human subject does not speak language so much as language 'speaks' (constructs) him or her; language pre-exists and is dominant in society and culture, and the subject becomes both an 'effect' and 'slave' of it. It was Lacan, in fact, who provided perhaps the most illuminating definition of the unconscious, a difficult concept to understand precisely because it refers to that inchoate space of repression and desire. While doing so, and even more explicitly than Freud, perhaps, it was also Lacan who turned the psychoanalytic account of subjectivity against the history of liberal humanism enshrined in Western philosophy. In what he described as 'modern man so sure of being himself', Lacan criticized the Western assumption that the 'individual' is based on the certainty of its being a 'conscious' and definable thinking self, a metaphysical assumption arrived at by seventeenth-century philosopher René Descartes, in his influential *Cogito*, 'I think, therefore I am.' Lacan, in a typically intricate and playful manner, unsettled Descartes's formulation, and by doing so he implied that the unconscious structure of subjectivity is as fragmentary and misplaced as it is potentially inaccessible: 'I think where I am not, therefore I am where I do not think.'

Lacan compounded his thesis in his discussion of childhood development. There, he argued that the child of 6–18 months effectively misrecognizes itself in the prelinguistic or imaginary *infans* 'mirror stage'. Looking in the mirror, the child mistakes the reflected image for a coherent and unified self, what Lacan calls its 'Ideal-I'. This image then constructs a false sense of self built from what is actually a 'misconstruction', steering the idea of subjectivity in what Lacan called an entirely 'fictional' direction. Put another way, according to Lacan, it is the image of 'the total form of the body' which 'symbolizes the mental permanence of the *I*'. And such images of unity and permanence conceal what is, for Lacan, a fundamental absence or lack of self-unity, a divided, unconscious self, only upheld as 'whole' in maturity by socially and culturally determined forces such as language. In addition, in Lacan's rereading of the Oedipus Complex, the boy still realizes the unattainability of the mother by experiencing the 'incest taboo' and the consequent fear of castration provided by the father. However, for Lacan, this fear of castration is also the moment in which the boy enters the 'symbolic order' of language, which is to say the authoritarian 'name' of 'the father'. The girl child, on the other hand, is not forced to give up her identification with the mother in her experience. In Lacanian analysis, she does not possess the phallus in the first place, and as a result she does not enter the symbolic order which Lacan sees as constitutive of (male) human subjectivity. She is thus condemned to a lifelong sense of lack, to a desire to fill the absence which becomes – not a desire for a material phallus (an actual penis) as such – but an empty signifier which gets filled with the 'significance' of whatever temporarily fends off desire.

Nowadays, there are vastly different psychoanalytic perspectives on Victorian literature in circulation. In classic 'psychobiographical' approaches, for example, such as Edmund Wilson's *The Wound and the Bow* (1941) and Lionel Trilling's *Sincerity and Authenticity* (1972), literary texts are treated as symptoms of the author's desires, repressions and neuroses. Such approaches have, however, been superseded by more sophisticated methods which draw on poststructural understandings of the text's contradictions and omissions. These do not focus on the author so much as on the language of the text; they attempt to reveal those silent or rather 'unconscious' elements of which the text is not 'conscious'. Modern psychoanalytic criticism tends to apply itself to the 'unspoken' of literature. It is partly indebted to what Pierre Macherey, in *A Theory of Literary Production* (1978), described as that which the text 'cannot' or ' does not say', which he reminds us is not the same as that which the text 'chooses not to say'. The analogy should not be pushed too far – texts are texts, not human beings – but one might envisage a Victorian poem, for example, as a traumatized patient full of unconscious desires and anxieties, albeit one which the therapy of psychoanalytic reading and interpretation can never cure, as it were, merely diagnose. Matthew Rowlinson, for instance, in *Tennyson's Fixations* (1994), approaches Tennyson's poetry in a formalist manner. He argues that Tennyson's work is typified by various rhythmic and thematic repetitions and repressions, which amount to the throb of Tennyson's secret desires for men and women, but which are also consonant with Freud's ideas about the subject's 'compulsion to repeat' the daily rhythms of childhood experience with the mother.

Unsurprisingly, then, in a period notoriously sheepish about 'speaking' of desire, there has been plenty of psychoanalytic attention to the sexual dimensions of Victorian literature. Critical works abound in this area, such as John Kucich's *Repression in Victorian Literature* (1987), Peter Gay's *The Bourgeois Experience: Victorian to Freud* (1986), and Christopher Craft's focus on the crisis of Victorian homosexuality in *Another Kind of Love* (1994). Some of the more exciting recent developments are those that combine such psychoanalytic perspectives with postcolonial theories and approaches, because they have enabled critics such as Daniel Bivona to arrive at key concepts like the 'colonial unconscious'. That Victorian fiction is uncomfortable with representing the British Empire has long been acknowledged. Edward W. Said, for instance, argued in *Orientalism* (1978) that the empire only obtains a 'shadowy presence' in the literature of the period. Of greater significance, perhaps, is the complex way in which the colonial unconscious becomes manifest in Victorian literature, as Lacan suggests, 'like a language', or, as Freud suggests, by a series of slips of the tongue or pen which betray the unconscious. The novels of Charles Dickens, for example, are full of 'Freudian slips' and suspicious silences around the question of empire, some more conscious than others. In *Nicholas Nickleby* (1839), Mrs Nickleby modestly points out to her daughter Kate that she must have had 'a dozen at least' of suitors before Kate's father. Her boast then turns to one such 'young gentleman' who mysteriously disappeared to the colony of Australia, in a series of revealing slips of the tongue or pen: '[the man] afterwards unfortunately went out to Botany Bay in cadet ship – a convict ship I mean – and escaped into a bush and killed sheep'. Mrs Nickleby corrects her slip here, but the term 'cadet' still obtrudes like one of Freud's 'screen-memories', as if to prevent the return of the colonial unconscious to the 'spoken' of the novel by displacing it onto another signifier. Her misreading of the Australian 'bush' as singular, and her comical equation between outback life and sheep, further indicate an uncomfortable – not to say guilty – awareness of the fact that Britain was using Australia as a prison colony for its criminals. In a similar incident, Betsey Trotswood in *David Copperfield* explains that her husband went off 'to India . . . and there . . . according to a wild legend in our family, he was seen riding on an elephant, in company with a Baboon; but I think it might have been a Baboo – or a Begum'. Intriguingly, Dickens's playfulness with the signifiers of empire in this example might well have been consciously executed. But what, to draw on Pierre Macherey's point, Dickens's text 'does not say', is that his pun on a Hindu title of respect, 'Babu', points again towards what Freud called the unconscious hostility of misnaming. The signifier 'Baboon' equates 'Babu' with monkeys, that most formidable legacy of eighteenth- and nineteenth-century 'scientific racism'. However humorously it was intended, for Freud and psychoanalysis, puns and jokes, like slips, are rarely innocent, and Dickens's 'joke' bears the burden of British imperial history in India. It marks, in this respect, an unconscious encounter between the Victorians and their empire which, although often repressed and silent, is, as with all repressions, always ready to return to language and make havoc in the present.

See also *Contexts*: Body, Childhood, Clothing, Family, Gender, Sex and sexuality; *Criticism*: Deconstruction, Feminism, Marxism, Postcolonialism, Queer theory.

Further Reading

Bivona, Daniel, *Desire and Contradiction: Imperial Visions and Domestic Debates in Victorian Literature* (Manchester and New York: Manchester University Press, 1990).
Gay, Peter (ed.), *The Freud Reader* (London: Vintage, 1995).

Queer Theory

Queer theory questions normative assumptions about identity based on sexuality and biology, especially those engrained in heterosexual ideologies. It does so by rereading a cultural field such as Victorian literature against the grain of heterosexual interpretation, 'querying' both the text and traditional criticism, so to speak. Queer theory as a critical practice took shape in the 1980s–90s. It emerged partly in response to the lesbian and gay rights movements, partly to feminism, and partly to the renewed climate of hostility towards homosexuals triggered by the AIDS crisis. Nowadays, queer critics draw on a range of ideas and critical perspectives made available by the advent of poststructuralism in the 1960s, and their work combines anything from Marxist to postmodernist perspectives.

Poststructuralism gave queer theorists a critical language with which to explore the constructed nature of sexuality and gender throughout Western history. Critics have then used this language to 'deconstruct' a society based on the binary opposition between 'normal' (heterosexual) and 'abnormal' (homosexual) sexualities, the 'violent hierarchy' of which underpins much of Victorian literature. Similarly, postmodernist queer theorists challenge the West's 'grand narrative' of heterosexual history, which has all but excluded homosexuals. In doing so, they attempt to rewrite history from a queer perspective which at once fragments the grand narrative into 'other' histories and undermines its totalizing 'truths'. Others challenge the assumption, sometimes implicit in society, sometimes explicit (as in Victorian literature), that human subjectivity is premised solely on its sexual orientation, and they call for a less reductive, less stable, notion of identity. They resist such an assumption because, broadly speaking, it has coloured the perception of homosexuality and contributed to much of the violence and oppression meted out against homosexuals in Western society throughout history, and most viciously in Britain since the beginnings of capitalist modernity c.1600.

The Victorian period is fertile ground for queer theorists. While lesbianism was not really recognized by society as a viable sexuality at all, homosexuality was condemned and criminalized throughout the period, and it is very much Victorian attitudes to gays and lesbians which are still being deconstructed in the twenty-first century. The terms 'homosexual' and 'heterosexual' were first coined in late nineteenth-century medical terminology, and homosexuality was pathologized in the eccentric explorations of a 'science' known as 'sexology'. The influential French historian of ideas, Michel Foucault, in *The History of Sexuality* (1976), tried to pinpoint the first use of 'homosexual' to 1870. He argued that it was, in fact, in nineteenth-century bourgeois discourse that the 'homosexual became a personage, a past, a case history . . . in addition to being a type of life . . . with an indiscreet anatomy and possibly a mysterious anatomy'. Foucault situated his theories in the context of a newly emergent capitalist-imperialist society that was still underpinned by a Christian ethos, and which saw the sexual congress of homosexuals as 'unnatural' and their 'wasted' semen as unproductive. By the nineteenth century, partly as a result of these attitudes, the Victorians were strengthening the legal mechanisms of discipline and punishment for homosexuals. In 1885, the Labouchère Amendment to the Criminal Law Amendment Act (1885) proclaimed that 'the commission by any male person of any act of gross indecency with another male person' was against the law and punishable by imprisonment, whereas between the sixteenth century and 1861 sodomy had been punishable by death. Only ten years later in 1895, after the most famous 'somdomite' [sic] trial of the century, Oscar Wilde was prosecuted for homosexual 'crimes against nature', and sentenced to two years' hard labour on a treadmill. But despite the furore which surrounded Wilde's case, and the sheer rampancy of gay love throughout the nineteenth century, homosexuality was, as Wilde's lover Lord Alfred Douglas put it, still very much 'the love that dare not speak its name' in Victorian society. And it is this silence, or rather submergence, which characterizes the image of homosexuality in the literature of the age, a repression which was repeated at the level of traditional literary criticism.

Victorian literature has undergone various queer readings since the 1980s. In *Love Between Men in English Literature* (1996), for example, Paul Hammond explores the blurring of male friendship and erotic love in a number of Victorian texts, such as Alfred Lord Tennyson's elegy for his friend Arthur Hallam. *In Memoriam* (1850) laments Hallam's beauty, and for Hammond, Tennyson repeatedly uses loaded terms of endearment to describe his affections, particularly 'dear' and 'love'. 'Love', in particular, features in one of the poem's sentiments which has long since passed into proverb, not to say cliché: "Tis better to have loved and lost / Than never to have loved at all'. But Tennyson's mournings are also, according to Hammond, overshadowed by the societal pressure to be silent about his illicit desires for Hallam throughout: 'And what I see I leave unsaid'. In terms of the Victorian novel, Jacob Press sees a complex homoerotics of 'Jewish Nationalism' (1997) in George Eliot's *Daniel Deronda* (1876). Press argues that Eliot's 'characterization of the Jewish male', Deronda, as 'outsider' in Victorian society, equates with the 'alienation' of homosexuals from 'the modern European imperative of aggressive heterosexual masculinity'. As with much feminist criticism, Press's work queries Victorian anxieties, by insisting on the

politics of the body in Eliot's work. He explores the physical and psychological effects of Deronda's 'unspeakable' circumcision, for example,
and Deronda's tangible fear of being touched by another male Jew,
Mordecai, as indicative of anxieties about homoeroticism, even though
Eliot contrives a 'marriage' of sorts between the two in her denouement:
'the marriage of our souls'. Elsewhere in Victorian literature, queer theorists have long since begun to see more than a platonic or sisterly relationship – 'Hug me, kiss me, suck my juices' – between Lizzie and Laura
in Christina Rossetti's sensuous 'fairy tale' of seduction and the marketplace, *Goblin Market* (1862), despite the fact that Rossetti also engineers
a heterosexual 'happy ending' for the girls.

Eve Kosofsky Sedgwick's groundbreaking work has, however,
provided an entirely different perspective for queer theorists. In
Epistemology of the Closet (1985), Sedgwick based her theory on the
notion that 'male–male desire' in literature can *only* become intelligible,
where at all, when 'routed through triangular relations involving a
woman'. Her ideas have consequently provided another way of looking
at the numerous 'male-bondings' that occur throughout Victorian
fiction, those which are a particular feature, say, of Charles Dickens's
novels. They throw new light, for example, on Samuel Pickwick and
Sam Weller's curious 'marriage' in *The Pickwick Papers* (1836–7) – 'which
only death will terminate' – and certainly on Pickwick's breach of
promise with a woman in the stories. But Sedgwick also discusses what
she calls the 'homophobia' of Dickens's *Our Mutual Friend* (1865), and
the homophobia of empire in his last novel, *The Mystery of Edwin Drood*
(1870), in which John Jasper is weakened and rendered effete – 'almost
womanly' – by his indulgence in the great Victorian drug of empire,
opium. Various queer theorists, such as Hammond, have, furthermore,
quarried the late Victorian works of Oscar Wilde for their many homoerotic codes and covert references to male love. In a concept similar to
what Diana Collecot in *Sexual Sameness* (1992) calls 'homotextuality',
Hammond suggests that a thematic sense of 'secrecy and the fear of
disclosure' haunts Wilde's only novel, *The Picture of Dorian Gray* (1891).
In Wilde's story, the exquisite young libertine, Dorian, famously remains
young and beautiful, whilst his picture ages and deteriorates. For
Hammond, though, the important point is that what actually transpires
during Dorian's 'descent into vice' in the East End of London's numerous low houses of entertainment in the novel is never, typically, fully
disclosed, only that these are 'ill-famed' places full of swaggering sailors
and, as Wilde writes, 'curious unpictured sins'.

Wilde's famous paradoxes and epigrams also suggest that his decadent novel set out to invert Victorian 'morality', what Foucault described

as 'reverse discourse', especially around questions of sexuality: 'For any man of culture to accept the standard of his age is a form of the grossest immorality.' Modern queer theorists working on Wilde have, on the other hand, often positioned themselves against earlier approaches to his work, such as those of Jeffrey Myers in *Homosexuality and Literature, 1890–1930* (1977). Myers's conclusions about Wilde's novel betray a certain pretheoretical and evaluative stance which seems to supply a misguided answer to an unnecessary question: '*Dorian Gray* is a failure as a novel because Wilde was unable to resolve the conflict between his desire for homosexual freedom and his fear of social condemnation'. Indeed, on the contrary, recent queer theorists such as Jeff Nunokawa have relished Wilde's 'conflicts' and 'irresolvable' contradictions as precisely part of the complex nature of homosexuality in his work. Moreover, for Nunokawa, such intricacies and tensions are integral to Wilde's problem of using his writings to represent the always subversive problem of homosexuality to an unforgiving and punitive Victorian society. In *The Importance of Being Bored* (1996), Nunokawa discusses what he describes as the central relationship between 'ennui' and 'desire' in *The Picture of Dorian Gray*, in which Wilde's sublimated references to homosexuality go hand-in-hand with the otherwise listless lives and sheer boredom experienced by Dorian Gray, Basil Hallward and Henry Wotton. Nunokawa argues that the many allusions to boredom in the novel are metaphors for the momentary satiation of homoerotic desire, or rather the sleepy afterglow of orgasm, although they also, at the same time, point towards a yearning for the 'death of desire', and so to an end to the chaos and uncertainty that such a desire creates. Intriguingly, for example, Dorian yawns repeatedly in the novel, lolls languidly on sofas smoking cigarettes, and the men make suggestive comments, such as 'It is such a bore putting on one's dress clothes'.

Another late Victorian novel which has also been heavily queried is *Dracula* (1897). To begin with, it is significant for theorists that Bram Stoker's famous Gothic pot-boiler emerged in the aftermath of Wilde's controversial trial for homosexuality. Numerous critics such as Hammond and Christopher Craft have speculated, for example, that Dracula's reservations in the novel about yielding Jonathan Harker to the bloodthirsty desires of his female vampires intimate an unspeakable, homoerotic attachment to Harker on Dracula's part: 'This man belongs to me!' In line with – but also in a sense complicating – Sedgwick's ideas, Dracula's intervention in this scene redirects, 'between men', the usual heterosexual nexus of vampire lust, in which vampire men sink their teeth into virginal women and suck their blood. Certainly, as Hammond points out, whatever happens in the time between Dracula's dismissal of the vampirellas, and Harker's waking up in his own bed, any hint of homoerotics in the text has fallen into the 'silence' between Stoker's chapters; it is repressed, that is, into the void beyond words, into that eloquent silence in which the Victorian 'love that dare not speak its name' can only haunt the text like a whisper. Meanwhile, Dracula himself, a little ruffled perhaps but none the worse for it, is later seen wearing some of Harker's clothes around the castle.

See also *Contexts*: Decadence and aestheticism, Sex and sexuality; *Texts*: Drama; *Criticism*: Deconstruction, Postmodernism, Poststructuralism, Psychoanalysis.

Further Reading

Kosofsky Sedgwick, Eve, *Between Men: English Literature and Male Homosocial Desire* (New York: Columbia University Press, 1985).

Kosofsky Sedgwick, Eve (ed.), *Novel Gazing: Queer Readings in Fiction* (Durham, NC and London: Duke University Press, 1997).

Structuralism

Structuralism was one of the most significant intellectual movements of the twentieth century. By the 1960s–70s – the heyday of structuralism – its ideas and theories, all of which were concerned, in one way or another, with the underlying 'structures' of human behaviour, had begun to have an enormous impact on numerous fields and disciplines, such as anthropology, psychology, semiology (the science of signs) politics, history, sociology, philosophy and literary theory. Definitions of structuralism are always hazardous, but Frederic Jameson, for example, in *The Prison House of Language* (1972), described it as 'an explicit search for the permanent structures of the mind'. In the same year, Jonathan Culler, in *Structuralist Poetics* (1972), defined structuralism as being, in its application to literature at least, not so much a 'search' for what texts mean but their 'conditions of meaning'. For Culler, structuralism was preoccupied, in other words, with the underlying 'structures' which determined *how* texts mean, rather than *what* texts mean.

The origins of structuralism lay mainly in the work of the Swiss linguist Ferdinand de Saussure, who developed a revolutionary theory of language in the period before the First World War. What originally motivated Saussure was his preoccupation with the 'structures' and conventions which underlie all language systems. It is important, in this respect, to have a fairly detailed understanding of some of Saussure's main theories about language in order to understand more fully the implications of structuralism and its focus on the ways in which literature uses, or is used by, the underlying structures of language. In his posthumously published *Course in General Linguistics* (1916), Saussure argued that language is a system of signs. He defined the sign as a complete linguistic unit, which combines a sound-image, the 'signifier' (the written word, the spoken word), and the idea that that sound-image denotes, the 'signified' (the meaning, the concept). The central point of Saussure's theory, especially for literary critics, was that the relationship between signifier and signified, word and concept, is purely arbitrary; that is, the relationship between the 'name' and the 'object' it denotes is neither natural nor inevitable, but merely a 'social' convention. For Saussure, there is no logical connection, for example, between the sound-image or written signifier, 'banana', and the concept of the yellow fruit being described. Similarly, there is no intrinsic or obvious reason why the signifier 'duck', and not the signifier 'cat', should designate the species of honking, semi-aquatic bird. Put another way, there is nothing 'duck'-like about the word 'duck', or indeed anything 'cat'-like about the word 'cat'. At the same time, there is no necessary or natural reason why the letters 'q', 'c' and 'k' should denote the sound [ke]; the relationship between the letters and their sounds, asserts Saussure, is also an arbitrary convention of society and culture. The only requirement for society, to ensure effective communication, is that the sign for 'c', for example, is not confused in written or spoken language with other signs, such as 'p', 't' or 'd'.

Language for Saussure is, as suggested above, a system of differences, where signs (words, letters) can exist only in negative opposition to other signs. And these signs, he explained, can only be identified by contrast with other similar signs, because their 'most precise characteristic is in being what the others are not'. That said, despite its arbitrary nature, Saussure never lost sight of the fact that language remains governed by certain rules and principles, and this is how its structures come to be 'meaningful' in society. As he puts it himself, 'the arbitrary nature of the sign explains . . . why the social fact alone can create a linguistic system'. Moreover, his own insight on this point is enough for Saussure to prove that language is not a natural or necessary process, but a highly constructed medium, a system of conventions solely designed by and for the community, so that even with the seemingly contradictory example of onomatopoeia, his theory proves to be the case. Onomatopoeic signifiers such as 'moo' or 'quack quack', needless to say, appear to imitate the 'concepts' they refer to, in this case the noises that cows or ducks make. But such signifiers are still arbitrarily chosen structures, as Saussure maintains; they are only 'approximate and more or less conventional imitations of certain sounds'. How, otherwise, does one explain the fact that English cows and ducks go 'moo' and 'quack', while French cows and ducks go 'meuh' and 'coin coin'? For Saussure, more importantly, *all* of our ideas and concepts are constructed by language, and not vice versa. He concludes from this that language is a system which precedes individuals and conditions our responses to a world in which there are 'no pre-existing ideas', and in which 'nothing is distinct before the appearance of language'. It is in this respect that his views went on to underpin both structuralist and post-structuralist theories.

In the 1950s–70s, structuralism was controversial, and it was criticized for removing the objects of study from their historical and cultural contexts. Worse, with its emphasis on the structures of forms and the centrality of language, and not people, it was thought to reek of 'anti-humanism'. However, one of the central tenets of structuralist thought is that everything, including such categories as 'humanity', 'subjectivity' and 'individual identity', are products of certain linguistic or cultural structures. As one of the groundbreaking structuralist (and later post-structuralist) critics, Roland Barthes explained in *Elements of Semiology* (1964) – a work which attempted to locate a single and universal system of signs – everything in society is structured like a language, and 'everything signifies': 'images, gestures, musical sounds, objects'. Barthes was interested, for example, in structures such as the 'language' of clothing, in which a particular set of garments might be structured and read like a 'sentence'. In an earlier work, *Mythologies* (1957), he had also looked into a variety of cultural images and artefacts for their underlying sign systems: in the theatrical gestures of wrestlers, for example, or in the greasy forelock on the heads of American actors which signified 'Roman' in Hollywood 'sword and sandal' epics. In his influential later piece 'The Death of the Author' (1968), by which time his work was becoming increasingly associated with poststructuralism, Barthes took the idea of the social and cultural determining powers of language to their most logical conclusion, in a point which was clearly indebted to the structuralism of Saussure: 'life never does more than imitate the book'. In terms of structuralist literary criticism, such ideas have had profound implications for the way in which Victorian literature is interpreted. Before structuralism, classic realist Victorian texts were supposed to have simply 'reflected' Victorian reality. According to the structuralist understanding of language, however, and certainly in Barthes's seemingly paradoxical point about 'the book', it is 'reality' which actually 'imitates' or is rather 'constructed' by the book, even while the book appears to hold the mirror of language up to reality.

Such ideas were pursued further by other major structuralist/poststructuralist thinkers, such as the French historian Michel Foucault, who extended them to his more historically based work. Foucault's research in *The Order of Things* (1966), *Madness and Civilization* (1967), *Discipline and Punish* (1975) and *The History of* Sexuality (1976) sought to uncover the underlying 'structures' of power in Western society, those which have governed the discourses of reason, madness, illness, discipline and sexuality throughout history. Similarly, in other important fields such as psychoanalysis, Jacques Lacan, who led a significant 'return to Freud' movement in the mid-twentieth-century period, argued in *Écrits* (1966) that the 'unconscious' is 'structured like a language'. For Lacan, human subjectivity itself is the result of the linguistic structures of signs, symbols, metaphors and dreams, and these structures are buried in all literary texts and systems of signification. Outside of France, the structuralist direction of the earlier 'Russian Formalist' movement was encapsulated by Viktor Shklovsky's proclamation in *Poetics* (1919), that the 'forms of art are explainable by the laws of art' alone, and not by anything external to them, such as historical context or content, a point which also, it seems, underlined Saussure's distinction between the structures of language and reality.

Structuralist approaches to Victorian literature have largely been superseded by poststructural approaches. The latter, being 'post', suggest that the idea of 'structures' in language, and the unity of meaning they point towards, are problematic. Some structuralist approaches, for example, such as that taken by David Lodge in *Working with Structuralism* (1981), now seem a little misguided from the poststructuralist perspective, as indicated by the somewhat old-fashioned sounding title of his chapter 'How Successful is *Hard Times*?' Lodge begins this chapter by questioning conventional twentieth-century criticism of Charles Dickens's 1854 novel. He finds the attempts of such criticism to ascertain whether or not Dickens's work was 'successful' in creating a 'truthful' account of Victorian 'hard times' in industrial Manchester, unsatisfying, and he suggests that the questions such critics ask are the wrong ones in the first place. He then points out, looking for his own 'structure' in the text, that it is the novel's 'persuasiveness rather than truthfulness' which should be its criterion for 'success' or 'failure', that this criterion can only be evaluated by way of a 'structuralist' appreciation of 'narrative technique', and that this appreciation will, in turn, illuminate 'what kind of novel' *Hard Times* is. Lodge sees in the novel a rapid compression of 'time' and a certain 'moralised theatricality'. He argues, for example, that the novel's underlying structures are 'borrowed from popular theatre', although he also concedes that it borrows from other fictional structures such as fairy tale, nursery rhyme and melodrama. As a result, Dickens's Louisa and Tom Gradgrind become the 'fairy-tale' innocent children in the text, Bounderby the industrialist is the evil 'giant in a castle', Coketown's factories are 'fairy palaces', and so forth; Dickens's places and characters are, for Lodge, more 'cartoon-like' in the novel than real. Furthermore, the novel's succession of 'suspenseful' events (Stephen Blackpool's redundancy, Slackbridge's trade unionism, Blackpool's falling down a disused mine-shaft) is also, for Lodge, part of its 'structure', although he maintains that these events have a more 'symbolic' than 'realist' function. Equally, these events are relayed, as Lodge puts it, by a 'reliable' and 'omniscient' narrator who sees the class 'structures' underlying everything in society at all times.

Lodge goes on to argue that another one of the underlying structures of Dickens's novel is the motif of 'ironic reversal' in fortunes, which most of the inhabitants of Coketown undergo. Stephen Blackpool, most obviously, already has a hard life as a poor weaver. Then his mad, embittered wife shows up, he falls down the mine, he is proven innocent of the theft, he is rescued from the mine, and then, in the bitterest 'ironic reversal' of all, he dies. But what most typifies the overall structure of the novel, according to Lodge, is that it resists the reader's identification with any single character. Lodge argues that Dickens rushes through multiple characters towards his classically sentimental Victorian conclusion without lingering on the interior lives of anyone. This form of narrative pressure binds Dickens to what Lodge calls a novelistic 'structure' which 'seems to evade the awkward questions about class, capitalism and social justice that he [Dickens] himself raised'. Indeed, it is in the moments such as these, in which structuralist approaches directly explore the 'political' structures of Victorian fiction, that their implications for the way in which we understand that fiction become more significant.

A more productive way into structuralist readings, perhaps, is to listen to the way in which, in an oddly Saussurean manner, Victorian literature can be heard playing around with the structures of language and meaning itself. In Lewis Carroll's nonsense world of Wonderland (1865), for example, Alice is continually querying the relationship between signifier and signified, word and meaning. At some points, her interrogations seem to unsettle the entire framework of language and meaning which underpinned the Victorian world: 'I don't know what you mean'; 'there's not an atom of meaning in it'; 'not that it signifies much'. When Alice falls down the rabbit hole, she seems aware that she has somehow acquired – in a distinctly Saussurean tone – the 'language' of things before the 'meaning', or rather the word before the 'idea': 'Alice had not the slightest idea what Latitude was, or Longtitude either, but she thought they were nice grand words to say'. After she has then further confused 'the antipodes', where she thinks she is destined, with 'the antipathies', the curious creatures of Wonderland go on with their curious linguistic disputes: '"Found *what*?" said the Duck. "Found it," the Mouse replied rather crossly: "of course you know what 'it' means."' Then, as the Eaglet puts it, during the same exchange: '"Speak English!" ... "I don't know the meaning of half those long words, and, what's more, I don't believe you do either!"' And later still, speculates the Mock Turtle, 'Why, if a fish came to *me*, and told me that he was going on a journey, I should say "With what porpoise?"' 'Don't you mean "purpose"?' said Alice. "I mean what I say," the Mock Turtle replied, in an offended tone.' While Alice blunders on through Wonderland, the relationship between language and meaning in the text becomes, in this way, even more unsettled, the relationship between signifier and signified increasingly arbitrary, as it does in the following exchange: '"Then you should say what you mean," the March Hare went on. "I do," Alice hastily replied; "at least – at least I mean what I say – it's the same thing, you know." "Not the same thing a bit!" said the Hatter. "Why, you might just as well say that 'I see what I eat' is the same thing as 'I eat what I see!"' At one point, as if to underline the typically Victorian tenor of one situating 'reality' *before* language, in an un-Saussurean manner, Carroll's Duchess even claims that 'the moral of *that* is – "Take care of the sense, and the sounds will take care of themselves."'

That the structure of language is bound up with the structure of power in Victorian society, and that dominance and superiority ultimately rest with those who control 'meaning', creates anxieties which are a feature of the *Alice* tales throughout. In *Through the Looking Glass* (1872) there are more, typically Carrollean debates over the signifier, and one, in particular, in which Humpty Dumpty stretches 'glory' to mean 'a nice knock-down argument'. When Alice says, equally typically, '"I don't know what you mean by glory"', Humpty Dumpty replies scornfully: '"When *I* use a word, it means just what I choose it to mean."' Not to be beaten, Alice then adopts what appears to be not so much a Saussurean or a structuralist, but a poststructuralist stance on the question of the signifier and its endlessly undecideable meanings in Wonderland: '"The question is," said Alice, "whether you *can* make words mean so many different things."' The despot Humpty Dumpty, however, is having none of that either. He may be a talking egg, and the *Alice* tales may well have been aimed at children, but his last words on the matter sum up exactly what, in terms of his tyranny over language, structuralists and post-structuralists alike are concerned with deconstructing throughout

Victorian literature: '"The question is," said Humpty Dumpty, "which is to be master – that's all."'

See also *Texts*: Mid-Victorian novel, Realist fiction, Social-problem novel; *Criticism*: Deconstruction, Feminism, Marxism, Postmodernism, Poststructuralism.

Further Reading

Barthes, Roland, *Mythologies* (London: Cape, 1972) (first pub. 1957).
Scholes, Robert, *Structuralism in Literature: An Introduction* (New Haven, CT, and London: Yale University Press, 1974).

Chronology

Historical and Political Events	Literary and Cultural Events
1800 Act of Union between Great Britain and Ireland drawn up (effective from 1801)	
1803 British Empire acquires Tobago and St Lucia	
1805 Battle of Trafalgar	William Wordsworth's *The Prelude* (began 1798–9)
1807 Atlantic slave trade abolished	
1811 First Luddite 'machine-breaking' troubles in England	Jane Austen's *Sense and Sensibility*
1812 Napoleon invades Russia. United States declares war on Britain	Birth of Charles Dickens
1814 Napoleon exiled to Elba. First steam engine	Walter Scott's *Waverley*
1815 Battle of Waterloo. Napoleon defeated. Corn Law passed, placing a tariff on grain imports and inflating bread prices	
1818 First steamer crosses the Atlantic	Mary Shelley's *Frankenstein*. Jane Austen's *Northanger Abbey* and *Persuasion*
1819 'Peterloo Massacre' in Manchester. Birth of Princess Victoria	Lord Byron's *Don Juan*. Walter Scott's *Ivanhoe*. Birth of George Eliot (Mary Ann Evans). James Mill's *Essay on Government*

Historical and Political Events	Literary and Cultural Events
1820 Death of King George III. Accession of George IV	Thomas Malthus' *Principles of Political Economy*
1824 First Anglo-Burmese War. Combination Laws repealed, relaxing legislation on trade unions	*Westminster Review* established. Death of Lord Byron
1825 First steam locomotive between Stockton and Darlington. Combination Laws reinforced	
1829 Robert Peel's Metropolitan Police established. Catholic Emancipation Edict promulgated	First Oxford and Cambridge boat race
1830 Death of King George IV. Accession of William IV	Charles Lyell's *Principles of Geology*. Liverpool to Manchester railway opened
1831 Mysore annexed by British East India Company. Charles Darwin sets out on voyage of the *Beagle*. Cholera epidemic infiltrates Europe	
1832 British electorate doubled by passage of First Reform Act.	
1833 Slavery abolished throughout British Empire. Factory Act establishes first factory inspectors	Thomas Carlyle's *Sartor Resartus*. Establishment of Oxford Movement
1834 Poor coerced into workhouses by passage of Poor Law Amendment Act. Fire damages Houses of Parliament. Tolpuddle Martyrs transported for seven years	First Hansom cabs on London streets

Historical and Political Events	**Literary and Cultural Events**

1835

Construction of Euston Station in London begins. Isambard Kingdom Brunel's Great Western Railway between London and Bristol is opened

1836

Children under the age of 13 no longer allowed to work over 48 hours per week after passage of Factory Act

Serialization of Dickens's *The Pickwick Papers* begins

1837

Death of William IV. Accession of Victoria to throne. Virulent smallpox epidemic

Serialization of Dickens's *Oliver Twist* begins in *Bentley's Miscellany*

1838

Anti-Corn Law League formed. Chartist movement for reform begins. Brunel's Great Western steamer crosses Atlantic. Railway opens between London and Birmingham. Afghan War begins

Licensing laws restrict opening hours for pubs. Pubs closed from midnight on Saturdays to midday on Sundays. Serialization of Dickens's *Nicholas Nickleby*

1839

Presentation of People's Charter formally initiates Chartism. First 'Opium Wars' between Britain and China. Custody of Infants Act permits women separated from husbands to apply for custody of children under the age of 7

Carlyle's *Chartism*. Invention of Daguerreotype photography

1840

Marriage of Queen Victoria to Prince Albert of Saxe-Coburg-Gotha. Penny postage introduced. Treaty of Waitangi annexes New Zealand. Nottingham laceworkers begin strike

Kew Gardens opened. Birth of Thomas Hardy

1841

Economic depression initiates 'hungry forties'

London Library founded. First publication of *Punch*

Historical and Political Events	Literary and Cultural Events
1842	
Second major Chartist petition. Hong Kong ceded to Britain from China (Treaty of Nanking). General Strike. Railways link London and Manchester. Pentonville Prison opens	Charles Mudie's Lending Library opens in London
1843	
Natal in South Africa becomes Colony. British take Sind, India. Factories Act limits hours worked by women and children to 12 hours per day	Dickens's *A Christmas Carol*. John Ruskin's *Modern Painters*. Carlyle's *Past and Present*. First Christmas cards sent
1845	
Failure of Irish potato crop creates Great Famine. Establishment of asylums in counties demanded by Lunacy Act. Sikh Wars	Benjamin Disraeli's *Sybil, or the Two Nations*. Frederich Engels's *The Condition of the Working Class in England*
1846	
Corn Laws repealed, initiating economic climate of free trade. First medical officer of health appointed	
1847	
'Ten Hours' Factories Act limits working day for women and children in textile mills to ten hours. Angela Burdett-Coutts founds Urania Cottage for prostitutes. First use of chloroform as an anaesthetic	Charlotte Brontë's *Jane Eyre*. Emily Brontë's *Wuthering Heights*. Serialization of William Makepeace Thackeray's *Vanity Fair* begins. Alfred Lord Tennyson's *The Princess*
1848	
Series of European-wide revolutions, known as 'Springtime of the People'. Cholera epidemic. Higher education for governesses opened to women for the first time at Oxford University. Last Chartist petition to parliament. Second Sikh War	Anne Brontë's *The Tenant of Wildfell Hall*. Elizabeth Gaskell's *Mary Barton*. Founding of Pre-Raphaelite Brotherhood. Karl Marx and Frederich Engels's *The Communist Manifesto*
1849	
Abolition of Corn Laws completed. British annex Punjab. Navigation Laws repealed	Charlotte Brontë's *Shirley*. Henry Mayhew's *London Labour and the London Poor*

Historical and Political Events	**Literary and Cultural Events**
1850	
Public Libraries Act for England and Wales. Invention of Bunsen burner.	Dickens's *David Copperfield*. Elizabeth Barret Browning's *Sonnets from the Portuguese*. Death of Wordsworth. Appointment of Tennyson to poet laureate. Tennyson's *In Memoriam*. Publication of Dickens's *Household Words* begins
1851	
The Great Exhibition opens in Crystal Palace. First and Second laws of thermodynamics published by William Thomson. Gold discovered in Australia	Ruskin's *The King of the Golden River*. First chess competition in London
1852	
French proclaim Napoleon III emperor. Dr Livingstone embarks on Zambezi expedition. Second Anglo-Burmese war. Houses of Parliament re-opened after reconstruction	Harriet Beecher-Stowe's *Uncle Tom's Cabin*. Death of Arthur Wellesley (Duke of Wellington)
1853	
Cholera epidemic. Union of Operative Cotton Spinners formed	Charlotte Brontë's *Villette*. Dickens's *Bleak House*
1854	
Crimean War begins (1854–6). Building of London underground begins	Tennyson's 'The Charge of the Light Brigade'. Serialization of Gaskell's *North and South*. Dickens's *Hard Times*. Coventry Patmore's *The Angel in the House*
1855	
London Board of Works approved to oversee construction of sewers. Self-government granted to Australian colonies. Victoria Falls 'discovered' by Dr Livingstone	Founding of *Daily Telegraph*. Death of Charlotte Brontë
1856	
Second 'Opium Wars' with China (1856–8)	

Historical and Political Events	Literary and Cultural Events
1857 Indian Mutiny. Divorce made available without act of parliament by Matrimonial Causes Act. Construction of Atlantic telegraph cable begins	George Eliot's *Scenes of Clerical Life*. Thomas Hughes's *Tom Brown's Schooldays*. Dickens's *Little Dorrit*
1858 Sewage in River Thames causes 'Great Stink', prompting louder calls for better sewage system. British government takes formal control of affairs in India	Hallé Orchestra established in Manchester. Founding of *English Woman's Journal*
1859 Charles Darwin's theory of evolution propounded in *On the Origin of Species*. Construction of Suez Canal begins	Tennyson's *Idylls of the King*. George Eliot's *Adam Bede*. Dickens's *A Tale of Two Cities*. Mill's *On Liberty*. Samuel Smiles's *Self-Help*
1860 Maori Wars in New Zealand. Italy achieves unification. Boxing with bare fists outlawed	George Eliot's *The Mill on the Floss*. Wilkie Collins's *The Woman in White*
1861 Death of Prince Albert from typhoid. Louis Pasteur's germ theory expounded. American Civil war begins (1861–5)	Dickens's *Great Expectations*. Ellen Price Wood's *East Lynne*. Francis Palgrave's *Golden Treasury*. Isabella Beeton's *Book of Household Management*. First English cricket tour of Australia
1862 Embargo imposed by American Civil War causes 'cotton famine' in Britain and implementation of poor relief	Mary Elizabeth Braddon's *Lady Audley's Secret*. Christina Rossetti's *Goblin Market*. Foundation of first football club, Notts County
1864 Prostitutes undergo examination after passage of first Contagious Diseases Act. Red Cross founded	
1865 Women's Suffrage movement founded by Barbara Bodichon. Reform League established to lobby for working-class male suffrage. Morant Bay rebellion in Jamaica	Lewis Carroll's *Alice's Adventures in Wonderland* Dickens's *Our Mutual Friend*

Historical and Political Events	Literary and Cultural Events
1866 Mill presents petition for women's suffrage to Britain. Founding of National Secular society. Cholera epidemic	Eliot's *Felix Holt*. Algernon Swinburne's *Poems and Ballads*
1867 Second Reform Bill gives vote to male householders in boroughs. Fenian terrorist campaign in Britain and Ireland. William Ewart Gladstone becomes leader of Liberal Party. Canada granted dominion status	Matthew Arnold's 'Dover Beach'
1868 Prime-ministerial rivalry commences between Benjamin Disraeli (Conservative) and Gladstone (Liberal), with Disraeli in office in February, and Gladstone in place by December. Trades Union Congress founded in Manchester	Wilkie Collins's *The Moonstone*
1869 Suez Canal opens. Debtors freed from imprisonment by Debtors Act. Anglican Church in Ireland dismantled	Arnold's *Culture and Anarchy*. Mill's *On the Subjection of Women*
1870 Elementary education for all children made compulsory by passage of W. E Forster's Education Act. Women gain monetary rights over wages earned after marriage, inheritances under £200, and some investments. Home Government Association founded in Ireland. Doctrine of Papal Infallibility promulgated	Dickens's *The Mystery of Edwin Drood* (unfinished). Death of Dickens
1871 Legalization of Trade Unions. Publication of Darwin's *Descent of Man*. End of Franco-Prussian war establishes Prussian dominance	Serialization of Eliot's *Middlemarch* begins. Founding of Football Association (FA) cup
1872 Union of Agricultural Labourers established. Thomas Cook provides 'round the world' holiday packages. Voting by secret ballot implemented	Thomas Hardy's *Under the Greenwood Tree*

Historical and Political Events	Literary and Cultural Events
1873 Ashanti war. Irish Home Rule league established. Beginning of 'Great Depression' (c.1870–96). Dissolution of East India Company	Walter Pater's *Studies in the History of the Renaissance*. Mill's *Autobiography*
1874 Establishment of Women's Trade Union League. Fifty-six hour week recommended by Factory Act	Serialization of Anthony Trollope's *The Way We Live Now* begins. Hardy's *Far from the Madding Crowd*. James Thompson's *A City of Dreadful Night*
1875 Non-violent picketing legalized. Age of consent raised to 16	Gilbert and Sullivan's *Trial by Jury*
1876 Alexander Graham Bell patents telephone. Disraeli proclaims Victoria 'Empress of India'	Eliot's *Daniel Deronda*
1877 Annexation of Transvaal by British Empire	Anna Sewell's *Black Beauty*
1878 Zulu war. Second phase of Afghan wars. Matrimonial Causes Act permits separation on the grounds of assault and cruelty. Establishment of Salvation Army. University of London opens degrees to women. Oxford University permits women to attend lectures. Light bulb invented	Thomas Hardy's *The Return of the Native*. Tchaikovsky's *Swan Lake*
1879 Pasteur identifies germs which cause puerperal fever. Suicide legally recognized as suicide, not homicide. Third phase of Afghan wars. Founding of Irish National Land League by Charles Stewart Parnell	George Meredith's *The Egoist*. Henrik Ibsen's *A Doll's House*. Publication begins of *Boy's Own Paper*
1880 First South African war. Elementary education from ages 7 to 10 made compulsory	Death of George Eliot

Historical and Political Events	**Literary and Cultural Events**
1881	
Some land reforms granted by Irish Land Acts. Death of Disraeli. Whipping abolished in armed services	Henry James's *The Portrait of a Lady*
1882	
Women gain full rights over property following passage of Married Women's Property Act. Egyptian war, and establishment of British protectorate. Mahdi uprising against Britain in Sudan	Death of Charles Darwin. Serialization of Robert Louis Stevenson's *Treasure Island*
1884	
All male householders acquire the vote after passage of Third Reform Bill. Founding of Fabian Society. Invention of machine-gun	First parts of *Oxford English Dictionary* published
1885	
Age of consent for girls raised to 16 and any sexual acts between men forbidden by Criminal Law Amendment Act. General Gordon killed at the fall of Khartoum in Sudan. British annexation of Burma. Discovery of gold in Transvaal. Leopold II establishes Independent State of Congo. William Gottlieb Daimler invents internal combustion engine. Invention of motor car	H. Rider Haggard's *King Solomon's Mines*. Formation of Football League to regulate professional matches
1886	
Defeat of Irish Home Rule bill in the House of Commons. Mothers granted rights over children, in the event of the father's death, following Infant Custody Act. Foundation of Indian National Congress. Repeal of Contagious Diseases Act. First bicycles produced in Coventry	Stevenson's *Dr Jekyll and Mr Hyde*
1887	
Victoria's Golden Jubilee. Riots in Trafalgar Square ('Bloody Sunday')	Arthur Conan Doyle's *A Study in Scarlet* (first Sherlock Holmes story). Giuseppe Verdi's *Otello*

Historical and Political Events	Literary and Cultural Events

1888

Willhelm II becomes Kaiser of Germany. British protectorates established over Borneo, Brunei and Sarawak. Slavery abolished in Brazil. Matchworkers' strikes. Invention of Kodak box camera. 'Jack the Ripper' murders of prostitutes in London

Rudyard Kipling's *Plain Tales from the Hills*. Oscar Wilde's *The Happy Prince*. Mrs.Humphrey Ward's *Robert Elsmere*

1889

Cecil Rhodes awarded Royal Charter for British South Africa. Employment of children under the age of 10 prohibited by Prevention of Cruelty to Children Act. Dock strikes herald first major triumph for unskilled male employees. Miners Federation founded. Naval rearmament begins in earnest, following perceived threat posed by Germany

W. B. Yeats's *The Wanderings of Oisin and Other Poems*. George Bernard Shaw edits *Fabian Essays*

1890

British Empire exchanges Heligoland for Pemba and Zanzibar

Ibsen's *Hedda Gabler*. James Frazer's *The Golden Bough*. William Morris's *News from Nowhere*

1891

Steam trams discontinued in London

Hardy's *Tess of the D'Urbervilles*. Wilde's *The Picture of Dorian Gray*. George Gissing's *New Grub Street*. United States outlaws literary piracy

1892

First automatic telephone conversations. James Keir Hardie becomes member of Parliament for Independent Labour party

Doyle's *The Adventures of Sherlock Holmes*. Wilde's *Lady Windermere's Fan*. Shaw's *Widower's Houses*. Kipling's *Barrack-Room Ballads*. Death of Tennyson

1893

Defeat of Irish Home Rule bill in House of Lords. Miners resist 25 per cent pay cut. Invention of diesel engine

George Gissing's *The Odd Women*. Wilde's *A Woman of No Importance*

Historical and Political Events	Literary and Cultural Events
1894 Opening of Manchester Ship Canal. British protectorate over Uganda proclaimed	Kipling's *The Jungle Book*. George Moore's *Esther Waters*. Wilde's *Salomé*. Establishment of International Olympic Committee
1895 Abortive Jameson Raid fails to overthrow Transvaal government. Wilde sentenced to two years in prison for homosexual crimes 'against nature'	Wilde's *An Ideal Husband* and *The Importance of Being Earnest*. Hardy's *Jude the Obscure*. Grant Allen's *The Woman Who Did*. H. G. Wells's *The Time Machine*. Max Nordau's *Degeneration*
1896 Oxford and Cambridge universities reject admission of women to degrees. First publication of *Daily Mail* as an evening newspaper	A. E. Housman's *A Shropshire Lad*
1897 Victoria's Diamond Jubilee. National Union of Women's Suffrage Societies elects Millicent Garrett Fawcett as president. 'Science' of 'sexology' heralded by Havelock Ellis's *Studies in the Psychology of Sex*. Invention of wireless radio	Bram Stoker's *Dracula*
1898 Discovery of radium by the Curies. Death of Gladstone. Reconquest of Sudan and Battle of Omdurman	Hardy's *Wessex Poems*. Wells's *The War of the Worlds*
1899 Boer wars (1899–1902). Discovery of aspirin	Serialization of Joseph Conrad's *Heart of Darkness* begins
1900 Boxer Rebellion in China. Foundation of Labour Party	Conrad's *Lord Jim*. Sigmund Freud's *The Interpretation of Dreams*
1901 Death of Victoria. Accession of Edward VII to throne. Employment of children under age of 12 in factories and workshops outlawed by Factory Act	Kipling's *Kim*. Edward Elgar's *Pomp and Circumstance*. Beatrix Potter's *The Tale of Peter Rabbit*

Historical and Political Events	Literary and Cultural Events
1904 British isolationism ended by *Entente Cordiale* with France	First performances of J. M. Barrie's *Peter Pan*
1910 Death of Edward VII. Accession of George V to throne	
1912–13 'Powder keg' of Balkan wars exacerbates national tensions and rivalries throughout Europe	D. H. Lawrence's *Sons and Lovers* (1913)
1914 Outbreak of First World War ends period known as 'long nineteenth century' (*c.*1815–1914)	James Joyce's *Dubliners*.

Index

The index is divided into three sections: (1) Concepts, Events, Figures; (2) Texts; and (3) Authors. Some important 'figures' and 'authors', such as Charles Darwin and Charles Dickens, appear in all three sections, while important entries such as those on 'Class' and 'Empire', or those on texts such as *Jane Eyre* and *Middlemarch* – all of which appear frequently in the text – are divided into sub-entries. In the Authors section, the names of significant texts are repeated where useful or appropriate. Each initial entry is capitalized. Capitalized entries and sub-entries refer to the 'concept' essays in the text, except for those which refer to proper nouns or idioms (some of which are in quotation marks). Un-capitalized sub-entries refer the reader to entries in both the index and the text.

Index of Texts Cited

Authors Cited

Acton, William, *Functions and Disorders
of the Reproductive Organs, The*, 125
Armstrong, Nancy, *Desire in Domestic
Fiction*, 224
Arnold, Matthew
Culture and Anarchy, 197
'Dover Beach', 121
Study of Poetry, 183
Essays on Criticism, 196
Austen, Jane, 98
Austin, Alfred, 75, 151
see also Poetry

Barthes, Roland, 205–6
'Death of the Author, The', 206,
237–40, 252
Elements of Semiology, 252
Mythologies, 252
Beeton, Isabella, *Book of Household
Management*, 45, 66, 68, 174
Belloc, Hilaire, 155
Belsey, Catherine, *Critical Practice*, 186,
221
Botting, Fred, 79
Bowen, John, 131
Braddon, Mary Elizabeth, *Lady Audley's
Secret*, 190
Brontë, Charlotte,
Caroline Vernon, 98
Jane Eyre, 95–6, 128, 130–1, 186, 198,
216–17, 234
Professor, The, 102
Shirley, xx, 69–70, 226
Villette, 72–3
Brontë, Emily, *Wuthering Heights*, 79
Browning, Elizabeth Barrett, *Aurora
Leigh*, 213
Browning, Robert
'My Last Duchess', 183
'Porphyria's Lover', 183
Bulwer Lytton, Edward
England and the English, xviii; 100
Harold, the Last of the Saxon Kings,
167
Last Days of Pompeii, The, 167
Last of the Barons, The, 167

Carey, Peter, *Jack Maggs*, 234
Carlyle, Thomas
A History of the French Revolution, 165

Chartism, 114, 118, 139
Hero as Poet, The, 183
*Occasional Discourse on the Nigger
Question*, 113–14, 175
Sartor Resartus, 122
Carroll, Lewis
Alice's Adventures in Wonderland, 156,
178, 233–4, 254–6
Through the Looking Glass, 255–6
Cixous, Hélène, *Newly Born Woman,
The*, 214–15
Coetzee, J.M., *Foe*, 239
Collecot, Diana, *Sexual Sameness*, 248
Collins, Wilkie
Moonstone, The, 115–16, 159
Woman in White, The, 190
Conan Doyle, Arthur
Adventures of Sherlock Holmes, The,
159–60
Conrad, Joseph
Heart of Darkness, 59
Nigger of the Narcissus, The, 59
Culler, Jonathan, *Structuralist Poetics*,
250

Darwin, Charles, see Evolution; Non-
fictional Prose; Science
De Beauvoir, Simone, *Second Sex, The*,
214
Defoe, Daniel, *Robinson Crusoe*, 156,
239–40
De Quincey, Thomas, *Confessions of an
Opium-Eater*, 49
Derrida, Jacques
Of Grammatology, 204, 209–10,
235–6
Positions, 211–12, 236
see also Deconstruction;
Poststructuralism
Dickens, Charles
A Christmas Carol, 46, 66
All the Year Round, 176
A Tale of Two Cities, 102, 167
Barnaby Rudge, 121, 167
Bleak House, 67, 91–2
David Copperfield, 169–70, 245
Dombey and Son, 58–9, 122, 134
Great Expectations, 234–5, 238–40
Hard Times, xiv–xv, 87–8, 253–4
Household Words, 176
Little Dorrit, 136, 143
Martin Chuzzlewit, 159